THE NORTH STAR

THE NORTH STAR

CANADA AND THE CIVIL WAR
PLOTS AGAINST LINCOLN

JULIAN SHER

ALFRED A. KNOPF CANADA

PUBLISHED BY ALFRED A. KNOPF CANADA

Copyright © 2023 Julian Sher

www.penguinrandomhouse.ca

Library and Archives Canada Cataloguing in Publication

Title: The north star : Canada and the Civil War plots against Lincoln / Julian Sher.
Names: Sher, Julian, 1953- author.
Identifiers: Canadiana (print) 20220259305 | Canadiana (ebook) 2022025933X |
ISBN 9781039000292 (hardcover) | ISBN 9781039000308 (EPUB)
Subjects: LCSH: United States—History—Civil War, 1861-1865—Participation, Canadian. | LCSH: Canadians—United States—History—19th century. |
LCSH: Lincoln, Abraham, 1809-1865—Assassination.
Classification: LCC E540.C25 S54 2023 | DDC 973.7—dc23

Text and jacket design: Matthew Flute
Image credits: (clouds) George Pachantouris / Moment / Getty Images;
(Ford Theatre) National Archives photo no. 66-G-22B(1)

Printed in Canada

10 9 8 7 6 5 4 3 2 1

FOR CHARLES AND CHLOÉ

*May they grow up in a world where
justice and equality are cherished*

Deep in our history of struggle for freedom, Canada was the North Star. So standing today in Canada I am linked with the history of my people and its unity with your past.

—MARTIN LUTHER KING JR., speaking in Toronto at the 1967 Massey Lectures, one year before his assassination

CONTENTS

CANADA EAST

CANADA WEST

St. Liboire

Montreal

Lennoxville

Halifax

St. Albans

Toronto

St. Catharines

Niagara

New York City

Chicago

Washington

UNITED STATES

THE UNION

Richmond

THE CONFEDERACY

CAST OF CHARACTERS

UNION ARMY RECRUITS FROM CANADA

ANDERSON ABBOTT — Canada's first Black doctor who works in Union hospitals

ALEXANDER AUGUSTA — Graduate from University of Toronto who becomes the highest-ranking Black doctor in the Union army

EDWARD P. DOHERTY — Quebec man who serves as a lieutenant in the US Cavalry and leads the hunt to track down John Wilkes Booth

EMMA EDMONDS — New Brunswick woman who disguises herself as a man to enlist as a Union nurse

CONFEDERATE SUPPORTERS IN CANADA

GEORGE TAYLOR DENISON III — Wealthy Toronto aristocrat

GUILLAUME LAMOTHE — Montreal's police chief and later the mayor

HENRY STARNES — Banker and twice a mayor of Montreal

CONFEDERATE OPERATIVES IN CANADA

THE LEADERS:

JACOB THOMPSON — Head of Confederate Secret Service operations in Canada

CLEMENT CLAY — Confederate commissioner, second-in-command in Canada

GEORGE SANDERS — Confederate agent and agitator

EDWIN LEE — Replaces Thompson in the final months of the war

MORGAN'S RAIDERS IN CANADA:

BENNETT YOUNG	Organizer of the attack on St. Albans, Vermont
THOMAS HINES	One of the leaders of the Northwest Conspiracy
JOHN HEADLEY	Heads the mission to burn New York City
JOHN CASTLEMAN	Plans and executes cross-border raids

THE DOCTOR:

DR. LUKE BLACKBURN	Mastermind of the yellow fever plot

THE COURIER:

SARAH SLATER	Carries secret dispatches between Richmond and Montreal

THE MAJOR HISTORICAL FIGURES

JEFFERSON DAVIS	President of the Confederate States
ABRAHAM LINCOLN	16th President of the United States
JOHN WILKES BOOTH	The assassin
JOHN SURRATT	Booth's fellow conspirator

AUTHOR'S NOTE

Language and the baggage it carries evolves as the politics of a society and the rights of its people progress. The terms *Negroes* and *colored* are used throughout this book when they are spoken by people or in contemporary newspaper accounts or in official titles, because they were commonly used during this period to describe Black Americans. In the nineteenth century, these terms were not necessarily seen as demeaning. Blacks themselves took pride in descriptions such as the "Colored Regiments" of soldiers.

In contrast, what today is described as the "n-word" always had a much more derogatory and explicitly racist weight to it. In this book, it appears as *n-----* only in direct quotations in order to accurately reflect the hatreds and prejudices of the person or organization speaking.

When the American Civil War broke out in 1861, the British colonies in North America were just six years away from becoming the Dominion of Canada under Confederation. In 1841, Upper and Lower Canada had been united as the British Province of Canada, made up of Canada West (what is now largely Ontario) and Canada East (Quebec). For the sake of convenience, the modern terms *Canada* and *Canadians* and the names of the provinces as they exist today are generally used throughout the book. In Quebec, many towns and streets that now have French names had English names, which have been kept in this book when referenced by the people at the time.

Some quotations from diaries, newspapers or other sources have been edited for minor grammatical or spelling mistakes.

Dooley's Bar at the St. Lawrence Hall in Montreal, near the poolroom where the assassin John Wilkes Booth played billiards just months before killing Lincoln (Courtesy McCord Museum)

'ABE'S CONTRACT WAS UP'

Mint juleps were available year-round in Dooley's Bar at the swank St. Lawrence Hall in Montreal. The libations were served just the way the Southerners from the Confederate States of America liked them: mint leaf, bourbon, some simple syrup and crushed ice, cold enough to allow a thin frost to caress the outside of the cup.

When the handsome Southern gentleman walked into the popular hotel bar on St. James Street one evening in October 1864, many of the patrons would have recognized him. Dark, curly hair, piercing eyes, an easy smile and the confident walk that came from being an actor of considerable renown—"A Star of the First Magnitude," as one glowing tribute had put it; "a muscular, perfect man," gushed another.

In the previous months, John Wilkes Booth had starred in performances in Nashville, Cincinnati, New Orleans and Boston. But in Montreal, he stayed away from the stage; he told people he was in town on "a pleasure trip," though in truth he would spend a lot of time conducting serious business with Confederate agents and sympathizers who flooded the city.

Perhaps the only person at Dooley's who was as well-known as Booth—at least to the locals—was the stocky man with the neat brown hair who was standing by the pool table in the billiards room next door to the bar. Joseph Dion sported a handlebar moustache that drooped below his chin and seemed to come all the way up to his ears. The Quebec billiards champion was enough of a celebrity to have his picture on a cigarette trading card.

"I was introduced to J. Wilkes Booth," Dion later recalled, "and indulged in a friendly contest of billiards with him in the saloon of that establishment which was to continue to a late hour in the evening."

There is no record of whether Dion was polite enough to let his American guest win. But it was the conversation rather than the competition that the billiards champion distinctly remembered about Booth. More specifically, "the wild ideas he expressed."

"Do you know, I have the sharpest play laid out ever done in America," Booth boasted. "I can bag the biggest game . . . just remember my address, you'll hear of a double carom one of these days," ostensibly referring to the rare pool trick of sinking two balls at once.

As the game and the evening wore on, Booth seemed to get more inebriated—and more political. The American elections were just a few weeks away; Abraham Lincoln's political future—and the uncertain future of his divided country—hung in the balance as the President fought for re-election.

For three years, Lincoln had been waging a war against the slaveholding Southern states that had broken away from the Union. His Emancipation Proclamation of January 1863, declaring "that all persons held as slaves" within the rebellious states should be free divided the country even more.

Booth, like most Confederate supporters, despised Lincoln—and made his views clear to his Canadian host. Many months later, when his words took on a much more ominous meaning, Dion recalled Booth saying that "it made damned little difference, head or tail, Abe's contract was nearly up."

———

It was no accident that the man who would become the world's most famous assassin found himself in Dooley's Bar just six months before he pointed his single-shot, .44-calibre derringer into the back of Abraham Lincoln's head.

In Montreal, Booth was among friends. The St. Lawrence Hall was a notorious hangout for Confederate spies in a city that was a hub for wartime plotters, assassins, mercenaries and soldiers on the run. A few hours' journey down a dirt highway or by slow train, Toronto was also a headquarters for Confederate money men and gunrunners. Canada in the 1860s was a country rife with espionage, a secret northern front in a civil war that was tearing apart its neighbour to the south. By early 1864, Jefferson Davis, the leader of the Confederate States, would order some of his most trusted aides to "proceed at once to Canada" to set up a well-funded secret service network. The Lincoln administration in turn sent its detectives and entice snitches to Canada to spy on the spies.

———

Today, Canadians take pride in having been on the "good side" in the battle against slavery, a refuge for thirty thousand Black men, women and children who fled to what they would call the "North Star" of freedom on the Underground Railroad. That heroic endeavour is only part of the story. Much less talked about is Canada's own history of racism, and the complicated role Canada played in the Civil War.

The truth is that not all Canadians were cheerleaders for "Honest Abe" in his fight against the rebel slave states. In fact, with support from powerful men in the ruling elites, the country provided a staging ground for Confederate kidnap plots, firebombings, bank raids and prison breaks. Shortly after Lincoln's assassination, Washington issued a formal proclamation explicitly declaring that "the atrocious murder" of the President was "incited, concerted and procured by . . . rebels and traitors against the government of the United States harbored in Canada." Five of the six alleged conspirators named in the indictment were operating out of Montreal and Toronto.

The sixth man, Jefferson Davis, was still in America. He was imprisoned after the defeat of his Confederate army, but once released on bail, Davis immediately fled to where many of his Confederate compatriots had already found refuge: Canada. He received a hero's welcome.

The echoes of the war to end slavery still linger today, in both America and Canada.

Many books about the Civil War focus mainly on the powerful politicians and generals, inevitably all men. *The North Star*, however, is about ordinary people who chose a life-altering path as they stood at history's crossroads. Some choices were made for them by their circumstances: the place of their birth, their class and social standing, their gender, their religion and the colour of their skin. But at key moments in their lives, each made critical decisions. Some changed careers, some changed countries; one of them managed, in a way, to change her gender.

Their choices would have extraordinary outcomes none of them could have envisaged when they took those first fateful steps. A farm girl from New Brunswick, disguised as a man, would fight in some of the bloodiest battles of the war as a Union soldier. A young Black man in Toronto whose parents fled slavery and racism in Alabama would become the first Canadian-born Black doctor, and would find himself at the Washington home where Lincoln lay dying from an assassin's bullet. A prominent and wealthy Toronto aristocrat would open his heart, his wallet and his home to the Confederate Secret Service leaders in Canada.

And a boy who grew up in a small village outside Montreal would become a respected lieutenant in a Washington cavalry regiment. Immediately after the assassin's bullet was fired at Ford's Theatre, he was tasked with leading the most famous manhunt in American history.

His prey would be the billiard player John Wilkes Booth, whose own choices would change the course of history.

*Soldiers from the 4th US Colored Infantry at Fort Lincoln, 1864
(Courtesy Library of Congress)*

PART ONE

'SAVE THE UNION'

(April 1861–February 1864)

If I could save the Union without freeing any slave
I would do it, and if I could save it by freeing all
the slaves I would do it; and if I could save it by freeing
some and leaving others alone, I would also do that.

—ABRAHAM LINCOLN, August 22, 1862

1.

'A MAGNIFICENT SPECTACLE'

The bodies and blood were everywhere, blanketing the Virginia hills and riverbanks in an early omen of the horrors that would devastate a starkly divided nation over the next four years.

"The sight of that field is perfectly appalling; men tossing their arms wildly calling for help; there they lie bleeding, torn and mangled." Such were the recollections of a nineteen-year-old Union army field nurse named Franklin Thompson, gazing across the Bull Run River on July 21, 1861. "Legs, arms and bodies are crushed and broken as if smitten by thunder-bolts; the ground is crimson with blood; it is terrible to witness."

For Thompson and the tens of thousands of new recruits, the First Battle of Bull Run was their initial experience of a war that had started just three months earlier. Everyone, from President Abraham Lincoln to the lowliest infantryman, expected the conflict to be, if not painless, at least mercifully brief. Like most battles in a new war, this one started with young men—many of them teenagers—pumped up on glory and cheers; like almost all the battles in a war that would drag on for four years, this one too would end with gore and weeping.

On a nearby hill, a 22-year-old recruit named Edward Paul Doherty witnessed the same kind of chaos that overwhelmed nurse Thompson. "We waded in great confusion," he wrote.

The American Civil War was the first war to be reported, recorded and remembered with an immediacy never felt before. The telegraph, invented just a couple of decades earlier, transmitted updates from the battlefields to generals and to newspapers. Breakthroughs in photography put wartime correspondents with clumsy cameras at the front lines; for the first time, people back home saw graphic pictures of the dead and dying while the smoke on the battlefields was still clearing.

The news from Bull Run quickly turned bad for the Federal forces, as Lincoln's men fighting for the central government were known. "We were immediately ordered to fall back and lie down, as the discharge from the enemy's battery was severe," Doherty wrote. To make sure as many soldiers as possible returned safely, Thompson helped the surgeons as they took over local buildings to refit them for taking care of the expected wounded. A rectangular brick structure with a wooden roof atop a small hill, known as the "old Stone Church," was chosen as a field hospital, and Doherty described how he and others desperately dragged wounded soldiers there.

Perhaps, amidst all the blood and screams of the wounded in that front-line hospital, the two soldiers ran into each other on that terrible battlefield. Their courage under fire was not uncommon. What set Thompson and Doherty apart was that they were both Canadians, willing to die in America's civil war. They had travelled far from the rural hamlets in New Brunswick and Quebec where they were born and raised. Like tens of thousands of Canadians, they had volunteered to fight for a country that was not theirs but a cause that spoke to them.

———

The Battle of Bull Run was unfolding just twenty-five miles southwest of Washington, DC. Lincoln's Union forces were so confident of victory that as the fighting got under way, a large crowd of spectators— including several members of the US Congress—gathered nearby, carrying picnic baskets and opera glasses. It was war as theatre: teach the upstart Southerners a lesson and then let's all go home. The soldiers on the battlefield stage shared that confidence. "The possibility of a defeat never seemed to enter the mind of any," Thompson noted. After all, they had almost all signed up as volunteers for just ninety days, assuming the war would be over quickly.

In the early dawn hours of that Sunday in July, Thompson described "a magnificent spectacle, as column after column wound its way over the green hills and through the hazy valleys, with the soft moonlight falling on the long lines of shining steel." The morning dawned bright and clear, Thompson recalled, the air resounding with the music from the regimental bands and the patriotic songs of the soldiers.

The men in Union blue initially outnumbered the Confederate greys, but delays by Northern forces in moving into action gave the South time to bring in an additional 10,000 troops. That pitted a roughly equal number of 30,000 soldiers on each side—almost all of them rookie volunteers. Mayhem and madness ensued.

"Now the battle began to rage with terrible fury," Thompson noted. "Nothing could be heard save the thunder of artillery, the clash of steel, and the continuous roar of musketry."

The Union forces took the upper hand in the morning, but by nightfall the Confederates—led in part by General Thomas J. Jackson, who earned the nickname "Stonewall" during the battle—were able to resist the onslaught and then turn the tide. "The news of this disaster spread along our lines like wildfire," Thompson reported. "Officers and men were alike confounded . . . and almost immediately the panic commenced."

The Northern troops were in retreat, but Thompson stayed behind to nurse the casualties huddled in the small church on the hill. "We saw stacks of dead bodies piled up, and arms and legs were thrown together in heaps," Thompson wrote. One soldier whose legs were crushed below the knees was in so much pain he was "insane, perfectly wild" as his comrades held him down as he died. Another pale-faced boy with "white lips and beseeching eyes" begged Thompson to write to his mother about his passing.

The dying men urged Thompson to flee before the Confederate cavalry arrived. The nurse soon made it back safely to Union lines. Edward Doherty would not be as lucky.

———

At Bull Run and subsequent battles, Franklin Thompson quickly earned a reputation for courage and devotion. A fellow soldier described him as "brave to the last degree." Official military records later took note that Thompson was "never absent from duty, obeying all orders with intelligence and alacrity, his whole aim and desire to render zealous and efficient aid to the Union cause."

Perhaps in the days leading up to their first battle, around the campfire or in the mess tents, Thompson had made mention of Canadian roots to the other nervous young recruits. There would be jokes about accents, teasing about unfamiliar hometown names and ribald humour over girlfriends and wives left behind. Thompson, one of the more well-liked soldiers, would have joined in the laughter and ribbing that soldiers everywhere use to ward off the fear of battle. A wartime buddy recalled Thompson as a "willing, cheerful soldier." Another noted that "the beardless boy was a universal favourite." But Thompson was also cautious. "He would choose his associates with discretion," one solder recounted.

That's because the popular Thompson had a much greater fear than the danger of battle: the dread that a deep secret would be revealed by mishap or malice. Because the brave field nurse known to all as Frank was actually Emma, a young woman from New Brunswick with big dreams and a thirst for adventure.

2

'THE WILDEST COLT'

It was bitterly cold that December in 1841, as all the winter months were in the backwoods of rural New Brunswick.

Sarah Emma Evelyn Edmondson came into the world on a bleak, isolated potato farm. She was the sixth child her mother Betsy had borne and, much to the displeasure of her father, Isaac, she was not a boy. He already had four girls and Emma's only brother was a sickly, epileptic boy for whom Isaac cared little. The fact that he had another daughter "set him off into a temper," friends and family later told Emma's biographer Sylvia G.L. Dannett.

Emma Edmonds—as she was later known—would never be described as pretty, but she had strong features: dark-brown eyes, a wide face with a tall forehead and thin lips. "Her features were almost too coarse to be those of a woman and too fine for a man," an acquaintance later described her. Though there is no evidence her father was physically violent with her mother and the children, his spite and mean-spiritedness marked the young girl for life. In contrast, the young girl adored her mother, writing that she was "as nearly a saint as we find on earth." Edmonds later said her mother passed on to her fierce independence and a "hatred of male tyranny."

"My infant soul was impressed with a sense of my mother's wrongs," Edmonds said, "although I managed to outgrow it immeasurably." In truth, she never did outgrow that anger. "In our family, the women were not sheltered but enslaved," she later recalled, in a newspaper interview in 1883. "Hence I naturally grew up to think of man as the implacable enemy of my sex."

The family tried to eke out a living in the hamlet of Magaguadavic, tucked into the southeast corner of the province, just twenty-five miles from the American border. The landscape of rolling hills and thick forests dotted by small lakes afforded the kind of rural isolation that was both vast and liberating, yet also too small to fulfill the hopes of an ambitious girl. Being raised in a farming family gave young Emma the opportunity to grow up strong and fit—planting potatoes, milking cows and chopping wood as well as learning how to fish and hunt. "She tried to be the boy her father had wanted," family and friends told Dannett. "On occasion she displayed her skill as marksman by bagging hare or partridge, thereby seeking to win words of praise from her father and make him forget her sex."

Fortunately, the girls were also afforded as good an education as could be had in rural nineteenth-century Canada. Edmonds attended the proverbial one-room schoolhouse, a parish building with no yard or even a privy. She was a good and attentive student, and also deeply religious, imbued with the hope that, despite her difficult upbringing, "God was there."

Emma's faith in God, however, did not stop her mother from raising concerns with the local clerical authority about her headstrong daughter. "I heard my mother once tell a Scotch Presbyterian clergyman she was afraid I would meet with some violent death," Edmonds recalled, "for I was always in some unheard-of mischief, such as riding the wildest colt on the farm, firing off my father's shot-gun, and climbing to the highest point of the buildings."

The brash young girl was a wild colt in her own right and paid scant attention to her religious elders. "When I was 13 years old," she later recounted, "one of those peculiar little incidents occurred which seems like God's own finger pointing out the way to a struggling soul."

A dishevelled peddler came by the farm one day and Edmonds's mother invited him for supper and a night's lodging. The man, in return, left Edmonds a book entitled *Fanny Campbell, The Female Pirate Captain, A Tale of the Revolution!*

A pulp novel that sold eighty thousand copies in a few months at twenty-five cents apiece, its cover showed a woman with short-cropped hair thinly disguised as a man on the deck of a ship, grasping her cutlass firmly in her right hand, a pirate flag in her left. When Edmonds and her sisters went to the field to plant potatoes, they packed a lunch—and devoured the rollicking adventure story. Fanny's childhood sweetheart, a sailor, promises to marry her after returning from his next sea voyage. Unfortunately, he and his shipmates are kidnapped by pirates. So the intrepid Fanny disguises herself as a young man and boards a ship to rescue him.

"When I read where 'Fanny' . . . stepped into the freedom and glorious independence of masculinity, I threw up my old straw hat and shouted," Edmonds remembered. "That was the most wonderful day in all my life. Surely, I must have been inspired . . . I was emancipated and could never be a slave again."

Still, even within the bounds of a pulp novel, respect had to be paid to nineteenth-century mores. The book ends on a traditional note with Fanny rescuing her man only to end up marrying him—and staying home to mind the children, her cutlass safely stored in the family closet. That fate was not to Edmonds's liking. "The only drawback in my mind was this: she went to rescue an imprisoned lover . . . and I regretted that she had no higher ambition than running after a man," she later wrote. "From that time forth I never ceased planning escape."

Escape was forced upon Edmonds four years later. One after the other, her sisters left the family farm, betrothed to local men. When Edmonds was just seventeen, it was her turn. "When her father made arrangements to marry her off to an old man whom she detested, that was the last straw," according to a later newspaper account of her life.

"Very early in life, I was forced to the conclusion from close observation and bitter experience that matrimony was not a safe investment for me," Edmonds recounted. "While the preparations were going on for the wedding, one starless night I most unceremoniously left for parts unknown."

Edmonds first made it to Fredericton and then Moncton, finding work making bonnets and hats. By 1858, she had settled in Saint John. The third-largest city in British North America with over thirty thousand residents, Saint John offered her the anonymity she seemed to crave. But she'd need to find a way to survive on her own rebellious terms. In the middle of the nineteenth century, well-paying jobs for women—much less exciting ones—were non-existent. So Edmonds took the rather unusual step of finding employment as a man.

Using the alias of "Frank Thompson," she answered a newspaper advertisement and secured a position as a travelling Bible salesman for a publishing company that operated out of the United States. It was a clever deceit: her employers were far away and would never see her; always on the road, she would never be in one place long enough to arouse suspicion. Edmonds put on some men's clothing and began to pass herself off as Frank. Her short hair, dark complexion and firm build from years on the farm surely helped. Edmonds soon found she could pull off the ruse fairly easily, concluding after many encounters with strangers that she must have come off as "quite a gentleman."

Soon, Edmonds decided to seek even better fortunes in the United States. She headed for Hartford, Connecticut, where she walked into the offices of a publisher and bookseller, still in the guise of Franklin Thompson. After a brief but financially rewarding stint selling books for her new employer back in Canada, Edmonds's wanderlust drove her west to the small town of Flint, just outside Detroit, Michigan. She rented a room from a local pastor, a fitting home for an ambitious Bible salesperson. "She had the appearance of a bright, active young man and her success proved her qualifications to be first class," a *New York Times* story later recounted. By the end of 1860 she had settled into a quiet life of sales trips on the road and regular church attendance. It seemed Emma Edmonds had found her independence and happiness.

Perhaps she would have lived the rest of her double life in peaceful anonymity. But events that were about to explode far beyond her city and her control set her on a path that would make Emma Edmonds one of the most famous disguised women in America.

3.

'THE BETTER ANGELS'

When Abraham Lincoln began his rise to the presidency, he was seen by many as an unlikely and uninspiring choice. "His weak, wishy-washy, namby-pamby efforts, imbecile in matter, disgusting in manner, have made us the laughing stock of the whole world," declared one newspaper. The stinging comments came not from the slave South but from Lincoln's home turf of Illinois. In Canada, the *Ottawa Citizen* dismissed him as a "fourth-rate Illinois lawyer."

In May 1860, the gangly politician surprised many by winning the support of the Republican Party as its candidate in the upcoming presidential election. At the time, Lincoln was neither well-known nor very popular. He had briefly served as an undistinguished Congressman for a smaller party known as the Whigs back in 1847. A decade later, as a Republican, he challenged the incumbent Democrat Stephen Douglas for an Illinois US Senate seat. They confronted each other in seven cities in what became known as the Great Debates of 1858—attended by thousands of people—which centred on slavery. Douglas was in favour of letting the system of bondage extend beyond the slave states of the South into what were called the free states like Illinois; Lincoln was vehemently opposed.

"It is the eternal struggle between these two principles—right and wrong—throughout the world," he said, arguing that expanding slavery would "blow out the moral lights around us."

Still, Lincoln the man of principle was also a prisoner of his time. He was opposed to the expansion of slavery, but not its existence. He had married into "a significant slave-holding family." As a young law-yer, he had represented a slave owner who sought to return a runaway woman and her four children and punish the people who had hidden them. "I am not, nor ever have been in favor of bringing about in any way the social and political equality of the white and black races," he said to much applause during one of the debates in Charleston. "I am not nor ever have been in favor of making voters or jurors of negroes, nor of qualifying them to hold office, nor to intermarry with white people; and I will say in addition to this that there is a physical differ-ence between the white and black races which I believe will for ever forbid the two races living together on terms of social and political equality . . . I as much as any other man am in favor of having the superior position assigned to the white race."

Lincoln lost the election for that Senate seat, but he had won the debates—and they cemented his reputation as a gifted orator. But now that he was running for president, Lincoln knew he was vying for the leadership of a country that largely accepted having four million people in bondage. Despite his iconic reputation today as the president who freed the slaves, Lincoln came to that role slowly and reluctantly. By 1860, he was courting the abolitionist vote by emphasizing "our convic-tion that slavery is wrong," but he also took pains to assure the Southern states that "wrong as we think slavery is, we can yet afford to let it alone where it is."

Consistently ranked today as the most popular president among Americans—if not around the world—Lincoln was a much more con-troversial figure in his time. It is easy to overlook how tenuous his hold on power was, even from the start. When Honest Abe went on to win the presidential election in November 1860, it was by the narrowest of victories. There were multiple parties and factions in a four-candidate race. Lincoln was elected by a majority of the electoral votes from the Northern states, but with less than 40 percent of the popular vote. It remains to this day the poorest showing by any winning presidential candidate in American history. Abolitionists in the North were furious at the new president's compromising stance on slavery; hardline Southern supporters of slavery were incensed that he dared to consider imposing limits on their cherished institutions. The new president's repeated attempts to find a dubious middle ground in what he had called the "eternal struggle between these two principles—right and wrong" ended up pleasing nobody and angering everybody.

———

One of the outraged Southern sympathizers was, like the new president, a rising star also known for his fine oratory and passionate performances. John Wilkes Booth was making headlines on the theatrical stage, though, not the political one.

By the age of twenty-two, Booth was already on his way to becoming a household name. He was born May 10, 1838, near Bel Air, Maryland, into a family of theatre royalty. His father, Junius Brutus Booth, was a famed Shakespearean actor who had emigrated from England. Athletic and daring, young John mastered horseback riding and fencing as a boy.

Booth quit school at age fourteen, not uncommon back then, especially when his father's death left the family short of money. His older brother Edwin followed the family tradition and was swiftly heralded as "the greatest tragedian" on the American stage; John Wilkes had a rockier start. At his stage debut in Baltimore at age seventeen, he missed some of his lines while acting in *Richard III*, prompting jeers from the audience. There was laughter three years later when on opening night in Philadelphia he suffered from stage fright and flubbed more scenes. But eventually Booth hit his stride. The critics soon raved about his "brilliant talents." The poet and writer Walt Whitman saw "real genius" in his acting. In October 1858 he played in *Hamlet* alongside his brother Edwin in the title role. Booth would later say that his favourite role of all Shakespeare's characters was Brutus, his father's namesake, the slayer of tyrants.

In December 1860, a month after Lincoln won the election, John Wilkes Booth penned a rambling twenty-one-page text railing against everything the new president represented. Apparently intended as a speech that Booth never delivered, the text lays out the future assassin's thoughts in heavy black ink and erratic handwriting. "Instead of looking upon slavery as a sin, I hold it to be happiness for themselves and a social and political blessing for us," Booth wrote, reflecting the white supremacist views that were at the heart of his ideology and his hatred of Lincoln. The South, he insisted, has "a right, according to the Constitution," to keep and hold slaves. "I have seen the black man whipped but only when he deserved more than he received," he declared.

Booth was far from alone in despising Lincoln's policies. On December 20, 1860, just over a month after the election, South Carolina became the first state to secede from the Union. By January 1861 six additional Southern states had joined in breaking away. In February, the Confederate States of America were formed. Jefferson Davis, the senator from Mississippi whose family had a large plantation with over a hundred slaves, was appointed its first president. "We recognize the negro as God and God's Book and God's Laws, in nature, tell us to recognize him," Davis said at the time. "Our inferior, fitted expressly for servitude." Davis and his supporters to this day would insist that the civil war that ensued was not about slavery, but states' rights. However that argument was disingenuous, because the rights states wanted to hold onto were all about keeping their slaves.

One of Davis's loyal friends and his earliest political ally was Jacob Thompson, another wealthy landowner from Mississippi. Like Davis, Thompson had a long history in Congress, serving in Washington from 1839 to 1851, and was named secretary of the interior by President James Buchanan, Lincoln's Democratic predecessor. He got to know many of Lincoln's future top advisers around that cabinet table. But the election of Republican Abraham Lincoln with his anti-slavery musings was too much for Thompson. On January 9, 1861, he resigned his cabinet post and enlisted with the newly formed Confederate army, first as its inspector-general and then as an aide to Brigadier General Pierre Beauregard. Thompson warned that a Northern majority "trained from infancy to hate our people and their institutions" would overthrow slavery and impose "the subjugation of our people."

He declared that in the South there was "but one feeling, all-absorbing, all-pervading . . . we will fight with stones, pitchforks, and scythe blades."

Before he quit his cabinet post, Thompson did perform a bit of spycraft for his Southern compatriots, leaking information to the Confederacy about Fort Sumter, the Federal military post that would become the flashpoint that ignited the Civil War.

It was not the last act of spying and subterfuge Thompson would carry out for the cause.

———

Across the border, Canadians were watching the political turmoil and debates over slavery with a mixture of fascination and horror.

Just over a week after Jacob Thompson quit the Federal government to take up the cause of the Confederacy, hundreds of people braved a January snowstorm in Montreal to make their way along the cobblestoned St. James Street to the ornate three-storey building known as Mechanics' Hall. They had come to hear about John Anderson, a runaway slave who was to be deported to the United States—and almost certain death. The start of the Civil War was still a few months away, but already its controversies and conflicts were whipping up passions in Canada as they were in the United States.

"The Hall was crowded to excess, and numbers were unable to obtain admission," one local newspaper reported, "so great was the interest and sympathy evinced by our citizens at large with regard to the unfortunate man whose sufferings have lately attracted the deep commiseration of the whole country." Anderson's sufferings had indeed galvanized much of the Canadian public. He had killed a slave master while fleeing bondage on a Missouri tobacco farm; like tens of thousands of fugitive slaves along what became known as the Underground Railroad, Anderson fled to Canada, where by law he was a free man the moment he crossed the border. But when his identity was discovered, he was arrested for murder and a lower Canadian court ordered him extradited.

"I maintain that it would be a crime on the part of our authorities—on the part of the people of Canada—to render this man up," thundered one of the speakers at the Montreal rally. A petition demanding Anderson's release gathered more than 2,700 signatures. "The cry here is throughout the land," the Anti-Slavery Society of Toronto declared. "Anderson is not a murderer but a Hero and he must not be given up." The public pressure had its effect: in February 1861 an appeal court released Anderson on a technicality and he was allowed to stay in Canada. Samuel Ringgold Ward, an escaped slave himself who became a newspaper editor and leading abolitionist in Canada, put it bluntly: "There is no country in the world so much hated by slaveholders as Canada."

———

However much the slaveholders may have hated Canada for harbouring what they considered their "runaway property," they naturally directed most of their fury against the man they felt threatened their very right to own, traffic and trade in human beings: the newly elected Republican president in Washington. Indeed, so serious were the concerns about assassination plots that Lincoln found himself in the ignoble situation of having to sneak his way into the Federal capital for his inauguration as president. In the months between his narrow election victory and his inauguration, Lincoln faced all kinds of threats, from poisoned ink to a spider-filled dumpling. To make the trip in a regular passenger train from Illinois to Washington for his swearing-in, Lincoln had to pass through Baltimore, a hotbed of Southern sympathizers. So he disguised himself in a soft wool hat and an old overcoat, often sitting in the shadows to avoid being recognized.

When he finally arrived safely and made his inaugural address on March 4, the sixteenth president of the United States once again sought that elusive compromise. He vowed to leave slavery in the South untouched, insisting he had "no purpose, directly or indirectly, to interfere with the institution of slavery in the States where it exists." Instead, in a turn of phrase that became legendary, he called on his fellow citizens to listen to "the better angels of our nature."

"We are not enemies, but friends," Lincoln declared.

Would that it were so. Lincoln's attempts at conciliation were soon drowned out by the sound of gunfire. Within a few weeks, Confederate forces had encircled Fort Sumter, a major military facility in Charleston, South Carolina. The South had demanded that the US Army abandon all its installations in the breakaway states. Lincoln refused, instead sending supply ships to the endangered fortress. At 4:30 a.m. on April 12, 1861, Brigadier General Beauregard opened fire on the fort with fifty cannons.

The Civil War had begun.

Running for president, Lincoln had warned that "a house divided against itself cannot stand." Now his nightmare had come true. He would need all his fiery oratory—and plenty of military firepower—to try to keep the United States from collapsing. Lincoln faced a formidable foe in Jefferson Davis. Prior to his becoming president, Lincoln's battles had been restricted to the courtroom tussles of a lawyer. Davis, on the other hand, was a West Point graduate and had even served as the US secretary of war from 1853 to 1857.

Both sides were more or less evenly matched, at least at the start of the war. Twenty states were in the Union; eleven were part of the Confederacy; five were considered "Border States," though they largely leaned towards the slave South. Their armies were roughly equal in strength, with than 200,000 soldiers on each side, but that parity did not last long. With more than triple the population to draw recruits from, the Northern forces eventually outnumbered the South by two to one, soaring to 600,000 men in uniform by the end of the war.

To get to that overwhelming show of force, Lincoln needed a lot of soldiers, and he needed them quickly. On April 15, just three days after the attack on Fort Sumter, Lincoln issued a proclamation calling for a 75,000-man militia to be formed almost overnight; the recruits were asked to sign up for only ninety days because everyone thought it would not take long "to suppress insurrection." The news flashed across the nation by way of hundreds of daily newspapers published in cities large and small. It was front-page news in papers across Canada as well, most of them more sympathetic to the South than to Lincoln.

In Flint, Michigan, one Canadian heard the newsboy on the street bellowing out the headlines that would change her life. "This announcement startled me, while my imagination portrayed the coming struggle in all its fearful magnitude," Emma Edmonds wrote in her memoirs. "War, civil war, with all its horrors seemed inevitable."

Then she asked herself the question that millions of Americans and Canadians would have to answer: "But the great question to be decided, was, what can I do? What part am I to act in this great drama?"

4.

'I FELT CALLED TO GO'

A chance encounter with friends, a quick conversation and a snap decision to sign up for a war: it took just a few minutes for Edward P. Doherty to take the first steps that would put him on the path to history in the Lincoln assassination saga.

On a brisk spring Saturday morning in New York City on April 20, 1861, five days after President Lincoln had issued his call for army recruits, Doherty was walking to work in New York City. "As I was proceeding to my place of business, I met a number of my friends who were members of the 71st regiment—who, after some parley, induced me to become a member of their corps," he recounted. Just like that, the 22-year-old from Quebec was a private in Company A of the 71st New York Volunteers. Doherty never elaborated on his reasons for enlisting so quickly, though his military diaries revealed a young man's thrill at the prospect of stirring battles and "gallant soldiers."

Little is known about Doherty's background. He was born to Joseph and Margaret Doherty, who hailed from Ireland, on September 23, 1838, in Wickham, a town of a few hundred souls in Canada East not far from Montreal. Like many settlements in what later became known as Quebec's Eastern Townships, Wickham had several English-speaking families, like the Dohertys, living in a largely French-speaking province. It was a sleepy, isolated existence. Doherty must have felt as trapped there as Emma Edmonds did four hundred miles to the east in New Brunswick. A small school had been opened in the local church in 1821. A nearby river was the main mode of transport until a decent road was built in 1822; a railway line didn't reach the community until 1875. Not much going on for a boy who had bigger dreams and the drive to accomplish them.

Doherty moved to Montreal to go to school, graduated from college and may have studied law with a local firm. Certainly, his precise and colourful articles about his war experiences that would appear in newspapers and his meticulous reports to the military brass reflected a solid education and a disciplined mind.

Even the bustling streets of Montreal—by then the largest city in British North America—apparently did not offer enough excitement for the young Doherty; by 1860 he found himself working in New York City as the Civil War broke out. With his friends on that Saturday, he walked to the Federal armoury on Broadway and enlisted. By evening, they got word that they were shipping out to Washington the next day.

At seven o'clock on Sunday morning, Doherty joined the three hundred men who were mustered at their armoury and then headed to the ships that would take them to war amid what Doherty called "the enthusiastic and vehement cheers of the largest assembly of people ever known in New York." Doherty no doubt was riding that high of new recruits who have not yet tasted the blood of battle, but he was not exaggerating the excitement or the size of the Northern crowds. "Every window, door, stoop, balcony and house-top were alive with human beings," the *New York Times* reported. "Cheers from ten thousand voices swelling in prolonged chorus . . . made the scene one of the most animated and exciting ever witnessed in the City."

———

About six hundred miles to the west, Emma Edmonds was watching the same kind of stirring military parades in Flint, Michigan, "with their bright bayonets flashing in the morning sunlight." Recruiting offices were filled with men as their women back home "were busily engaged in preparing all the comforts that love and patriotism could suggest." That traditional woman's role of sewing uniforms or preparing food had no appeal for the fiercely independent Edmonds. "I could only thank God that I was free . . . and was not obliged to stay at home and weep," she said.

Unlike almost all the young recruits rushing to join the militias, this was not her country—and, arguably, not her war. "It is true, I was not an American—I was not obliged to remain here during this terrible strife," she wrote. "I could return to my native land where my parents would welcome me to the home of my childhood." Still, Edmonds's heart—and her religious upbringing—pushed her to join what she saw as a righteous fight for her adopted country. "I had no motive to enlisting than love to God, and love for suffering humanity. I felt called to go and do what I could for the defense of the right."

The problem, of course, was that, unlike Edward Doherty, as a woman Emma Edmonds could hardly enter an army office and enlist. But she decided that if she could sell Bibles as Franklin Thompson in a suit, why couldn't she carry a gun and wear a uniform as the same man? "I spent days and nights in anxious thought in deciding in what capacity I should try to serve the union cause," Edmonds recalled. "I could best serve the interest of the Union cause in male attire—could better perform the necessary duties for sick and wounded men, and with less embarrassment to them and to myself as a man than as a woman."

Nursing, like all of medicine, was still largely a man's world, though women were slowly becoming more common in the profession. But even where they were accepted, female nurses were largely kept in hospitals far from the front. Edmonds had no intention of waiting for the wounded to arrive "and then in some comfortable hospital sit quietly and fan the patients, after the Surgeon had dressed their wounds." That was not her style; she hungered for what she called "all the excitement of the battle scenes."

In late May 1861, Edmonds walked into a recruiting station and signed up as "Franklin Flint Thompson" (her new middle name likely inspired by her adopted hometown). Desperate for volunteers, the army had no formal medical checkups; basically, if you had a pulse and looked reasonably in shape, you were in. Edmonds, as she later recalled, "had always been a remarkably strong, healthy girl accustomed to hard work" and was immediately accepted. At nineteen years old, the girl who had shouted with glee when reading about a female pirate was now officially a private in Company F, 2nd Michigan Volunteer Infantry. Edmonds and her militia soon boarded a train on their way to the capital of a very dis-United States fighting for its very survival.

———

Edward Doherty, too, was making the exhausting trip to Washington with the men of the 71st Regiment, though his trip by boat was longer and even more gruelling than Edmonds's journey by rail.

He wrote of his early days in the American army in a remarkably detailed series of five letters printed in the Montreal *Gazette* under the title LETTER FROM THE SEAT OF THE WAR. FROM A MONTREALER IN THE U.S. ARMY. Penned between May 4 and May 30, they were published just days later, a testament to how fast news of the war travelled.

The men on the troopship slept on bare floors, with not enough room to stretch out. The food, Doherty wrote, was as bad as the beds—some salt beef, two biscuits per day and a cup of coffee. The Confederates had already blockaded the Potomac, so Doherty and his fellow recruits had to trek the final miles by foot. Just two hours outside Washington, they spotted a force of two thousand Confederate men "mounted on horse with artillery." While no attack came, it showed how precarious the situation was for the Federal forces. To modern readers, Lincoln's prolonged battle with "the South" conjures up images of a president huddled safely in Washington plotting war against his Confederate enemies somewhere far away in Mississippi and Alabama. In reality, the Civil War was a messy brawl in a family that was close-knit geographically if not politically: the "South" began in Virginia, just across the Potomac. On a clear day, with field glasses, Lincoln in the White House could see a Confederate flag fluttering in Alexandria, Virginia.

When they finally made it to the capital, Doherty and the rest of the 71st Regiment were billeted at the Washington Navy Yard. The President himself came by to visit the troops soon after: "On Sunday, we were honored by a visit and a how do you do shake hands," Doherty reported. There was even time for some relaxation with a recently invented game called baseball. An amateur team comprising members of Doherty's regiment defeated a club called the Washington Nationals by a score of 41–13.

On May 3, Doherty and the other volunteers were formally sworn in for three months of service. "I belong to the crack company of the regiment—and in fact the tigers of the empire city—composed of merchants, brokers, clerks, etc.—all highly respectable men," he boasted. "We are all anxious to have a brush at someone, and we have the metal in our regiment."

———

Not far from the Navy Yards where Doherty was anxiously awaiting battle, Emma Edmonds had her hands full tending to the casualties in the already overwhelmed and under-equipped hospitals that dotted Washington. *Hospital* was a polite term; aside from a few buildings, most were makeshift tent cities of the wounded and the dying. "The troops came pouring in so fast," she noted. "I would find a number of men there delirious with fever . . . but no physician to be found in attendance," she remarked. Typhoid fever—with a frightening mortality rate of 60 percent—had begun to sweep its way across the camps. Edmonds went from tent to tent, ministering to helpless men.

There were hundreds of thousands more to come. Edmonds was witnessing the beginning of what remains to this day the deadliest conflict in American history. An estimated 750,000 soldiers would die in the war. As hard as it may be to fathom, that death toll is higher than the total American combatants who perished in all the conflicts since, including the two world wars in the twentieth century, as well as Korea and Vietnam. What is just as shocking is that as many as two-thirds of those deaths came not from guns but from germs. Soldiers were more likely to be struck down by pneumonia, diarrhea, malaria and the typhoid that Edmonds and the other medical staff were battling with little success.

———

As Emma Edmonds was doing her best to treat the wounded, for his part Edward Doherty was equally determined not to become one of them.

Doherty got another chance to see Abraham Lincoln when the President made a return visit to the Navy Yard. This time the troops pulled off "the largest and most fashionable assemblage of the season" with a marching band. "The President sat in his accustomed seat in the portico," Doherty reported, "and seemed to enter fully into the spirit of the lively scene before him."

But in less than a week, the spirit changed and Lincoln and Doherty were mourning their losses after what might be described as a lethal game of capture the flag.

In the early morning hours of Friday, May 24, 1861, Doherty's regiment were finally given orders to move into action. Their mission: to cross the Potomac into rebel Virginia and take possession of Alexandria. Virginia's secession from the Union had just been ratified by referendum on the previous day. Lincoln and his cabinet were certainly displeased to have a rebel slave state just across the river; what must have enraged them even more was that large Confederate flag Lincoln could see from Washington, flying defiantly on the rooftop of an inn called Marshall House in Alexandria.

After a day of fighting, Doherty and his fellow fresh recruits took the town and tore down the rebel flag, though not without their first casualties of the war. "Everyone you meet seems as [if] he had lost a relative or friend," Doherty reported. As he walked through the streets of Alexandria, now under Union occupation but still filled with Southern sympathizers, Doherty saw signs that the slave trade had been temporarily halted—but only partly. A business that advertised "Dealers in Slave Males, and Females at a bargain" was shut down. Still, the ugliness of racism was ever-present. Doherty remarked that "16 black men were publicly whipped in the market of Alexandria by order of the Mayor." He also recorded a "very romantic and exciting incident" when an escaped slave whom he described as "a beautiful intelligent young creole" came up to the men pleading for help, with tears in her eyes. "She stated that she had just been beaten by her master and exhibited cuts on her arms and neck," he wrote. Four constables grabbed her, dragging her away, presumably in order to return her to her master. Doherty reported the Union soldiers were about to intervene when their commanding officer ordered them to stand down and "the four constables carried off their prize."

The anecdote serves as a reminder that, at least at this early point in the war, the battle for most people was still far from being motivated by the righteous cause of freedom for the enslaved people.

———

For Doherty and Edmonds, along with the tens of thousands of other eager young recruits, it was hard not to get swept up in the enthusiasm that envelops armies at the start of every war.

After the small skirmishes with the enemy in May, Doherty was itching for a full-fledged battle—and revenge. "The first blood has been shed," he wrote. "The troops are marching upon the enemy and we will have what we want—fighting."

The news they had been waiting for came in late July 1861. "Marching orders received today," Emma Edmonds wrote in her journal from Washington on the eve of the First Battle of Bull Run.

"The Army of the Potomac was soon to meet the enemy for the first time . . . Oh, what excitement and enthusiasm that order produced—nothing could be heard but the wild cheering of the men."

5.

'DESTRUCTION AND DEATH'

On that cool July evening before the first major battle of the Civil War, it all felt eerily peaceful. "We found many engaged in writing by the glimmering light of the camp-fire," Emma Edmonds wrote. "Some were reading their bibles, perhaps with more than usual interest; while others sat in groups, conversing in low earnest tones."

Bibles did little to stop the bullets when the carnage at Bull Run began.

The Civil War had none of the high-tech, long-range weapons that American soldiers would rely upon in the conflicts a century later. This was brutal close-contact conflict, with cannonballs, bayonets and muskets, that often ended with hand-to-hand combat. According to one account of the battle, Edward Doherty killed a horse from underneath a Confederate colonel from Georgia and then killed the colonel, capturing his sword and sash.

Doherty and his fellow soldiers were better armed than their adversaries, equipped with the new Minié rifled muskets invented just over a decade earlier in Europe that fired bullets with more speed, range and accuracy. The Confederates, cut off from Europe by a Federal blockade and without the manufacturing base of the richer North, relied initially on older "smoothbore" muskets and cannons that suffered from lesser range and accuracy. But screaming hot metal pouring down from the skies and piercing men's bodies could be just as deadly no matter how outmoded. Typical ammunition was the "grapeshot," a cluster of lead or iron balls held together like a bunch of grapes that broke up when fired. It was an early form of anti-personnel bombing, spraying a deadly shower over a wide number of targets.

Edmonds witnessed the resulting "confusion, destruction and death" as she put it. All around her, she saw men "being mown down like grass by the rebel batteries" through "the cloud of flame and smoke rolling from the hill."

Still, they fought on. "Come on boys, the rebels are in full retreat," shouted one commander, but as Edmonds noted, the bravado was short-lived: "The words had scarcely been uttered when he fell, pierced to the heart by a bullet."

In the heat and chaos of the battle, after Doherty had left some of his comrades at the church that had been turned into a hospital, he took a shortcut across the fields to what he supposed was his regiment about half a mile away. He was badly mistaken: they were Confederates.

The enemy took Doherty back to the church, which became a sort of tomb for the dying and a dungeon for the living as the number of wounded men in the small building quickly climbed to over 250.

———

On the other side of the battlefield, a young Confederate soldier was equally horrified by the devastation, though he was on the winning side.

Edwin Gray Lee had just turned twenty-five, serving as an aide-de-camp to General Thomas J. "Stonewall" Jackson. "The strife and carnage was fearful," he wrote his mother. Lee's courage during the battle earned him praise from another commander—his cousin Robert E. Lee, who went on to become the most prominent Confederate general. Edwin himself was destined for bigger things as well, though he could not have envisioned in three years he'd be commanding Confederate operations not in a Southern valley but in Canada.

"Thank God for our victory," Lee wrote of Bull Run. "We drove the enemy entirely off in ignominious defeat."

The battle was mercifully brief, lasting only one day. By Civil War standards the toll was nothing compared with the massacres to come. Still, it came at a steep cost. Bull Run was the bloodiest and largest battle to date of a conflict that was only three months old. The Confederates had over 1,800 men killed and wounded; the Union suffered over 1,500 casualties and another 1,300 missing or captured.

———

Edward Doherty had been one of those many Union soldiers who had been taken prisoner. Trapped in the church turned hospital that Edmonds as a nurse had been forced to abandon, he tried to tend to his wounded brothers. But death seemed certain during the night for those who lay in heaps of mangled bodies and shredded limbs. For those who survived, the prospects looked almost as bleak: the healthier prisoners were being marched away to Richmond. Doherty had no intention of being forced deeper into enemy territory, much less of being left behind to die. Escape from the thinly protected hospital seemed like a better option, if a desperate one.

Doherty later chronicled his adventures at Bull Run in a lengthy article for the *New York Times*. As he described it, five days after the battle, on Friday evening at 5 p.m., he and two other captured soldiers made a break for it. They snuck by the guard, crawling on their hands and feet until they got out of earshot of the other sentinels. They ran all night and the next day. By 4 p.m., they came upon an old man and asked for directions, pretending to be soldiers separated from an Alabama Confederate regiment. "Were you in the fight Sunday?" he asked. "I am glad, boys, you guys escaped from the slaughter. Those damned Yankees, I would like to see every man of them strung up."

The three "damned Yankees" kept going late into the evening, across railroad tracks, fields and forests. At one point, they were fired upon by Confederates on horseback. But by 5 a.m. on Sunday—seven days after they had survived the war's first major battle—the three exhausted Union fighters finally made it to safety across the Potomac.

The Montreal *Gazette* reported that Doherty's "narrative of the battle, care of the hospital and escape is very graphic and must commend him to the notice of his superiors." Doherty's bravery and resourcefulness indeed helped him move up the ranks, to the seat of power in Washington and eventually a very special mission. But for now, all the man from Quebec wanted was a warm supper and a good night's sleep. The next day, Doherty rode back to the Bull Run River to see where so many of his comrades had fallen.

"I visited the field of battle on horseback," Doherty recounted. "I saw there numbers of our comrades, unburied." As he looked over the hills littered with rotting bodies, it was not the blood or the disfigured faces and torn limbs that struck him, but the smell.

———

The disaster at Bull Run had disabused Abraham Lincoln, his generals and everyone else in the North of the notion that the revolt by the Southern states was a minor "insurrection" that could be quelled with untrained volunteers.

Just two weeks before the battle, Lincoln had gone to a special session of Congress to ask for money and troops "for making this contest a short, and a decisive one." But Jefferson Davis and the Confederacy had shown that the war would be neither short nor decisive. "We have broken the back bone of invasion and utterly broken the spirit of the North," the *Richmond Examiner* exclaimed triumphantly.

The North was reeling, forced to retreat.

"The hospitals in Washington, Alexandria and Georgetown were crowded with wounded, sick, discouraged soldiers," Emma Edmonds recounted as she struggled to cope. "That extraordinary march from Bull Run, through rain, mud, and chagrin, did more toward filling the hospitals than did the battle itself . . . Measels [*sic*], dysentery and typhoid fever were the prevailing diseases after the retreat."

"The 'Soldiers' Cemetery' was being quickly filled with new-made graves," she wrote.

———

Edmonds and Doherty were witnessing this ghastly toll because they had chosen to fight in another country's war. They were not alone: an estimated 30,000 to 50,000 English and French Canadians enlisted in the Civil War—overwhelmingly on the Union side. Some were doctors and lawyers. Most of the recruits were ordinary workingmen—day labourers, factory workers, farmers, fishermen.

Some, like Edmonds, did it out of conviction that the cause was a just one. Others, like Doherty, did it for the sense of adventure. Many enlisted for the money: the signing bonus of $200, plus the $13 monthly pay for soldiers (and between $100 and $200 for officers), went far for struggling families in the 1860s. It certainly meant a lot to the tens of thousands of French-Canadian economic migrants who had already settled in the northeastern states, looking for work. Between 15,000 and 20,000 *Canadiens* would fight in the Union army. As many as 5 to 10 percent of some regiments in Maine, Massachusetts and Michigan were francophones. The Canadians fought valiantly: at least twenty-nine earned Medals of Honour; five of them became Union generals. And many paid the ultimate price for valour: an estimated 5,000 to 7,000 died.

But among the ruling elites in Canada—French and English—there was much less enthusiasm for Lincoln's cause. "Such unfortunate young men . . . fooled by false promises by an even falser people," bemoaned *La Minerve* newspaper. "A report of the Confederate victory in the war's first battle [at Bull Run] elicited a spontaneous cheer in Canada's legislature," writes historian John Boyko. Canada, as would become clear over the next four years, was just as divided as America over what to do about slavery and the increasingly savage war to end it.

6.

'THE STAR OF HOPE'

The Americans on the wrong side of the war were oppressors.

They had blood on their hands and no respect for race or creed.

They deserved to lose. Their leaders were bloodthirsty despots who trampled on basic freedoms.

In the pages of the Canadian newspapers filled with stories of the Civil War, those criticisms were directed not at the slaveholding Southern states but at the Northern states led by Abraham Lincoln. Such views were not surprising, as the publications echoed the beliefs of their wealthy owners. Large parts of the business and political ruling classes—along with many church leaders in both English and French Canada—expressed affinity with, and at times open endorsement of, the slave-owning aristocracy.

Canadian political leaders, while taking care not to openly offend Abraham Lincoln as the duly elected leader of the United States, did not hesitate to show sympathy for his opponents in the slave states. Three years before he became Canada's first prime minister, John A. Macdonald spoke eloquently to the delegates at the 1864 Charlottetown Confederation Conference about "the gallant defence that is being made by the Southern Republic."

"[A]t this moment they have not much more than four millions [*sic*] of men," Macdonald said, "yet what a brave fight they have made."

While tens of thousands of ordinary Canadians had signed up to fight and die with Lincoln's forces, Canada's elites largely supported his enemies.

———

Canada's leaders were in step with the rulers of the British Empire in England, which, under the guise of neutrality, gave much-needed support to the Confederacy. British North America at the time was a scattering of provinces with about four million people, out of which a third were French-speaking and 100,000 were Indigenous peoples. The country was rapidly evolving from a sleepy colony into a bustling industrial nation. The first train in Canada had billowed smoke the length of its fifteen-mile route along the St. Lawrence River in 1835; the first clicks of the telegraph wire were heard in 1846 between Toronto and Hamilton. By mid-century, trains and telegraphs had connected much of Canada together and, equally important, had bound Canada ever closer to the United States. Convenient travel by train and the many steamers that criss-crossed the Great Lakes—along with porous borders with no surveillance, much less passports—made travel between the United States and Canada easy and frequent.

Though only a few years away from becoming a distinct country under Confederation in 1867, Canada was still firmly within the British colonial empire and followed its lead on the American Civil War. England had played a leading role on the world stage in abolishing slavery throughout most of its territories. But the industrial capitalism that underpinned "Rule Britannia" ran on profits, not principles.

Lincoln had tried to strangle the South by imposing a sea blockade along the coastline all the way from Virginia to Texas. But British ships conducted a brisk trade to buy Southern cotton—80 percent of England's cotton came from America—providing Jefferson Davis's fledgling secessionist states with much-needed cash. The Confederates raised funds in the London financial markets and built their navy ships in British shipyards. Understandably, Lincoln's government did not take kindly to this state of affairs. While England declined to formally recognize the Confederate government, its actions amounted to almost the same thing. It gave the secessionist states credibility and status by treating them on par with Lincoln's government—two supposedly legitimate sides of an unfortunate family squabble. Many in the Canadian business elite, like their counterparts in the mother country, made fortunes trading with the South, prompting the *New York Times* to snipe: "Our Canadian neighbors are imitating their 'mamma' in sending aid and comfort to the slavocracy of America."

Given the conservative bent of the English-speaking business elite across Canada and of the Catholic Church in Quebec, many of the newspapers they owned or sponsored reflected their anti-Lincoln bias. Even before the Civil War started, French-language papers showed their true colours. The widely read *Le Canadien* published a laudatory biography of Jefferson Davis and dismissed Lincoln's inaugural address as "colourless, confusing and contradictory." When the cannon fire erupted in April 1861, *Le Canadien* insisted the Southern slave states had "the right to autonomy" while the *Courrier du Canada* blamed Lincoln, arguing that civil war is "natural and almost obligatory" when "despotism leads to the abuse of freedom." The leading French paper in Montreal was *La Minerve*, considered a house organ for John A. Macdonald's Conservative Party and his francophone ally, George-Étienne Cartier, both future Fathers of Confederation in Canada. As the Civil War raged on, *La Minerve* had no shame in praising the Confederacy for fielding one of "the most intelligent armies we have known in America," lauding the bravery of Southern troops. Describing Confederates as "compatriots," it ran stories about imperilled whites in Louisiana threatened by Black mobs and railed against Lincoln's plan to create "Coloured regiments."

English Quebec saw the same pro-Southern bias, with almost all of the six main newspapers slanting their coverage and opinions against Lincoln. The *Montreal Witness* was a solitary voice decrying the evils of slavery. "Such a gigantic wrong cannot exist on the same continent with us without affecting the people of Canada in one way or another," the newspaper declared. But the much more influential *Gazette*— published by two close friends of Macdonald and Cartier—decried what it called the North's "unlawful war." The same day the *Gazette* began running its series of letters from Edward Doherty, it also published a letter from an unnamed Canadian, this one in Alabama. "The Southern movement did not originate with a few wealthy slaveowners," he assured the newspaper's readers. "All white men, who are planters, are necessarily slave-owners, and of course, interested in the preservation of their lives and property." Another commentator in the *Gazette* wondered fearfully if "the blacks be permitted to rise and massacre their masters and their families." In Quebec City, the *Morning Chronicle* was equally inflammatory. Typical was a headline mocking "a French-Canadian gentleman" who had been given command of a "n----- regiment" made up of what the newspaper called "unbleached Americans."

In Ontario, the voices against Lincoln and the North were even more shrill. The *Niagara Review* denounced Lincoln as a "mad, blood-stained despot at Washington." In the week that the Civil War started, the *Toronto Leader*, arguably the most consistently pro-Confederate paper in the country from the start of the war, praised Southern soldiers for being "hearty in their cause" and warned "innocent women and helpless children are to be butchered" by armed slaves.

The Confederate leanings of most Canadian papers infuriated the pro-Lincoln press in the Northern states. "By far the greater number of the leading journals show an unmistakable hostility to the federal cause," complained the *New York World*. But that bias delighted the slave state leaders back in Richmond. They sent an emissary to Canada to gauge public opinion, and after travelling for two months through small and large towns he was thrilled to conclude that "the South's only adversary in the Canadian press" was a single newspaper.

But it came with a loud voice.

———

There was one publisher in Canada who was the most consistent in urging Americans to fight for what he called "the suppression of the inhuman traffic that disgraced their land." He was George Brown of the Toronto *Globe*, Canada's largest and most influential English-language newspaper.

Brown was the leader of the Reform Party, allied with the Quebec Liberals and a fervent opponent of John A. Macdonald's Conservatives. He was elected to Parliament at various times from 1851 to 1865 and even served briefly as the co-premier of Canada West. The fact that Brown openly mixed his political affiliations with his paper was not unusual for the times. What made Brown unique among his fellow newspaper barons was his passionate commitment to use his press and his power to fight what he called the "sum of all human villainies."

Born and raised in a well-to-do family in Edinburgh, at the age of eighteen Brown had followed his father to New York City. When his father set up a reform-minded newspaper, Brown learned the tools of the journalism trade; like his father, Brown received a schooling in politics by getting involved in the growing abolitionist movement in the Northern states. Brown brought his newspaper skills and his new-found abolitionism to Canada when he moved to Toronto to start the *Globe* in 1844; by October 1853, Brown was printing tens of thousands of copies daily.

"The question is often put: What have we in Canada to do with American slavery? We have everything to do with it," Brown proclaimed. "We are alongside of this great evil. Our people mingle with it; we are affected by it now, and every day enhances the evil."

By profession, Brown was a man of words; on principle, he would take action to confront "this great evil." When hundreds of people had gathered at City Hall on February 26, 1851, the *Globe* described it as "the largest and most enthusiastic meeting we have ever seen in Toronto." It was perhaps a forgivable exaggeration, given that the meeting was held to create the Anti-Slavery Society of Canada—and the newspaper's publisher, George Brown, was one of its founders. "We, the anti-slavery men of Canada, have an important duty to discharge," Brown later declared. "Slavery is the one great cause of the American rebellion, and . . . the success of the north is the death-knell of slavery."

The Society brought together pillars of the white establishment, like Brown and Oliver Mowat, the future premier of Ontario, with emerging leaders of the Black community, such as Wilson Abbott, a successful businessman who had become an outspoken advocate for civil rights and equality. Their goal was nothing less than "the extinction of slavery all over the world" and offering sympathy and support for the "victims of slavery flying to our soil."

———

Canada was an ideal refuge for escaped slaves not just because it was America's northern neighbour. Like the United States, Canada had its own sorry history of human bondage. Discrimination and racism still ran deep. But at least on paper, when it came to the written law and statutes, Canada had excised its demon of slavery.

The first slaves in what was New France in the 1600s were Indigenous peoples; African slaves soon followed. In 1629, in the first recorded slave sale in Canada, English traders sold a six-year-old boy from Africa to a French clerk. By the mid-1700s there were about 3,600 enslaved people in the country. Perhaps the best-known was Marie-Josèphe-Angélique, a young Portuguese-born Black woman who, while trying to escape, was accused of setting a fire that burned down much of Montreal in 1734. She was tortured with wooden planks that crushed her legs in order to force her to confess, then paraded through the city streets in a garbage cart, hanged in front of the Notre-Dame Basilica, burned and then, as the court had ordered, "her Body then Reduced To Ashes And Cast to the Wind."

More enslaved people came to Canada—now under the control of Britain—in the 1780s when the United Empire Loyalists fled the American Revolution and brought about 2,500 slaves with them. It was not unusual to see advertisements like the one that ran in the Montreal *Gazette* three days after Christmas in 1795:

FOR SALE: A Young healthy Negro wench between 12 and 13 year of age, lately from Upper Canada where she was brought up.

Following the lead of the British, though, Upper Canada ruled in 1819 that "negroes are entitled to personal freedom through residence," and by 1833 the British Imperial Act formally abolished slavery throughout the British Empire. Thus began Canada's reputation as a land of freedom.

Frederick Douglass, a former slave who became America's most influential abolitionist leader, set up his base in Rochester, New York, just across the Erie Canal from Canada. He called his newspaper the *North Star*, a reference both to the celestial light that would guide fleeing slaves and to the beacon of freedom that the Northern states and Canada became. "To millions, now in our boasted land of liberty, it is the STAR OF HOPE," Douglass exclaimed.

Making it safely to that North Star was difficult and treacherous, and so a system of elaborate escape routes emerged that came to be known as the Underground Railroad. Rochester, from where Douglass waged his crusade, was one of its last stops. "Conductors" used wagons and boats to carry the "cargo" of runaways to hundreds of hidden "stations" such as barns, homes and churches of abolitionist sympathizers. One of the most prominent conductors was Harriet Tubman, who escaped from a Maryland plantation and made at least thirty trips, shepherding hundreds of ex-slaves to Canada. Tubman and other rescuers relied heavily on the growing Black population in towns such as St. Catharines, Chatham and Windsor, which served as "terminals" for the railroad.

There are no precise figures on how many people rode the Underground Railroad to freedom in Canada in the decades between 1820 and 1860—understandably, given that it was a clandestine enterprise. Activists claimed it was as many as 60,000 to 75,000; most historians estimate that at least around 30,000 fugitive slaves had settled in Canada by the time the Civil War broke out. By all accounts it was certainly in the tens of thousands. "Almost every ship or boat coming into Toronto harbor from the American side of Lake Ontario seemed to be carrying a runaway slave," the *Toronto Colonist* reported in 1852.

The flight of people to the Northern states and Canada was such a serious concern that in 1850 the US Congress, still under the sway of the slave owners, passed the Fugitive Slave Act. A harsh and unforgiving law, it in effect obliged Northerners (and by extension Canadians) to become collaborators in the slavery machine, requiring law enforcement officials to arrest suspected runaways and threatening any ordinary citizen who aided a former slave with heavy fines and imprisonment. (When Lincoln became president a decade later, he said that while he was morally opposed to the law, he would enforce it.) It was this law that American authorities invoked in their bid to repatriate John Anderson, the escapee who became a symbol of Canada's resistance to Southern bondage. *Globe* publisher George Brown, like many abolitionists, denounced "the atrocious Fugitive Slave Law, compelling the freemen of the north to become . . . hounds on their own farms after the human chattels of the slave-holders of the south."

Ironically, the Act only increased the flood of people to Canada. There were stories of one hundred members of one Black Baptist church in Buffalo and another hundred parishioners in Rochester, New York, fleeing en masse to Canada. In Pittsburgh, Black waiters at one hotel took up arms and made their way to the Canadian border, declaring they were "determined to die rather than be captured."

The repressive Act also inspired one woman helping runaways flee to Canada to write a book that in many ways would hasten the beginning of the Civil War.

———

Harriet Beecher Stowe was the daughter of a preacher, schooled in a seminary and surrounded by outspoken abolitionists as she grew up. A teacher and writer, she settled in a small town in Maine about 120 miles from the Canadian border where she and her family harboured several runaway slaves. In 1851, she began publishing a series of stories in the paper that would be published in book form under the title *Uncle Tom's Cabin*, a monumentally influential work with a decidedly mixed legacy.

On the one hand, Stowe's book—certainly by today's standards—was poisoned by the condescension that often marked the world view of the white religious abolitionists at the time. Stowe may have thought of her title character as a "noble hero" but "Uncle Tom" became a derogatory term describing an overly servile Black man, too eager to please his masters. Other characters reinforced the stereotypes of the joyful "mammy" and the lazy "happy darky." Nevertheless, despite its flaws as seen through modern eyes, back in the 1850s the book played a seismic role in exposing the atrocities of slavery. It became the most-read novel of the nineteenth century and reportedly the second-bestselling book of that century, behind only the Bible. When Lincoln met Stowe shortly after the Civil War began, the story went that he told her: "So this is the little lady who started this great war." While the quote is generally considered to be apocryphal, it reflected the immeasurable impact the book had in stirring up Northern passions and the drumbeats of a war against slavery.

In fiction and in reality, the book also cemented Canada's image as a North Star, a haven from bondage and brutality. Four of the characters in Stowe's book cross Lake Erie to find freedom. The novel was said to be inspired in part by the real-life story of Josiah Henson, who, unlike the meek and subservient Uncle Tom, was a courageous and resourceful fighter. Born into slavery in Maryland, he was taken from his parents, sold twice and beaten badly enough to injure him for life. Henson escaped, fled with his wife and four children and crossed the Niagara River into Upper Canada in late 1830. Near what is now Dresden, Ontario, he built a two-hundred-acre settlement of farms, mills and schools. To raise money for his project, Henson published his autobiography in 1849, three years before Stowe's book, *The Life of Josiah Henson, Formerly a Slave, Now an Inhabitant of Canada.*

Henson went on to become a conductor of the Underground Railroad, helping to recruit Black Canadians to fight in the Union army against the slave states he had fled.

―――――

If Harriet Beecher Stowe used words that hastened the Civil War, John Brown used weapons. Like Stowe, his actions inflamed the political passions that would lead to war; and like Stowe, his struggles had strong connections to Canada.

Brown was a firebrand abolitionist who had not shied away from violence in the service of a righteous cause. In 1856, when the Kansas

Territory was plunged into a series of deadly confrontations between pro- and anti-slavery factions, Brown and four of his sons stabbed and hacked to death five pro-slavery men with swords. Brown had grown tired of the pacifist abolitionists. "These men are all talk," Brown had once said. "What we need is action—action!"

To plan his action, Brown needed safety and support. He chose Chatham, Ontario—a terminus for the Underground Railroad where about a third of the six thousand residents were escaped slaves—as a secure place from which to plan wider insurrection. While there, Brown met with Harriet Tubman, the Underground Railroad leader who was frequently in Canada. He also earned the backing of prominent local abolitionists like Mary Shadd, the first Black woman publisher in North America, whose newspaper, the *Provincial Freeman*—"Devoted to anti-slavery," as its slogan proclaimed—was a tireless voice not just for abolition but for school equality, integration and civil rights.

On May 10, twelve white men and thirty-three Blacks gathered in secret at the First Baptist Church in Chatham to plan guerrilla warfare in the United States that they hoped would inspire a slave uprising. With more righteousness than realism, they adopted a "provisional constitution" for the "citizens of the United States and the oppressed people." Recording the proceedings as secretary was Osborne Perry Anderson, a free Black man from Pennsylvania who had moved to Canada to become a printer. Brown quietly returned to the US, where for the next year he led sporadic raids to liberate enslaved people while still dreaming of a major assault he quixotically hoped would spark a slave insurrection. Then, on October 16, 1859, he struck.

Brown led a small band of twenty-two men, including five free Black men, on a raid of the Federal arsenal in the quiet Virginia enclave of Harpers Ferry. They easily captured the unprotected armoury, but a pitched battle ensued when a company of US Marines arrived. For thirty-six hours the battle raged, but Brown's tiny band was no match for the government army. Ten of Brown's men were killed, including two of his sons and a 23-year-old Canadian named Stewart Taylor—the only member of Brown's raiding party not born in the United States.

One of the few lucky survivors who managed to escape was Osborne Anderson, the American-born printer from Chatham. Brown was put on trial and found guilty of "inciting servile insurrection" and treason against the state. At eleven o'clock on the morning of December 2, 1859, Brown was taken from his jail to the gallows sitting on top of his own coffin in a wagon pulled by two white horses. He died swinging at the end of a noose in a very public display meant to discourage any other anti-slavery rebellions.

———

As Brown's life had slipped away in those final moments on the gallows, a young actor watched the execution with a mixture of animosity and awe. John Wilkes Booth was taking a break during a rehearsal at a Richmond theatre when he caught sight of men from the militia known as the Virginia Grays, boarding a train to Charles Town to provide security at John Brown's execution. Booth asked the volunteer militia if he could join them; a uniform was found and the young man was on his way to witness history.

"I saw John Brown hung and I may say that I helped to hang John Brown," he later said, exaggerating his role somewhat. As a Confederate sympathizer whose support for slavery was unwavering, Booth had nothing but "unlimited, undeniable contempt" for the "traitor and terrorizer," as he put it. But as a performer who loved the theatrical, Booth also admitted he was impressed by how calmly the condemned man had faced his final moments. As Booth later wrote to his sister, John Brown was a "brave old man" whose "heart must have been broken when he felt himself deserted" and no one had come to rescue him from the gallows.

However misguided and ill-planned Brown's raid was in the eyes of many, it did indeed spark "fear and trembling in all the Slave States," as he had vowed. Six days after his execution, a senator from Mississippi rose in Congress to warn that "a thousand John Browns can invade us" while the "Black Republican Government," as he called Lincoln's administration, did little to protect white Southerners. "Have we no right to allege that to secure our rights and protect our honor, we will dissever the ties that bind us together, even if it rushes us into a sea of blood," he thundered. The senator's name was Jefferson Davis, and by the next December the Southern states indeed started severing their ties to the union and plunged the country into a sea of blood.

———

North of the border, John Brown was seen as a hero by many ordinary Canadians. In Montreal, over a thousand people attended a memorial at the St. Bonaventure Hall and voted for "resolutions of sympathy." Another large service for the executed hero was held at Toronto's St. Lawrence Hall, where funds were raised and forwarded to Brown's widow. The *Globe* thundered that the Harpers Ferry leader would be remembered as "a brave man" who dared to challenge "the money-hunting, cotton-worshipping American world."

When the Civil War erupted just over a year after he was hanged, "John Brown's Body," in various versions, became a popular folk song. Union soldiers picked it up as they marched through the South, adding more militant words against the Confederacy to the lyrics. Emma Edmonds heard the song around the army campfires with her fellow troops preparing for battle. "John Brown is still remembered there," she wrote. "[T]he spirit of John Brown does seem to march along wonderfully fast."

Edmonds and her fellow soldiers would need all the inspiration they could get. The war was going to get a lot uglier and a lot bloodier— and Lincoln, however reluctantly, soon made the abolition of slavery, the cause that had so inspired Stowe and Brown, the central issue in the conflict.

7.

'FIELD OF CARNAGE'

The cold and rain and mud were everywhere.

On March 17, 1862, tens of thousands of troops in Major-General George B. McClellan's Army of the Potomac had landed at Fort Monroe, on the southern tip of the Virginia Peninsula. Like her fellow soldiers, Emma Edmonds—still successfully pulling off her disguise as Franklin Thompson—was hungry for warmth and food, but also for battle and revenge. Having seen too many friends perish, Edmonds wanted to fight on the front lines, not just cope with the carnage in the hospitals. "I did not enjoy taking care of the sick and wounded as I once did," she admitted, "but I longed to go forth."

She would get her wish.

McClellan had assembled the largest armada America had ever seen, using dozens of boats to ferry more than 121,000 men, 1,150 wagons and over 15,000 horses from Alexandria, on the outskirts of Washington, to Fort Monroe. His plan was to push up through the peninsula with the goal of capturing the Confederate capital of Richmond, just eighty miles northwest. The Peninsula Campaign, as it came to be known, was a five-month march of folly that ended with the loss of tens of thousands of lives.

As a soldier, a nurse and a sharp-eyed chronicler, Edmonds would witness it all.

It helped that thirteen days before reaching Fort Monroe, she had been given a new assignment that resulted in access to more than her own small unit. Colonel Orlando Poe, who commanded the 2nd Michigan

Regiment, issued an order "that Private Franklin Thompson of Company F be appointed mail carrier." Edmonds was later promoted to postmaster for the entire regiment. Many years after the war, when Edmonds's true identity had been exposed, Poe remarked: "As a soldier 'Frank Thompson' was effeminate looking and for this reason was detailed as mail carrier to avoid taking an efficient soldier from the ranks." The colonel was perhaps trying to retroactively explain away his failure to catch on to a woman serving under his command. But Poe was nonetheless right that her small size (and her skill with horses) made her the perfect fit for the job.

For Edmonds, dashing from one camp to another at all hours of the day and night was the ideal assignment. It made hiding her gender easier because she was often on the road and away from the crowded and cramped Union outposts; it made her popular with her fellow fighters; and it gave her a front-row seat for the adventure she craved.

———

On May 4, the Confederates had deserted Yorktown, twenty-five miles from Fort Monroe.

McClellan and his Army of the Potomac gave chase to the retreating Confederates, confronting them the next day at the Battle of Williamsburg. It was the first serious encounter of the Peninsula Campaign, and a harbinger of what was to come: inconclusive skirmishes with the only certainty being the mounting body count. "[T]he thunder of cannon and the crash of musketry reverberated through the woods and over the plain," Edmonds noted as 41,000 Union soldiers faced 32,000 Confederates. "When morning came still there were hundreds found upon the field. . . found in heaps, both dead and wounded piled together in ravines, among the felled timber, and in rifle pits half covered with mud." The heaps of bodies amounted to four thousand killed and wounded on the two sides.

Sixteen days later and about forty miles up the peninsula, the armies yet again confronted each other, this time in the Battle of Seven Pines. The two days of fighting, like much of the Peninsula Campaign, ended inconclusively. "Many brave soldiers lay down on that gory field—the weary to sleep, and the wounded to die," Edmonds noted after the first day of fighting. The morning brought sunlight and more savagery; the final tally of casualties reached eleven thousand. Edmonds made her way to what was called the "hospital tree" in the hamlet of Fair Oaks where the wounded waited for the saws and knifes that would amputate their limbs.

"The ground around that tree for several acres in extent was literally drenched with human blood," Edmonds remarked. "It was enough to make angels weep to look down upon that field of carnage."

———

In between and sometimes during these pitched battles, Edmonds was also racing through woods, ravines and rivers to carry mail and messages from camp to camp, at times covering dozens of miles at a stretch with several heavy bags of letters. Once, while on a delivery, Edmonds discovered that Confederate troops had moved in between her and the Union lines. "[M]y ear caught the click, click of a dozen rifles," she wrote. "My colt took fright at this unexpected salute, and plunged into the woods in another direction with the speed of lightning."

By all accounts—not just hers but those of her comrades-in-arms— Emma Edmonds was a courageous and committed fighter. A fellow soldier, William Morse, reported that "her faithfulness, bravery and efficiency . . . won the respect, admiration and confidence of both officers and men." Indeed, even commanders from other regiments took note of her. She rode "with a fearlessness that attracted the attention and secured the commendation of field and general officers" during the hellish disaster at the December 1862 Battle of Fredericksburg, according to Major Byron M. Cutcheon of the 20th Michigan Regiment, whose memories of her figured large later in Edmonds's life. Still, Edmonds apparently felt the need to embellish her tales of front-line nursing and perilous mail deliveries for the book she eventually published, *Nurse and Spy in the Union Army*. Her role as a nurse was demonstrably true, the designation as "spy" somewhat less so.

In Edmonds's telling, her induction into the military spy world came in February 1862 when a Union spy was captured in Richmond and a replacement was urgently needed. "I was becoming dissatisfied with my situation as nurse, and was determined to leave the hospital," she wrote. "I am naturally fond of adventure, a little ambitious and a good deal romantic." Edmonds claimed she had an interview with Union general George B. McClellan and other officials—though no record of such a meeting exists—and got the job as an army spy.

For her first mission to penetrate the Confederate stronghold of Yorkton, Edmonds said she created a "complete disguise" as a Black worker. She used silver nitrate to make sure her "head, face, neck, hands and arms were colored black as any African" and wore "a wig of real negro wool." She claimed that she hauled wheelbarrows of gravel and pails of water, while secretly gathering information and making sketches of Confederate fortifications, cannons and mortars. Upon her safe return to Union lines, Edmonds reported to General McClellan and received his "hearty congratulations."

The second spy adventure behind Confederate lines, according to Edmonds, took place in May 1862 when she donned the outfit of an Irish female peddler. If Edmonds was aware of the irony of her situation, she didn't acknowledge it, but there she was, a woman disguised as a male soldier in the Union army who wears another disguise to pass as a female to mix with the Confederate army. When some important papers fell out of a soldier's pocket, she recounted scooping them and bringing back the valuable military intelligence.

Her book was filled with other harrowing adventures behind enemy lines. "While in the 'Secret Service' as a 'Spy,' . . . she penetrated the enemy's lines, in various disguises, no less than eleven times, always with complete success and without detection," her publisher boasted in the introduction to her book.

However, Edmonds could never have been in the official United States Secret Service, since it was only created shortly after the Civil War ended in 1865. There were numerous Union spying operations, most notably one operated by Allan Pinkerton, whose private company helped protect Lincoln. Pinkerton regularly filed military intelligence reports to McClellan, but historian Edwin C. Fishel found "no information attributed" to Edmonds in the Pinkerton documents. Fishel, who rather dismissively refers to Edmonds as "the transvestite spy," concluded that "she almost certainly was never a spy at all."

It is possible, of course, that some of Edmonds's alleged adventures as a spy were unofficial excursions that were never recorded. It is also true her mail delivery assignments could have afforded her occasions to roam more freely and surreptitiously than most soldiers. Certainly, the legend of her spy missions only gained traction over time. From the official account of Michigan's Civil War activities, commissioned by the state government in 1879, to most popular biographies in the twentieth century, her spy adventures were taken for granted. As late as December 2020, the *Globe and Mail*, as part of its "Moment in Time" history feature, extolled Edmonds's reputation as "a daring spy."

But unlike many other events in her memoirs that can be corroborated by eyewitnesses and written records, we only have Edmonds's account—replete with her usual poetic and religious embellishments—of her secret operations. Edmonds herself seemed to cast doubt about her spying sagas in her later years, when she fought for a military pension. "I make no statement of any secret services," she wrote in a sworn affidavit. "In my mind, there is almost as much odium attached to the word 'spy' as there is to the word 'deserter.' There is so much mean deception necessarily practiced by a spy that I much prefer everyone should believe that I never was beyond the enemy's lines rather than fasten upon me by oath a thing that I despise so much. It may do in wartime, but it is not pleasant to think upon in time of peace."

The lies people tell about themselves can be more revealing than their truths. Not content with being just a brave soldier and a nurse, Edmonds—perhaps inspired by her childhood heroine Fanny the pirate—added more excitement and adventure to her story. Her spying tales were filled with sympathetic encounters with oppressed Blacks in the South or dying Confederate soldiers she cradled in her arms. In her exaggerated tales as a military spy, Edmonds was painting a very real portrait of the compassionate person she was, or at least the caring and daring person she wanted to be.

8.

'THE PROMISE OF FREEDOM'

The pink-and-white magnolia trees that decorated Washington, DC, were a colourful distraction from the dreary grey of the battlefields. For a few weeks in the middle of 1862, Emma Edmonds had a brief respite from the front-line dangers. She was sent to Washington to deliver letters and packages to soldiers in hospitals there. At least in the capital in all its July glory, Edmonds could let down her guard and relax. She visited the halls of Congress, the museums and a camp of former slaves who "all were happy, because they were free."

But in her bones, the battle-weary Edmonds knew she was a soldier, not a tourist. More comfortable with the dirt, sweat and blood of the front than with "the aristocratic spirit" she felt pervaded the city, she had nothing but scorn for the military officials she saw in their "plumed hats, scarlet lined riding cloaks . . . and gaily caparisoned horses."

Within a month, Edmonds found herself far from the pretense and plumage of Washington. By August, she was plunged into the Second Battle of Bull Run on the same grounds in northern Virginia where she had first seen fighting back in 1861. Like the first Bull Run conflict, it was a crushing blow to Union morale. An emerging Confederate hero, General Robert E. Lee defeated his Union opponents, leading to fourteen thousand dead and wounded—almost a quarter of the men in blue on the battlefield. Edmonds, still acting as a mail carrier, was one of those injured. On her way back from Washington, she was desperate to get the mail and messages to Union lines before the worst of the fighting had got under way. Looking for shortcuts, she rode through fields, jumping over fences. It was a costly mistake.

Attempting to cross a wide ditch, her mule reared and she was thrown headlong onto the ground, hurting her left leg and chest. She managed to retrieve the mud-splattered mailbags and get back to her camp. But Franklin Thompson the intrepid mail carrier had a problem worse than "his" injuries: any full medical examination risked exposing Edmonds's real gender. "I made no report of the accident but simply said that I had hurt my leg and it was very painful and asked him [the surgeon] for something to relieve the pain," she recounted.

"Being a *woman*, I felt compelled to suffer in silence and endure it the best I could, in order to escape detection of my sex," she wrote many years later. "*I would have rather been shot dead* than to have been known as a woman and sent away from the army under guard as a criminal." The italics are hers, reflecting how determined she was to keep her secret.

Despite her injuries and her need for a constant disguise, Edmonds soldiered on as the regiment's devoted and deeply appreciated mail carrier. Damon Stewart, one of Thompson's closest friends, noted that "he was faithful and brave . . . and gained all hearts by his cheerful, obliging activity." Orlando Poe, the regimental leader, had come to rely on her constantly. In mid-October he wrote to his wife: "I am very busy—twenty persons waiting to transact business, and I can't write much for Thompson is waiting to carry this to Washington." Two months later, on December 3, 1862, he told his wife that letters were not the only things Edmonds made sure to deliver to her commanding officer: "Frank Thompson (mail carrier) has just returned from Washington," Poe wrote. "He brought me a pocket full of apples and doughnuts, and a very nice orange."

Poe evidently thought highly enough of his young postmaster that he made Thompson his aide-de-camp—in essence his personal assistant—that same month. The timing could not have been more consequential: it gave Edmonds another front-row seat for the final battle of 1862, one that turned out to be yet another disaster for Lincoln's cause.

———

On December 11, no fewer than 120,000 Union soldiers were set to lay siege to the Confederate strongholds at Fredericksburg, Virginia. Facing them was the seemingly indomitable Confederate Robert E. Lee, with 79,000 men under his command. The Union plan was to storm the heights near the city on the way to a triumphant march to Richmond. Lincoln desperately needed a victory—for morale as much as military reasons.

From the start, it did not go well.

"While I write the roar of cannon and musketry is almost deafening, and the shot and shell are falling fast on all sides," Edmonds recorded in her journal on December 13. "This may be my last entry in this journal. God's will be done." Her fear was justified. Over and over again the Union commanders ordered their men to charge a well-protected ridge west of the city, with horrific results. Ever the dutiful soldier, Edmonds was unwilling to criticize the foolhardy generals. But her graphic descriptions stood as a merciless condemnation. "I never saw, till then, a man deliberately shoot himself, with his own pistol, in order to save the rebels the satisfaction of doing so, as it would seem," she recounted. "The field was literally piled with dead."

When it was over, the Union army counted more than twelve thousand casualties—more than twice the Confederates' losses. Southern papers hailed the Battle of Fredericksburg as "a stunning defeat to the invader." Lee's reputation as a splendid commander was solidified. Lincoln's standing, on the other hand, had suffered another in a series of endless setbacks. "It was not a battle, it was a butchery," one governor told the President after returning from the front. Lincoln, as always, captured the moment in a few powerful words: "If there is a worse place than hell, I am in it."

The President knew he was beloved and despised, perhaps in equal proportions, by his citizens. It was typical of his daring that if 1862 was to end in hell for him, he would start 1863 with a bold act that would only inflame the passions of his supporters and enemies.

———

Abraham Lincoln had long been ambivalent about abolishing slavery. That he personally hated the institution of enforced bondage was never in doubt. "If slavery is not wrong, nothing is wrong," he once said. "I cannot remember when I did not so think, and feel." But Lincoln the person and Lincoln the president were at war with each other, the human heart all too often losing out to the cold calculus of politics. That turmoil was perhaps best reflected in a public letter Lincoln wrote in August 1862 to Horace Greeley, an influential New York newspaper publisher:

> My paramount object in this struggle is to save the Union, and is not either to save or to destroy slavery. If I could save the Union without freeing any slave I would do it, and if I could save it by freeing all the slaves I would do it; and if I could save it by freeing some and leaving others alone, I would also do that . . . I have here stated my purpose according to my view of official duty; and I intend no modification of my oft-expressed personal wish that all men everywhere could be free.

Rather than liberating slaves, Lincoln was initially more interested in relocating them—and the millions of freed Blacks. Though little known today, a policy widely touted by his administration was voluntary "colonization." Schemes included sending Blacks to work on sugar plantations in the Caribbean or in coal mines in Colombia. "You and we are different races," Lincoln told a visiting delegation of Black leaders. "Even when you cease to be slaves, you are yet far removed from being placed on an equality with the white race . . . It is better for us both, therefore, to be separated."

The Black abolitionist leader Frederick Douglass best captured Lincoln's dilemma: "President Lincoln was a white man, and shared the prejudices common to his countrymen towards the colored race," he observed. "Viewed from the genuine abolition ground, Mr. Lincoln

seemed tardy, cold, dull, and indifferent; but measuring him by the sentiment of his country . . . he was swift, zealous, radical, and determined."

In the end, Lincoln found a way to accommodate his personal beliefs
with his presidential burdens. In September 1862, he unveiled plans
for his historic Emancipation Proclamation. But despite his legendary
status today as the "Great Emancipator," Lincoln did not free all the
slaves. He vowed that at the start of the following year he would take
advantage of his war powers to free those in bondage only in the
Southern states—if and when those jurisdictions each fell under Union
control. It was a deft political move, framing the partial ending of slavery not as a matter of principle but as a "military necessity" to weaken
the South. It left almost one out of four slaves untouched and unfreed,
including a half million of them in the so-called neutral Border States
between the South and the North. What's more, it did not challenge the
legality of slavery, which was still enshrined one way or another in several clauses of the US Constitution.

Nevertheless, when, on January 1, 1863, Lincoln's single most
famous act came into force, it struck a blow at the very underpinning
of the Southern slavocracy. The white masters of the South were
appalled—and afraid. Confederate president Jefferson Davis—who
before the war had owned a cotton plantation in Mississippi enriched
with the toil of slaves—told his secessionist Congress on January 12
that this was "a measure by which several millions of human beings of
an inferior race, peaceful and contented laborers in their sphere, are
doomed to extermination, while at the same time they are encouraged
to a general assassination of their masters."

Pro-South newspapers in America and Canada mocked or denounced
any notion of emancipation. The Montreal *Gazette* quoted a Richmond
paper which snickered that "the proclamation will be little more than an
indecent exposure of Lincoln's rage and fiendishness." George Brown,
the fervent abolitionist, was once again out of step with many in the
Canadian establishment. His *Globe* lavished praise on the President.
Lincoln was "wise and right; the whole force of freedom must be arrayed
against the slave power," Brown's paper intoned. "[N]othing short of the

actual undoing of Slavery, and the inauguration of universal freedom can either compensate the sacrifices or destroy the causes of this war."

Lincoln's proclamation is best remembered today for helping to free the slaves in the South. But almost hidden in the fourth-to-last line of his Emancipation Proclamation were a handful of words that also had a huge impact on the outcome of the war and civil rights: the President officially opened the doors for Blacks to fight for their own freedom. Henceforth, they would be "received into the armed service of the United States to garrison forts, positions, stations, and other places, and to man vessels of all sorts in said service."

Arming free Black men was tremendously empowering; in the words of one of Lincoln's top generals, it amounted to "the heaviest blow yet given to the Confederacy." And the promise within that single sentence in the Emancipation Proclamation would change the lives of countless people—among them, two pioneering doctors from Canada.

9.

'THE TIME HAD
NOW COME'

His letter to "His Excellency Abraham Lincoln, President of the U.S."
was full of hope.

Six days after the Emancipation Proclamation came into effect on
January 1, 1863, Dr. Alexander Thomas Augusta wrote to its author
from his home in Toronto. "Having seen that it is so intended to garrison the U.S. forts with colored troops, I beg leave to apply to you for
an appointment as surgeon to some of the colored regiments," he asked
the President. "I was compelled to leave my native country and come
to this [one] on account of prejudice against color . . . I am now prepared to practice . . . and would like to be in a position where I can be
of use to my race."

Augusta, like many Blacks born free in America, had fled to Canada
for a chance at a better life. Like many exiles, he kept up the fight
against prejudice in his adopted country as well. A month after sending
his application to Lincoln, Augusta attended the twelfth annual meeting of the Anti-Slavery Society of Canada at Toronto's Music Hall. It
was a snowy night on February 4, but the *Globe* reported there was a
"large and respectable attendance . . . including a sprinkling of our
coloured citizens."

"If anyone had been of the opinion that the [anti-]slavery feeling was
dying out in Canada, the proceedings of [the] night and the speeches . . .
showed that there was still plenty of that feeling in Canada," Augusta

said to much applause. "The coloured people have a duty to perform at the present time, and the eyes of the whole world are set upon them. The time had now come."

The same day that Augusta was making his speech, another doctor from Toronto—a younger man whom Augusta had mentored—was following in his footsteps by also applying to serve in Lincoln's army. Anderson Ruffin Abbott sent a letter to Edwin M. Stanton, the secretary of war. "I learn by our city papers, that it is the intention of the United States government to enlist 150,000 colored troops. Being one of that class of persons, I beg to apply for a commission as Assistant Surgeon," he wrote, like Augusta making race a central part of his bid to join the Union ranks.

Both men would make history by breaking through the colour barriers in Canada and in the United States. Abbott and Augusta, like many Blacks in Canada, were not about to rely on the kindness of well-meaning whites and the all too frequent condescension of Northern abolitionists. That was a lesson they and their families had learned the hard way in their struggles for freedom and equality on both sides of the border.

———

Alexander T. Augusta was born in Norfolk, Virginia, in 1825 as a free Black, but a man shackled by the prejudice that blocked him from pursuing his dreams of a medical career. He secretly learned to read and write with the help of a sympathetic local church leader and then used private tutors to study medicine while working as a barber. But when Augusta applied to the Faculty of Medicine at the University of Pennsylvania, he was refused and so he fled to the North Star.

In 1850, Augusta moved to Toronto and soon became Canada's first Black medical student when he was admitted to the University of Toronto's Trinity Medical College. Augusta's work was so impressive the university president hailed him as "one of his most brilliant students." In between his studies, Augusta found the time to get involved in politics and community work. He founded the Provincial Association for the Education and Elevation of the Coloured People of Canada, a literacy group that provided funds, books and other school supplies to Black children.

Augusta also took direct aim at politicians who were unnerved by the independent spirit and increasing clout of Canada's growing Black population. A politician from Essex County named John Prince stood up in the Legislative Council for Canada West to denounce Blacks as "the greatest curse ever inflicted upon the magnificent counties which I have the honour to represent." Dismissing them as "necessary evils, only submitted to because white servants are so scarce," Prince suggested Ontario's Blacks be exiled and isolated on Manitoulin Island in Lake Huron. The outraged Black communities in Chatham, Windsor and Toronto held protest meetings against Prince. Augusta drafted a petition signed by four hundred people condemning "the disgusting and despotic language . . . as a base slander of our character as citizens, calculated to foster prejudices against us and to degrade us." They demanded Prince be forced "to resign his seat . . . immediately, as being morally unfit" for office. Prince kept his seat but was defeated in the next election by a Reform candidate backed by local Blacks.

Politics did not distract Augusta from finishing his studies. His portrait shows a confident, handsome man with short-cropped hair, a thick but well-trimmed moustache and a neatly tied cravat atop a white shirt. When he graduated in 1856, he became Canada's first foreign-born Black doctor. It did not take long for a Canadian-born Black student to follow in his footsteps.

———

When Anderson Ruffin Abbott was born on April 7, 1837, he was doubly lucky. For one, he was fortunate just to be alive and healthy. In the previous five years, his mother had lost her first three children within days or months of their births. He also had the good fortune to be born a free Black in Canada. Abbott's parents had fled the racist laws and violence of the American Deep South to pursue new dreams north of the border. They passed on their drive and determination to the young boy who would grow up to become a civil rights champion.

Anderson's father, Wilson Abbott, a free Black man in Mobile, Alabama, ran a general provision store and bought several properties, earning enough to buy the freedom of several enslaved people. Anderson later wrote with a measure of pride that his father had "incurred the hatred of the pro-slavery class who considered that Wm. Abbott set a dangerous precedent in the community." Wilson got a tip his store would be attacked; he put his wife on a steamer to New Orleans and stayed behind only to watch his store burn to the ground before being forced to flee to save his own life.

The Abbotts headed north, stayed for a brief time in New York and eventually crossed into Canada in late 1835 or early 1836, settling in a warren of streets and shacks in Toronto known as the Ward. Today that area is dominated by glistening office towers and the bustling Eaton Centre shopping mall, but back then it was a sprawling, hardscrabble home to some of the city's most downtrodden populace: eastern European Jews, the Chinese, the Irish and newly arrived Blacks from the US. Anderson grew up in one of the nicer homes in the area, on the corner of Terauley and Albert, behind what is now Toronto's Old City Hall.

Wilson Abbott became a successful businessman and real estate broker, eventually owning several dozen real estate holdings in Toronto, Hamilton and Owen Sound. But Anderson Abbott later noted that men like his father had to constantly battle for recognition and equality. "They did not come in response to a friendly invitation . . . They were not given a choice in the matter. They were exiles, and forced to seek a refuge in some asylum where they might be permitted to live and enjoy unrestricted those rights and privileges which pertain to every human being."

In 1840, Wilson Abbott began to fight for those rights and privileges. Prosperous and confident enough to run for city council, he won a seat as the representative for St. Patrick's Ward, with a margin of forty votes, becoming by some accounts the first Black person elected to office in Canada. He did not shy away from using his new-found clout. It was common then for Blacks to be portrayed as bumbling simpletons in minstrel shows featuring white actors in blackface. Anderson's father put together a petition with eighty-five signatures demanding that city council ban the performances "which, by ridicule and holding up to contempt the coloured population, cause them much heart-burning and lead occasionally to violence." The city council argued it did not have the power to censor the offensive acts, but it did oblige the travelling troupes to get a licence. Three years later Wilson Abbott agitated again to stop them, and this time the city agreed to grant performance licences only "on the condition of their not singing Negro songs—this to save the feelings of the gentlemen of color."

By the time Anderson was ten, his father was directly taking on the evils of slavery. He founded the Provincial Union Association, a Black-led relief association dedicated to helping refugees from America settle in Ontario and to "remov[ing] the stain of slavery from the face of the earth." When the Anti-Slavery Society of Canada was set up by George Brown and other liberal members of Canada's white establishment in 1851, it was only natural that Wilson Abbott would be one of the three Black members of the executive. Anderson Abbott's mother, Ellen, joined in the abolitionist fight as well. She was the first president of the Queen Victoria Benevolent Society, which helped fugitive slaves with shelter, education and comfort.

Growing up as a young boy in such a charged atmosphere, Anderson would have heard talk of these early battles around the dinner table and in church. His parents not only inspired him; they made sure to put him on a path of education that would help him break through the barriers they had fought so hard against. Wilson Abbott—along with the newly graduated doctor Alexander Augusta, who had become a family friend—fought hard to open the doors to better schooling for Blacks in Canada. The Anti-Slavery Society in which both men were active campaigned ardently against segregated schools, which forced Black students into crammed classrooms with poorly paid teachers. Wilson Abbott joined Augusta's Provincial Association for the Education and

Elevation of the Coloured People of Canada; Augusta in turn supported Abbott's work to develop a bold new schooling experiment, the Elgin Settlement in Buxton, near Chatham. The Settlement became the largest and most successful of several self-sufficient Black communities that had sprung up in southern Ontario, at its peak offering a home and hope to over two thousand residents. In Buxton, Blacks ran prosperous farms, mills, businesses—and a school that was so successful, white parents eagerly sought to enrol their own children there.

Abbott attended classes there from about age fourteen to seventeen—and it marked him for life, giving him a confidence, a boldness and an unyielding striving for racial equality. His classmates went on to become doctors like him, teachers, missionaries and even a Congressman in the United States. By 1854, the Abbotts moved back to Toronto. Anderson enrolled at the Toronto Academy of Knox College as one of the school's first three Black students. By 1857, he was studying chemistry at University College and the next year he enrolled in medical school at King's College, taking a wide range of classes, from "Surgical Anatomy" to "Diseases of Women and Children." In 1861, Abbott became what he called a "licentiate"—possessing a licence to practise medicine—from the College of Physicians and Surgeons Upper Canada, though he still had to complete his bachelor of medicine degree. That made Anderson Ruffin Abbott Canada's first native-born Black doctor.

———

It is not known when or how Canada's first Black doctors, Alexander Augusta and Anderson Abbott, initially met. When Abbott began studying medicine in Toronto in the late 1850s, he almost certainly would have heard of the path-breaking Black doctor from America. What is known is that around 1858, Abbott began a four-year "supervised placement" with Augusta in what became Toronto General Hospital. Abbott learned more than medicine from his mentor; he saw the value of community service. Both men worked together to take care of patients at the House of Refuge, a poorhouse in eastern Toronto where the needy received free medical care in exchange for letting the doctors and medical students observe and study them.

Abbott also learned that a medical degree did not cure racism. Soon after graduating, Augusta had applied to be the coroner for Chatham, in Kent County. When he was turned down, Abbott was predictably enraged: "[H]is application was sent in," Abbott wrote later. "How was it treated? Why, it was thrown in the scrap basket and . . . an Irishman received the appointment instead."

Both men could only hope they would have more luck in their fight to join Lincoln's army. While they had made history by graduating and working as Black doctors, history is not just about achievements, it is about timing. For Augusta, returning to his home country in the midst of a war for freedom was a natural extension of his life's battle for equality. For the Canadian-born Abbott, joining the Union army was an equally natural choice. He had grown up witnessing his parents' fight against slavery in America and racism in Canada.

Neither of them was willing to stand on the sidelines now.

10.

'I DO NOT LOVE YOU LESS'

Emma Edmonds was miserable.

After an emotionally draining year of dangerous, often inconclusive battles and risky mail missions, the accumulation of fighting and fatigue had taken its toll. In the early spring of 1863, she lay in her tent, racked with fever and despondency. When a shell burst nearby, the noise and smoke sparked hours of weeping. "All my soldierly qualities seemed to have fled, and I was again a poor, cowardly, nervous, whining woman," she recalled. "All the horrid scenes that I had witnessed during the past two years seemed now before me with vivid distinctness, and I could think of nothing else."

The fear of being uncovered as a "nervous, whining woman" must have only added to what today would be called PTSD. For two years, she had led a very clandestine and—under military law—illegal life. She had kept up her impersonation of a man, thanks to a combination of courage and circumstance. The military routines during the Civil War helped. The men wore loose-fitting clothes, often several layers thick. They did not wash frequently, bathed in their undergarments and often slept in their clothes. Instead of using the open-air latrines, many soldiers took to the streams and woods in conditions that were bad for sanitation but good for subterfuge. Asked many years later if the men ever had their suspicions, Frank Thompson's good friend Damon Stewart said: "Never!"

In retrospect, there were plenty of clues that should have given her away. "We jested about the ridiculous little boots and called Frank 'our woman,'" remembered Stewart. "I readily recall many things which ought to have betrayed her," her commanding officer Orlando Poe rather sheepishly recalled long after the war was over, "except no one thought of finding a woman in soldier's dress."

Still, the constant pressure to keep up her pretense as a man—and the potential consequences of discovery—must have weighed heavily on Edmonds. She knew that a woman disguising herself in a man's army could face not just humiliation but jail or even execution. There was a news report about a woman in an Iowa regiment who shot herself upon being discovered. For two years, Edmonds had shrewdly manoeuvred to fight her way into Lincoln's army and had worked skilfully to stay hidden as a man in the Union blue uniform. But by the middle of 1863, her ruse started to unravel and she was faced with the hard choice of finding a way out.

It would not be an elegant departure.

―――

In her memoirs, Edmonds presented the exit of Franklin Thompson as an officially sanctioned release due to physical and mental fatigue: "I sent for the surgeon and told him I was not able to remain longer—that I would certainly die if I did not leave immediately," she wrote. "The good old surgeon concurred in my opinion, and made out a certificate of disability, and I was forthwith released from further duty as 'Nurse and Spy' in the Federal army."

Like several other stories in her book, this one does not stand up to scrutiny. It was highly unlikely any surgeon would have let a soldier leave the army in the middle of a war simply because they complained of stress and fatigue. More problematically, Edmonds put these events after the Union victory at Vicksburg in July 1863. But by then she had been out of the army for at least three months: the official military records show that Franklin Thompson did not leave with a doctor's note but with dishonour, listed as a "deserter" in April of that year.

Over time, Edmonds adapted her exit story to include the fact that she had deserted, but she insisted it was forced. Long after her book was published, in letters to friends and in affidavits, she repeated the description of illnesses, but with an important twist: she was worried that any medical examination of a serious illness would reveal her as a woman. "From my standpoint, I never for a moment considered myself a deserter," she wrote. "I simply left because I could hold out no longer, and to remain and become a helpless patient in a hospital was sure discovery, which to me was far worse than death." In a personal letter from 1897, she wrote that her departure was necessitated not by a serious fever but by internal injuries to her lungs that she suffered during the Second Battle of Bull Run in August 1862 when she had been thrown by her mule while delivering the mail. A medical examination of her lungs would have been out of the question for Edmonds.

Regardless of the ever-shifting details of her stories, there was an underpinning of truth in her public explanations of her desertion. Her fever and illnesses were confirmed by her fellow soldiers in later testimony to Congress about her war record. "[H]er health became greatly impaired by reason of . . . arduous service," they wrote. "At this juncture, she felt impelled to ask for leave of absence . . . which being denied she left the army." It was also true that any extensive medical treatment would have revealed Edmonds's true gender.

This version of events proved to have popular appeal: a brave woman whose disguise as a male soldier was threatened by a wartime illness or injury, forcing her to be wrongly branded as a deserter. For many decades, that storyline—much like her spying adventures—was echoed in countless newspapers articles, books and academic journals, and, more recently, on tribute pages on Internet websites ranging from the US Congress to Canada's History Society. It made for a gripping tale. But it was false, or at the very least incomplete. For what ultimately pushed Emma Edmonds out of the army was not so much her bad health as a broken heart.

———

In Edmonds's telling, she encountered Jerome Robbins by accident, in the chaos of a battle and the carnage of a field hospital. It was June 27,

1862, and the Battle of Gaines' Mill was raging in Hanover County, Virginia. It was the third in what became known as the Seven Days Battles and—like most of the ill-fated Peninsula Campaign—it was not going well for the Union. Edmonds had been given the task of warning the hospitals along the battle lines to retreat. During her mission, she came across one especially brave hospital worker at a Union supply depot and field hospital called, apparently with no sense of irony, Savage Station. "One of the noble-hearted nurses refused to leave . . . I marked that noble boy's countenance, dress and general appearance, and by making inquiry afterwards I found out that his name was J. Robbins, of the Second Michigan Regiment," she wrote.

It was a single paragraph in a four-hundred-page book, a passing reference to a seemingly random encounter on the battlefield. One clue that the man named Robbins was someone special to her is that this is the only time in her published memoirs that Edmonds uses the real surname of one of her fellow soldiers. But Edmonds never let on that he was central to her life, her heart and her mysterious departure from the Union army. It was only in 1963 that Betty Fladeland, a legendary historian of the abolitionist movement, discovered Robbins's detailed diary in the Michigan archives and wrote about it in various historical reviews. His contemporaneous accounts provide some of the most extensive documentation we have of Edmonds's wartime experiences aside from her own, often unreliable words—revealing deeper secrets and a much richer tale.

His full name was Jerome J. Robbins, and he was a college student from Michigan described as "a handsome man, with dark wavy hair, strong cheekbones and dark, inky eyes." Three months shy of his twentieth birthday, he was mustered into the 2nd Michigan Infantry on May 25, 1861, the same day Edmonds signed up in the same regiment as Frank Thompson. According to the diary, they appear to have first met as soldiers not in the midst of battle in 1862, as Edmonds claimed, but in the early fall of 1861, when Robbins was visiting a friend at the hospital where Edmonds was stationed. By November, Robbins's diary entries were full of references to the "good noble-hearted fellow" who had become "one of the few cherished friends" in the ranks.

The pair grew closer as they went for pleasant walks together, two college-educated young people with deep religious beliefs and a shared revulsion for the hardships of war. They ended up being assigned to the same hospital; Robbins started as a private in the hospital dispensary, then graduated to be a hospital steward. They went to prayer meetings together and even managed to arrange a joint visit to Washington. "No greater blessing at present could be mine than the society of a friend like Frank, full appreciating the noblest sentiments that the heart should possess," Robbins wrote.

Yet from the start there was something nagging at Robbins about his new companion. "A mystery seems to be connected with him that is hard to unravel," he wrote in his first diary entry mentioning Frank Thompson, repeating two weeks later that the mystery "is impossible for me to fathom."

Robbins was worried about where this might lead: "Not for the world would I wrong a friend who so sincerely appreciates confiding friendship."

———

In the late fall of 1861, the truth came out.

Robbins recorded that he had "a long and interesting conversation with Frank" in which she described her childhood in New Brunswick. For the first time, he uses the female pronoun in describing his friend. "Though frankly never asserted by her, it will be understood that my friend Frank is a female," Robbins wrote at the end of a long and troubled diary entry on November 16, 1861.

Suddenly, this friendship between two army buddies became very problematic. Not the least because Robbins had revealed that he was engaged to a young woman back home named Anna Corey, which put Frank in a very "disagreeable manner." Meanwhile, Edmonds—once exposed as a woman—likely confessed deeper feelings towards Robbins. "God knows in my heart that towards her I entertain the kindest feelings, but it really seems that a great change has taken place in her disposition," Robbins remarked.

In December, the distance only seemed to grow. In a series of diary entries, Robbins noted that Frank was "somewhat displeased" then "very reserved" and finally "much out of humour." By Christmas Day, their relationship had reached its lowest ebb. "There is not so warm friendship existing between us as there formerly has been," Robbins wrote with regret.

Still, even as their bonds frayed, Robbins to his credit never betrayed his good friend's secret over the next few months as the war raged on. By the summer, they were both embroiled in the run of military disasters that made up the Peninsula Campaign. On June 29, 1862, the Confederates seized the medical outpost known as Savage Station— where Edmonds recounted meeting the "noble-hearted" Robbins in her book—and captured the young soldier. Robbins spent the next five months in a prison camp, which somehow only seemed to draw the two companions closer. Edmonds, "whose sympathies seem to be with me most earnestly," wrote to Robbins at least eleven times and he replied on eight occasions.

The two old comrades joyfully reunited after Robbins was finally released in December 1862, in one of the regular prisoner exchanges between the warring armies. "A very agreeable time have I passed" with "Frank," Robbins noted in his diary on Christmas Eve. Two weeks into the new year, Edmonds penned what can only be described as a love letter from Falmouth, Virginia. Though she seems to have reconciled herself to Robbins's pending marriage, the letter reveals her troubled heart:

> Dear Jerome, I am in earnest in my congratulations & daily realize
> that had I met you some years ago I might have been much happier
> now. But Providence has ordered it otherwise & I must be content.
> I would not change it now if I could—if my life's happiness
> depended upon it. I do not love you less because you love another,

but rather more, for your nobleness of character displayed in your love for her—may God make her worthy of so good a husband.

Your Loving friend, Emma

But then things got murkier, as affairs of the heart often do. While Robbins was in prison, Edmonds seems to have transferred her affections—as restrained as they had to be under the conditions—to another man. His name was James Reid. Like Robbins, he was a handsome fellow—tall, blue-eyed—but he also happened to be married. Like Edmonds, he had fought at the First Battle of Bull Run in 1861 and may have come across Edmonds at the Battle of Fredericksburg in early December 1862, when both of them were aides to the senior commanders. In any event, by the time Robbins had reunited with Edmonds after his release from prison, he noted with more than a hint of displeasure that she and her new acquaintance Reid were "particular friends." Reid, Robbins noted bluntly, "is very fond of Frank."

It is uncertain if Reid knew at the time that Frank was a woman. Were they just close friends, as Robbins and Edmonds had first been, or was something else going on? In any event, Edmonds's interest in another male soldier seemed to make Robbins jealous—even though he had rebuffed Edmonds's affections. "It is a sad reality to which we awaken when we learn that others are receiving the *devotion* of one from whom we can only claim friendship's attention," he wrote in a note on April 4, 1863.

Events moved quickly—and for Edmonds quite tragically—in the following hectic weeks of April. Reid had given notice on April 1 that he was resigning shortly from the army, ostensibly because of his wife's "very precarious" health. Then, on April 11, Orlando Poe, the commander who had promoted, befriended and to some degree sheltered Edmonds, left the regiment amidst many tears from the soldiers under his command. In a matter of days, Edmonds had lost a soldier for whom she had affections; she had said goodbye to a commander who protected her; and she had upset her closest friend and ally, Jerome Robbins.

The "wildest colt" had run out of room to run.

Edmonds was last seen by her comrades on April 16. "I was surprised this evening upon making inquiry after Frank Thompson to hear he had not been seen since yesterday noon," Robbins recounted. "Frank has deserted for which I do not blame him," he stated calmly and sympathetically enough. "His was a strange history."

It got stranger. On April 20, James Reid made good on his announcement that he was leaving the army. What precisely he said and did as he left remains murky; a cryptic entry in Robbins's diary said only that Frank had been "betrayed by his friend R." Reid likely spread the word that the missing Franklin Thompson was a woman. He may have gone further, boasting—truthfully or not—in a private conversation with Robbins that he and Edmonds had become lovers. Whatever he said, it left Robbins saddened by what he called the ingratitude, deception and "almost every petty attribute of a selfish heart" in the woman he knew as Franklin Thompson.

———

By May 1863, one month after her desertion, Emma Edmonds was reborn, after a fashion. Safe in Washington, she planned on providing much-needed nursing help—this time openly as a woman—in the Union's overwhelmed hospitals. She did not have to worry that the authorities would ever come after the deserter Franklin Thompson; he literally did not exist, except on paper in the military records. Few people knew her real name and no one had any way of tracking her down.

On May 10 she wrote a deeply affectionate and intriguing letter to Robbins. "Dear Jerome," she began. "This is Sabbath afternoon and I am sitting in the parlor of a private boarding house . . . and anxious to drop you a line." She implored Robbins to tell her what Reid had confided to him and offered a token of affection: "If tomorrow is fine, I shall have some photographs taken and will send you one. I want you to send me one of yours without fail."

There is no record of Robbins replying to her or sending his picture. Still, he must have treasured her note, for he kept it for decades; it was found in his papers when he died. Edmonds had made clear in her letter that her true love lay with Robbins, not Reid: "Oh Jerome, I do miss you so much," she wrote. "There is no person living whose presence would be so agreeable to me this afternoon as yours." And then, as if to correct her impetuousness with a man who was to be married, she asked about his fiancée: "How is 'Anna'? May God bless you both and make you faithful to him and to each other." She signed the letter:

Goodbye my dear boy,
E. Edmonds

It was indeed goodbye. That appears to be the last communication between the two close confidants. On May 16, Robbins made the final entry in his diary about his strange companion—for the first and only time calling her "my friend Emma E. Edmundson."

Robbins remained in the army for two more years, until the war was over. He ended his military service as an assistant surgeon and eventually became a successful doctor once he was back in Michigan. As it turned out, he never did marry his fiancée Anna. He fell in love with another woman and raised a family of three children. To his dying day, Robbins kept Emma Edmonds's secrets. He had ordered that the sections of his diary about her be sealed. "Please allow these leaves to be closed until the author's permission is given for opening," he stated. When the glued pages were opened a century later, some of the lines written in pencil had been erased.

11.

'THE NEW DESTINY'

For some, getting into an army can be as difficult as getting out.

By the middle of 1863, at the same time as Emma Edmonds was desperately if awkwardly trying to end her military career in Lincoln's army, the two Black doctors from Canada—Alexander Augusta and Anderson Abbott—were just as eager to fight their way in. Lincoln's army badly needed medical staff, as the casualties in the now two-year-old civil war reached into the tens of thousands. And yet it took several months of delays and obstacles before Abbott and Augusta got to put their medical skills to the service of the Union cause. For all its vaunted opposition to the Confederacy, Lincoln's Northern army was still struggling to come to terms with the idea of accepting Blacks into its ranks.

Abbott was more skeptical than Augusta about their chances. "I don't know why he should have been sanguine enough to think that the government would commission a colored man as a surgeon," he wrote. But three months after he had first sent his enlistment request to Lincoln in January, Augusta got word that seemed to indicate he had been accepted. The assistant secretary of war wrote back to him, instructing him to show up in Washington for a routine exam by a medical review board, which was set for March 25, 1863. "Augusta had his misgivings," Abbott recalled, "but being of a hopeful nature, he determined to risk the ordeal."

Clearly, based on the explicit remark Augusta had included in his letter about wishing to be of "use for my race," at least some of the top officials in Lincoln's war administration knew very well that the applicant from Canada was Black and were not bothered by that. But the furor that erupted next made the front page of the *New York Times* with the simple headline A COLORED ASPIRANT FOR MEDICAL HONORS. The story recounted how the army had "received an application from a person in Canada to be examined before the Medical Examining Board . . . Permission was of course granted." Before the test began, a permit signed by a senior doctor had to be given to a board official— "the papers being handed to him by a respectable looking colored man," the *Times* reported, "whom he supposed was the would-be Doctor's servant, never dreaming that the colored gentleman was himself the candidate."

When Augusta then presented himself as a surgeon to the astonished president of the board, Dr. C. Clymer told him in no uncertain terms that "it was not the custom of the Board to examine colored men for admission into the medical corps." Clymer then wrote to the Surgeon General insisting "There has been a mistake in this case" because the applicant was "a person of African Descent." The *New York Times* reported that "opinion is divided here as to the action" to be taken "in this novel but inevitable case."

Augusta, for his part, was furious. "I have come near a thousand miles at great expense and sacrifice, hoping to be of some use to the country and to my race at this eventful period," he told the Army Medical Board on March 30. Fortunately, the officials in Lincoln's War Department were more broad-minded than the examining doctors or the bureaucrats. They directed the Surgeon General to force the medical board to examine Augusta, and on April 1 he passed easily as an "exceptionally qualified" doctor.

Even after Augusta had won, his success did not sit well with the medical army brass. A few days after the examination, the Surgeon General spoke to Clymer, the head of the review board.

"I say, how did you come to let that n----- pass?" he asked.

"The fact is," Clymer replied, "that the n----- knew more than I did and I could not help myself."

Hard as they tried, the board bureaucrats could not stop the march of history. On April 14, 1863, the 38-year-old Alexander T. Augusta was commissioned as a surgeon and a major in the Union army—the first Black man to be awarded that rank in the United States military and the highest-ranking Black officer at the time. Though American-born, he would be described with pride by Black publications as "the colored surgeon from Canada."

———

Back in Toronto, Anderson Abbott's delight with his colleague's victory must have been tempered by growing frustration over his own lack of progress.

Abbott had sent in his application to join the army a month after Augusta had, back in February. But by the spring, he still had received no reply. The rebuff would have rankled: in his personal archives he kept a copy of a news clipping that told of a white Canadian medical student who was not even a doctor yet but, unlike Abbott, was easily accepted into the Union army.

But Abbott had been raised to never back down from a fight. On April 30, almost three months after his first effort to join the Union army, Abbott tried once again. Perhaps, he hoped, the ground was shifting with Augusta's breakthrough. Abbott wisely decided to invoke his ties to the first Black surgeon in the US Army. "I have been a pupil of Dr. T. Augusta for several years," he noted. "He will give you the information you may require concerning my character and attainments."

To further increase his chances, Abbott applied for the lesser post of medical cadet rather than surgeon. It worked. Abbott was hired as a contract surgeon and awarded the honorary rank of captain. Abbott, the son of freed Blacks from America, was thrilled. "I am a Canadian first and last and all the time," he later wrote, "but that did not deter me from sympathizing with a nation struggling to wipe out a great iniquity." He and his fellow Black doctors would have a chance "to give to other nations a higher conception of the value of human liberty."

Liberty seldom comes easily, however. Just reporting for work would turn out to be an ordeal for both men.

————

As the first Black commissioned as a medical officer in the US Army, Augusta became an instant hero to the Black community. Two days after his official enlistment, he attended a celebration at the 15th Street Presbyterian Church in Washington. "The appearance of a colored man in the room wearing the gold leaf epaulettes of a Major," reported the *Evening Star*, elicited "much applause and [con]gratulation with the assembly." In another part of the capital, an enthusiastic if nervous crowd of newly recruited Black soldiers gathered for the mustering of the first two "coloured" regiments. Augusta's appearance elicited tremendous excitement. He looked "splendid among the shabby field hands . . . The sight of his uniform stirred the faintest heart to faith in the new destiny of the race for Dr. Augusta wore the oak leaves of a major on his shoulders," according to one account.

Enthusiasm for the new destiny was one thing; the harsh reality of the old ways was quite another.

Two weeks after being cheered as a hero of high rank by the newly enlisted Black soldiers in Washington, Augusta suffered a starkly different reception while attempting to board a train from Baltimore to Philadelphia. The headline in the *Globe* on May 8, 1863, reprinting a *New York Tribune* story, was blunt: DR. AUGUSTA MOBBED. The brief article explained that Augusta—described as "a negro Major"—was in full uniform when he was attacked and beaten by a crowd of several hundred persons, amid cries of "'Kill him!' 'Hang him!'"

Reflecting the esteem in which Augusta was held in Toronto—at least in the eyes of Brown's *Globe*—the newspaper prefaced its coverage by saying "We are sorry to see . . . that Dr. Augusta has been mobbed in Baltimore." Meanwhile, in America, the *Douglass' Monthly*, a journal put out by the Black civil rights leader Frederick Douglass, made the attack much more political in its headline by blaming it not on an anonymous mob but on "Baltimore secessionists."

Augusta provided his own account of the affair in a lengthy letter published in the *Globe* and several American newspapers a couple of weeks later. At the train depot, he had purchased his ticket and taken his seat when "a boy about fifteen years of age . . . came up behind me and swearing at me, caught hold of my right shoulder strap and pulled it off." The teenager and an older man who joined him then ripped off the officer epaulettes from Augusta's left shoulder and stepped up the attack, threatening to strike Augusta with a club. A gang of "eight to ten roughs" quickly surrounded the doctor. A nearby policeman declined to intervene, but Augusta found better help when a group of provost guards—in effect soldiers acting as military police—offered their protection.

The doctor could have quietly resumed his trip at this point, but Augusta was always more concerned about principles than personal self-interest. "I was determined to stop back so as to have the parties punished, knowing full well that the same thing might occur again, unless a stop was put to it at once." He went with the military police to their nearby headquarters, where a sympathetic commander ordered a lieutenant to accompany Augusta back to the station. He spotted one of his attackers, who was taken into custody. That's when things turned even uglier.

On the way back to the provost office, another man leaped in front of Augusta and assaulted him; he too was arrested. Accompanied by armed guards, he weaved his way through the increasingly dangerous streets as the angry mob grew larger.

A young man then walked up and punched Augusta in the nose and mouth, as the crowd chanted, "Lynch the scoundrel" and "Hang the Negro!" Somehow, Augusta made the rest of the journey to the train safely. "I washed the blood from my face and prepared to take my seat when an officer . . . came up to me and told me he was going to Philadelphia and offered to protect me at the risk of his own life," Augusta said. Other soldiers came to Augusta's aid, surrounding him with drawn revolvers until the train started.

The rest of the trip went off without further incident, but controversy around the mob attack continued to swirl. Augusta acknowledged in his letter to the newspapers that many people blamed him for inciting the event by daring to wear a uniform in a city well-known for its antagonism towards Blacks: "[T]he people of Baltimore are opposed to it; and even Union men do not wish to see coloured men wearing the United States uniform," Augusta admitted. "I have always known Baltimore as a place where it is considered a virtue to mob coloured people." Still, Augusta insisted there were "higher grounds" to consider. He pointed out that as a Union army doctor, he had signed up to treat not just Blacks but whites, and even wounded Confederate soldiers should they come his way.

"I hold that my position as an officer of the United States entitles me to wear the insignia of my office and if I am either afraid or ashamed to wear them anywhere, I am not fit to hold my commission, and should resign at once," he stated forcefully. "The question has no doubt been frequently asked: 'What has been gained by this transaction?' I will answer. It has proved that even in rowdy Baltimore, coloured men have rights that white men are bound to respect."

That respect never came easily, even inside the army. Two weeks after the mob attack, Augusta found himself in Washington. One of his first assignments as a doctor in the Union army was to treat wounded Black soldiers. What made things worse was that they had been injured not by Confederates but by white men in Union blue. According to the *New York Herald* of May 20, 1863, the Black men were marching on the eastern slope of Capitol Hill when soldiers from the 5th and 15th Pennsylvania reserves started pelting them with stones. "The attack was entirely unprovoked, and was not resented by the negroes, who behaved with much more manliness and propriety than their cowardly assailants," the paper reported.

In defiance, that evening the Black battalions returned to parade in the streets around Capitol Hill.

———

Still in Toronto getting ready for his departure for Washington, Anderson Abbott followed the news coverage of the Baltimore attack against his friend Augusta with a mixture of astonishment and admiration. "It was a wonder that he escaped with his life," Abbott wrote. "But he was of that bulldog tenacity that cannot be destroyed by fear." When he finally set off for his deployment in Lincoln's army in July, Abbott would get his own taste of racial animus in America.

Accompanied by Augusta's wife, Mary, Abbott had taken the train from Toronto to Washington, passing through New York. It was early on Friday evening, July 10, when they pulled into the downtown station. Facing a wait of several hours for their connection, the two travellers were resting in the station when two white men "began to abuse us in the coarsest language, threatening to stamp out our lives and do many other dreadful things," Abbott later wrote.

They could not find a policeman; a train watchman was uninterested in helping. But when several soldiers entered the room and convinced the "toughs" to go outside with them, the pair made their escape. The frightened travel companions succeeded in making it to a restaurant, staying there until it was time to get their train. It was only after he arrived safely in Washington that Abbott realized how narrowly he and Mary Augusta had missed a race riot of deadly proportions, which broke out just three days after Abbott managed to escape from the city. "[W]e had been marked out as the first victims of the New York draft riots," he surmised.

Tensions had been rising in the North since April, when an unpopular military draft imposed by Lincoln came into effect. Blacks were exempt from military service because they were not considered "citizens," while wealthy whites could easily buy their way out of conscription by paying a $300 "commutation fee" to hire a substitute to enlist in their place. Coming just months after Lincoln's Emancipation Act, the draft, in the eyes of many white working-class men, meant they were being forced to risk their lives to free enslaved Blacks. Opposition politicians stoked the fires of hate by suggesting the freed slaves would move north to steal jobs.

Real fires and racial anger exploded on the streets of New York on that Monday morning, July 13, 1863, and continued for three unnerving days. It was volunteer firemen, ironically, who set the first blaze, burning down a draft office because they were upset at losing their traditional exemption from conscription. Mobs moved on to Newspaper Row, repelled from attacking the *New York Times* only because the editor and his staff, remarkably, resorted to using Gatling guns, a forerunner of the machine gun, to defend their building. It did not take long for the protesters to turn their venom on innocent Blacks.

The rampaging whites destroyed tenements and boarding houses, and targeted dance halls frequented by Blacks as well, ripping off the clothes of the businesses' white owners and attacking white women married to Blacks. The Colored Orphan Asylum on the corner of 44th Street and Fifth Avenue was burned to the ground, though miraculously, all 237 children made it out safely. "It seemed to be an understood thing throughout the city that the negroes should be attacked wherever found," the *Times* reported. "There were probably not less than a dozen negroes beaten to death in different parts of the city during the day."

In an ugly echo of what was happening in the Deep South, the streets of New York saw the horrific spectacle of lynchings of at least eleven Black men. One of them "was attacked by a crowd of about 400 men and boys who beat him with clubs and paving stones till he was lifeless, and then hung him to a tree . . . Not being satisfied with their devilish work, they set fire to his clothes and danced and yelled . . . around his burning corpse."

By the time a semblance of peace had been restored on July 16, more than two thousand people had been injured. The official death toll was never calculated, but most historians put it at around 120, making the New York draft riots one of the worst race riots in American history.

———

While Abbott and Augusta fought hard to get into Union uniforms as doctors, thousands of Canadian Blacks were just as determined to enlist as ordinary soldiers, risking their lives to fight the Confederate South. An estimated 2,500 Black Canadians signed up, joining about 180,000 American Blacks in the Union army (and another 20,000 in the navy)— eventually making up an impressive 10 percent of Lincoln's forces.

Josiah Henson, the fugitive slave whose escape had partly inspired *Uncle Tom's Cabin*, offered money to help the families of any army volunteers from Canada and accompanied a group of them across the border. Mary Shadd, the firebrand publisher, worked tirelessly with the Colored Ladies' Freedmen's Aid Society to ship supplies to the untrained and ill-equipped Black fighters in battle. In a battle made famous by the Oscar-winning movie *Glory*, the 54th Massachusetts Colored Infantry—the first Black regiment in the North—stormed Fort Wagner in South Carolina on July 18, 1863. Half the men, including four Black Canadian recruits, perished that day. Their sacrifice came two days after the lynchings and other attacks in the New York City draft riots had finally stopped. "It wasn't because the colored troops were colored that we admired them," Anderson Abbott wrote. "It was because they were brave men, worthy of respect."

Blacks were not given their freedom; they fought for it in slave revolts, earned it in perilous escapes to Canada, and paid for it with their bodies scattered in Union blue on the many Civil War battlefields.

12.

'BEAUTIFUL RIGHT AND UGLY WRONG'

Every war feels like a forever war when you are caught up in the middle of it. A few months or years down the road, any history student will know the date your nightmare ended, the year some kind of peace came. But when you are living the horror of history in the making, all there is to do is endure.

Midway through 1863, no one could have guessed that the Civil War was only at its halfway point: two punishing years gone, two even more cruel years to go. All that anyone knew for certain was that the struggle for the soul of America between a slaveholding South and a free North could go either way. If anything, the South seemed to be holding its own, a victory of sorts against a much stronger North.

By coincidence and circumstance, the three people who ended up becoming the most famous Canadians in the Union army—Emma Edmonds, Edward Doherty and Anderson Abbott—all found themselves in Washington, DC, by the fall of 1863. Though they never met, their lives did intersect. Emma Edmonds and Anderson Abbott were both helping the wounded in local hospitals, though racial segregation ensured their paths would never cross. Edward Doherty, meanwhile, would be transferred to the military regiment tasked with protecting the nurses, doctors and civilians in the endangered city.

———

It is hard to grasp today how encircled the city of Washington—and Abraham Lincoln—must have felt during the Civil War. The Confederates were always just a day's ride from the Union capital. Washington was like a medieval fortress, hoping to withstand imminent siege. More than eighteen thousand artillerymen stood behind the nine hundred guns that lined the thirty-seven miles of fortifications protecting Washington. Edward Doherty became one of the soldiers assigned to defend Washington—but not before he overcame a brief setback in his military career.

By early 1862, Doherty was serving as a second lieutenant in Company C of the 1st US Sharpshooters whose specialty was the killing of Confederate targets of high importance. Whether it was due to the stress of that job, the after-effects of his prison escape during the Battle of Bull Run or his personal inclinations, Doherty appears to have developed a drinking problem, which was serious enough that he was forced to resign in February 1862. His commander noted in his record that he abandoned his post, "under the influence of liquor most of the time for the past six weeks."

But Doherty's time away did not last long. Nine months later, the army was eager to have him back. On November 18, 1862, Doherty was mustered as a captain in the 155th Regiment of New York Volunteers. Doherty's military record is full of praise from his superior officers regarding his role as a soldier and a leader. "I can cheerfully testify to his intelligence, faithfulness and efficiency in his performance of his duty as an officer and a gentleman," wrote one general. "His reputation for gallantry in the field as admired by his brother officers is second to no one in the service," said another commander. Even his Confederate foes had strikingly similar praise for the Canadian. One of them described Doherty as "that gallant officer." Perhaps more important to Doherty was the admiration he earned from his fellow soldiers, who would later salute his bravery "on lonely scout and daring raid[s], and in the secret night watches . . . [in] the by-paths, thickets and wilds of Virginia, its mountain passes and guerilla haunts."

Military records show that Doherty resigned briefly in May 1863 for undisclosed "family reasons," but he returned within four months. On September 12, 1863, Doherty arrived in Washington thanks to a promotion to first lieutenant in the 16th New York Cavalry. Doherty's new regiment had just returned from Gettysburg. Now he and his brethren were handed a prestigious and important assignment, "covering the Defences of Washington, D. C., and operating against guerrillas." At one point, Doherty and the 16th New York Cavalry had made a brief foray sixty miles southwest of the capital towards Culpepper, Virginia, hoping to secure a railroad bridge and freight depot. They expected little resistance, but were vastly outnumbered and beaten back by an entire division of Confederate infantry. Doherty was singled out by his superiors for "his gallant and stubborn resistance" leading two hundred and fifty against an attacking force three times as strong. "[H]e firmly held the enemy in check, allowing the command to escape from overwhelming numbers."

Doherty was making a name for himself in Washington, which would come with unintended consequences. He couldn't know that within two years his name would rise to the top of the list when it came time to fulfill a military assignment no one could ever have imagined.

———

Emma Edmonds, for her part, had taken off her soldier's uniform, but in her heart she was still very much a soldier and a nurse, and her thoughts were never far from the comrades she had left behind. "The war still continues—our soldiers are daily falling in battle, and thousands are languishing in hospitals or in Southern prisons," she wrote.

By the spring of 1863, she was staying at a private boarding house in Washington, visiting wounded soldiers in the hospitals. "My intention is to go at once into the missionary work notwithstanding the protestations of my friends to the contrary," she wrote to a friend. She never became a missionary, but she kept up her mission as a nurse: within a few months, Edmonds was volunteering at a military hospital in St. Louis, Missouri, under dreadful conditions that must have reminded her of the battlefield medicine she was used to. "The beds all dirty and disgusting; men sleeping in their clothes; no sheets or bed clothes," wrote one health official.

———

As for Anderson Abbott and Alexander Augusta, the conditions they faced in treating Black soldiers were even more appalling than what Edmonds encountered. The Civil War was particularly deadly for Black soldiers. Even though they had joined only halfway through the fighting, forty thousand of them perished—about one in five, more than 35 percent higher than the already alarming mortality statistics for white soldiers. As with white soldiers, sickness was the leading cause of death for Black soldiers. Three out of four deaths of Black recruits in the Union army came not from bullets but from infection and disease.

The segregated Blacks had to cope with much worse medical care. By the middle of 1863, Abbott and Augusta—having survived the New York race riots and a Baltimore mob—began their efforts in the Union army at what was known as the "Contraband Hospital" in Washington. The term "contraband" came about as Union forces pushed deeper into the South, classifying freed slaves as "contraband of war"— freeing them, but essentially dehumanizing them as captured enemy property. By 1863 around ten thousand escaped former slaves had made their way to Washington, mainly from Virginia and Maryland, which were just across the river. The hospital was located in a swampy northwest corner of Washington in what are now the comfortable city blocks between 12th and 13th Streets. The government had put up a one-storey building and tents to handle the destitute Blacks, along with the growing number of soldiers in the "coloured regiments." It was a ramshackle site of rain-soaked tents, wooden barracks and unclean water, a poor imitation of what a proper hospital should be.

This was the dire situation Alexander Augusta faced when he was named, in May 1863, as the surgeon-in-charge—the first Black man in American history to become the administrator of a hospital. Running the Contraband Hospital was a mixed blessing: a path-breaking appointment but a morale-breaking burden. "The water inside the camp appears to produce diarrhea, and the wells in the neighborhood where we receive our supply from, are drying up," he warned in a stern letter to the military brass on June 17.

A week later, Anderson Abbott was at Augusta's side. "On June 26th, I was commissioned and placed on duty in the same hospital under Dr. Augusta who was a surgeon in charge," he wrote. Together with other newly recruited Black doctors—one of them also a Canadian medical graduate—they laboured tirelessly to improve the conditions there. By October 1863, Augusta was transferred out of the hospital and appointed senior surgeon for the United States Colored Troops stationed near Baltimore. But Abbott would stay for at least another year.

As was his custom, Anderson Abbott refused to give in to pessimism, rising above the misery and suffering to take a broader view of the stakes in the Civil War. "It became a struggle between beautiful right and ugly wrong," he wrote. "It determined whether civilization or barbarism should rule, whether freedom or slavery should prevail upon this continent."

13.

'A NEW BIRTH
OF FREEDOM'

Attending stage plays was one of Abraham Lincoln's preferred pastimes; he visited Ford's Theatre, just a few blocks from the White House, no fewer than ten times during his presidency. In early November 1863, he showed up to see *The Marble Heart*, a lighthearted comedy about a French sculptor whose works come to life. What made the performance special for Washington's elite crowd was that the man playing the lead role was a national star named John Wilkes Booth.

Lincoln was as entranced with the renowned actor as everyone else. Booth was at the height of his career and fame—though his outbursts offstage did cause him some trouble. Early that year, the actor had been arrested in St. Louis for making "treasonous" threats against the government. Booth had been overheard declaring that he "wished the President and the whole damned government would go to hell." Booth was released after paying a small fine and the incident earned little attention.

For the performance of *The Marble Heart*, Lincoln and his family sat as always in the presidential box to the right of the stage. "Twice Booth in uttering disagreeable threats in the play came very near and put his finger close to Mr. Lincoln's face," according to a later but much disputed account by Mary Clay, one of the President's guests.

"Mr. Lincoln, he looks as if he meant that for you," she remarked.

To which Lincoln replied, "He does look pretty sharp at me, doesn't he?"

The play ended with much applause and praise for the actor. Lincoln went back to his work at the White House, preparing for a speech that would make history.

———

Five months after the dead at Gettysburg had been buried, a tired and troubled President Abraham Lincoln travelled to the outskirts of a small town in Pennsylvania to utter perhaps his most famous words.

The Battle of Gettysburg in July 1863 had left between 46,000 and 51,000 men from both armies dead or wounded. More American soldiers perished in those three days than in the entire Korean War, and almost as many Americans lost their lives in that single battle as during the war in Vietnam. Gettysburg was not so much a decisive victory for Abraham Lincoln's Union as it was a demoralizing defeat for Jefferson Davis's Confederacy. Two years into the war, at last it felt as though the North—with three times the population and eventually twice the number of soldiers—was not going to lose outright. But victory was still not assured and it certainly would not come quickly.

On the morning of November 19, 1863, a sombre crowd of fifteen thousand gathered to dedicate a sprawling seventeen-acre cemetery for the fallen of Gettysburg. With his army's victory in that battle coming on July 4, the same day America had declared its independence eighty-seven years earlier, Lincoln chose to signal the anniversary in the immortal opening words of his speech.

"Four score and seven years ago our fathers brought forth on this continent, a new nation, conceived in Liberty, and dedicated to the proposition that all men are created equal," he said. "Now we are engaged in a great civil war, testing whether that nation, or any nation so conceived and so dedicated, can long endure." He praised the brave men, living and dead, who consecrated the ground at Gettysburg, but he quickly turned, as he knew he must, to "the unfinished work . . . the great task remaining before us."

Then came his stirring conclusion: "We here highly resolve that these dead shall not have died in vain—that this nation, under God, shall have a new birth of freedom—and that government of the people, by the people, for the people, shall not perish from the earth."

It was only 272 words and took less than three minutes to recite, but the Gettysburg Address changed the course of the war, and arguably the country. The Civil War may have begun as a dispute over states' rights; it may have been waged by a Union and a president reluctant to take on the curse of slavery. It was now indisputably a war about principles, a war about freedom and a war against slavery.

———

But beyond the stirring rhetoric, as doctors in Lincoln's army, Alexander Augusta and Anderson Abbott found that principles could only get them so far.

In his new role as senior surgeon for the 7th Regiment of the United States Colored Troops, Augusta faced an awkward situation—or rather his white colleagues did. As a major, he outranked his fellow white surgeons, something they found intolerable even though they professed to be open-minded enough to work in Black regiments. "We claim to be behind no one, in a desire for the elevation and improvement of the colored race in this Country," they said in a letter to the White House and the War Department in February 1864. But there was a catch—their support only went so far. "Judge of our surprise when, upon joining our respective regiments, we found that the Senior Surgeon of this Command was a Negro," they wrote, referring to Augusta. For even the liberal white doctors, that was a "degradation" and an insult to their "proper self-respect." They demanded that "this unexpected, unusual, and most unpleasant relationship" be terminated with Augusta's removal. While Augusta remained as a senior surgeon, eventually being promoted to lieutenant-colonel, he was moved on from the 7th Regiment to other assignments.

Augusta always cut an impressive figure in his dark-blue uniform, a small, smart cap on his head and the major's gold oak leaf on his epaulette. Early on the chilly and rainy morning of February 1, 1864, the doctor was on his way to his hospital to pick up some important medical files. He was to testify at a court martial against a white private charged with killing a Black man who had died at the hospital. At the corner of 14th and I Streets, Augusta stepped onto Car No. 32 of the City Railway Company. But the conductor sternly warned him that "it was against the rules for colored persons to ride inside," Augusta reported in a letter he wrote later that day to the army's judge advocate.

The conductor insisted Augusta stand with him in the open area of the carriage at the front, which would have exposed Augusta to the cold and rain. "I told him, I would not ride on the front, and he said I should not ride at all," Augusta recalled. "He then ejected me from the platform."

Never one to take a racial offence lightly, Augusta fired off his angry letter to the army brass and then a longer note to the assistant secretary of war. He asked that "the offender . . . be arrested and brought to punishment," but on a wider scale he demanded "that something may be speedily done to remedy such evils as those we are now forced to submit to."

Senator Charles Sumner, a staunch abolitionist, took up Augusta's complaint and read his letter into the *Congressional Globe*. A gifted orator, Sumner thundered: "An incident like this, at this moment, was worse than a defeat in battle. It makes against our cause and excites distrust." Sumner had been pushing for regulations to force the railway companies in the capital to stop segregating passengers and Augusta's story added impetus to his cause. Legislation was eventually passed forbidding streetcar discrimination in Washington. Anderson Abbott had been following the battles waged by his colleague and later proudly reported: "It was through Dr. Augusta that . . . the colored people of Washington enjoy the privilege of riding in the street when and where they like."

––––––

By early 1864, Augusta and Abbott had spent almost a year in the Union army, battling disease and discrimination. It had been a trying yet rewarding journey. The two doctors were justifiably proud to be among the handful of Black surgeons working in the Union army. Why not pay a visit to the man who had made it possible?

It was a cool winter evening in Washington. To help lift the spirits in the capital, President Abraham Lincoln was holding one of his regular "levees" or evening parties for the elite establishment in Washington. The two Black doctors from Canada decided to crash it.

"One evening we appeared at the White House in full uniform," Abbott recounted. "The White House was a blaze of light. Soldiers were guarding the entrance. Carriages containing handsomely-dressed ladies, citizens and soldiers were continually depositing the elite of Washington at the entrance to the porch."

Abbott and Augusta were ushered inside a wide hall and taken to the President, standing just inside the door. Lincoln seemed pleased to see two Black men dressed smartly in Union blue: "Mr. Lincoln, on seeing Augusta, advanced eagerly a few paces forward, grasped his hand," Abbott reported.

But Lincoln's son Robert was aghast:

[Robert] came up to the President and asked a question very hastily, the purport of which I took to be, "Are you going to allow this invasion?" referring, doubtless, to our presence there! The President replied, "Why not?"

Then the President turned again to Augusta and gave his hand a hearty shake and then I was introduced and the President shook hands with me also. Then we passed on to a position in front of Mrs. Lincoln and were introduced to that lady.

Abbott and Augusta made their way to the East Room, where they continued to turn heads:

The moment we entered the room, which was crowded and brilliantly lit up, we became the cynosure of all eyes. I had never experienced such a sensation as I did when I entered the room. We could not have been more surprised ourselves nor could we have created more surprise if we had been dropped down upon them through the skylight.

. . .What made us more conspicuous, of course, were our uniforms. Colored men in the uniforms of the United States, military officers of high rank had never been seen here before. I felt as though I should have liked to crawl into a hole.

The Black doctors had fought long and hard to get accepted into the Union army. They were not about to let the prejudices of Washington high society turn them back now:

> But as we had decided to break the record, we held our ground. I bit my lips, took Augusta's arm and sauntered around the room . . . Some stared at us merely from curiosity, others with an expression of friendly interest, while others again scowled at us in such a significant way, that left no doubt as to what views they held on the Negro question.

Abbott recounted how the two men stayed in the room, facing down "monocles and lorgnettes . . . stares and fascinating eyes." After a tense half-hour, they gathered their winter outerwear and left. It had been a stressful, even intimidating evening—but Abbott was glad they had forced the issue. It was a head-spinning moment: a free Black forced to flee the United States to pursue his dreams of a medical career and the son of another free Black who fled to Canada to fight for equality and civil rights were standing there in their uniforms, shaking hands with the President in the White House.

"I do not know whether we were really the first colored guests to visit the President of the United States at one of his levees but I am inclined to think we were," he concluded. "We had broken the ice." In his personal records later donated to the Toronto Metro Library archives, there is a short news clipping he obviously treasured that appeared in the *Washington Star* the following day: "During the evening Dr. Augusta, the colored Surgeon of the District [of Columbia] colored regiment, dressed in his major's uniform and also Assistant Surgeon Abbott (colored, of the same regiment) paid their respects to the President and were kindly received by him."

Fourteen months later, Anderson Abbott would again be near Lincoln, but in much more tragic circumstances that nobody at that Washington party could have imagined.

*St. Albans raiders outside the Montreal jail.
George Sanders is in the middle of the back
row; Bennett Young stands on the front right.
(Courtesy McCord Museum)*

PART TWO

'TO ROB AND PLUNDER'

(March 1864–January 1865)

In this great struggle, this form of Government and every form of human right is endangered if our enemies succeed. There is more involved in this contest than is realized by every one.

—ABRAHAM LINCOLN, August 18, 1864

14.

'A SECRET MISSION'

The Confederacy was hurting badly: losing battles, losing men, losing time.

After their crushing defeat at Gettysburg, which had cost Robert E. Lee a third of his army, the Confederates lost Vicksburg and, with it, control of the Mississippi River. By February 1864 they were driven out of Meridian, an important industrial centre in Mississippi that was vital to their military supply lines. In early March, the Union armies pushed into Louisiana. "The year of 1864 opened gloomily for the Confederacy," admitted Thomas Hines, a Confederate soldier who eventually ended up in Canada. "Her arms had everywhere sustained reverses."

It was time to open up a new front of warfare and sabotage. For that, Jefferson Davis chose a trusted political ally. On April 7, 1864— almost three years to the day after the Civil War started—he sent a short, cryptic telegram to an old friend, summoning him to Richmond: "If your engagements will permit you to accept service for six months, please come here immediately," Davis wrote.

———

The man Davis reached out to was Jacob Thompson, the former cabinet minister in Washington who, when Lincoln was elected, had resigned his seat to side with the slave South. It made sense that Davis would have confidence in Thompson's political loyalty; his qualifications as a military or intelligence leader were less obvious.

Friends described Thompson as "a typical Southern gentleman of the old school." For decades, he had been well entrenched as a privileged member of the slave-owning aristocracy. Born and raised in Virginia into a comfortable family, Thompson married into more money. His wife inherited a large plantation and slaves; the wedding present from her parents was a truck filled with gold. Thompson himself over the years would amass great wealth, including two plantations, a sawmill, a hotel and three cotton gins.

Little wonder that after serving six terms in Congress, when the Civil War broke out, Thompson had left Washington in a huff, warning that the slave states faced "common humiliation and ruin" if they remained in the Union. When he resigned his cabinet post, the Northern press predictably denounced him as "a traitor" swayed by "the ideas of cotton-growing chivalry." But back home in Oxford, Mississippi, he was greeted by musical bands and cheers. Thompson served the next two years in the Confederate army and then took a seat in the Mississippi state legislature.

To answer Jefferson Davis's call to duty in the spring of 1864, Thompson had to leave his plantation mansion. "The slaves all gathered together by their master," according to one pro-Confederate biography of him, "and after his talk, pledged their loyalty to him and were very much overcome at telling him goodbye." Perhaps the loyal goodbyes from his enslaved workers were a bit forced. The biography also made note that Thompson employed a vicious overseer who "had such perfect control over the slaves that plantation owners for miles around sent their incorrigible slaves to him for discipline."

———

No record remains of what words Davis used to describe Thompson's mission when they met privately in the capital of the Confederacy. Details were kept as confidential as possible. But about two weeks later, the Confederate president followed up with a formal, if deliberately vague, letter:

Richmond, Va., April 27th, 1864.
Hon. Jacob Thompson:

Sir:—Confiding special trust in your zeal, discretion and patriotism, I hereby direct you to proceed at once to Canada; there to
carry out the instructions you have received from me verbally, in
such manner as shall seem most likely to conduce to the further-
ance of the interests of the Confederate States of America which
have been intrusted to you.

Very respectfully and truly yours,
(Signed) Jefferson Davis.

What instructions had Thompson received verbally?

In his memoirs published long after the war, Davis tried to down-
play the mission, presenting it merely as a diplomatic endeavour to
engage in talks with Northern politicians who wanted to end the war:
"A commission . . . was accordingly appointed to visit Canada, with
a view to negotiate with such persons in the North as might be relied
on to aid the attainment of peace." But Davis, as the losers of war are
wont to do, was trying to rewrite history. In reality, he had appointed
Thompson to head a Confederate Secret Service in Canada, and he
was entrusted with massive funds to carry out the mission.

In a secret session of the Congress of the Confederate States held a
couple of weeks earlier, $5 million—worth an astonishing $88 million in today's currency—was set aside for clandestine operations,
and a hefty chunk of that money was earmarked for operations in
Canada. Two days before Davis issued his written instructions to
Thompson, on April 25, his Executive Office issued $1 million "pay-
able in foreign countries" for secret operations abroad from funds
under the Secret Service Act that Jefferson Davis had signed into law
on February 15, 1864.

Thompson's work was to be overseen by the powerful Confederate
secretary of state, Judah Benjamin. Benjamin was somewhat of an

oddity in the Southern government elite: a Jew among white suprema-
cists, the owner of a plantation with 140 slaves who eventually sold
them to become the only minister in Davis's cabinet without enslaved
Blacks. He was clever and confident, and—perhaps because, as a Jew,
he could never threaten Davis for the top position—he had the
Confederate president's ear and his trust.

Thompson must have sensed the weight of his new assignment.
Perhaps also realizing that his political skills did not easily translate
into spying and sabotage, he "hesitated to accept the appointment,"
according to one fellow politician. "But difficult and embarrassing as
was the mission, hopeless as he considered it . . . he felt it to be his duty
to serve his country." Within a few days, in early May, he was on a
ship headed towards the eastern shores of Canada.

––––––

Thompson had gone from Richmond to North Carolina to take a
stealthy steamer "painted gray . . . so that she could scarcely be seen at
night." The ship would run the Union blockade and get him to his destination on a circuitous and dangerous route. On board with Thompson
was a second commissioner named by Davis, Clement Claiborne Clay.
Like Thompson, Clay was a long-standing and loyal Confederate politician. He served in Washington as a senator from Alabama from 1853
until January 1861, when he and several other Southern sympathizers
resigned their seats. Even by the standards of the slave states, Clay—a
slave owner himself and "the intimate friend" of Jefferson Davis—was
considered an unrepentant hard-liner. Vehemently opposed to any
compromise with Lincoln, he had advocated restarting the African
slave trade.

Unlike Thompson, who had made a quiet departure from Congress,
Clay delivered an unapologetic defence of white supremacy. "No sentiment is more insulting or more hostile to our domestic tranquility,
to our social order, and to our social existence, than is contained in
the declaration that our negroes are entitled to liberty and equality

with the white man," Clay declared. He went on to sit as a senator in the rebel Confederate Congress from 1862 to 1864 and was popular enough to have his portrait adorn the Confederate one-dollar bill. His friend Jefferson had offered him the powerful position of Confederate secretary of war, but Clay declined because of ill health. He was at best a reluctant recruit as a spymaster north of the border, writing to Jefferson Davis that he doubted his fitness for the mission and confiding to a friend: "I am on my way to Canada . . . [for] a difficult & delicate duty for which I am not suited by my talents tastes or habits."

Thompson and Clay shared a devotion to the Southern cause but little else. If Thompson was seen as a smooth if at times overconfident backroom political operator, Clay was "peevish, irritable and suspicious," according to one Confederate soldier who would end up serving under him in Canada. Another colleague worried that the rivalry between Clay and Thompson was "the source of constant embarrassment, and proved one of the most potent obstacles to success."

Still, they would have to learn to collaborate as the designated leaders picked by Davis, joined by William Cleary, who would serve as their secretary. Together the three Confederates survived treacherous waters and enemy patrol ships while they navigated their way from North Carolina to Bermuda, a common stopping point for blockade runners, and then northwards to Halifax aboard a ship called the *Alpha*. "We waited until it was quite dark," recalled Cleary, "creeping along and twisting our devious and perilous way."

Thirteen days later, on May 19, they landed in Nova Scotia. They quickly got a taste of just how much sympathy their Confederate cause inspired in Canada.

———

Halifax, as one Confederate courier put it, was "a hot Southern town— they hate the Yank as bad as we do." When a Confederate warship, the *Tallahassee*, docked at the harbour for repairs, the Halifax Volunteer Band came to play "Dixie" for the crew. The *Halifax Journal* urged local citizens to remember "the treatment of defenceless Southern women and children by Yankee ruffians."

The Nova Scotian port, not far from the United States by land or sea, had become a hub of Southern exiles and sympathizers. Canada's supposed neutrality in the American war did not stop Halifax from doing brisk business with the Confederacy. Most of the city's elite and the political class backed the Southern cause, so much so that many local businesses flew Confederate flags and used Confederate currency.

Thompson and Clay stayed at the Waverly Hotel, favoured by the many Confederates who had flooded the city. They must have felt more relaxed than in the besieged Southern cities—if not at home, then at least safe and welcome. While in town, Clay met with Thomas Connolly, the prominent and powerful Catholic archbishop of Halifax. An unapologetic supporter of the Confederate States, Connolly often hosted Southern agents at his home in Halifax. Like many among Canada's ruling class, the clergy feared that a powerful Lincoln government, if it defeated the South, would turn its expansionist and annexationist eyes towards Canada. Clay had first encountered Connolly just two weeks earlier, during his brief stopover in Bermuda. The archbishop was at a dinner party hosted by a leading Confederate official on the island and was reported to have described Clay as "a good type of true Southern gentleman."

Clay returned the compliment, praising the Canadian archbishop as one of the "foremost" supporters of the slave states. When they met up again in Halifax, Connolly told Clay he was willing "to traverse the United States as an advocate of peace, or to do anything to promote that end that was compatible with his duty to his church and Queen." The church leader also gave Clay a gushing letter of reference, praising him as "one of the eminent men" from the South in Canada, conducting "important public business duly credited by the Confederate States." It was, the archbishop stressed, "a cause that commands the respect and sympathy of the world" and therefore worthy of "the attention and kindly services of every Catholic Bishop and Priest and layman with whom he may come in contact."

The blessings from powerful church leaders were most welcome. But what Clay and Thompson needed even more were soldiers to carry out their mission. They would find their best fighters from a fearsome gang of Confederates who came to be known as "Morgan's Raiders."

15.

'PROCEED TO CANADA'

They were feared because they struck suddenly and swiftly, deep inside Union territory. More akin to stealthy guerrillas than a traditional, slow-moving army, the elite force were heroes to many in the South for disrupting supply lines and terrorizing Union forces from Kentucky to Tennessee and as far north as Ohio.

Their leader was a charismatic, skilled marauder named John Hunt Morgan. "Colonel Morgan issued a stirring proclamation calling upon the young men of Kentucky to rally to his standard," recalled Bennett H. Young, one of the first to answer the call. "Their hearts were thrilled with the story of his adventures and his triumphs."

Young, along with three other of his comrades, would bring to Canada the skills and tactics they learned as guerrillas under Morgan's command, becoming the backbone of what developed into the Confederates' secret army north of the border.

———

All four of the raiders who would play a leading role in Canada were Kentucky boys—not even adult men yet, but in their late teens. They were, in Young's words, "made up of the cream of Kentucky's gentility," coming from families with deep Confederate roots in a state where almost one out of four inhabitants was a slave.

Young, raised by devout Presbyterian parents who were wealthy slave owners, was a month shy of his eighteenth birthday when the war broke out. He was studying to become a minister but postponed his education to enlist with the Confederate cavalry. Young later told his comrades that a band of marauding Union troops committed an "outrageous insult" against the woman he was hoping to marry, which led to her death; he quickly enlisted, "burdened with grief and longing for vengeance." Whatever his motivation, Young was bold, shrewd and a smooth talker. Morgan "gave war a new glamour," as Young aptly put it—and he would apply that lesson to become the most famous and successful Confederate operative in Canada, both during the war and long after its end.

Another recruit, John W. Headley, was trapped working at his father's store in the hamlet of Nebo, worried he'd never see the promise of battle: "All wanted to get with Morgan. Our exalted ideas in the beginning, of generals commanding armies, had changed," he wrote. "Morgan had been the first man in history to raid far in the rear of the enemy's great armies and successfully defy overwhelming numbers."

John B. Castleman was also chomping at the bit for a piece of the action. He grew up in Fayette County, Kentucky, at a sprawling colonial homestead that boasted a mansion with spiral staircases, rosewood and mahogany furniture, and the twinkling lights of glass-and-silver candelabras. His father was a prosperous merchant and farmer, a ruling elder in the Presbyterian church—and, of course, the owner of many slaves.

Like most white Southerners, Castleman was oblivious to the injustices of human bondage, convinced of "the ties of affection that existed between the master and the slave." "These slaves were part of every family. Their work was not hard, and their hours of leisure were many," he insisted. "The young slaves were generally the playmates of the white children . . . and happiness prevailed." Castleman was not about to let Lincoln destroy the slavocracy that so benefitted his family and his state. At nineteen he was studying law at university, but as soon as the hostilities began, he recruited more than three dozen men for Morgan's regiment.

Thomas Henry Hines also swapped his school books for bullets. A grammar school principal and university professor, Hines seized the imagination and admiration of the others. "He was athletic and capable of endurance," his fellow raider John Headley noted. "In manners he was captivating . . . endowed with varied talents and unflinching courage."

John Morgan led his men into the Battle of Shiloh in southern Tennessee in the spring of 1862, and by the summer he launched his first raid deep into Kentucky, a three-week assault that led to the capture of more than a thousand Union troops. And while the fast guns and horses of Morgan's Kentucky boys contributed much to the effort, so did the fast fingers of a telegraph whiz kid from Canada. "The story of how he misled his foes, and deceived them," said Bennett Young, "is not only one of the most amusing but one of the most surprising of the war's happenings."

———

His name was George Ellsworth, and by the nickname "Lightning," he became one of the best-known Canadians to join the Confederates.

Born in July 1843 in Prince Edward County, about fifty miles southwest of Kingston, by the tender age of 14 Ellsworth headed south, already a skilled operator in the relatively new technology of the telegraph. Infatuated with "the daring deeds" of Morgan's Raiders, the Canadian teenager gamely walked up to the famed guerrilla leader in the early summer of 1862 with a great sales pitch: "I could be of assistance by use of the Telegraph in throwing the enemy off his track and off their guard."

The timing could not have been better. Morgan brought Ellsworth along to assist in his first major raid into Union territory in Kentucky. With deviousness and every so often a dash of whimsy, he knew how to hack into Union telegraph lines to help spread what would today be called "fake news" and disinformation. Near a vital supply route along a railroad, Ellsworth got to work in the middle of a raging thunderstorm—which earned him the nickname "Lightning." Using a small pocket device, he deftly cut into the telegraph lines unbeknownst to Union operators. On another occasion near Midway, deep in Kentucky territory, he sent out false instructions supposedly signed by a Federal general which led to three thousand Union men marching in the wrong direction.

"Captain Lightning" and his commander were not above having some fun at the Union army's expense. With Morgan's prodding, Ellsworth once sent a spoof message requesting that two barrels of whiskey be sent two hundred miles south to a Union officer in Nashville—which was done with much wasted time and expense. Once, when suspicious Union operators at the other end of the line wanted to know who was at the keys, Ellsworth, at the end of a successful mission, boasted of his notoriety.

"I am Ellsworth—G," he tapped over the wires.

"You damn wild Canadian," came the furious response.

————

Luck for Morgan and his men ran out in the summer of 1863 during a stunning assault of more than a thousand miles that started in Tennessee and ran through Indiana, Kentucky, Ohio and even West Virginia, a Border State that had just been admitted into the Union. It was the farthest north that any uniformed Confederate soldiers would ever reach. But a desperate attempt to cross the Ohio River under heavy enemy fire turned disastrous. Ellsworth escaped, but Morgan and several hundred of his battered band surrendered.

While Morgan had the bad fate of getting captured, he had the good fortune of being jailed with perhaps the most talented officer in his ranks, Captain Thomas Hines. The former university professor had somehow convinced the authorities in the Union prison outside Columbus, Ohio, to provide him with some reading material, including Victor Hugo's Les Misérables. Inspired by what he called the "vivid delineations of the wonderful escapes of Jean Valjean," Hines and his comrades—with nothing more than a couple of stolen knives—over six weeks dug a twenty-five-foot tunnel and made their escape.

But John Morgan never fully regained the confidence of the Confederate generals after his failed Ohio adventure. He led a few other raids well into 1864 but was eventually surprised by Lincoln's forces near Greeneville, Tennessee, and shot dead in the back while attempting to retreat. "The minds of many of the young men were stirred by the strange exploits of Morgan," Bennett Young summed up their history, knowing the famed raiders were too talented to waste. With their leader gone, they expected new and daring assignments.

What surprised the veteran fighters was where they were sent.

———

It was Hines who first came up with the idea, perhaps inspired by his miserable time in the Ohio prison. The South's army was badly outnumbered by its Union foes; why not organize attacks—from Canada— to rescue the tens of thousands of Confederate soldiers suffering in prisons along the Canadian border? In early 1864, Hines met in Richmond with Jefferson Davis and other leaders, who liked his idea. The goal of freeing prisoners remained a central focus if not an obsession of the Confederates; it motivated John Wilkes Booth to undertake one of his early plots against President Lincoln.

The written orders Thomas Hines received directly from the Confederate secretary of war James Seddon in March 1864 were explicit and succinct: "You are detailed for special service to proceed to Canada . . . collecting there the men of General Morgan's command who may have escaped." Headley got similar instructions. "I was also detailed to report to . . . Toronto, Canada, for service . . . along the northern borders of the United States."

Bennett Young eventually joined them through a rather more circuitous route. He had been imprisoned in the notorious Camp Douglas near Chicago, where more than four thousand detainees perished. After one failed escape attempt, he endured a month in an underground dungeon. His next attempt succeeded, and from Illinois it was a short run to Canada. George "Lightning" Ellsworth also made his way back to his native Canada to lend a hand.

It was shortly after dispatching these veteran fighters that Davis had sent Jacob Thompson and Clement Clay to Canada with the money needed to underwrite their military work. If Morgan's Raiders had been so successful striking at the Union's underbelly from the South, it stood to reason they could spark the same terror and turmoil with surprise attacks from where Lincoln would least expect it: his unprotected northern flank in Canada.

16

'ENTERPRISES OF WAR'

After bitter guerrilla fighting in the South and gruesome conditions in Union prisons, the tranquility of Toronto in April of 1864 offered a welcome reprieve for the tired exiles who had once been the stalwarts of Morgan's Raiders.

John Headley found upon his arrival in that city that while Canada might be colder in temperature, it was warm in its welcome of the dispirited fighters from the South. "Within a few days we had met, perhaps, a hundred Confederates and prominent citizens of Kentucky, Missouri, West Virginia, and Maryland, who were refugees," he remarked. With another soldier who had escaped a Union prison, Headley enjoyed a boat ride on Lake Ontario. "The city presented a grand front when viewed from a distance out in the bay," he recalled, a far cry from the dark prison cells and burned-out Southern towns he and his fellow combatants had left behind. "There was everything in the prospect at Toronto to make a sojourn enjoyable," Headley added. "The leading newspapers of Canada were published here and the South got a friendly comment on the course of events. All the news of the war and from the front of the armies was published daily."

Thomas Hines was also discovering the pleasures of Toronto, especially the luxurious Queen's Hotel. Hines quickly realized that the Queen's Hotel was the place for a spy to be. "Toronto at the time must have been like Lisbon during World War II," his biographer James Horan noted. "Agents of the Confederacy, and detectives for the Union, walked in and out of the Queen's bar, buying, selling and trading information."

As for Bennett Young, he found his solace in Toronto, albeit briefly, through religion. He enrolled in divinity classes at the University of Toronto but in May 1864 he abandoned his studies and headed to Halifax, eager to join the rebellion once again. There he met Clement Clay who had just arrived in Canada along with Jacob Thompson to get the Confederate secret services organized.

Clay was impressed with the zeal and the plans for military strikes being hatched by the 21-year-old Kentuckian. "After having satisfied me that his heart was with us in our struggle," Clay wrote to Judah Benjamin, the Confederate Secretary of State, "he developed his plans for retaliating on the enemy of the injuries and outrages inflicted upon the South."

Clay dispatched Young to Richmond to get official sanction for his schemes. The eager young rebel and the veteran Confederate politician had just set in motion what in five short months would become the most controversial Confederate attack from Canada into the United States.

While Young was talking military missions with Clement Clay, Thomas Hines was helping Jacob Thompson—the newly appointed head of Confederate operations in Canada—with money matters. It was a bright spring morning, May 29, 1864, when the two men met up in Montreal, where Thompson had just arrived after a long land journey from Halifax.

If Toronto during the Civil War has been compared to Lisbon in World War II, Montreal was its Casablanca—a mysterious, treacherous city that Union (or Federal) detectives flooded into in order to spy on the growing number of Southern exiles there. The Montreal police chief estimated there were at least 300 to 500 Confederate agents and soldiers in his town. With its easy access by train and by ship, Montreal was one of the largest and grandest cities in North America. With over ninety thousand inhabitants, it was twice the size of Richmond, the

Confederate capital, and it far surpassed Toronto as a financial and cultural hub of the Canadas. There were theatres, numerous banks, restaurants and even the continent's first indoor skating rink—not to mention a hundred houses of prostitution.

Thomas Hines had little time for tourism. He found the city unsafe, even as a seasoned guerrilla fighter. The politician apparently shared the soldier's distrust of Montreal. "We can't stand here, Captain," Thompson told Hines. "There are too many Federal detectives. It is best we move on to Toronto."

But first they had important business: the head of the Confederate operations in Canada needed to open a bank account "for the ample funds at his command," as one of his operatives put it, and Montreal was the financial capital of British North America. It did not take long for Thompson to find a suitable establishment to help the Southern cause.

———

Henry Starnes looked and acted like the stereotypical mid-nineteenth-century banker and political heavyweight that he was. Always elegant in his three-piece business suit and sporting fashionable mutton chop sideburns, he had solid roots in Quebec's establishment. Born in Kingston to a United Empire Loyalist father and a French-Canadian mother, he went to school at the elite Montreal Academical Institution and the Petit Séminaire de Montréal, where he met future prominent leaders including George-Étienne Cartier, a Father of Confederation. He prospered in the food importing business until he turned his interest to banking, becoming the general manager for the Montreal branch of the Ontario Bank in 1859.

Starnes also flexed his political muscle. He had served on Montreal's city council from 1852 to 1855 and was mayor from 1856 to 1858. He then moved up to provincial politics, sitting in the Legislative Assembly from 1858 to 1863. At ease with English and French politicians of all stripes, as the *Montreal Daily Star* put it, Starnes was "always sure to be found in the Government ranks, no matter the color of the flag or uniform." Starnes was just the kind of well-placed political and financial operator the Confederates needed.

On May 30, a day after arriving in Montreal, Jacob Thompson walked into Starnes's bank, situated in a stately three-storey building on Place d'Armes, across the street from the imposing Notre-Dame Basilica. He set up what would in effect become the slush fund for the Confederacy's war of sabotage and subterfuge waged from Canada against Lincoln and his government. Robert Anson Campbell, the chief teller at Starnes's Ontario Bank, testified at the conspiracy trials after the Civil War that Thompson opened his account in May 1864 with two deposits totalling $109,965. Over time, Campbell said, the bank records showed Thompson's account grew to at least $649,873.28, the equivalent of more than twelve million dollars today. Thompson and his associates also used banks in Toronto and St. Catharines, but by far the biggest chunk of the finances flowed through Starnes's institution. The Montreal bank was central to keeping the Confederate machine well-oiled—and secretive.

Campbell explained how huge amounts of untraceable cash were siphoned into Starnes's bank. "Thompson has bought from us several times United States notes—greenbacks as they are commonly called," the chief teller testified.

"In large sums?" he was asked.

"Yes, sir," he said—citing two examples over a short period when Thompson transferred $15,000 and then $19,125 from abroad over a short period.

All of this—quite legal, if perhaps ethically dubious—was going on with the full knowledge by the bank that they were aiding and abetting the Southern cause. Thompson became a regular enough customer at Starnes's bank during his frequent trips to Montreal that the chief teller grew familiar with him. "Oh, yes, I know him well," Campbell later told American investigators.

Starnes's bank did more than move large amounts of cash for the Confederate cause; in effect, it helped the slave states launder money. Campbell explained that, "as a general thing," cheques at the bank were issued "payable to the bearer"—that is, a specific person. But the bank facilitated Thompson's discreet work by issuing many cheques "payable to order"—in other words, anonymously. More details into how the scheme worked came from Daniel Eastwood, the assistant bank manager. He testified that bills of exchange, signed by the secretary of the treasury of the Confederate States, with an address in Liverpool, England, were deposited into the "large fund" at the bank. The deposits were initially made out to a sympathetic newspaper publisher in New York, but his name "was erased at Mr. Thompson's request" and Eastwood's name was put on the paperwork "to make the draft negotiable without putting any other name" on it.

Eastwood was asked if he knew where the money ended up. "I have no knowledge," the banker said. "By the account it will be seen that there was a considerable amount . . . purchased at one time and another, but we were not acquainted with the use it was put to."

———

Though Thompson never had a formal title as their commander and would try to disavow some controversial actions by his men later on, it was clear to the Confederate agents in Canada that, as Thomas Hines put it, "his authority . . . was almost autocratic over the Confederate agents and officers who were ordered to report to him." Especially because he controlled the purse strings.

The Confederacy could claim that Thompson was on nothing more than a "diplomatic mission," but the pretense wore thin very quickly. He told agents like Hines that their true mission was "to cripple and embarrass the military policy of the Federal Government by the destruction of military and naval stores . . . but to carefully avoid all transgressions of the laws of war."

It was an intractable contradiction. Either Thompson was a diplomat operating within Canadian laws or he was the leader of a secret rebel force—a force made up of trained and experienced killers from Morgan's Raiders. Either he and his agents respected Canada's neutrality or they ignored the border to carry out military forays and sabotage.

It was a conundrum that the Confederates in Canada could never fully resolve, and it would plague them until the end of the war. After all, Hines's explicit orders from the secretary of war made any compromise all but impossible: Seddon had put him in charge of "effecting any fair and appropriate enterprises of war against our enemies . . . in any hostile operation"—hardly compatible with avoiding transgressions of the laws of war.

John Castleman, a military man with a sharp mind, summed up the Confederacy's doublespeak regarding its Canadian operations by describing it as "the elastic verbal instructions given by President Davis."

———

His all-important bank account opened and operational in Montreal, Thompson headed to Toronto, his final destination. Flush with Confederate money, he could afford the best in accommodations in the bustling Ontario city. He chose, naturally, the Queen's Hotel, the sprawling, elegant, three-storey establishment at the corner of Front and York (where the Fairmount Royal York now stands). "It may be said that we found Confederate headquarters here at this hotel," John Headley recalled, noting that Thompson took over no less than a suite of rooms.

But Toronto, like Montreal, was full of Union spies trying to keep close surveillance on the Southerners. "Colonel Thompson cautioned us on our arrival against any stranger who might claim an acquaintance," John Headley recalled, "as a swarm of detectives from the United States, male and female, were quartered in Toronto."

Thompson and his operatives would need a more private and secure place than the Queen's Hotel to plot their campaign against Lincoln. Fortunately, they could rely on a wealthy member of one of Toronto's most elite families, whose sympathies for the Southern cause ran as deep as his pockets.

17.

'A STRONG FRIEND'

It was as close as you could get to a Southern plantation home, considering it stood in the middle of a wooded estate on what were then the western outskirts of Toronto.

"The red-brick mansion had a distinctly southern style, with a wide veranda supported by Doric columns, a Grecian pedimented entry, shuttered windows, and eighteen-foot ceilings," as one historical archive described it. A rose garden was adorned "with rustic bridges, wild strawberries, and trilliums." It was called Heydon Villa, and its owner, a wealthy and powerful aristocrat named George Taylor Denison III, sought to emulate more than the architecture of the slave South—he was an avowed ally and supporter of the Confederacy.

"I became very friendly with Colonel Thompson . . . at my house," Denison wrote. "There were a number of escaped prisoners . . . and many other officers of lower rank, with whom I was in the habit of frequently discussing military matters."

Denison offered more than the comforts of a Southern-style mansion to the Confederates in Canada. He provided money, refuge, political support and even some help in spying—in effect, becoming a co-conspirator in some of their most ambitious enterprises.

———

The affinity George Taylor Denison III felt for the Southern aristocracy came naturally. What his distinguished family lacked in originality when it came to naming their sons, they more than made up for in passing on their privileges. Born in 1839, Denison led a life of the pampered and powerful. His father was one of the wealthiest landowners in Upper Canada. The Denison property, with lush forests, fields and a creek that ran all the way to Lake Ontario, extended from what is now Queen and Ossington to College and Dufferin—a vast expanse of real estate that took up what today, in modern Toronto, is ten city blocks east to west and twelve city blocks north to south.

He attended Upper Canada College but by all accounts wallowed at the bottom end of his class. He then went on to Trinity College, only to be expelled for being rude to an instructor. He eventually graduated with a law degree from the University of Toronto and went into practice with his brother. But the law never much interested Denison; the military did.

As a boy, Denison had devoured books on Napoleon and the Duke of Wellington. He loved to soak up the lore passed on to him from generations of uniformed Denisons: tales of how they battled the American revolutionaries who fought for independence from Britain in 1767 or suppressed the Canadian rebels who clamoured for democracy in 1837. "The recollections of the glorious victories won by our fathers in these campaigns will continually be handed down by tradition," Denison recalled, "and in case of future trouble be an inspiration and encouragement to our people."

He learned to ride, to shoot and to wield a cavalry sabre. As he grew into early manhood, Denison came to his military standing the same way he got his wealth and pretty much everything else in life: through inheritance. At age fifteen "he was commissioned as an officer in his father's troop. Two years later, he inherited it as lieutenant and commanding officer." By the age of twenty-two Denison had been made a major, and he climbed the ranks over the next five years. "I was the youngest cornet, lieutenant, captain, major and lieutenant-colonel we have ever had in the Canadian Cavalry," he noted proudly in his memoirs. He also fought, and won, in the political arena. By the 1860s he sat on Toronto's city council, as his father had before him, representing the St. Patrick's Ward that bordered his family estate.

Outwardly, George Taylor Denison III exuded the self-confidence of the entitled. But he confided in his diary that he was haunted by his father's admonition that "if a man does not make his mark or be in a fair way" early in life, he is a failure. Denison was determined to make his mark the way his forefathers had—with tales of "glorious victories." In the end, the master of Heydon Villa didn't have to go looking for a war; the war had come to him.

———

In 1864, the year Jacob Thompson arrived in Canada, Denison was only twenty-five, but already he had parlayed his family's inheritance and social connections into a personal fortune, marrying Caroline Macklem, a niece of the Bishop of Niagara and granddaughter of one of the wealthiest landowners in the Niagara Peninsula. It is not known when or how Denison first met Thompson, but the connection between the two men was all but inevitable. Denison was the perfect Toronto ally for the Confederate plotters. He was conservative and had militia training, political clout as a city councillor and the fuel every insurrection runs on: money. Thompson, a Southern politician in a strange northern land, needed someone he could trust—and Denison came with an impeccable family background. His uncle, George Dewson, had just arrived back in Toronto after he had spent several years in the South, where he had risen in the ranks of the Confederate Secret Service to become a colonel. The Confederate secretary of state had dispatched Dewson to Toronto in September 1864 to build support for the cause. "His presence at George Denison's home was an open invitation to the numerous Confederate agents . . . to congregate for entertainment and more serious business," as the Denison family biography put it.

Heydon Villa, sheltered in the woods of the vast Denison estate far away from both the common masses and the prying eyes of the authorities, was a perfect place for Jacob Thompson and George Denison to figure out how to try to help the South win the war. Denison knew all too well that while Thompson's lodgings at the Queen's Hotel were pleasant, it was not the safest location for a Confederate undercover operation. "There were a number of spies of the Federal Government sent there to watch him," he wrote. "Colonel Thompson had the greatest difficulty in keeping up any communication with his Government in Richmond."

Denison was only too happy to offer a solution. He opened up his Southern-style villa to the Confederate plotters he so admired. "I was a strong friend of the Southern refugees who were exiled in our country, and I treated them with the hospitality due to unfortunate strangers driven from their homes," he wrote.

Those unfortunate strangers included Thompson himself, his secretary William Cleary, as well as top Confederate leaders, generals, sympathizers and spies. And the hospitality Denison offered them would eventually land him in a mess of trouble.

18.

'THE WORK OF MURDER'

They called it the Black Vomit.

Once you had reached that stage of the illness, you were already close to death.

Many of the patients suffering in the crowded corridors of the hospitals and makeshift clinics in the Bermudian islands in April 1864 had the early signs of the disease: muscle aches, headaches, dizziness and loss of appetite. Then came the toxic phase: abdominal pain; bleeding from the nose, mouth and eyes; liver and kidney failure; delirium; and the distinctive symptom that gave the disease its name—a yellowing of the skin.

Yellow fever had swept through the British colony, just six hundred miles off the American coastline. With a frightening mortality rate of 30 to 50 percent and no known cure, any outbreak caused alarm and fear. Making the rounds in the sweltering heat at a hotel and a boarding house that served as improvised hospitals was a handsome, confident American doctor named Luke Pryor Blackburn. In his late forties, he looked distinguished with his short-cropped, thinning brown hair, clean-shaven face and deep-set light eyes. Blackburn's reputation preceded him: having wrestled with several outbreaks of yellow fever in the United States, he had become a de facto expert on a disease that still puzzled the medical world at the time.

Blackburn asked for no fees for his services in Bermuda. Because secretly, his mission went beyond medicine. He doggedly began collecting soiled clothes and linen from the diseased and the dying. His goal:

an early form of bioterrorism, what he cold-bloodedly described to a co-conspirator as "an infallible plan directed against the masses of Northern people solely to create death."

———

Born in 1816 into a large family of thirteen children in Kentucky, Luke Blackburn displayed his talents for medicine before he ended his teenage years. As an apprentice, he fought a cholera outbreak in the 1830s and he got his medical degree three months before his nineteenth birthday. By 1848 he was elected health officer for the city of Natchez, Mississippi, and battled a yellow fever outbreak there. His expertise was also called upon when the pestilence killed thousands in New Orleans in 1853 and New York in 1854. He knew all too well the human toll of disease: his wife died in a malaria epidemic in 1856.

Blackburn—like many well-off Mississippians—owned enslaved Blacks. His family had twenty-one people in bondage while he was growing up; he acquired eighteen slaves as an adult and co-owned another seventy-four with his brother. In Natchez, his "circle of friends" included a rising political star named Jefferson Davis, and Blackburn naturally shared Davis's visceral rejection of Lincoln's plans to free the slaves. When the war started, Blackburn acted as an envoy for the governor of his home state of Kentucky, trying to procure weapons. In 1862, as an aide-de-camp for a Mississippi general, he delivered messages about troop movements across the South and also managed to round up eight thousand guns for the badly depleted army.

There was a bit of the wannabe spy in Blackburn. He proposed a complicated scheme for running the Union blockade, which the Confederacy approved. Appointed as "Mississippi's agent in Canada," Blackburn headed north in August 1863, stopping in Halifax on his way to Toronto. There, he obtained a boat and loaded it with ice. The vessel made it back to Alabama, where the Confederates took the ice and other goods and gave Blackburn cotton to be swapped in Cuba for "arms, ammunition and money." It was bad luck for Blackburn when Union troops captured the vessel, but he was fortunate the authorities assumed he was just a civilian passenger, not the mastermind of the smuggling operation, and let him go.

————

After that adventure Blackburn returned to Canada, and towards the end of 1863 his plot to weaponize yellow fever began to take shape. As an engaging Kentuckian with plenty of war stories, Blackburn easily made friends with the many Confederate agents he met, including their official leader, Jacob Thompson. It was a tight, secretive circle, and as rebels in a foreign country they had to trust each other. John Headley and another of Morgan's men, Thomas Hines, took lodgings at a rooming house while Blackburn found a room at a boarding house run by a Kentucky man whose brother had served with the raiders.

In the boisterous crowd of Southern sympathizers, an unassuming man from Little Rock, Arkansas, seemed to have ingratiated himself with everyone. His name was Godfrey Hyams and he claimed to have escaped from a Union prison. "He was a very smart fellow and had managed to establish the closest confidential relations with Colonel Thompson," recalled John Headley. Hyams was later described rather inelegantly by the *New York Times* as being "of small stature, of dark complexion, and Israelitish features, and is said to be of the Jewish persuasion." Born into humble origins in Manchester, England, in 1833, Hyams immigrated to the United States in 1857 and eventually settled in Helena, Arkansas, eking out a living as a shoemaker. When Union troops marched into the state in 1862, Hyams, like many other civilians in the South, had to endure their marauding and plundering. He claimed in a letter to military authorities that Lincoln's men had confiscated his home and burned his furniture.

Though he appears to have had no overt political leanings, Hyams was briefly locked up in a wretched Union prison designated for suspected Confederate guerrillas, spies and sympathizers in 1862. By the spring of 1863, like so many other disaffected Southerners, he made his way to Toronto. Hyams found work again as a shoemaker, living in what he later described as a "state of destitution" in a shabby apartment on Terauley Street. Hyams, with a pregnant wife, was desperate: "I have not a cent to help her," he wrote. Perhaps still seething at being driven out of his home by Lincoln's forces, Hyams named his newborn son Stonewall Jackson after the Confederate hero general.

But as a downtrodden Confederate hiding out in Toronto, Hyams was looking for cash, not a cause. He thought his fortunes would change when, according to his later account, he met the well-to-do Luke Blackburn in Toronto in December 1863. "He took me upstairs in a private room; and he . . . offered his hand in friendship that he would never deceive me, and wanted to place confidence in me for an expedition," Hyams recalled. Blackburn promised to pay $100,000, an irresistible fortune for a poor shoemaker.

"He then told me that he wanted me to take a certain quantity of clothing—he did not state how much, but he said they would consist of shirts and coats and underclothing—into the States," Hyams said. Blackburn now had a plan, and all he needed was a plague. Four months later, yellow fever struck Bermuda.

The doctor quickly packed his bags and left Canada to head to the infected islands.

———

In the Bermudan clinics where Blackburn tended to the sick, staff around him noticed some rather odd behaviour. One nurse noticed that instead of letting fresh air soothe the afflicted, the doctor would wrap a sickly patient with covers, then place the sweat-soaked blankets in his trunk. A second nurse saw Blackburn stay all night next to a dying patient, but the next morning the corpse was covered with a shroud and his clothes were gone. "One of the hospital nurses said that whenever one of his patients was sick, he would stretch out a handkerchief to catch the black vomit, and afterward wrap up the handkerchief and carry it away with him," another witness later recalled.

Over several weeks, Blackburn managed to pack five trunks full of soiled clothing and linen and ship them to Canada. In early June, he wrote to his keen accomplice, Godfrey Hyams, and told him to meet him in Nova Scotia. Blackburn arrived in Halifax by July 12, content that he had managed to get his dangerous biological weapon to Halifax undetected; now all he had to do was smuggle the cargo into the Northern states.

He told Hyams what to do next: retrieve the trunks from the steamer and bring them back to the hotel to repack them, taking care to chew camphor and smoke strong cigars to avoid getting infected. There was also a "very nice valise with some very elegant shirts and other things infected with fever or small pox." Upon learning that Blackburn wanted him to send those clothes to the White House, addressed as a gift for President Lincoln, Hyams later claimed he balked: "I objected to taking it, and refused to do it."

But Hyams had no qualms with helping Blackburn in his scheme to infect thousands of ordinary citizens, as the good doctor explained, "to destroy anybody—it did not matter who—that they came in contact with." Bribing a captain at the Halifax port with a twenty-dollar gold piece, Hyams arranged for the trunks to be smuggled into the northeastern states. The clothing was shipped and sold in Boston, Philadelphia and two cities with a heavy Union troop presence—New Bern, North Carolina, and Norfolk, Virginia. Blackburn had given Hyams special instructions for the largest trunk, which he nicknamed "Big No. 2," to be delivered to Washington.

Satisfied he had accomplished everything Blackburn had asked, Hyams returned home to Canada, expecting the generous reward promised for his murderous mission.

————

How much did Confederate officials know about Blackburn's meticulous plans to spread the poison of a deadly disease among innocent civilians in the North? Certainly, the top conspirators in Canada must have had a good idea what was afoot. When Godfrey Hyams arrived by train in Hamilton after his shipping spree in the United States, he says he was greeted by none other than Clement Clay, one of the two Confederate commissioners sent by Davis to direct the secret operations in Canada, along with one of Clay's associates. "They both rose up and shook hands with me, and congratulated me on my safe return and upon my making a fortune," Hyams recalled. "So I understood at the time, from that . . . that they must have known all about it."

Hyams then telegraphed Blackburn, who was staying at St. Lawrence Hall in Montreal, and the next night, around midnight, there was a knock at his door.

"Come down, Hyams, and open the door," Blackburn cried out. "You're like all damned rascals who have been doing something wrong—you're afraid the Devil is after you."

Hyams came out to find the doctor accompanied by Bennett Young, one of the former Confederate raiders. Hyams told Blackburn how he had disposed of all the goods in the targetted American cities and the doctor seemed very pleased.

"Well," he said, "that is all right as long as 'Big No. 2' went into Washington: it will kill them at sixty yards' distance."

Hyams, who could barely feed his family, expected he would finally get paid. Blackburn assured him that he would contact Jacob Thompson and make arrangements for the money. But things did not go as Hyams had hoped when, on August 11, he went to see the Confederate commander in Canada. Thompson offered only $50 and promised a second payment when Hyams provided written proof he had sold the goods. Hyams promptly contacted the Washington auction house to get evidence of the sale, but received only another small cheque: "Received from Jacob Thompson $100, in full, on account of Dr. Luke P. Blackburn," read the receipt.

They may have tried to cheat Hyams out of his promised reward, but there is no record of Thompson or any of the other top Confederate leaders in Canada ever voicing objections to the yellow fever plot. Nor apparently did Jefferson Davis. In a letter unearthed by Lincoln historian Edward Steers, a Southern chaplain who had no qualms about military violence in the name of the cause warned the Confederate president that germ warfare was crossing the line:

> [I]t cannot be our policy to employ wicked men to destroy the persons & property of private citizens, by inhumane & cruel acts. I name only one. $100 of public money has been paid here to one "Hyams" a shoemaker, for services rendered by conveying and causing to be sold in the city of Washington at auction, boxes of small-pox clothing. . . There can be no doubt of the causes of the failure of such plans. It is only a matter of surprise that, God does not forsake us and our cause when we are associated with such misguided friends.

It is not known if Davis read the letter, but he certainly never admonished his "misguided friends" in Canada about the "inhumane acts." Thompson had been on his official "diplomatic" mission for less than three months and already his network was sanctioning and financing biological terror.

———

That "$100 of public money" from the Confederate treasury was a far cry from the fortune Hyams claimed he had been promised. Disappointed, he sent a letter to Blackburn in Montreal, where he was staying in a fancy hotel. "I wrote down to him at Montreal, and told him I wanted some money, and that he ought to send me some," Hyams noted. Even angrier when he received no reply, Hyams made his way to Montreal to confront the doctor in person: "I asked the doctor for money but he laughed at me," the hapless conspirator complained. "He . . . then got into his carriage and rode off to some races, I think, and left me, and never gave me any more satisfaction."

Luke Blackburn and Jacob Thompson would come to regret their dismissive treatment of the shoemaker from Arkansas. With his betrayal of Godfrey Hyams, the doctor had turned a desperate accomplice into a disgruntled one. By the time Hyams was through with his former fellow conspirators, the damage he inflicted would be immense.

Partnering with and then snubbing an unreliable collaborator such as Hyams was one of two fatal flaws in Blackburn's scheme. More significantly, Blackburn's idea for a nineteenth-century form of bio-terrorism was crippled by a nineteenth-century misunderstanding of yellow fever. What Blackburn and other doctors did not know was that infected mosquitoes transmitted the disease, not people or their clothing. That medical discovery did not come for another four decades, in 1901.

At the time, though, Blackburn had no reason to doubt his "infallible plan . . . to create death." In the early fall of 1864, the town of New Bern, North Carolina—one of the places Blackburn had told Hyams to ship clothing—was hit by what one survivor called "a sweeping pestilence, so completely decimating," which claimed the lives of hundreds of people.

To Blackburn, it appeared that the Black Vomit had done its dirty work as he had planned.

19.

'A CONSTANT MENACE'

"All that is needed for our success is unflinching nerve."

Jacob Thompson was eager to show his superiors in the Confederate capital of Richmond that, though once a politician, he was now a determined man of action. Over the summer of 1864 and into the fall, he and his co-conspirators unleashed a flurry of sometimes coordinated, sometimes random operations across the border that grew in their intensity and violence. The people in the North, he told his Confederate leaders, "are weary of the war" and with just a little push of sabotage and sedition, they could be nudged into open rebellion.

For most of these schemes, Thompson and his partner Clement Clay could rely on the expertise and daring of the hardy bunch of veterans from John Morgan's Raiders now residing in Canada—experienced soldiers such as Bennett Young, Thomas Hines, John Castleman and John Headley. But Thompson would also get unsolicited help from a fellow Southerner who was as impulsive as Thompson was cautious. While Thompson vigilantly worked in the shadows as much as possible so as not to antagonize the Canadian authorities, George Nicholas Sanders vociferously sought the spotlight.

"I never knew of another man like him," recalled former Morgan Raider Castleman, who had seen more than his share of all kinds of soldiers and scoundrels. Thomas Hines, no stranger either to the wild men of war, was "fascinated as well as repelled by his evil genius." Sanders more than any other person was the Confederate in Canada the pro-Lincoln press loved to hate, denouncing him over the years as "a zealous and unscrupulous Southerner," one of the Confederacy's "drunken, unprincipled adventurers" and "the notorious rebel . . . engaged in visionary political schemes."

He proved to be all those things—and more.

———

George Sanders was raised on a family estate in Lexington, Kentucky, called Grass Hills, 1,200 acres of cattle, thoroughbred horses—and, of course, plenty of enslaved people. A hustler with a sharp eye for mixing business with politics, at age thirty-six he managed to convince the Hudson's Bay Company, which owned the rights to the vast Oregon Territory, to hire him as a business agent. He hoped to make a fortune selling the land to the US government, but the deal fell through in no small part because of his underhanded tactics and dishonesty.

In 1851, after buying a newspaper in Washington, DC, Sanders "became attracted by the power and splendor of politics," as a close friend put it. He used his paper to successfully back Franklin Pierce, the Democratic candidate who became an avid pro-slavery president in 1853, enforcing the repressive Fugitive Slave Act and defending what he politely called "involuntary servitude" as an "admitted right" under the Constitution. Pierce promptly rewarded Sanders with a prestige posting as America's consul in England. "He sees everybody, talks to everybody, high and low," wrote one newspaper. "Sanders . . . was considered one of the most adept political wire-pullers in the country." He threw lavish parties, "never without money or beautiful women." Remarked Castleman: "The name of George N. Sanders was daily on the tongues of men of nearly every Christian nation." It was not meant as a compliment.

Sanders's own quick tongue got him into trouble. In Europe, he was friendly with democrats like Victor Hugo but also with revolutionaries seeking to overthrow tyrants. At a well-attended and well-publicized dinner in London, he toasted "do[ing] away with the Crown Heads of Europe"—which was seen as a veiled call for assassinations. That and other inflammatory outbursts did not go over well back home in

Washington, and the Senate refused to confirm him as consul. His diplomatic career had lasted only three months.

Nevertheless, as soon as the Civil War broke out, Sanders was primed to try to help the Confederacy (and himself) make money and mischief. He started off marketing weapons, using Southern cotton as credit in Europe to buy six ironclad merchant vessels that would help the war effort and, as he gleefully admitted, be "worth a fortune" for his pocketbook. To arrange the purchase, Sanders had to sneak over the Canadian border on his way overseas. According to the gushing Confederate account called *The Adventures of George Sanders*, he walked across the suspension bridge linking the American and Canada sides of Niagara Falls disguised as a poor Cornish miner. He wore a seedy coat, a coarse shirt and a jagged straw hat, carrying tools in one hand and, in the other, an old and dirty carpet bag. Inside the bag he had stashed secret papers, dispatches and money for Confederates.

The ruse worked. Once safely in Canada, Sanders went straight to the Clifton House, a stately hotel overlooking Niagara Falls and a favourite Confederate hangout in Ontario. At first they balked at the shabbily dressed vagabond until he produced a thick wad of American greenbacks.

While negotiating for the vessels, Sanders recruited his family to set up a courier service to clandestinely get dispatches from the Confederacy to its supporters in Europe. One son, Reid, organized speedy schooners to make the trip from the South to Halifax. Another son, Lewis—whom Sanders had arranged to get appointed as a Confederate agent in Nova Scotia—directed the boats to Europe. Richmond agreed to pay Sanders $600 a month, a juicy contract. But, as it turned out, it came at a terrible cost. His son Reid was captured by Union forces during one of the operations in late 1862. He was freed in a prisoner swap, only to be captured once again in South Carolina two months later and jailed in the harsh Union prison system, where many did not survive.

———

The Union disruptions of Sanders's courier operations cost him his contract with Richmond. His options and opportunities running out in the embattled South, George Sanders returned to Canada in June 1864. Sporting a long, pointed beard and curly hair, "constantly unkempt and unshaven," he managed to charm or bully people with his undeniable charisma and force of personality. Unlike Jacob Thompson and Clement Clay, who had been appointed as commissioners, Sanders had no official status, though he later claimed in a letter to Jefferson Davis that he had been "encouraged by your approval of my suggestion . . . to visit Canada." But formality and rules never bothered Sanders, "living affluently in a room overlooking the bay" in the Queen's Hotel in Toronto. "It is said that he borrowed and spent thousands on champagne alone," according to one account. "He liked to think of himself as a promoter."

"Mr. Sanders is remarkably well-adapted for a mission," noted one pro-Lincoln paper. "He has a large head well-stocked with brains; has no modesty to interfere with a great project . . . He is well-calculated to do our cause mischief."

Thompson, always the proper politician, never took a liking to the gregarious Sanders. "Between him and myself there existed a political antagonism," Sanders admitted. "There is such a thing as spoiling broth by having too many hands in it," Thompson complained to Clay, who agreed. Clay in turn told Richmond he wished Sanders were "in Europe, Asia or Africa."

Sanders, though, was much closer than that, on his way to St. Catharines to try to ingratiate himself with Clay, who had set up quarters there. The picturesque town near Niagara Falls was more suited than Toronto or Montreal to the temperament of the former senator, who missed his home in Alabama. It also helped that many of the town's citizens were sympathetic to the cause, eager to provide what the local newspaper called "a haven for fugitives from the wrath of the United States government." Clay had already endured one miserable winter in Canada, spending a fair amount of time and money buying his wife expensive gifts such as silk dresses and French hats, not easily available in the embattled South. Now he was about to be sucked into one of Sanders's sales pitches. "Commissioner Clay soon yielded entirely to his

influence," recalled Castleman. "[M]ost men were swayed by his plausible theories, and he was a constant menace."

Sanders had wormed his way into power, becoming a member
of what the *Philadelphia Inquirer* aptly called "the Canadian junta" of
Confederates north of the border. By the early summer of 1864, Sanders
had come up with a "peace plot" that impressed Clay and the other
leaders. Sanders was a showman but he was astute; he realized a badly
out-gunned Confederacy could perhaps outwit their foes on the political battlefield. "Conscious of the fast-waning vitality of the Confederacy,
and well-acquainted with the strength of the Federal arms," as he put
it, Sanders decided to play a game of high-stakes diplomatic poker.
"I determined to make a direct move upon President Lincoln."

———

Everyone was exhausted and embittered by the war, now well into its
third year—Southerners, because the tide had turned against them
and their states were being ravaged by the advancing Union armies;
Northerners, because they were losing loved ones on the battlefields in
distressing numbers. What's more, many whites in the Union increasingly objected to any more sacrifices made on behalf of Blacks. "Tens
of thousands of white men must yet bite the dust to allay the Negro
mania of the president," cried out one anti-Lincoln paper in Ohio.
The lynchings and burning of Black homes during the draft riots in
New York—less than a year earlier—were still fresh memories.

The Confederates in Canada shrewdly decided to play on these
anti-war sentiments in the North. "The Yankees are sick of war and
anxious for peace," Clay wrote. To pull off their scheme, Sanders
needed to reel in a peace advocate of unimpeachable prestige and
principle. That man was Horace Greeley, arguably the most powerful
newspaper publisher in the country. His pro-Lincoln *New York Tribune*
was the most widely read paper in the nation's biggest city. When
Greeley spoke, the President listened. When Greeley grew frustrated
with Lincoln's reluctance to abolish slavery early in the war, he penned
a scathing editorial in 1862 blasting the President for being "timid"

instead of doing everything "to fight Slavery with Liberty." Those words were what had prompted Lincoln's famous reply, which he probably later regretted: "If I could save the Union without freeing any slave I would do it."

With calculated vagueness, Sanders let it be known through an intermediary who was friends with Greeley that "confidential agents of the Confederate government" in Canada had the "general power and knowledge of the wishes" of Richmond and were ready to talk peace. It was Sanders at his manipulative best; in truth, he had no power to declare that the Canadian Confederates could speak officially on behalf of Richmond in any peace negotiations, much less to insert himself into the process. But Greeley took the bait. Two days later he wrote to Lincoln about Sanders's peace overture, pointedly reminding the President that "your bleeding, bankrupt, almost dying country also longs for peace; shudders at the prospect of fresh conscriptions, of further wholesale devastations, and of new rivers of human blood."

Lincoln was skeptical, so in his letter of response he added the stringent caveat that any peace talks had to embrace "the restoration of the Union and the abandonment of slavery"—in effect, a surrender by the Confederacy. He sent his private secretary John Hay to accompany Greeley to Niagara Falls to meet the Confederates. In the end, both sides were bluffing. Sanders had misled Greeley into thinking he and his colleagues had authorization to act on behalf of Jefferson Davis's government. Greeley in turn didn't tell the Confederates about Lincoln's impossible preconditions. Sanders waited for Lincoln's envoys in the bar at the Clifton House. It should have been history in the making—a possible end to a devastating civil war. But when he met Sanders, Greeley was unimpressed with the "seedy looking Rebel" with greying whiskers. Nevertheless, he gave the Confederate officials the letter from Lincoln reiterating the President's insistence on the abolition of slavery and the preservation of the Union.

The Confederates in Canada were predictably outraged with the conditions. Greeley was similarly disheartened when he learned he wasn't really dealing with official ambassadors. The "peace" negotiations fell apart before they even began. It looked, at least initially, as if the plans had failed—another example of Sanders "always promising some glorious fruits of the schemes" he concocted, as Clay put it.

But Sanders would show them that even if they could not win at the peace table, there was a way to score victories in the war of public opinion.

———

Sanders promptly orchestrated the leaking of Lincoln's letter to the press, along with the Confederates' blistering response, painting Lincoln as an untrustworthy warmonger. "Instead of the safe-conduct which we solicited," they wrote, Lincoln offered only a hard line of "no bargaining, no negotiations, no truces with rebels, except to bury their dead." The gambit worked, at least by giving the anti-Lincoln press even more fodder. The *Philadelphia Age* complained that "the grinning, chattering, autocrat Lincoln says there shall be no peace." The Toronto *Leader* blasted Lincoln for wasting "such a favourable opportunity of bringing about peace" by imposing conditions that were "insulting to every Southerner who might read it." Even the *New York Times* was forced into trying to minimize the damage, dismissing the "great Peace Conference" in Niagara Falls as nothing more than an "electioneering dodge" and singling out Sanders for his machinations on behalf of "the ruffians of the Slave states."

Clay, once dismissive of Sanders's schemes, was now celebrating the "glorious fruits" of all the plotting, bragging to his boss in Richmond, Judah Benjamin, that "we lost nothing and gained much." He boasted to his president, Jefferson Davis, that the Confederates in Canada had scored a rare victory against their foe in the White House. "[A]s the matter now stands, it has weakened the Administration."

Even as Clay was exulting at victory to his bosses, privately he was consumed with dread that the Confederates were losing their breakaway republic and the slave system upon which it was built. In a remarkably frank letter that he wrote to friends in August 1864 from his home in St. Catharines, he admitted, "[W]e need peace even more than the NORTH does . . . Our BEST men have been, or are being killed or maimed and disabled." Then, referring to the runaway and freed Blacks fighting in Union ranks, Clay seethed: "[W]e have been robbed of fully a million of slaves who have been destroyed or are employed to destroy us."

Even more enraging for Clay was the fact that the Blacks still under bondage in the South were being encouraged to revolt. "Our slaves are being daily more demoralized, armed and incited to murder, arson, rape and other crimes." The Confederate commissioner in Canada then made a frightening proposal, going so far as to propose the possible genocide of adult Black males in the South:

> We may be constrained, in self-defence before long to commence
> RIDDING OURSELVES of the male slaves above fifteen, to save
> our innocent women and children from destruction. It is a horrible
> thought, at which my heart revolts, but less horrible than the fate
> of the victims of their brutal passions, incited by our white foes of
> more cunning heads and more devilish hearts. Besides, their extermi-
> nation is inevitable if the war continues a few years more.

Clay's conclusion was bleak: "The interests not only of the white race of the SOUTH, but the preservation of the black, demands that we shall soon put an end to the war." The enslaved people held in chains under Clay's Confederacy would disagree that their interests aligned with those of their white overlords, but Clay was right that he and his fellow Confederates in Canada would have to come up with even more daring—and violent—schemes if they wanted to end, much less win, the war.

———

Lincoln himself seemed to acknowledge that he had been outplayed by Sanders in the peace talks fiasco, confiding in a friend about "the harm

they are doing." People were now "attacking me for needlessly pro-
longing the war for purposes of my own," the President complained.
"Their mission was subterfuge."

Subterfuge was what Sanders did best—and he was not finished. In
early September 1864, he got the devastating news that his son Reid
had died in a dingy Union cell in Boston after twenty-one months
behind bars. "His long imprisonment and the hopeless chances of
exchange seems to have worn out his body," Sanders's other son Lewis
wrote, filled with grief.

George Sanders's machinations against Lincoln had always been
political. Now his revenge would also be personal. If his fellow conspirators in Canada—not to mention Lincoln's government—were
already wary of him as a "constant menace," they had not seen anything yet.

Emma Edmonds as "Franklin Thompson" (Courtesy State Archives of Michigan)

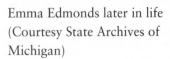

Emma Edmonds later in life (Courtesy State Archives of Michigan)

Drawings from Edmonds's book showing her in battle and delivering the mail (Reprinted from *Nurse and Spy*)

Application of Discharged Soldier for Arrears of Pay, &c.

Edmonds's application in 1882 to clear her name as a deserter and get her pension (Courtesy US National Archives)

Edward P. Doherty in full uniform shortly after the manhunt for John Wilkes Booth (Courtesy US National Archives)

Doherty's tombstone at the Arlington National Cemetery honours him for leading the cavalry detachment that "captured President Lincoln's assassin." (Courtesy Michael Hill, FindaGrave)

Dr. Alexander Augusta in uniform (Courtesy Oblate Sisters of Providence Archives, Baltimore, Maryland)

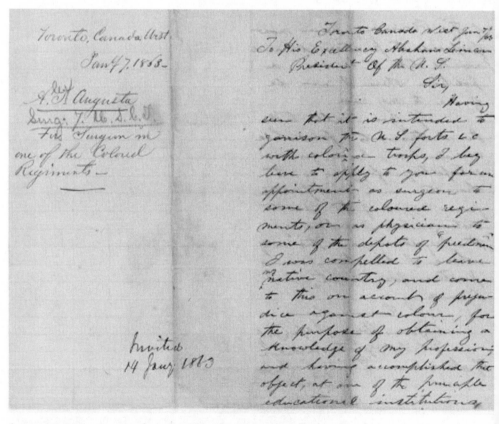

Augusta's January 1863 letter to President Lincoln offering to serve in the Union army (Courtesy US National Library of Medicine)

Dr. Anderson Ruffin Abbott
as a Union army surgeon
(Courtesy Oblate Sisters of
Providence Archives)

A drawing called "True Defenders of the Constitution." Black soldiers had a 35 percent
higher mortality rate than whites in the Union army, mainly from infection and disease.
(Courtesy US Library of Congress)

George Taylor Denison III in his library around 1912 (Courtesy Library and Archives Canada). Below, his estate known as Heydon Villa (Courtesy Toronto Public Library

Bernard Devlin, Montreal city councillor, prosecuted the St. Albans raiders. (Courtesy McCord Museum)

George Brown, publisher of the *Globe*, fought to end slavery. (Courtesy McCord Museum)

Guillaume Lamothe was forced to resign as Montreal's chief of police. (Courtesy Archives de Montréal)

Judge Charles-Joseph Coursol freed the St. Albans raiders. (Courtesy McCord Museum)

Henry Starnes (left), manager of the Ontario Bank of Montreal (bottom), which handled the finances of the Confederates (Courtesy McCord Museum)

A bank draft for John Wilkes Booth signed by Starnes for the equivalent of about $300 in US gold (Courtesy US National Archives)

20.

'OUR PLAN WAS DARING'

John "Bowie Knife" Potter, the American consul general in Canada, was not your typical diplomat.

He had earned his nickname as a congressman back in 1860 when, in an explosive encounter with a pro-slavery rival politician, he was challenged to a duel. Potter chose the bowie knife as his weapon of choice; his opponent—who went on to be a Confederate general—demurred.

Once the war began, Potter was equally willing to pick a fight with any apologists for slavery. As one of the "Radical Republicans" inside Lincoln's party, he pushed for much more of a hard line against the South and slavery. So when the President appointed him in 1863 to be America's consul general to Canada, based in Montreal, Potter never held his tongue when it came to the Southern sympathizers who, in his mind, infested the city. He tried to keep tabs on what he saw as these "enemies of the United States, scoundrels too cowardly to stay at home and fight, too indolent to labor." He decried the fact that Canada "harbored, entertained and treated with consideration" the Southern rebels.

Potter and the other American diplomats had plenty of spies and sources monitoring the Confederate operations. By late August 1864, Potter was reporting to Washington about more plots for raids from Canada:

Leading rebels unusually busy visiting Toronto, Niagara, Hamilton + Windsor. Within last month many people arrived who claim to be deserters from the rebel Army. Send 2 or 3 active + shrewd detectives.

———

Bowie Knife Potter was right to be concerned. Over the summer and into the early fall of 1864, the Confederates in Canada tried to orchestrate a triple assault on Lincoln's America: attacks on prisons to try to free Southern soldiers; an armed insurrection to topple pro-Lincoln governments in the northwest states; and the takeover of a political party. In Southern lore, it became widely known as the Northwest Conspiracy.

The men behind the plot had survived in the dark, damp cells of Union prisons. They witnessed their friends waste away and die. The memories, and the wounds, were still all too raw and fresh for the Confederates in Canada.

Thomas Hines had been interned at Johnson's Island, an isolated outpost on Lake Erie, but then managed to escape after he was transferred to another prison in Ohio. Bennett Young had broken out of Camp Douglas in Chicago, probably the worst of the Federal prisons, where nearly one in five inmates died from sickness, starvation and cold. John Castleman had thus far avoided jail time, but he had seen too many of his comrades perish behind bars.

Prison fatalities were deplorably high during the war—almost one in ten deaths among soldiers on both sides were men behind bars. More than 215,000 Confederates spent time in Union jails during the war; 26,000 of them died. The Union had about the same number of its men imprisoned in the South, but with an army twice the size, the impact on its ranks was proportionally not as serious. The much smaller Confederacy, on the other hand, desperately needed its troops who were trapped in the prisoner-of-war camps. Its depleted ranks suffered even more by the middle of 1863, when what up until then had been a well-functioning prisoner exchange program broke down— in large part because the South started to classify captured Black soldiers as "fugitive slaves" instead of POWs, which led an enraged Lincoln government to more or less stop the prisoner swaps.

Castleman summed up the dire math all too accurately: "In 1864 Confederate prisoners held by the United States numbered a force well-nigh equal to the efficient numerical strength of [the] army." In other words, the weakened South had just as many of its men behind bars as on the battlefield.

If exchanges could not free them, escape was the only option.

Several of the biggest Union prisons were strategically placed far away from the South, which put them close to the Canadian border—and the many Confederate agents stationed there. Jacob Thompson was eager to step up the attacks against Lincoln from Canada—perhaps even more so when he got news that, on August 22, Union troops had burned and destroyed his expansive estate in Mississippi. He decided to ally with—and bankroll—a group of the opposition Democrats known as "Copperheads" who were pushing to abandon the war and appease the slave South. Thompson found the perfect partner in an ambitious politician he had known from his days in Washington. Clement L. Vallandigham, a three-time representative for Ohio in the US Congress, was one of the most forceful leaders of the Copperheads.

Vallandigham had denounced Lincoln for having "plunged the country into a cruel, bloody and unnecessary war," railing against what he saw as "the enslavement of the white race, by debt and taxes and arbitrary power." By May 1863, the Union government arrested Vallandigham under a strict military law that barred "disloyal" statements against the war, and Lincoln—in what many considered an abuse of presidential power—had him exiled to the Southern Confederacy.

But if Lincoln thought he had silenced a meddlesome opponent, he was rudely surprised. Two months later, Vallandigham turned up in Canada where he found plenty of support for his cause among the country's elites. He was feted by railway barons in Quebec City and toasted at an exclusive social club for the business class. He was invited as an honoured guest to the Legislative Assembly and praised by leading politicians. From headquarters he had set up in a two-room suite of a Windsor hotel with a view of Detroit across the river, Vallandigham even tried to run for governor of Ohio. He ended up losing the election by over 100,000 votes. Defeated at the ballot box, Vallandigham turned to sedition. He became the "Supreme Commander" of the Sons of Liberty, an underground organization of extremist Democrats and disgruntled Lincoln-haters.

In the summer of 1864, Jacob Thompson went to Windsor to plot strategy with Vallandigham. It was an easy trade of men for money. Vallandigham boasted to Thompson he had upwards of 160,000 fighters who would join the many men newly freed from Union prisons by the Confederates in Canada. Together, they would overthrow the governments in Missouri, Kentucky, Ohio, Illinois and Indiana. Thompson offered generous amounts of cash.

Vallandigham also planned to attend the Democratic Party's national convention scheduled for Chicago on August 29, 1864, to push for a radical "peace plank" that amounted to a Union surrender to the South.

A few days after negotiating with Thompson, Vallandigham snuck back into the US under disguise. The prison targets were chosen. Castleman would lead an attack on Rock Island, at the western tip of the state, where five thousand men were jailed. Meanwhile, Hines would strike at Camp Douglas in Chicago, packed with even more prisoners of war. Joining Hines were two other men who had ridden with John Morgan. One was George "Lightning" Ellsworth, the telegraph whiz who wrote that he was in Chicago "waiting in breathless suspense day after day" for the street fighting to erupt. The other was Bennett Young, eager to avenge his prison stay there, even at the cost of murder. "Our plan was daring enough," he explained. "We were to shoot down the guards and let out the 10,000 prisoners."

The Northwest Conspiracy was ready for launch. Guns were procured from New York for $30,000 in gold and smuggled to Toronto in boxes labelled as school and prayer books. On August 28, Hines gathered sixty former Confederate soldiers at the Queen's Hotel in Toronto and gave them each $100 and a train ticket for what he hoped would be a "powder keg" of insurrection in Chicago. "Arms were ready," recounted his fellow soldier John Headley, noting that they had the time and the money to prepare. "Everything was arranged for prompt action."

———

Everything, that is, except secrecy.

What the Confederates did not know was that the Sons of Liberty, a ragtag organization at best, had been easily infiltrated by Union spies. As early as May, a double agent had wormed his way high up in the ranks and was reporting on their plans to the authorities. Large numbers of Federal troops were sent into Chicago on the eve of the Democratic convention. There was a sweep of arrests of dissidents and troublemakers. The Sons of Liberty, who had already dithered and delayed throughout the whole summer, were spooked. "On the part of the timid, timidity became apparent," Headley noted caustically.

The night before the convention, the Sons of Liberty leaders met with the Confederates from Canada in a Chicago hotel room—and backed out. They had bragged of tens of thousands of members, but none seemed willing to take to the streets. Veteran fighters like Ellsworth and Hines were furious with those who had "promised so much and did so little." It would not be the last time the Canadian conspirators would be betrayed by Copperhead boasting.

As the prison break plans collapsed, so did the political plotting. On the convention floor, Vallandigham and his supporters got their "peace at any cost" plank into the Democratic Party platform, calling for an immediate end to all hostilities followed by quick negotiations with the slave South—in order words, capitulation. But much to their dismay, George McClellan, Lincoln's former general who won the party's nomination, soon repudiated that position. Vallandigham would campaign only half-heartedly for the divided Democrats in the fall. He never successfully regained his political career or his clout.

Hines was seething over what he called the "fiasco at Chicago." But good soldier that he was, he was not quite ready to give up yet. He considered striking at a smaller prison—but the Sons of Liberty couldn't produce even the small force needed for that. Hines then led a small group to set fire to army warehouses in Mattoon, Illinois. John Castleman and his men, meanwhile, tried to burn five Federal supply ships in St. Louis, but the authorities got wind of the plans and

Castleman was arrested. He was now a captive in the prisons he had sought to liberate.

The Northwest Conspiracy had fizzled.

———

While Castleman was cooling his heels in a Union jail, Luke Blackburn was battling heat and disease in the British colony of Bermuda.

Since his first attempt at biological terrorism earlier that spring, the doctor had stayed close with his fellow Kentuckian Confederates in Canada—Castleman, Hines, Bennett Young and John Headley. So much so that, according to his biographer, Blackburn was supposed to lead "diversionary forces against Boston" while the prison breaks in Illinois were under way. But his mission was called off when the attacks were scuttled.

The collapse of the Northwest Conspiracy, however, did not deter the good doctor from helping the cause. Yellow fever had returned to the Bermudas and so had Blackburn. In September he volunteered his services once more, caring for hundreds of patients. He refused all payment for his work, "being desirous only of benefiting this community," a suspicious American consul reported, but the doctor also "never neglected to advertise on all possible occasions the cause of the rebels." What the American diplomat never suspected was that, yet again, Blackburn was at least as interested in harm as he was in healing. He filled several more trunks with soiled clothing and linen that he believed to be infected with the deadly disease. He found a local man who would store the goods until he could make arrangements for them to be shipped once again to Halifax.

Satisfied with his efforts on behalf of the Confederacy, Blackburn sailed to Canada.

A grateful British government, which ruled Bermuda as an overseas territory, praised "the philanthropic conduct" of such an "eminent physician" and offered him a gift worth over $20,000 in today's currency as a reward for his "humane services."

———

Back in Canada, Jacob Thompson had watched the collapse of his plots to attack Union prisons by land. He decided to make one more desperate gamble by attempting to lay siege to the prisons by water. Thompson recruited John Yates Beall, a veteran of the Confederate infantry and navy who had made a name for himself as a buccaneer seizing Union ships on the Potomac and Chesapeake Bay. With a handful of men, Beall took control of a small steamer called the *Philo Parsons* on Lake Erie. The plan was to use it to capture the much larger Union warship called the USS *Michigan*, turning its guns on a prison on Johnson's Island to free Confederates there and then attacking nearby cities. "It would put the cities and towns of New York, Ohio, Illinois, Michigan, and Wisconsin at the mercy of this warship under Confederate command," Thompson confided in one of his men.

But the plan sank when an agent Thompson had planted aboard the *Michigan* was uncovered and Beall faced a mutiny among his own men once the odds of their success collapsed. The botched battle on the Great Lakes enraged the Americans, embarrassed the Canadians and put Thompson—who had always claimed to respect Canadian neutrality—in a tough spot. PIRACY ON LAKE ERIE! cried the *Globe*, denouncing it as a "shameless outrage" and slamming the Confederates for "their disgraceful work from Canadian soil."

"With the failure of Beall's enterprise, all efforts to conduct belligerent operations on the lakes was abandoned," fellow raider Thomas Hines noted with regret.

The schemes over the summer to break their comrades out of Northern jails had failed. Piracy on the Great Lakes had faltered. But the Confederates in Canada knew they still had the advantage of being so close to the vast undefended border that separated the two countries. It fell to Bennett Young, the youngest but perhaps the boldest of Morgan's Raiders stationed in Canada, to come up with an audacious plan—with bigger risks but greater reward.

21

'REIGN OF TERROR'

The only thing military men hated more than witnessing their side lose badly was not being able to pick up a gun to do something about it.

Former Confederate guerilla fighters like Bennett Young were seething, as they drowned their bitterness in the bars and taverns of Toronto, Montreal and Halifax. In the early years of the war, they had been the ones inflicting untold damage in Union territory—raiding towns, causing mayhem and sometimes murder. Now they were rebels in exile, reduced to reading the grim news in the Canadian and American papers: the Shenandoah Valley was burning. During the late summer and fall of 1864, the Union army under Major General Philip Sheridan unleashed a campaign in Virginia of destruction and pillage upon the civilian population, vowing to turn Confederate lands into "a barren waste."

From the safety of Canada, Young plotted revenge. During the Northwest Conspiracy, he had been sent to Chicago to help Hines with the aborted attack on Camp Douglas. But he had another mission while there: Young met and recruited around twenty Confederate soldiers, who had on their own escaped from other Federal camps. On August 20, Secretary of War James Seddon had sent a secret message to Young telling him it was time to exact revenge for Union rampages in the South; he wanted Young to reconnoitre towns along the border. "It is but right that the people of New England and Vermont . . . should have brought home to them some of the horrors of such warfare," Seddon wrote.

Instead of attacking well-fortified prisons, why not launch terror attacks on sleepy border towns?

———

By the next month, Young was in St. Catharines, calling on Clement Clay to fill him in on his progress. "He proposed . . . passing through the New England States, and burning some towns, and robbing them of whatever he could convert to the use of the Confederate Government," Clay later told his superiors back in Richmond. "My instructions to him, oft repeated, were to destroy whatever was valuable; not to stop to rob; but if, after firing a town, he could seize and carry off money, or treasury or bank notes." Which was a polite way of saying: do you what you want and what is necessary for the cause.

Shortly after, Bennett Young wrote to Clay to confirm he was ready to strike. "I will never return," he wrote, "until I have done something. If nothing else, may I destroy the northern border of Vermont and New Hampshire for 150 miles?" Bank receipts preserved in Clay's family papers show he provided thousands of dollars for the eager marauder and his mission.

The men, munitions and money were lined up; all that was missing was the target. Young selected the quaint Vermont town of St. Albans. Conveniently just twelve miles from the Canadian border, its population of four thousand made it big enough to host several banks but small enough to lack a Federal garrison. Many adult males would be away fighting the war. It also happened to be the home of the state governor. George Sanders, who had long pushed for cross-border raids, was pleased with the choice. "They know how defenceless the town is," he wrote, "against a sudden attack of men thoroughly armed with the best of revolvers."

As the autumn leaves began to display their full colours in early October 1864, Young and about twenty of his men slowly infiltrated their way from Montreal across the border into the town of St. Albans, dressed not in Confederate grey but as Canadian tourists. Over several days, they registered at local hotels and boarding houses and took in the local sights. The handsome Young found time to charm the locals. Newspaper accounts described him as "tall, good-looking . . . a man of talent, coolness and of good education." By claiming to be a theology devotee from Montreal, the former divinity student finagled a visit with the governor and his wife, who found him "a nice mannered man." At the hotel where he was staying, he also bewitched a young lady with his Bible talk, taking a stroll with her to the town square known as the village green.

When Young's team walked into his hotel room in the mid-afternoon on October 19 for a last-minute planning meeting, they found him praying by his bedside. Thirty minutes later, Young was all action. Brandishing his weapon on the porch of the American House hotel, he declared to the local citizenry: "In the name of the Confederate States, I take possession of St. Albans! I have been sent here to take this town, and I am going to do it; the first that offers resistance I will shoot him."

If at first the townspeople were not inclined to take this 21-year-old Kentuckian too seriously, they quickly changed their minds. As a church clock struck three o'clock—the signal the robbers had decided upon for action—Young's men stormed three banks in a swift, well-coordinated attack.

One of his most aggressive men was Thomas Collins—like Young, the son of a minister, deeply religious and also a veteran of Morgan's Raiders. "We are Confederate soldiers," Collins told the shocked people inside the St. Albans Bank, "detailed . . . to come north and rob and plunder, the same as your soldiers are doing in the Shenandoah Valley and in other parts of the South."

Assistant cashier Cyrus N. Bishop recalled how the robbers "pointed large navy revolvers at me . . . threatening to blow my brains out if I made any resistance or gave any alarm." Not missing a chance to put on a show, the men also humiliated the Vermonters in the bank by forcing them—at gunpoint—to pledge allegiance to the Confederacy.

At the nearby Franklin County Bank, four well-dressed men marched in and stunned the tellers and customers into silence when they pulled out their guns. One client who raced for the door was told he would be shot dead "if you move an inch." The same kind of threats faced the people at the invaders' final target: the First National Bank. "We have come to retaliate for the acts committed against our people by General Sherman," explained Caleb Wallace, a robber who happened to be the nephew of a former governor of Kentucky. "You have got a very nice village here, and if there is the least resistance, we'll burn it to the ground."

Young's gang struck three banks in less than fifteen minutes, making off with at least $208,000—over $3.7 million in today's currency. It was a sizable haul for a Confederacy desperate for cash.

"Keep cool, boys! Keep cool!" Young shouted to his men. But that proved to be not so easy as pandemonium spread and the Confederates tried to herd a frightened populace towards the village green. "The reign of terror in the village of St. Albans, during the attack and immediately following it, was fearful," recalled lawyer Edward A. Sowles, who would later act on behalf of the banks in the subsequent trial. "They had magnificent arms . . . and as fast as one weapon was unloaded, they drew another and kept up the fusillade."

In the first few minutes of the raid, no one had been seriously injured, much less killed—but as panic reigned and bullets flew, tragedy struck. Elinus Morrison, a contractor at a local hotel, ran towards the commotion. Outside Miss Beattie's millinery shop, he crouched down, his hand clutching his stomach. Staggering to the newspaper office next door, he cried out: "They have shot me through the body." A bullet—several witnesses said it was fired by Young—had cut through his hand and lodged in his abdomen. Morrison died two days later.

Cries of "Robbers and murderers!" and "Stop them, stop them!" rang out. The Confederates decided to make their escape. "We're coming back and we'll burn every damned town in Vermont," they shouted as they fled on stolen horses. A quickly formed local posse gave chase, shooting and badly wounding one of the bandits, Charles Higbee. As they galloped out of town, they lobbed bottles filled with incendiary fluid against some of the buildings, but none of the fires lasted long.

And neither, as it happened, would their freedom.

As they made their dash to sanctuary back in Canada, the Confederate rebels could take no small measure of pride in the fact that they had succeeded in their primary goal: spreading fear in the Northern states that had seen little of the Civil War's devastation. It would go down in history as the most northerly attack carried out in the entire Civil War.

St. Albans lawyer Sowles recalled the terror spread along the entire northern frontier: "It was the prevailing opinion that these raiders were but the advance guard of an army from Canada . . . carrying all the horrors of war to our doors." Residents of Plattsburg in the neighbouring state of New York had torn up rail tracks over five acres, "fearful that another train filled with hostile Confederates might arrive." Newspapers on both sides of the border were aghast at the daring of the raid. "With our homes sacked and the blood of our kindred crying for vengeance, we will not be content to leave the punishment of these cutthroats to the tedious and reluctant consideration" of Canadian courts, the *New York Herald* warned. The Montreal *Gazette* tried to pass off the raid as "a simple bank robbery," insisting "there is not a particle of evidence to show that the robbers were Confederates, or in any way acting under Confederate authority." But as the truth quickly emerged, even the normally pro-Southern paper had to admit that "to surprise a peaceful town and shoot people down in the streets, at the same time committing robbery, is not civilized war; it is that of savages."

Lincoln's military commanders, understandably, were furious. Major General John Dix, who led the Federal forces in the east, had a deeper understanding of Canada than most Union generals: he had gone to school in Montreal and learned French. But now he couldn't care less about the niceties of borders and ordered the Confederate thieves to be caught at all costs: "[I]f the rebels cannot be found this side of the line pursue them into Canada, if necessary to destroy them."

Fortunately, that kind of military invasion turned out not to be necessary. The unofficial Vermont posse had crossed into Canada and was doing a good job of hunting down the raiders. The *Gazette*, typically, seemed angrier at the pursuers than the bandits, criticizing "the troops of Yankees" for conducting themselves "in the most reckless and disgraceful manner." But working with Canadian authorities, the Vermonters quickly and safely nabbed most of the fugitives. Perhaps too cocky after the excitement of their adventure, Young's men foolishly had taken refuge in small towns north of the border instead of making it all the way to Montreal, which would have offered more places to lie low. Two were arrested entering a hotel, two more as they slept in their rooms in a tavern, another walking on a sidewalk, one at a railway station and two more fast asleep in a hayloft. Within twenty-four hours, at least a dozen of them were behind bars.

On October 20, when he learned that most of his crew had been captured, Young—exhibiting a leader's admirable sense of honour—made a bold decision to give himself up. Fourteen men were now behind bars; the remaining handful of men were never caught. At least two of them made it to Montreal and escaped with $50,000, the papers reported. "Since then, all traces of them have been lost." In the end, only $87,000 of the stolen loot was recovered in the hands of the arrested bandits.

Young and the other captives were taken to a jail in the nearby town of St. Johns (now called Saint-Jean-sur-Richelieu). They faced a serious battery of charges—robbery, assault, attempted arson, horse theft and murder. To frightened Vermonters, it must have looked like a speedy end to the story: banks robbed, criminals caught, justice to be served.

But when it came to the Confederates in Canada, nothing was ever simple.

———

The first sign of trouble came at the jail in St. Johns.

Instead of treating the apprehended Confederates as suspected criminals, the guards "manifested the warmest friendship for the prisoners," noted fellow Confederate John Headley. "They extended every courtesy, and the citizens were likewise friendly and hospitable." A correspondent from the *Globe* found Young and his men in a joyous enough mood to be singing.

Upon their arrest, the raiders quickly reached out for help from their leaders—and the person they went to was George Sanders. "We are captured. Do what you can for us," read the telegram they sent. Sanders—always accustomed to fine living and dining—dispatched his son Lewis to the jail in St. Johns "providing wine and a variety of edible delicacies." He would soon provide much more invaluable help.

Bennett Young also immediately launched a very public and unabashed defence of his actions. "I went there for the purpose of burning the town and surrounding villages in retaliation for the recent outrages committed in the Shenandoah Valley, and elsewhere in the Confederate States," he told the *Montreal Evening Telegraph* in a letter written just a day after his arrest and reprinted on the front page of the *New York Times* a few days later. He scolded complacent Northerners for forgetting that they were "in the midst of war, and ruled by a man despotic in his actions, and supreme in his infamy." Young was equally unrepentant when a group of citizens from St. Albans came to visit him, pleading for a return of all the money because "many widows and orphans would suffer in consequence of his depletion of the vaults of the banks at St. Albans."

George Sanders was even blunter when he met with the St. Albans visitors in St. Johns, warning that the attack on their town was "merely the starting point of a system of warfare that would carry destruction all along the frontier, that there were no less than twenty thousand men in Canada, eager to enter upon raids across the American border."

"Many Yankee sons of—would be killed," he declared, according to later court testimony in which the profanity was deleted. "[M]en were ready to sack and burn Buffalo, Detroit, New York, and other places." Sanders revelled at being the centre of attention. "The notorious George Sanders is here, managing the cause of the rebels," the *Globe* reported. His only complaint about the St. Albans raid was that "it was conducted on too small a scale." Remarkably, Sanders saw no contradiction in spewing out these bellicose threats but then insisting: "My mission here is one of peace."

The tension in the St. Albans affair ratcheted up when the case moved from the jails to the courts. The judge assigned to the case was Charles-Joseph Coursol, a well-connected political player. He had married the daughter of Sir Étienne-Paschal Taché, a premier of the Province of Canada and future Father of Confederation. Coursol secured the post of coroner in Montreal when he was still in his twenties and then was named inspector and superintendent of police in his thirties, which made him a "judge of the sessions of the peace"—essentially, a police magistrate. "He was what we should call a fast man," the *New York Times* later complained. "He is one of that class . . . who rise to fame by some extraordinary exhibition of utter incapacity."

In the first of several dubious decisions, when he showed up in St. Johns, Coursol immediately opted to shift the trial away from the border towns to Montreal, where Confederate sympathies were stronger. Then, in what turned out to be a fateful move, he handed the seized loot to Guillaume Lamothe, the Montreal chief of police.

Lamothe was an odd choice to head the police department of Canada's largest city. The son of a fur trader, militia officer and Indian Department official, he sought adventure in Europe as a young man, spending most of his twenties abroad. That included taking part in the storming of the Tuileries Palace in France in 1848 during a popular revolt against the monarchy. Back in Canada, Lamothe dabbled in business and rose through the ranks of the militia before being picked as the city's top cop in 1861. In a private memoir he wrote for his son decades later, Lamothe admitted his appointment had little to do with police experience—of which he had none—and everything to do with his political connections, which were plentiful. "I always took an active part in politics," he wrote, "and I often gave of myself and of my money to the Liberal Party, of course." The ruling Liberal Party gave him the plum posting, thanks to the efforts of what Lamothe described as *"la cabale pour mon compte"*—loosely translated as "backroom intrigues on my behalf."

Now, as Montreal's chief law enforcement official, he found himself at the centre of more such intrigues. The judge's abrupt decision to hand him the stolen money worried St. Albans lawyer Edward Sowles. But Coursol assured Sowles that the monies had to be turned over "for their safe-keeping" and "to be used as evidence." The money—and the accused men—were promptly moved to Montreal.

Within days after the raid, the intrigue got darker. On Sunday, October 23, a meeting took place at the city's fashionable Donegana Hotel on Notre-Dame Street. In attendance were Judge Coursol, Chief of Police Lamothe—and George N. Sanders. "Nothing transpired at that interview except information to us in regard to the capture of the prisoners and their condition," Sanders later insisted. That was a lie, as a scandal over the seized money later revealed. But Sanders's attempt to justify the meeting was beside the point. Under no circumstances would it be proper for the judge presiding over the case and the police chief handling the bank loot to huddle with the Confederate agent organizing the defence of the jailed men.

At the time few people knew about this secret gathering, but many already doubted justice would be served in such a politically fraught case. Lawyer Edward Sowles expressed his fear that "Canada was so friendly with the South and so inimical to the North that the raiders would be safe, whatever atrocities they might commit."

He had no idea how right he was.

22

'I AM GOING TO HELL'

The year had not been easy on John Wilkes Booth.

Professionally, he remained one of the most popular performers in America. The actor had stayed in the North for much of 1864, performing in cities such as Boston and New York. But on a personal level, Booth was not as lucky. He had spent the summer in Pennsylvania, losing a lot of his savings in a failed oil business venture. When he visited his elder, more famous brother Edwin in August, there were "stormy words," as his sister recalled. Edwin, a Lincoln supporter, belittled John's Confederate passions and John stormed out of the house.

By September, Booth had channelled his fury into a plot to kidnap the man he blamed for "this horrid war": Abraham Lincoln. Like the Confederates in Richmond and in Canada, Booth was consumed by the fate of the tens of thousands of Confederates suffering in Union prisons. He figured a captive president would force the release of the men, giving the South the troops it needed badly and a desperate last chance to win the war. Booth outlined his scheme when he met with two childhood friends at the Barnum Hotel in Baltimore, sipping wine and smoking cigars. Samuel Arnold had attended a military academy with Booth when they were both teenagers; Michael O'Laughlen had lived across the street from Booth. Both men, having served briefly in the Confederate army, listened intently as Booth outlined a daring kind of military mission. "We drank and freely conversed about the war," Arnold recalled later in his memoir. "Booth then spoke of the abduction or kidnapping of the President, saying that if such could be accomplished . . . he thought it would bring about an exchange of prisoners."

After his two friends consented to join him, Booth told them where he was going next to carry out his plot. "Booth left to arrange the business north," Arnold recalled. "First to New York . . . from there to Boston and finally to Canada."

A trip north of the border would be more than a distraction for the moody Booth. It would also afford him a chance to meet with Confederate conspirators as he mulled over his plots against Lincoln. Friends asked Booth where he was heading.

"I am going to Hell," he replied.

———

John Wilkes Booth could not have picked a more tumultuous time to visit Montreal. He had arrived in Canada on October 18, 1864, the day before the St. Albans raid began. Like all the other Confederate sympathizers who had flooded into the city, he was soon swept up in the excitement over the cross-border military adventure, covered in the papers with frantic headlines and breathless articles.

The Confederates in Canada were delighted with the boldness of the attack. They flocked to Montreal to observe the trial and the political fallout—as did the Union spies who tracked them. The St. Lawrence Hall was overflowing with guests, three or four to a room. But John Wilkes Booth had Room 150 all to himself. "He was a most genial gifted man in many ways, a fine actor, and a great favorite," said Henry Hogan, the hotel's owner and one of Booth's biggest admirers. Surrounded by fellow Southerners, Booth must have felt much more at home than he had in Lincoln's Northern states—and enjoying the comfort and elegance an actor of his stature demanded.

The St. Lawrence Hall, on the northwest corner of St. François Xavier and St. James Streets, boasted that it was located "in the most salubrious and fashionable part of the city," with a concert room, a well-supplied reading room, a renowned billiard room and imported wines and liquors. Orchestral music filled the halls every evening from

6 to 9 p.m. The dining room—offering fare that ranged from green turtle soup to salmon in lobster sauce—was "elaborate and gilded, with the crystal pendants of its chandeliers flashing in the gaslight."

By Hogan's own admission, in "the exciting times during the Civil War . . . the St. Lawrence Hall was the headquarters of the 'Confederate Junta.'" Some of the most colourful details of Booth's stay in the city came from the hotel owner, who—well aware that his establishment was a nest of intrigue for rival spies from the South and the North— had installed a peephole in his office to allow him to do some spying of his own, with a view of the entire main parlour. Booth devoured the latest news about the St. Albans raid and other Confederate actions. "A victory for the soldiers in gray would send him scattering small silver pieces round among the newsboys and bell boys," Hogan recalled.

Booth was spotted playing cards with an all-star cast of Confederates. Sitting with him around the table was James D. Westcott, a former Florida senator described by Hogan as "a most bitter hater of everything 'Yankee' who thoroughly despised every soul from the North." There was Beverley Tucker, a Virginia newspaper editor and diplomat for the Confederacy posted to England and now Canada. Rounding out the party was none other than Luke Blackburn, the yellow fever plotter. "[Blackburn] was one of that clique of men who were together known there as Confederate men," observed Hosea Carter, a Union spy who was stationed at the St. Lawrence Hall for six months.

For more distraction—and perhaps inspiration—Booth borrowed some books by Walter Scott, filled with tales of swordplay and sacrifice. At one point, Booth tried a little adventure of his own in what was probably the coldest city he had ever visited. He put on a heavy coat and yellow fox-skin cap and rode a horse to Lachine, eight miles from the centre of the city. "A Canadian winter was a novelty to Booth," one of his acquaintances later wrote. "A breeze at twenty below zero was more than he bargained for or cared to repeat."

Not far from Booth's hotel stood the Theatre Royal, a fixture of the city's cultural scene. John Buckland ran the theatre, along with his actress wife Kate, a stage beauty who, according to her official biography, "befriended" Booth. John Deveny, an American draft dodger in Montreal at the time, later testified at the Lincoln assassination trials that he had read in the local newspapers that Booth "had been trying to make an engagement with Buckland, of the Theatre Royal." So when Deveny saw Booth in the city, he asked if he was going to appear on the stage.

No, answered Booth.

"What are you going to do?" Deveny pushed.

"I just came here on a visit, a pleasure trip," replied the actor.

No doubt Booth found plenty of distractions in the city. "His spending was profuse and reckless and his habits intemperate," one Montreal newspaper later recounted. The excuse Booth gave for his unusual trip to Canada was that he wanted to arrange a way to get around the Northern blockade and send two trunks of his theatrical gear to the South. But it does not take ten days to ship some costumes.

Booth's trek north to Montreal was not a pleasure trip, it was business. He had already met with his two friends in Baltimore to begin plotting the kidnapping of Lincoln. Now he was taking steps to put his plan into action—and the Confederate haven of Montreal was the place to do that.

———

Booth had arranged to transport his trunks through Patrick C. Martin, a former Baltimore merchant who was now a prosperous Confederate blockade-runner in Montreal. But Martin was more than a shipper. He was, as one unflattering newspaper account put it, "a rather excitable, meddlesome man who went off on the first desperate venture of war to aid the South." Connected with Confederate leaders, he was close enough to Jefferson Davis to write him personal letters. Martin had also been instrumental in an earlier attempt authorized by Richmond to seize a ship in Canada and attack a Northern prison on the Great Lakes in order to free captured Confederates. He was, in other words, an important operative with the connections Booth needed.

Martin gave Booth important letters of introduction to the Confederate network in Maryland—a Baltimore police marshal who had
been imprisoned for his rebel sympathies and a well-connected doctor
named Samuel Mudd. Not the kind of contacts a travelling star of the
stage would normally seek out, but just what a conspirator plotting
to kidnap a president needed to escape out of Washington through
Maryland to Richmond. Booth would end up using that route the night
he killed Abraham Lincoln.

Martin also helped Booth with his finances. As Jacob Thompson
and others had done, Booth chose Henry Starnes's Ontario Bank
branch on St. James Street to do his banking, doubtless because of its
favourable reputation among Confederates.

"How often did you see J. Wilkes Booth in Canada?" the bank's
chief teller, Robert Campbell, was asked months later, during the trial
after Lincoln's assassination.

"I could not say. He might have been in the bank a dozen times; but
I remember distinctly of seeing him once." A dozen visits, if Campbell
was accurate, would mean Booth came into Starnes's bank every day
he was in Montreal, a remarkable frequency for someone with a bank
balance of a few hundred dollars at the branch.

The one visit Campbell remembered in detail was October 27, the
day before Booth left the city. Booth walked in with Patrick Martin
and asked for a bank draft.

"I am going to run the blockade," Booth told Campbell openly,
clearly not worried that the bank would have any objections. "[I]n case
I should be captured, can my capturers make use of the exchange?"

"I told him no, not unless he endorsed the bill: the bill was made
payable to his order," recalled the ever-helpful banker.

The bank happily issued Booth a bank draft in English currency—
about "sixty-one pounds and some odd shillings"—worth about $300
in US gold at the time. In essence, bank drafts were in the nineteenth
century what traveller's cheques became in the twentieth: a safe way
to travel without having to carry cash. Like all such documents, it was

made official with a signature from the bank president, Henry Starnes.

Campbell was pushed at the trial about how this kind of "disbursement" could be used.

"We can never tell. We never ask a man anything about that," answered the discreet banker. "A man doing business with us deposits what he likes; and we never ask any questions. He draws checks for what he likes; and we do not know what he is going to do with it."

———

There is no written evidence that Booth met either of the official Confederate commissioners for Canada—Jacob Thompson or Clement Clay—while in Montreal: no hotel registries, diaries or other accounts. Both men were in Quebec City on October 14 on other business. Clay was back at his residence in St. Catharines by October 19, so on the train trip back to Ontario he could in theory have crossed paths with Booth in Montreal on the actor's first day in the city. Thompson, on the other hand, did not make it back to Toronto until October 21. Where was he during that week after Quebec City? His activities have never been accounted for, and he would have had at least four days to meet up with Booth.

The one Confederate leader in Canada whom Booth certainly did talk with was the ubiquitous George Sanders. Sanders stayed in Room 169 at the St. Lawrence Hall—with a typical flourish, in the hotel registry he wrote his city of residence as "Dixie"—not far from Booth in Room 150, and by the accounts of at least three witnesses, they spent much time together in Montreal. Hosea Carter, the Union detective who was stationed at the hotel for months as a more or less permanent spy, said he "frequently" observed Booth "in intimate association with Sanders." John Deveny—the American who had asked Booth if he was going to appear onstage in Montreal—was coming out of the post office across from the St. Lawrence Hall when he spotted the two men talking rather secretively, standing against a pillar. He saw them another time as they headed into Dolly's Chop House, a popular eatery on St. James Street, just a few steps from the hotel.

What did the two Confederate diehards discuss? No one overheard their meetings, which were "always confidential, always whispered," according to Deveny. It seems likely, given Sanders's well-known radicalism and thirst for action, that Booth would have been eager at the very least to share his plans to kidnap the president. Perhaps to get advice; perhaps to encourage Sanders to reach out to officials in Richmond to let them know what was afoot.

Did the two men go further than that—to discuss killing, not just kidnapping, Abraham Lincoln? After all, during his time as a consul in Europe a decade earlier, Sanders had expressed open sympathy for what Continental revolutionaries called "the theory of the dagger," based on the premise that murdering tyrants was justified. His views did not seem to lose any of their ardour over time. While Sanders was taking part in the aborted peace talks in Niagara earlier that summer of 1864, a Union colonel dressed in civilian clothes was sent to spy on the proceedings at the Clifton House hotel. He reported that he overheard one of the Confederate negotiators—almost certainly Sanders—"urging a plan to assassinate Lincoln just before the November elections."

There was one more clue about what Sanders was plotting, with Booth or with others. Sanders talked at length with a journalist from England's *Daily Telegraph* named George Augustus Sala who was in Montreal at the time. Sanders boasted about "justifiable retaliatory war" and went on to warn: "In fact, Sir, we shall do such deeds within the next three months as shall make European civilization shudder."

———

If Montreal was the Casablanca in the American Civil War, Dooley's Bar in the St. Lawrence Hall was Rick's Café. All the usual suspects gathered there, to drink away their worries and shoot some pool. "Booth would hurry over to the Hall and down to Joe Dion's billiard rooms to play with the best in the city," recalled Henry Hogan. The reference was to Joseph Dion, the Quebec pool champion who was a fixture at the hotel.

The night Booth challenged Dion to "a friendly contest at billiards," the actor seemed to be holding his liquor well, if not his tongue. "My opponent seemed to have been indulging freely in stimulants, not appearing intoxicated at all," Dion recounted. "He was a young man of means, given to a gay, rollicking life." As the evening wore on, Dion was struck by "the wandering character of his conversation . . . indicating a rather immoderate dissipation and a slight mental derangement or excitement."

But then Dion noticed that "a sudden thought seemed to flash upon" Booth's mind. The actor raised his pool cue and continued in an excited manner to boast to his Canadian pool partner about pulling off the "double carom" of sinking two balls with one shot, bragging that he could "bag the biggest game." It was clear Booth was no longer talking about pool but about politics. The November presidential elections were fast approaching, and Booth issued an ominous warning explicitly about Abraham Lincoln: "Whether re-elected or not, he would get his goose cooked."

"I paid little regard to his remarks at the time," Dion remembered, "supposing them to proceed from the ordinary fancies of a person in his condition." But in Booth's mind, they were more than fancies. As the game wrapped up, Booth clapped Dion on the shoulder and pointed to his local clothing. "I like your Canadian style," he said. "I must post myself in Canuck airs, for some of us devils may have to settle there shortly."

The implication was that Booth was plotting something so "devilish" that he might need a safe place to hide, north of the border.

———

Booth checked out of the St. Lawrence on October 28. Less than two weeks later, Abraham Lincoln handily won the elections that Booth had told his Quebec billiards partner would not matter. Lincoln defeated his former general, George McClellan, garnering 55 percent of the popular vote.

Booth was despondent about the fate of the Confederacy and desperate to do something. On November 24, 1864, he penned a kind of manifesto. He gave it to his brother-in-law in a sealed envelope, and it was only after the assassination a few months later that it came to light. It began with what in hindsight reads like a startling prediction of what was to come:

TO WHOM IT MAY CONCERN:
Right or wrong. God judge me, not man. For
be my motive good or bad, of one thing I am
sure, the lasting condemnation of the North.

"[L]ooking upon African Slavery," Booth wrote, "I for one, have ever considered it one of the greatest blessings (both for themselves and us)." Then, in twelve words, Booth crystallized everything that made Lincoln such an existential threat to him and to the white supremacy of the South: "This country was formed for the white, not for the black man," Booth stated bluntly.

As if performing an overwrought soliloquy onstage, Booth used the word *blood* no fewer than four times in four paragraphs in his angry declaration. Then he signed off:

A Confederate doing duty upon his own responsibility.
J. WILKES BOOTH.

John Wilkes Booth was a man on a mission. As St. Lawrence Hall owner Henry Hogan said of his famous visitor: "[I]t was recalled by the friends of Booth that just before leaving Montreal he told them that they would hear in a short time of something that would startle the world."

23.

'TO BURN NEW YORK'

John Wilkes Booth was not the only person in the South—or the North for that matter—whose rage was reaching dangerous levels. By the late fall of 1864, the tensions and hatreds were so inflamed that both sides began to fight fire with fire.

One Union general, Philip Sheridan, had already laid waste to the Shenandoah Valley in Virginia; Major General William Tecumseh Sherman was about to launch the same "scorched earth" campaign in Georgia from Atlanta to Savannah. The Confederates were eager to respond with the same brutality. "There is one effectual way, and only one that we know of, to arrest and prevent this and every other sort of atrocity—and that is to burn on the chief cities of the enemy," cried out the *Richmond Examiner* in an editorial on October 1. "It is not immoral or barbarous to defend yourself by any means, or with any weapon the enemy may employ for your destruction," the newspaper argued. "We may so use their own weapon as to make them repent, literally in sackcloth and ashes."

In italics, the Southern opinion makers suggested who could carry out such a "barbarous" attack:

The men to execute the work are already there. There would be no difficulty in finding there, here or in Canada, suitable persons to take charge of the enterprise and arrange its details.

The fact that a leading newspaper in the Confederate capital would single out Canada as a likely place to recruit arsonists to burn down Union cities was a testimony to the reputation the country was earning as a hotbed of sabotage and resistance. What the *Richmond Examiner* perhaps suspected but probably did not know for certain was that there were already "suitable persons" in Canada planning to burn not just any town, but the largest metropolis in the country: New York City.

———

From his base in Toronto, John Headley had been following—and would later carefully chronicle—the exploits of his former companions from Morgan's Raiders as they attempted prison breaks, piracy on the Great Lakes and bank robberies. Finally, in November 1864, it would be his turn to take centre stage. He met with the leaders of the Confederate Secret Service, Jacob Thompson and Clement Clay, in Toronto. The election date of November 8 "was deemed an opportune time for the blow to be struck," Headley recounted in his memoirs, entitled *Confederate Operations in Canada and New York*.

Despite the earlier failures of the Northwest Conspiracy, Thompson had not given up on sparking a revolt among disaffected Northerners. The plan was for Headley to lead the attack on New York. The irrepressible Luke Blackburn would join a group that would set fire to Boston. Thomas Hines would handle Chicago, trying once again to organize a prison break at Camp Douglas and Rock Island.

For his New York operation, Headley assembled a team of seven other men, several of them, like him, veterans of Morgan's cavalry. Typical of the recruits was a young hothead named Robert Cobb Kennedy, who had just turned twenty-nine and displayed more bravado than brains. Coming from a Louisiana family that owned dozens of slaves, Kennedy's devotion to the South was deeper than his discipline. He had been kicked out of the West Point military academy for drunkenness and other violations. Captured early in the Civil War, he managed to break out of the grisly Union prison on the coast of Lake Erie. As the *New York Times* later described Kennedy: "[H]e was regarded as wholly useless in planning or executing matters requiring caution or delicacy of manipulation, but as the best man of the force for anything reckless, devilish or foolish."

Headley, Kennedy and the others slipped into New York City late in October to make preparations. Headley met with anti-Lincoln Northerners he hoped could help spark rebellions. James McMaster was typical of the blowhards the Confederates relied on—radical but hardly reliable. A Roman Catholic newspaper editor of extreme right-wing views, he had been jailed early in the war for his rantings against Lincoln. He was not above calling for the assassination of abolitionist leaders. McMaster promised Headley that he and his fellow Copperheads had twenty thousand men and arms at the ready. Headley's plan was simple: arson in the service of an armed uprising on the date of the presidential election, November 8. "It was determined that a number of fires should be started in different parts of the city," he wrote, "which would bring the population to the streets and prevent any sort of resistance to our movement."

———

Headley and Thompson had tried to keep their plans secret, limiting the number of people in the know in Toronto to a bare minimum and maintaining a low profile in New York. Still, given the determination of Union spies to infiltrate the often porous Confederate operations, the plotters in New York should probably have expected some hints of their plans to slip out. Sure enough, on November 3 the *New York Times* ran a small but alarming news item:

ANTICIPATED RAIDS FROM CANADA

Rebel Conspiracy to Burn North Cities

The story revealed that several mayors had received a warning from officials that "there is a conspiracy afoot to set fire to the principal cities in the Northern States on the day of the Presidential election." The next day, General Benjamin Butler moved into New York with ten thousand troops to protect the city.

On election day, November 8, the *Times* thundered: "Let trouble show itself in whatever quarter, whether from raiding parties over the Canadian border, or from unruly demagogues and riotously-disposed persons in the streets of the city, it will meet with swift and speedy suppression." Butler later disclosed in his memoirs that "confidential agents and detectives" had supplied tips about rebel plans. What's more, the Confederates had not exactly been silent about the plans of burning Northern cities. The *Times* reminded its readers that the Richmond papers had been "lately urging the rebels stationed in Canada and in the North to give a helping hand to the sinking Confederacy."

The heavy presence of Federal troops shattered what little backbone the Copperhead braggards like James McMaster had left. In much the same way Clement Vallandigham's boasts during the summer's Northwest Conspiracy in Chicago had proved empty, McMaster was all talk and no action and pulled out of the New York plot. "This left us practically at sea," Headley admitted. But even after election day had passed, Headley told his men they could still "set the city on fire and give the people a scare if nothing else."

Headley went to a basement apartment on Washington Place to meet the chemist who had prepared the weapons: Greek fire, the nineteenth-century version of the Molotov cocktail—an incendiary device consisting of a mixture of flammable liquids (usually phosphorus) inside a bottle. A heavily built, elderly man with a heavy beard handed over a leather valise two and a half feet long. Headley dragged the dangerous cargo to a streetcar, so weighed down by its bulk he had to change hands every ten feet or so. Once he was on board, passengers grew suspicious about the odd smell of rotten eggs. "There must be something dead in that valise," one unsuspecting citizen quipped as Headley finally disembarked.

Once back at his hotel room with his crew, Headley opened the valise to find 144 bottles to set a city ablaze. "We were now ready to create a sensation in New York," Headley later said.

———

By November 16, after Lincoln's undisrupted re-election, the Federal troops had gone from the streets of New York and it looked as though the threat of Confederates attacks had passed. The *Times* snidely dismissed the Southern sympathizers in the city for being "too slothful or cowardly to brave the dangers and fatigue of the battlefield." What the esteemed newspaper pointedly chose to ignore was that, just the previous day, the Union army had demonstrated its own willingness to set civilian targets ablaze. On November 15, General Sherman destroyed more than three thousand businesses, hospitals, homes and schools in Atlanta—an inferno made famous by Hollywood decades later in *Gone with the Wind*. "Behind us lay Atlanta, smouldering and in ruins, the black smoke rising high in air, and hanging like a pall over the ruined city," Sherman boasted.

Headley was outraged at Union hypocrisy: "[W]hen General Sherman had burned the city of Atlanta, Georgia," he complained, not unjustly, "the Northern papers and people of the war party were in great glee over the miseries of the southern people." It was time for payback. "Thus far, the South had borne all the trials, endured all the privations," explained Robert Kennedy, Headley's youthful partner, "and it was [with] the purpose of turning the tables that these raids were undertaken."

The new target date was Friday, November 25, giving each conspirator time to register at multiple downtown hotels. "Our fires would be started in the hotels, so as to do the greatest damage in the business district on Broadway," Headley explained. "It was agreed that our operations should begin promptly at 8 o'clock p.m., so that the guests of hotels might all escape, as we did not want to destroy any lives." What he never bothered to explain was how they thought they could set the city ablaze, with downtown hotels erupting in flames, without destroying any lives.

Each man took ten bottles, wrapped in paper and stuffed in their coat pockets or small valises. Headley had made reservations for himself at four hotels. He started at the Astor House, the city's premier luxury hotel, stretching over an entire city block, adorned with Greek pillars, elaborate ballrooms, arched ceilings and a rooftop garden. At 7:20 p.m. in Room 204 on the top floor overlooking Broadway, he hung the bedsheets over the headboard and piled chairs, dresser drawers and newspaper on the bed, soaking them all. "I opened the bottle carefully and quickly and spilled it on the pile of rubbish," he wrote. "It blazed up instantly and the whole bed seemed to be in flames before I could get out. I locked the door and walked down the hall and stairway." The plot leader then headed off to the other hotels on his list. As he gazed back at his room in the Astor, "a bright light appeared within but there were no indications below of any alarm." It was an early indication that perhaps things would not go as planned.

One by one, his men repeated the same actions at more than a dozen hotels in busy Manhattan. "They were described as being rather gentlemanly in the deportment, neatly and unostentatiously dressed, appeared inclined to attract as little attention as possible," the *New York Herald* later reported. "They carried small black leather valises, signed fictitious names on the hotel books and carried their own baggage to their rooms."

Flames erupted on the fifth floor of the United States Hotel around 8:30 p.m.; thirteen minutes later at the St. James; no fewer than four rooms were burning at 9:05 p.m. at the St. Nicholas; fifteen minutes later, fire started on the third floor at the Lafarge; by 10 p.m., the front room on the upper floor of the Metropolitan facing Broadway was engulfed in smoke; at Lovejoy's, a fourth-floor room was struck at 10:30 p.m. and then, at midnight, a second fire; the New England House was hit at 11 p.m. It was not just packed hotels that became targets. Headley walked down to the North River wharf. "I picked dark spots to stand in, and jerked a bottle, in six different places," at barges and vessels, he boasted. "They were ablaze before I left."

Making his way back to the crowded streets, Headley was surprised to see people in a panic streaming out of the Barnum Museum, a popular site for freak shows and entertainment. It was not on their list for arson, but when Headley bumped into Robert Kennedy, the young Confederate blurted out that it "was simply a reckless joke." As he later admitted: "The Museum was set on fire by merest accident, after I had been drinking and just for the fun of the scare."

———

In the Winter Garden Theatre that evening, patrons had paid top dollar for a special performance on Broadway of *Julius Caesar*, Shakespeare's powerful play about what was until then probably the most famous assassination in history. What made the show even more of an attraction was that it featured the three Booth brothers—Edwin, Junius and John— as part of a benefit performance to raise money for the bronze statue of Shakespeare that still stands today in Central Park. The only time the Booths would appear onstage together, "[i]t was a proud moment for their mother who sat in a private box," the *Montreal Herald* reported.

Edwin, the best known and most talented actor of the three, played the lead character of Brutus, the tyrant's killer. But as Marc Anthony, John Wilkes Booth got to perform many memorable lines, including an eerily ominous passage:

> *The evil that men do lives after them,*
> *The good is oft interred with their bones.*

As the second scene of Act 2 was unfolding, there were cries of "Fire! Fire!" and the odour of smoke coming from the Lafarge Hotel next door. "The excitement became very intense among the closely-packed mass of human beings," the *New York Times* reported. Edwin Booth, taking a break from Brutus's assassination plots, calmed the audience from the stage, assuring them "there was no danger."

"There was the wildest excitement imaginable," Headley recounted as he stood on Broadway. "There was all sorts of talk about hanging the rebels to lamp posts or burning them at the stake." The newspaper headlines in the city—and indeed around the country and in Canada—screamed out the news. "The city was paralysed last evening by the loud and simultaneous clanging of fire-bells in every direction," a lengthy front-page story in the *New York Times* said, "and the alarming report soon spread from street to street that a pre-concerted attempt was being made by rebel emissaries . . . to burn New York and other Northern cities." The *Herald* too devoted entire pages to what it denounced as "a vast and fiendish plot . . . which if successful, would have been accompanied by such unspeakable horrors." New Yorkers "had escaped, as by a miracle, from a dreadful calamity which might have left half the city in ashes and consigned thousands of innocent people—men, women and children—to the most horrible of deaths."

The fact that no one died had more to do with luck than any planning on the part of the arsonists. "We desired to destroy property, not the lives of women and children," Kennedy admitted, "although that would of course have followed in the train." In just one example of near death, a mother and her child who were asleep when Room 108 burst into flames at the Tammany Hotel were rescued by firefighters at the last minute. The property damage to more than nineteen targeted buildings was steep—by some estimates more than half a million dollars. But there was no inferno of flames engulfing New York as the Confederates had imagined, just isolated pockets of potentially lethal fires that were mostly suppressed by midnight.

"It appeared that all had made a failure," Headley admitted glumly. He blamed sabotage—someone who "had put a job on us" and doctored the incendiary devices. But it was science, not scoundrels, that defeated the Confederate plot to burn down New York City. "However shrewd and skilful they proved themselves in other respects, they committed one fatal blunder at the close of their work," the *New York*

Herald explained. The problem was ventilation. The arsonists had kept all the doors and windows in the hotel rooms closed, depriving their fires of the oxygen they needed to spread.

Still, the New York hotel arson strike—like the St. Albans raid but on a much grander scale—accomplished what all terror attacks seek to do: sow fear and panic. The Confederates from Canada had struck not small-town Vermont but the very nerve centre of the Union's financial and cultural base. Over breakfast the next morning in New York, John Wilkes Booth and his brothers—having finished their Shakespearean benefit show—quarrelled over the fires. Booth, echoing almost word for word the rationalizations used by Headley and his men, justified the deed "as an act of war in retaliation for Union atrocities." The older and more moderate Edwin—who had voted for Lincoln two weeks earlier—disagreed. A furious Booth lambasted the President.

Perhaps Booth would have found more enjoyment in the company at another busy restaurant, this one on Broadway and 12th. There, John Headley and his fellow arsonists, having slept in until 10 a.m., were enjoying good food and the morning papers. "It was crowded but everyone was reading a newspaper," Headley recounted. "[T]he entire front pages were given up to sensational accounts of the attempt to burn the city." Despite their pride at having sparked so much fright if not flames—the *Times* called it "diabolical . . . one of the most fiendish and inhuman acts known in modern times"—there was reason for Headley's gang to start worrying. The papers also had fairly accurate descriptions of the suspects from witnesses at the hotels.

"The chief conspirator is believed to be a member of Morgan's old command," the *New York Herald* reported from police sources—which was true, given Headley's service with John Morgan. That may have been just a lucky guess, since they got some of the other details wrong about the suspect. But what the papers and the police got right was the Canadian connection. As the *Herald* put it in one of the headlines:

THE PLOT ORIGINATED IN CANADA

"In the first place it was ascertained beyond a doubt that several rebel officers left Canada, from Toronto and its vicinity to come to New York," the newspaper said. "The parties detailed by the rebel skulkers and desperadoes in Canada to perform this work were guerillas, who had served their apprenticeship under the footpads that infest Tennessee, Kentucky and Missouri." It looked as if the authorities were closing in on the suspects—and if they got caught, there would be little mercy. Major General Dix—who never missed a chance to flex his military muscle—issued General Order 92 the day after the fires, which gave him the legal authority to hunt down the "Rebel emissaries and agents" under "martial law and penalty of death."

"They will be immediately brought to trial before a military commission, and if convicted, executed without the delay of a single day," he vowed.

Even the usually cavalier Kennedy was unnerved: "I expected then that I should be caught and if caught I expected to die," he later recalled. He and the others found an 11 p.m. train to Albany, glad that they had boarded two hours early and were safely in their berths as they gazed out the train windows to see detectives scrutinizing the passengers still checking in. Headley contemplated shooting it out if confronted by the police in the train, but "to our great relief the train pulled out on time."

Once safely back in Toronto, Headley reported to his boss. "I gave a full account of our operations in New York City to Colonel Jacob Thompson, upon whose orders the enterprise had been undertaken," he wrote in his memoirs. Thompson was delighted. "A most daring raid has been made to fire the city," he told his superiors in Richmond, though he cautioned them that "the Greek fire has proved a misfortune" and they would not take a chance with it anymore.

Two days later, Thompson dropped by the boarding house where Headley was staying to warn him that Union detectives had been snooping around the Queen's Hotel, looking for Headley, Kennedy and others in the gang. They hired a top lawyer in case they were arrested and faced extradition and hid out in a small, secluded cottage in the suburbs of the city. Nothing came of the police investigation. But Robert Cobb Kennedy, always the most reckless of the gang, yearned to return to the South for more combat. "I was restless however and wanted to rejoin my command," he admitted. He boarded a Grand Trunk Railroad train from Toronto, but not far from Detroit he was spotted by two federal detectives and arrested. Imprisoned at Fort Lafayette in New York harbour, he faced execution if found guilty before a military court.

———

John Headley had no time to rest in Toronto; Thompson had a new mission in mind for the veteran Kentucky raider. Despite the failure by John Yates Beall to seize the USS *Michigan* in the fall, Thompson had not given up on piracy on the Great Lakes. He purchased a steamer called the *Georgian* for $16,500. His good friend George Taylor Denison, the Toronto aristocrat and politician with deep Southern sympathies and deeper pockets, would eventually foot the bill. Ostensibly the *Georgian* was supposed to be hauling timber, but Thompson dreamed of turning it into a kind of Confederate warship. Headley was to join Beall for a new adventure. "It was intended that Beall should shell and capture Buffalo, if possible, or make the authorities ransom the city," Headley wrote. "Then our navy would take the towns along the shore to Cleveland."

It was fanciful stuff, but the Confederates were serious about their weaponry, with plans for cannons and torpedoes. American and Canadian authorities, though, grew suspicious about activity around the *Georgian*. In early December, they arrested several men who were awaiting the ship's arrival in Collingwood, Ontario, with guns and ammunition packed in boxes. The vessel was eventually seized and lay useless in Collingwood harbour—far from any mischief it could cause on the Great Lakes.

Undeterred, two weeks later Thompson and Headley attempted a train hijacking. They had got word that several prominent Confederate generals were being transferred by rail to a prison in upstate New York.

Headley and Beall were tasked with stopping the train and effecting a rescue—and, while they were at it, robbing the safe on board. "It was distinctly understood that nothing should be taken that belonged to passengers," Headley recounted with measured politeness, before adding: "But if passengers interfered, we should shoot them."

They crossed the border stealthily and waited for the train at a small town west of Buffalo, only to discover that there were no Confederate generals on board. They tried to stop another train by placing an iron rail covered in snow over the tracks, but that only created slight damage as the locomotive barrelled through it "without any trouble."

Defeated once again and dejected, the men headed back to Canada. Headley and several of his gang made it across the bridge linking Buffalo to Fort Erie. But Beall, having fallen asleep while waiting for a train at a border restaurant, was arrested by the police.

Union major general John Dix dragged Beall in front of a military commission for a speedy trial whose outcome—and a death sentence—was never much in doubt. Like Kennedy, Beall awaited his fate in a dungeon-like eight-by-four cell in New York State, "unkempt, roughly clad, dirty," as he recounted in his memoir. "I am a stranger in a strange land."

Beall and Kennedy conspired in Canada but were unlucky enough to be arrested and jailed in the United States. Their fellow plotters who had carried out the St. Albans raid had the good fortune of being arrested in Canada; they would discover the prison conditions—and their legal prospects—were much brighter north of the border.

24.

'KINDNESS TO
THE PRISONERS'

Bennett Young liked to call it "Payette's Hotel."

"My jailer, Payette, was very indulgent and I had plenty of visitors," the ringleader of the St. Albans raiders boasted. Louis Payette's official title was Keeper of Her Majesty's Common Gaol. As Montreal's jailer, he ran the prison housed in the impressive stone building that remains to this day at the foot of the Jacques Cartier Bridge. Its majesty belies the many executions that took place there—the most notorious being the hanging of the Patriotes, heroes of the 1837–38 popular rebellions.

Now, almost thirty years after those events, Payette had other rebels to take watch over—only the treatment reserved for the Confederate raiders awaiting trial on charges of robbery and murder in St. Albans was decidedly more upscale.

"The jailer set aside his parlors for the accommodation of the prisoners," recorded Confederate John Headley with amusement. "They were permitted to occupy outside bedrooms and their meals were served in the jailer's family dining room. There were no indignities and none of the restrictions incident to imprisonment in a jail." Admirers flocked to visit. "The large number of Southern people who were sojourning in Montreal vied with each other in kindness to the prisoners," Headley noted. "The citizens of the city were equally conspicuous in their manifestations of friendship, sympathy, and courteous attentions."

The *New York Times* reported that the fine ladies of Southern families in Montreal "countenanced the robbers by sitting by them in the court-house during all the trial, providing them with luxuries in prison." A special visitor who would prove exceptionally friendly—and useful—was none other than the daughter of the presiding trial judge. Mary Coursol brought fruit and flowers to the jailed men. "She was an attractive girl about my age and I scented a chance to find out how our case was progressing," Young later recalled. "I encouraged her to come again."

All the pampering infuriated Edward Sowles, the lawyer representing the St. Albans banks. "Their apartments were furnished with all the modern hotel improvements," he noted. "Their dinners were served with 'bills of fare,' not omitting 'the wine list,' by competent attendants, such as would grace the table of a prince." As if to rub it in, George Sanders also arranged for regular shipments of chilled wine and cold chicken for the prisoners. Sanders took the time to pose for a photograph outside the gate of the jail building with the contented St. Albans raiders in their stylish dark suits, white shirts and gold watch chains.

Sanders wanted to make sure his men were not just well-fed but well-defended. He launched an opening salvo by writing a letter to the pro-South Montreal *Gazette* on October 27. "This enterprise was conducted without unnecessary violence and by an open and public declaration that they were acting as soldiers under the orders of the southern Confederacy," Sanders declared, perhaps not realizing that his words implied he considered bank robbery and murder to be necessary violence for his cause. But Sanders was also foreshadowing what would be the cornerstone of the robbers' defence: that they were acting under official orders of a legitimate army. To pull that off, Sanders would have to obtain the sharpest legal minds money could buy.

———

If Sanders was gleeful, Clement Clay was embarrassed by the political storm the St. Albans raid had created. "I am no less surprised, shocked and disturbed than you can be," he wrote to his fellow Confederate commissioner Jacob Thompson on October 22. "I have full proof that

I discountenanced it. I did not know that anything would be attempted." Clay was lying to conceal his responsibility: he had met with Bennett Young in September, giving him full approval and cash for the raid. Moreover, on the same day he wrote that apologetic disavowal to Thompson, Clay's bank receipts show that he sent $6,000 to Sanders for the "defense of St. Albans prisoners." More money flowed in from Southern sympathizers in Montreal. Henry Hogan, the proprietor of the St. Lawrence Hall, recalled that "the 'Southern Junta' at 'the Hall' were raised to action to support and defend their young countrymen, and after several meetings funds were forthcoming for the best legal talent in the country."

Sanders hired three top lawyers, led by John C. Abbott, the dean of McGill's law faculty and a Conservative member of the Legislative Assembly. (He would later become Canada's third prime minister.) Abbott would use his oratory and his considerable legal acumen to portray his clients as "daring and devoted patriots" condemned for acts that many in the American South "held to be praiseworthy, if not heroic."

Representing the government's case was Bernard Devlin, a Liberal politician but also as liberal in every sense of the word as Abbott was conservative. Born in Ireland, he started a progressive newspaper, the *Freeman's Journal*, when he was only twenty and then became a crusading lawyer. His motto—quite unconventional for the times—was "justice and equality to all classes and creeds, undue favor to none." Looking younger than his forty years, he had a drooping moustache with thick, bushy tips that hung an inch or so below his chin. He was a city councillor for the St. Lawrence ward, which included the St. Lawrence Hall, one of his—and the Confederates'—favourite hangouts.

When the full trial got under way for Bennett Young and a dozen of his men in front of Judge Charles-Joseph Coursol in Montreal on November 2, 1864, the proceedings were narrowly focused on the events at only one of the three places they had robbed: the St. Albans Bank. The American authorities had formally requested that Bennett Young and a dozen of his men be extradited to the US. But sympathy for the defendants ran high in the local press. "The accused are all young men, respectable-looking," the Montreal *Gazette* reported. "They bore the scrutiny with coolness, self-possession and good humour." Sanders, who had organized and paid for the defence, attended the proceedings, as did Jacob Thompson. George Taylor Denison, the Confederates' Toronto benefactor, was also on hand, visiting the men when they were in jail (and after the ordeal was over, he had a few of the men visit him in his villa).

Abbott and the defence team had their work cut out for them. After all, their clients had boldly and openly admitted to the crimes. A good portion of stolen loot had been found in their hands. Day after day in court, a parade of witnesses relived the frightening moments of the attack on their town. They easily identified the culprits sitting in the dock. Ten days into the trial, on November 12, Judge Coursol asked Bennett Young: "Having heard the evidence, do you wish to say anything in answer to the charge?"

"Whatever was done at St. Albans was done by the authority and order of the Confederate Government," Young declared in a measured and confident voice. "The course I intended to pursue . . . was to retaliate in some measure for the barbarous atrocities" committed by the North. Young asked for a thirty-day suspension to obtain "important testimony . . . from Richmond" that would prove he was acting under Confederate orders. It was a stunning and politically explosive defence. In effect, the St. Albans raiders were trying to prove they were innocent—by admitting they were guilty of participating in an organized military plot sanctioned by Richmond and run out of Canada. They were not traditional bank robbers—after all, they did not wear masks—but belligerents in a war for which Canada had pledged its neutrality. George Brown's *Globe* was outraged at the implications of this tactic: "Has Mr. Jefferson Davis power to make what seems to our common sense an act of robbery simply an act of war?"

It appeared so. Judge Coursol agreed to suspend the trial for a month. Now the Confederates had to figure out how to smuggle official military papers from Richmond through Union lines, across several

Northern states and an international border, into a Canadian court-room.

———

George Sanders was not one to stand around waiting for paperwork to arrive. He enjoyed being at the centre of the action—and attention—too much. "Beautiful women flocked about Sanders," according to one Confederate biographer. "He began giving the lavish parties he loved so much. There was much champagne, fine food, music and laughter in his suite" at his hotel in Montreal. He boasted to a visiting correspondent from the *St. Albans Messenger* that "the raid on St. Albans is merely the starting point in inaugurating our frontier warfare against the North."

Bennett Young, too, seemed to be enjoying his comfortable jail time. He penned a sarcastic letter to the *St. Albans Messenger*, asking for two copies of the paper. "I am extremely sorry that I cannot visit your town and subscribe for your valuable journal in person. My business engagements in Montreal prevent my coming at present," he wrote, enclosing a small bank note as payment—which the newspaper pointedly remarked "did not come into Young's possession honestly." Young also wrote to the manager at the hotel in St. Albans where he had stayed, apologizing for not settling his bill and asking about a shirt and a flask of whisky he might have left behind in his room. "Please remember me to the lady next door," he said, referring to the young woman he had charmed. "Make to her your best bow."

While Young was having fun at St. Albans's expense, Sanders was working very seriously. He had already managed to arrange his secret meeting with the sitting judge and the chief of police at the Donegana Hotel just days after the arrests. That was just the start of a brilliantly executed scheme. Five days before the trial was set to resume on December 13, Sanders talked again with Montreal police boss Guillaume Lamothe. It was a Thursday, December 8. Under questioning about the events later, Sanders couldn't recall if they met at the St. Lawrence Hall or at Dolly's Chop House, nor would he disclose what the two men discussed. But under any circumstances it was suspicious, if not improper, for a police chief to be meeting alone with a Confederate agent in the midst of a trial. Then, on Sunday, December 11—just two days before the resumption of the trial—Sanders reached out to Young and his fellow accused. "I ordered the boys to have their things put in their trunks, with their names written upon them." It certainly seemed that Sanders knew something about the trial's outcome that no one else did, though later he insisted he was only acting on the hope they would be freed soon and he wanted to get "everything ready lest they should be caught napping."

Getting things ready for a verdict that could go either way was one thing; what Sanders did next shows how he colluded with powerful players to make sure the outcome would serve the Confederates. On Monday, around 4 p.m., Sanders paid a visit to a broker he knew well. John Porterfield had the look and manners of the Southern aristocrat he was: a Nashville banker who was, in effect, the Confederacy's financial agent in Montreal. "Porterfield is on very intimate terms with Thompson and Sanders," the trial against Lincoln's conspirators would later be told. Porterfield had set up his broker's office right near the St. Lawrence Hall and the Ontario Bank, managed by Henry Starnes. When John Wilkes Booth was in Montreal in October, carrying out business at Starnes's institution, he had been spotted at least once coming out of Porterfield's office. Porterfield had always been keen to lend his business acumen to the Confederate cause. With Confederate money, he purchased a large amount of gold on the New York market in an effort to depress the value of gold and undermine the Union's finances. Now, in early December, the financier was taking steps to become, literally, a Confederate bagman.

Just hours before the trial was set to resume, Sanders dropped by Porterfield's office accompanied by an important guest: Chief of Police Guillaume Lamothe, who had been entrusted with the nearly $90,000 in stolen bank loot for "safe-keeping." "I was introduced to him by George N. Sanders," Porterfield later recounted. "The chief called on me to know if I had any authority to receive the moneys . . . We went to a corner of the room and spoke in an undertone." The chief and the Confederate obviously came to a quick understanding, because Porterfield then immediately issued specific instructions to Sanders about what to do with the stolen cash. "I suggested to Mr. Sanders . . . to have it placed in the Ontario or some other bank."

Lamothe later admitted he had been told by the judge ahead of time that "the prisoners would be entitled to the possession of the money." That afternoon, Sanders dropped off the money at Starnes's bank. "It was a middle-size carpet bag, rather much worn, and heavy for me to carry in one hand," recalled the accountant who handled the transaction, Kirkland Finlay Lockhart. Starnes, whose bank was already playing a major role in helping the Confederates disburse and launder their money, was only too happy to help. "Where other men were carried away by political passions, he remained cool and solved many problems in a quiet matter of fact way," as one newspaper account put it.

It is hard to exaggerate just what a remarkable and highly suspicious set of circumstances had just occurred: the day before the most watched trial in Canada during the Civil War was about to resume, two Confederate agents conspired with the Montreal chief of police and a cooperative banker to store the stolen loot that was at the very centre of the case. It said everything about why Montreal was such a favoured nest of sympathizers and scoundrels for the Confederacy.

That evening, according to Lamothe's own account, he received two visitors at his home. At 6 p.m., a worried Bernard Devlin came to see the city's top cop, who cared little for the government lawyer. ("He was known to be quite a scoundrel," Lamothe later wrote.)

"Where is the money?" Devlin asked the chief.

"I have done my duty" was all Lamothe was willing to let on.

"I don't know what I will do—but I will hold you responsible," Devlin warned, taking his leave.

Ninety minutes later, another knock on Lamothe's door. This time it was "a gentleman of the South"—as Lamothe described him—who took out of his pocket a large envelope, stuffed with what the police chief assumed was a huge wad of money.

"I was tasked with giving this to you, as was agreed between us," the man said.

Lamothe later claimed he was insulted by the apparent bribe. "I was indignant," he wrote. He stormed off to the St. Lawrence Hall to confront Porterfield, who told him a list had been drawn up of people who should be paid off for their services—with "a big sum" set aside for the chief. Porterfield told Sanders he had his doubts Lamothe would take the money and had sent a man to make the delivery "with some hesitation."

Even if Lamothe's account of refusing the money is true and not self-serving, what is still shocking is that Montreal's police chief by his own admission knew about active attempts by accused Confederate criminals to bribe and corrupt officials—and yet he did nothing to report or stop the illegal activity. "If you had made noise about this . . . it could have done a lot of damage for us," Porterfield later told Lamothe, "but you didn't; and I thank you for me and our cause."

Lamothe was not finished helping the cause. When Judge Coursol called his court back in session the next morning, he and Porterfield—along with Sanders, the banker Starnes and the Confederates' lawyers—were ready to pull off an intricately timed plan to, in effect, steal the money a second time.

25.

'CONSPIRED WITH SOUTHERN AGENTS'

"The whole of the proceedings are wrong."

The moment the trial of the St. Albans bandits picked up again on December 13, their lawyers launched a broadside attack. Given that the evidence against their clients appeared overwhelming, the defence had little choice but to challenge the very legitimacy of the court.

They argued that the extradition law under which the raiders had been charged in Canada had not been granted royal assent in England; therefore, the arrest warrants were invalid and a local police magistrate such as Coursol could not try the case. The judge adjourned the court; he would render his decision after lunch.

What few in the court knew was that Judge Coursol had already met privately with the defence team for the raiders to discuss their objections. The ever-charming Bennett Young had an even more personal conduit to what the judge was thinking: his daughter. Young later claimed that he had seduced Mary Coursol into becoming his lover, presumably taking advantage of the comfortable lodgings at "Payette's Hotel" that was supposed to be a jail. "She came often and even told what her father had said at the breakfast table about our case," Young boasted. "One day in excitement she said 'You have nothing to fear, Father is going to order a discharge for lack of jurisdiction.'"

Sanders later disclosed that he too knew in advance what was likely to happen, which might in part explain why he wanted to get the money ready for a quick snatch. At 2 p.m., Bennett Young, the leader of the robbers, handed Porterfield a written receipt for the money "before the judgement was rendered."

One hour later, at 3 p.m., the judge returned to the courtroom to reveal publicly the ruling that his daughter had already disclosed to the bandits. "I have and possess no jurisdiction," he announced. "Consequently, I am bound in law, justice, and fairness, to order the immediate release of the prisoners from custody upon all the charges brought before me." Bernard Devlin, the lawyer representing the US government and the banks, leaped to his feet, pleading with the judge to hear his arguments "on a matter of such importance." He pointed out that the court had only examined evidence about one charge involving a single bank; Coursol had not even begun to look at the five other accusations.

"When men charged with robbery and murder are allowed to go free, without all the cases being investigated, our good name for justice and fair-play was at stake," Devlin warned.

The judge would have none of it.

"Let the prisoners be discharged," he declared.

———

Pandemonium erupted in the courtroom.

Edward Sowles remembered "rounds of applause and screams never before heard or known in a court of justice, in which all seemed to participate. Then there was a rush for the doors and streets, and the news spread through the city and country with great celerity."

Amidst the confusion, Sanders and Porterfield carried out their plan with military-style precision. "I had understood that Mr. Devlin was very sharp, and that I would have to act like lightning to get the money," Sanders noted. Porterfield was ready before the prisoners had even left the courtroom. "I was the first man out," he said. He met police chief Lamothe in the courtroom lobby to get the written authorization for the release of the money. "I went immediately to the Chief," Porterfield recounted, "and there he gave me the order."

Montreal's top police officer had dutifully fired off a note to Starnes's bank:

THE ORDER.
Montreal, Dec. 13, 1864

Mr. Henry Starnes will please deliver to
Mr. Porterfield ... the carpet bag put in
trust into his hands.

(Signed)
GUIL. LAMOTHE
Chief of Police

With Lamothe's note in hand, Porterfield dashed outside. "I had my sleigh at the door and I drove immediately to the Bank," he reported. "I then called at the bank to see whether the package was there and I was told by Mr. Starnes that it was."

"It was in a sealed and labelled carpet bag which I did not open," he continued. "I delivered it to the owners that night as soon as I could find them." For a Confederate banker like Porterfield (and apparently the judge and the police chief) it was the robbers—not the Union banks—who were "the owners" of the stolen cash. Free from jail and flush with cash, Young and his fellow raiders were delighted as they rifled through the bag of stolen loot now back in their hands. "There was more than they expected," Porterfield recalled.

As the men exclaimed to Sanders: "The money, all right and a little plus."

———

Back in court, Devlin and his team were scrambling to stop the robbers and the stolen bank money from slipping away. As far as Devlin was concerned, the Confederate thieves had not been acquitted: only part of the case against them had been dismissed—incorrectly—on a technicality. (In fact, Judge Coursol was wrong about not having jurisdiction.

The extradition treaty had in fact been recognized in England through an order-in-council, giving him full rights to hear the case.) Within fifteen minutes he and his colleague Thomas Ritchie had filed a fresh complaint against the men for their robbery at the First National Bank. Not able to find a judge in chambers at the courthouse, they raced to the private home of one judge, who dismissed them because it was "after the usual hour of business."

They had more luck with Superior Court Justice James Smith, who agreed to issue an arrest warrant for the very same men Judge Coursol had freed just hours earlier. With a warrant in hand, Devlin felt they had a good chance of recapturing the Confederates before they fled that night. By 6:30 p.m. they had made it to the police station in Jacques Cartier Square, only to be told that Chief Lamothe was not there. A deputy chief of police refused to enforce the warrant without Lamothe's okay, even though the warrant authorized "any constable or peace officer" to act.

Ritchie then went to the chief's home, finding him asleep on the sofa in a dark room. "Mr. Lamothe seemed a little annoyed at our visit," the lawyer recalled. "He said he had no orders to receive from me or anyone else." Ritchie tried to explain these were not orders from a lawyer but a judicially authorized warrant. Still Lamothe balked. Ritchie pressed on, explaining he was worried that Young's men would be taking an 8:15 p.m. train out of the city. The chief told him he had to dine first and think about it, perhaps sensing he was about to be thrust into the middle of a scandal that would not end well for him. "I was not in a good mood and I decided to have nothing to do with the affair of the raiders," Lamothe later wrote.

Frustrated, the lawyers went to the home of Adolph Bissonnette, a senior constable on the force, and convinced him to accompany them back to Lamothe's house. Bissonnette emerged fifteen minutes later to say that Lamothe still wanted more time to decide. Ritchie, in desperation, took Bissonnette to the home of Judge Coursol, who gave a "verbal order" for the police to to act—a bizarre twist of events since he was sanctioning a warrant issued by a judge for the arrest of the men Coursol had just released.

But by then it was too late. Most of the St. Albans raiders had fled successfully, never to be brought to justice again. Ritchie went home, dejected and furious. "It was mortifying in the extreme for me to find . . . that it was apparently an absolute impossibility to execute a Judge's warrant in the city of Montreal, merely owing to the delay or reluctance to act of the Chief of Police," Ritchie lamented. The *Montreal Witness* was blunter, insisting it was not procrastination but political sympathies: "There are circumstances about the case so suspicious . . . [that they] indicate strongly the good feeling of some of our officials towards the raiders."

———

One of the fugitives had never even had to worry about court. Charles Hunt Higbee, who had been shot through the shoulder while fleeing St. Albans, had made his way to Montreal back in October, where he found refuge with the Saint-Jean-Baptiste Society, a Quebec nationalist group with strong sympathies for the Southern cause.

Higbee was more than a mere bank robber. He had blood on his hands as a killer in one of the worst civilian massacres of the war, when, in August 1863, Confederate raiders attacked the town of Lawrence, Kansas, known for its opposition to slavery. They executed more than 150 men and boys, targeting Black Union soldiers and white abolitionists. Higbee was accused by his fellow Confederates of making off with much of the plundered loot and fleeing to Canada.

Now, after the St. Albans raid, he found himself on the run again— but the Saint-Jean-Baptiste devotees took good care of their fugitive. They arranged for a Confederate doctor based in Montreal to visit and treat Higbee until he was well enough to escape back to the United States.

Bennett Young was glad Higbee and most of the other raiders had escaped, but he and four others were not as lucky. On December 20 five men, including Young, were found in Quebec City and rearrested, and now faced a new trial. But nothing could undo the political damage that had already been done. In the United States, a war of words erupted. The

St. Albans Messenger decried that Judge Coursol "has not only written himself down as an ass, but laid himself open to the very serious charge of being bribed." The *New York Times* repeated the unproven but widespread allegations that the stolen loot had been "liberally divided" among the judge, the police chief and George Sanders himself. "It is useless to mince matters," the *Times* fumed. "The Canadian people have given shelter and friendship to men who have robbed and murdered American citizens . . . It has not only set the outlaws free, but has secured them their plunder." Other papers issued open calls for an invasion of Canada. "Take her by the throat and throttle her as a St. Bernard would a poodle pup," the *Chicago Tribune* bellowed. The Montreal *Gazette* worried that "we shall find ourselves dragged into the war . . . and the country on both sides [of] the line made red with murders."

Lincoln made his displeasure clear, using the high-profile platform of his State of the Union address to Congress to single out his northern neighbour. He softened the blow by diplomatically noting that the "authorities of Canada are not deemed to be intentionally unjust or unfriendly toward the United States." But then the President went on to denounce in no uncertain terms "the insecurity of life and property in the region adjacent to the Canadian border, by reason of recent assaults and depredations committed by inimical and desperate persons who are harbored there." Lincoln's tolerance for Canada's so-called neutrality was past the breaking point. Washington threatened to scrap the Reciprocity Treaty, which allowed for the free flow of many goods across the border, and the agreement that barred military vessels on the Great Lakes. For the first time, passports were also imposed on any Canadians seeking to come into the United States.

The pro-Lincoln *Montreal Witness* told its readers that the fury of Americans loyal to the President was justified in the wake of the St. Albans fiasco: "When all this was going on, they could come to no other conclusion than they arrived at, that Canada was a safe base of operations against the North."

———

Two nights before Christmas, on Friday, December 23, the visitors' gallery at Montreal's City Hall was packed as the mayor called the special council meeting to order. A single item on the agenda: the fate of Chief of Police Guillaume Lamothe.

For the previous nine days, the municipal police committee had held hearings about the St. Albans affair. Bernard Devlin, the lawyer for the US government, was also a sitting council member. Having lost in court, he brought two charges before the committee against police chief Guillaume Lamothe for "unlawfully" handing over the money to the robbers and for refusing to execute the new warrants for their arrest.

Devlin did most of the grilling of the witnesses. Rodolphe Laflamme, one of the lawyers for the raiders, was also a councillor and did his best to shield the Confederates—and the police chief—from embarrassment. There was no judge, no jury, no legal consequences, but in many ways this was the most thorough trial of Confederate activity in Canada that would be held during the Civil War. No other legal proceedings would ever probe as deeply into the clout of Confederate agents in Canada and the collusion of their Canadian accomplices. Important operatives like George Sanders and John Porterfield gave sworn testimony. Most of what we now know about the behind-the-scenes scheming and plotting for the money and the raiders' escape came from these hearings.

First up was the chief himself, who made the ludicrous claim that he had received the money as an individual and not as "an officer of the Corporation"—and therefore was not subject to the city's jurisdiction. He insisted that he thought himself "legally bound" to return the money to men who had been, in his words, "illegally arrested." Devlin quite rightly called the chief's actions "an outrageous violation of his official duty."

Judge Coursol was next. He appeared ready to throw his colleague Lamothe under the proverbial bus, or sleigh as it were. He insisted he had "no such power" to give a legal ruling on the money. Questioned about what instructions he had given Lamothe, he dithered: "I cannot really recollect."

John Porterfield was equally cagey. When asked what he did for a living, the well-known Confederate banker and broker demurred: "I am not engaged in any business for the moment."

Three times Devlin tried to push him on the fundamental issue, asking if "arrangements were made . . . for the escape of the prisoners in anticipation of a judgement being rendered in their favour." In other words, did the Confederates have advance knowledge of the judge's call? Each time, other councillors raised objections that the questioning was "illegal and irrelevant" and might also incriminate Porterfield, so he was never forced to answer directly. All he would say was that Bennett Young, expecting to be released shortly, "asked me if I would assist him in getting off from the city immediately after his discharge."

George Sanders—ever the braggart—was slightly more forthcoming during two days of testimony, describing in detail his meetings with the police chief, the judge and Porterfield. Still, he was duplicitous. He denied being "the representative or agent of the Confederate States" though he had openly boasted of being exactly that. When asked outright if any bribes were paid, Sanders chose his words carefully. "No portion of this money so far as the Chief of Police is concerned, has, to the best of my knowledge, gone to him," he said. "I decline further to answer what has become of it."

As the embarrassing details kept spilling out, it was not looking good for Lamothe. "Seldom has a public official been so universally condemned as Lamothe," the *Globe* pronounced. "It is simply monstrous that a man holding so responsible a position . . . should be so wanting in moral principle." On December 17, the beleaguered police chief returned to the committee to submit a written statement. "Feeling that personal motives and enmity do not allow me to expect fair justice from the Committee," he said, "I therefore resign the office of Chief of Police." To many, it was an admission of guilt but it was also a tactic to avoid any more uncomfortable revelations or punishment. His lawyer immediately tried to quash any further proceedings, arguing that his client was no longer a public officer. But the investigation continued for another five days. Then, on December 23, in front of the full city council, came the vote on whether or not to accept the resignation of the Montreal chief of police.

Bernard Devlin made a speech as impassioned as any he had delivered in court. "Disguise it as you may, it will ever appear that Mr. Lamothe conspired with Southern agents for the delivery of this money," he declared. "If he did not, why put himself into the hands of Mr. Sanders? Why hold private interviews with Mr. Porterfield? Why deposit the money in the Ontario Bank the day before the judgement for Mr. Porterfield's convenience? Why wait in the passage leading into the court room with an order already prepared for delivery of the money? What a thoughtful and delicate act of courtesy this was!" Devlin ended his speech with a stirring warning that Canadians must ensure they acted on the right side of history, denouncing "our mistaken and ill-judged sympathy with the wily agents of the South who are here plotting and planning."

The crowd of Montreal citizens burst into loud applause. The final vote was fourteen to eleven. The chief was out.

Judge Coursol's days were numbered too. It's never a good sign for a judge when the attorney general denounces you as "this wretched prig of a police magistrate," as John A. Macdonald did. Coursol was suspended early in the new year. Quebec Superior Court judge F.W. Torrance was appointed to investigate the "failure of justice in the matter of the St. Albans raid." Torrance found no evidence of "bribes or corruption"—but he was relying solely on the predictable denials of Sanders, Porterfield and Bennett Young. Still, he was scathing towards Coursol for his "grave dereliction of duty" and concluded he was "indictable for a malfeasance of his functions as a justice of the peace."

Torrance's inquiry also found that Lamothe's refusal to act on the warrant to rearrest Young and the raiders after Coursol had freed them was "an indictable offense," but the police chief was never disciplined much less charged. None of the stolen money that had been handed back to the St. Albans gang was ever located. But years later Bennett Young confessed where most of it went: "Whatever we had was handed over to the Confederate treasury."

Lamothe, though disgraced, was not finished helping his Confederate friends.

26.

'THE CURSE IN THIS COUNTRY'

John Headley, still licking his wounds from his headline-grabbing but ultimately disappointing New York arson attack, contemplated the distressing state of affairs of the Confederates in Canada. It struck him that most of their attention was now centred on prisons—but not ambitious plots to free thousands of Southern soldiers; instead, at this point, they were simply trying to free their own captured agents and operatives.

"Now many of our best men were in prison," Headley complained. "It appeared that the Confederate Department in Canada was without practical purposes for a longer existence except to wind up its business and the protection of our friends who were in prison."

Indeed, the roster of Confederates from Canada who were behind bars on both sides of the border by the end of 1864 was dispiriting. Robert Kennedy, who had accompanied Headley to New York, and John Yates Beall, who had joined him in the train hijacking plot, were in the United States facing trials and possible execution. John Castleman was in solitary confinement in a seven-foot-square cell in an Indianapolis prison after the failure of the Northwest Conspiracy. Bennett Young and four other St. Albans raiders still languished in jail in Montreal, awaiting another trial.

The secret service operation in Canada was in turmoil. One leader would quit, one would try to hold on to his job, and a new man would be sent from Richmond to try to strengthen the Confederacy's attacks on Lincoln as the war ground on.

———

The year 1864 had been a hectic if not always successful time for Jacob Thompson and his Confederate Secret Service operations in Canada. The plans were certainly bold, but the execution left something to be desired. The yellow fever plot and the arson attacks failed because of a bad understanding of science. The peace plot was bad politics, the prison breaks were badly planned, and the piracy on the Great Lakes was a victim of bad luck. On December 3, Thompson wrote a long letter to his boss, Secretary of State Judah Benjamin. It was part report card, part self-promotion, part defensiveness, as Thompson tried to justify the money and the men he had deployed in the eight months he had been in Canada. "I have relaxed no effort to carry out the objects the Government had in view in sending me here," wrote the wealthy plantation owner from Mississippi, now huddled in his Queen's Hotel room in cold Toronto. "I had hoped at different times to have accomplished more, but still I do not think my mission has been altogether fruitless."

Thompson admitted his plots to spark a revolt in the northwest states and to embarrass Lincoln with a peace plan fizzled; the piracy on the Great Lakes to free Confederate prisoners "was well conceived and held out the promise of success" but failed because of "some treachery." The attempt to burn down New York with Greek fire "has proved a misfortune." The only real success—the St. Albans raid—was an operation that Thompson had little to do with.

Thompson, not unjustly, had complained to Richmond about how much his activities had been hampered by surveillance and Union infiltrators. "The bane and curse of carrying out anything in this country is the surveillance under which we act," he wrote. "Detectives, or those ready to give information, stand at every street corner. Two or three cannot interchange ideas without a reporter."

(The irony was that at the same time as Thompson was grumbling about Union surveillance, John Potter, the consul general in Montreal, was sending yet another of his intelligence reports to Washington based on his spies and infiltrators. He warned that "rebel agents [were] being reinforced" by a new batch of disbanded fighters coming from Kentucky while at the same time Confederate infiltrators were finding it easy to sneak back into the US to carry out attacks because they had Canadian passports.)

If Thompson's year-end results were grim, it was not for lack of money. "The entire expenditures as yet, on all accounts, are about $300,000," he reported to Richmond, noting that he also gave Clay close to another $100,000. "Should you think it best for me to return, I would be glad to know in what way you think I had best return with the funds remaining on hand." Much to Thompson's embarrassment, what he did with the rest of the Confederate riches in Canada would later become a subject of much scandal and controversy.

Perhaps hoping to save his dignity if not his imprisoned agents, Thompson was not ready to be pushed aside. "I should remain here for the present, and I shall obey your orders," he told Secretary of State Judah Benjamin, if "that is your wish."

―――――

For his part, Clement Clay, Thompson's co-commissioner and uneasy partner, had had enough.

"I do not see that I can achieve anything by remaining longer in this province," he wrote to Richmond in despair. "I am afraid to risk a winter's residence in this latitude and climate." He left St. Catharines in early December, spent a few weeks in Montreal and Quebec, and then made his way to Halifax, where he had a farewell dinner with his good friend and supporter Archbishop Thomas Connolly before booking passage by boat to Bermuda and then to Charleston, South Carolina, in early January.

His return ocean trip was even more hazardous than his stormy maiden voyage to Halifax back in the spring of 1864. This time he barely survived a shipwreck. "Ran aground . . . abandoned ship & took to life boats," he recounted in his diary. "I waded to shore, carrying what baggage I could in my hands." He eventually made it back to Georgia, where—ever careful as the congressman turned conspirator—"he destroyed a number of papers relating to his Canadian stay."

Getting rid of the evidence, however, would not save him from punishment when the time came for the Union to settle accounts with the Confederates who had used Canada as a staging ground for their attacks.

———

With Clay gone and Thompson trying to cling to his job, Richmond decided there was a need for new, more decisive leadership to take over the secret service work north of the border. On December 30, Judah Benjamin sent a letter to Thompson: "From reports which reach us from trustworthy sources, we are satisfied that so close an espionage is kept upon you that your services have been deprived of the value which is attached to your residence in Canada," he said. "The President [Jefferson Davis] thinks that it is better that you return to the Confederacy."

It was time to replace the hesitant politician Thompson had been with someone with a stronger military pedigree. Edwin Gray Lee had come a long way since serving as a junior aide-de-camp in the Battle of Bull Run back in 1861. Despite ailing from chronic lung disease, he had fought in at least four major battles, been captured, imprisoned, and freed in a prisoner exchange.

In 1863, as a captain in the Confederate navy, he partnered with John Yates Beall—an old friend—to run a raiding and piracy operation they set up with Jefferson Davis's approval on the Lower Potomac and Chesapeake Bay. Lee's career was helped no doubt by the fact that he was a cousin of the Confederacy's most famous general, Robert E. Lee. Edwin had fought with Robert against John Brown's insurgents at Harpers Ferry and in the First Battle of Bull Run.

By the end of 1864, Lee had become a brigadier general and his battlefield shifted to Canada. With his wife Susan, Lee set sail for Halifax on December 27 from Bermuda on what was becoming the Confederate commuter line to Canada: the steamer *Alpha*, the same vessel that had brought Thompson, Clay and Blackburn north. Doctors had recommended that a cold, dry climate would be better for his poor lungs, which provided a convenient medical cover for his mission.

"Certificate given to avert suspicion of my real business in Canada," he wrote.

In Montreal, he settled into what had become the unofficial headquarters of Confederate spies, the St. Lawrence Hall. As a kind of rite of passage, he had his portrait taken at the famous photography studio of William Notman, known as the "Photographer to the Queen." Political and popular luminaries such as John A. Macdonald and Harriett Beecher Stowe had graced Notman's Montreal premises. So did pretty much every prominent Confederate in Canada—from Jacob Thompson and George Sanders to the St. Albans raiders.

Lee had now joined the club, and he would serve it well.

27.

'A WAR FOR HUMANITY'

Emma Edmonds had described reading the adventures of Fanny, the swashbuckling young woman who disguises herself as a pirate, as "the most wonderful day in all my life." For a farm girl trapped in the traditions and restrictions of rural New Brunswick, it was a liberating tale of breaking boundaries and adventure. Perhaps it was time for her to return the favour and inspire a new generation of young women.

While volunteering in Union hospitals after she had left the army, Edmonds somehow found time to write a four-hundred-page memoir. Her one-room schoolhouse education in New Brunswick came in handy as she recounted her wartime escapades in flowery but at times quite moving prose that mixed war reportage with lyrics from songs and religious verses. She approached the same publishers for whom she had sold books as a man, this time revealing her true gender and what must have seemed to them a shocking but potentially lucrative tale. The first version of the book came out sometime in 1864 with a lengthy, if not lurid, title page:

UNSEXED:

OR,

THE FEMALE SOLDIER.

THE

THRILLING ADVENTURES, EXPERIENCES AND ESCAPES

OF A WOMAN.

AS NURSE, SPY AND SCOUT, IN HOSPITALS, CAMPS
AND BATTLE-FIELDS.

BY

S. EMMA E. EDMONDS

The Publishers' Notice at the beginning of the book started by stating "no apology is necessary for adding one more" volume to the ever-increasing pile of Civil War books. But in fact much of the notice was an apology for Edmonds's daring duplicity in passing herself off as a man. "Should any of her readers object to some of her disguises," the publisher pleaded, "it may be sufficient to remind them it was from the purest motives and most praiseworthy patriotism, that she laid aside, for a time, her own costume . . . hazarding her life for her adopted country, in its trying hour of need."

Perhaps to make Edmonds's story more acceptable, the book was reissued in 1865 under the simpler and presumably less controversial title *Nurse and Spy in the Union Army*. The book featured what were called "Embellishments"—nine black-and-white engravings of Edmonds in battle. The more numerous embellishments, though, were in her stories, often more fiction than fact. Her accounts of penetrating behind enemy lines as a spy were almost certainly not true and, in any case, unverifiable. And there were other scenes in her book that rang false. She wrote exciting accounts of the Battle of Antietam in September 1862—at the time the bloodiest day in United States military history—but in fact her regiment never fought there. At the end of her book, she made much of the siege of Vicksburg, but that drawn-out battle ended three months after she left the army. Many years later, she was asked by an interviewer if her book "can . . . be regarded as authentic?" "Not strictly so," Edmonds answered. "Still, most of the experiences recorded were either my own or came under my observation. I would like, however, to write differently of that portion of my life."

Despite or maybe because of the exaggerations, Edmonds's book enjoyed a tremendous success. "The book was widely read and discussed for years after the Civil War," the *Detroit Free Press* reported. The publisher claimed it sold 175,000 copies, which if true made it a remarkable bestseller. Edmonds insisted the proceeds from the book sales go to wounded and needy soldiers; the publisher reported he had turned over "hundreds of dollars from the profits of the book" to her causes.

For all its scandalous nature as a "tell-all" book, *Nurse and Spy* did keep one closely guarded secret. Edmonds never revealed the name she used as her alias—Franklin Thompson—nor did she identify her regiment. She was, in effect, still an anonymous female soldier in disguise. Most of the men in the 2nd Michigan Volunteer Infantry with whom she fought still did not know the private story of the buddy they called Frank.

———

Emma Edmonds's book was full of accurate and unnerving accounts of battlefield nursing and medical care. As doctors in Washington, Anderson Abbott and Alexander Augusta saw the carnage every day. Eighteen sixty-four had been the first full year that Blacks had been on the front lines as members of the United States Colored Troops. With inferior military training and equipment and inadequate medical care, they suffered a much higher mortality rate than white combatants.

Struggling as a surgeon in Washington, Anderson Abbott didn't need statistical reports to witness the devastation in front of his eyes. He saw it in the endless and often brutal amputations, heard it in the agonized screams, smelled it in the pus and sores on untreated infections. By late 1864, the dilapidated and woefully inadequate Contraband Hospital had been moved several times. It finally found a decent location at a former army medical facility and was eventually renamed the Freedmen's Hospital, under the control of the Bureau of Refugees rather than the army.

Abbott briefly served as the senior administrator. "The Hospital contained a capacity for 300 beds," he later recalled with pride. "It was used for the treatment of Freedmen and Colored soldiers. It was fully equipped with a competent staff of nurses, laundry women, cooks, stewards, and clerks." It was still far inferior to what white soldiers could expect in their hospitals, but at least it was a step forward.

Still, Abbott and Augusta continued to suffer indignities, small and large. In the fall of 1864, Abbott—along with another Black Canadian doctor serving at the hospital—was accused of "indulging in the use of intoxicating drinks" at a celebration in a local Presbyterian church to hail the new constitution passed in the Maryland Legislative Assembly that prohibited slavery. Nothing came of the complaint, but it was another example of the humiliation facing Abbott and his colleagues.

On a more serious level, from the moment they were accepted into the Union army, Black surgeons and soldiers had to suffer the indignity of grossly unequal pay. Lincoln's Emancipation Proclamation opened the ranks to Blacks; they could enlist, be wounded and die in greater numbers than the white soldiers, but at about half the pay. A Black private typically was paid $7 a month, compared with $13 a month for his white counterpart. Abbott's first contract as a surgeon (with no official rank) earned him $80 a month, at least $40 less than white physicians under contract were paid. Augusta managed to get a monthly salary of $169 as a major. But then, in early 1864, the army bureaucrats insisted he be paid the same measly $7 a month that went to all other Blacks in uniform.

As always, Augusta fought back. He wrote to the chairman of the Senate's Committee on Military Affairs and got his salary reinstated. By June 1864, Congress passed legislation that guaranteed equal pay for soldiers regardless of race. State legislatures followed suit.

Anderson Abbott put everything in the wider context of a fight for equality. "There never was such a gathering of men of all races . . . moved by a common impulse to sacrifice their lives for a great principle as in that Civil war," he later remarked. "It was not a war for conquest or territorial aggrandizement, racial, social or political supremacy. It was not a war for white men or black men, red men or yellow men. It was a war for humanity."

To wage that war, Abbott and other Blacks wanted more than better pay from the army; they wanted to attain the ranks of power. There were a growing number of "Colored Regiments," but they were all commanded by white men. On January 16, 1865, Abbott joined several non-commissioned officers—including two sons of the famed civil rights leader Frederick Douglass—to write a petition to the secretary of war calling for nothing less than "a number of colored regiments to be officered exclusively by colored men." They argued that "while many of the noblest of our race have sprung to arms with alacrity in defence of the Government," many others had hesitated to enlist because they saw the continued discrimination within the ranks of the Union army. "We confidently believe that the removal of this bar to a soldier's ambition would result in an uprising of the colored people, unsurpassed even by the enthusiastic response to the President's first call."

Meanwhile, outside the army, there was momentous change in the very makeup of a country gripped by civil war. Two weeks after Abbott and his Black colleagues submitted their petition, on January 31, Congress passed the historic Thirteenth Amendment to the Constitution that abolished slavery. "Neither slavery nor involuntary servitude . . . shall exist within the United States," it declared in a few simple words that would shake a nation.

Abraham Lincoln had not started the Civil War with the intention of abolishing slavery, but before the war was over, he would bring an end to human bondage in America. What Anderson Abbott and his fellow petitioners—along with the politicians and the public—could not know was that the war had less than four months left to run its course.

And President Abraham Lincoln had only four months left to live.

*An official portrait taken of Lincoln on February 5, 1865,
two months before his assassination (Courtesy Library of Congress)*

PART THREE

'SORROW'S DARKEST NIGHT'

(January 1865–April 1865)

If I am killed, I can die but once; but to live in
constant dread of it is to die over and over again.

—ABRAHAM LINCOLN

28.

'SHE WORE HER VEIL'

She almost always remained in the shadows, hidden and mysterious.

While images abound of almost every figure in the Lincoln assassination saga, there is a single grainy photograph some claim could be the elusive spy Sarah Slater, though even that is unlikely. Diaries and letters from other people and hotel registries give us some dates of her travels, but except for a will she wrote, there are no documents in her own words. She went by many names and aliases and lied about her age.

She was universally described as beautiful, with dark eyes and hair. But usually only a fleeting glimpse of her would be caught, for she often covered her face. "She was a rather slim, delicate woman," one Confederate later told investigators. "I think she wore her veil down nearly all the time."

Perhaps Confederate secretary of war James Seddon was also taken by the striking young woman who walked into his office in late January 1865. But he wasn't looking for beauty; he needed bravery. The accused St. Albans robbers were in serious legal trouble in Canada and Seddon needed a courier to smuggle north the documents that could save their lives.

It would be one of many dangerous missions Slater carried out for the Confederacy to and from Canada, right up until the days immediately before and after the assassination of Abraham Lincoln. Her name came up repeatedly during the trials and investigations in the wake of Lincoln's murder, but the authorities could never find her.

———

She was born Sarah Antoinette Gilbert on January 12, 1843, in a small town in Connecticut. Church records listed ten children born in the family, but only five survived—Sarah, along with three brothers and a sister. Their father, Joseph Gilbert, was born on the French island of Martinique; her mother, Antoinette Reynaud, in Trinidad. Slater would later claim her mother was born in France; either way, her parents spoke French, as did young Sarah, an indispensable skill when she became a spy making frequent trips to Quebec.

By the time she was fifteen, Sarah had moved to North Carolina and by age eighteen she had married Rowan Slater, who ran a "Dancing and Waltzing Academy." It was June 1861, less than sixty days after the onset of the Civil War. Her name was now Sarah N. Slater—the N standing for Nettie, a more easily pronounceable and American-sounding abbreviation of her mother's first name. Two of her brothers signed up early with the Confederate army. Her husband Rowan started as a purchasing agent for the Confederate government, then enlisted in the 20th North Carolina Infantry and was eventually taken prisoner in 1864.

Sarah Slater was not about to sit back and let the men do all the fighting.

––––

By the start of 1865, the embattled Confederacy was plunged into its darkest days.

Food and fuel were scarce in the encircled Southern cities and countryside. Desertion plagued the army, as starving soldiers abandoned their posts. It said a lot regarding what the war was really about that even in the midst of all that desperation, the Southern states found the time to carry out a brisk trade in humans. On January 3, "about three hundred negroes were sold in Augusta [Georgia] . . . at auction, at an average of $8,000," one newspaper announced. Rebel president Jefferson Davis was so desperate for cash early in the year, he sold three of his horses—and two of his slaves, for the much lower price of $1,612.

It was not a great time for 22-year-old Sarah Slater to be asking for a favour from embattled Confederate officials. Anxious to visit her mother, who had settled in New York, she secured the support of two Confederate congressmen for safe passage across enemy lines. "She has lost her only brother in the Confederate Army and we have no hesitation in vouching for her loyalty and her high social position," they wrote to the authorities. It was the first of many lies Salter would spin over her career. The dead sibling was not her only brother and he had died of natural causes. Her two other brothers had served in the Confederate army—but only briefly, before they deserted.

Her request was forwarded by the army all the way up to the office of the secretary of war, James Seddon. There are two interpretations of what happened next. The more conspiratorial accounts argue that by this time Slater was already a Confederate agent and that the letter from the possibly duped congressmen was just a "cover." The more romantic accounts have the striking 22-year-old Slater grabbing Seddon's attention the moment she walked into his office. "He liked what he saw. She was beautiful, unafraid, spunky, and daring," as one history of espionage put it. Regardless of which interpretation was closer to the truth, by the time the first month of 1865 was over, Sarah Slater was a full-time Confederate agent.

Her services were urgently needed. Back in Montreal, the on-again, off-again trial of the recaptured St. Albans bank robbers was resuming. Bennett Young and his men needed official documents from Richmond to prove that they were acting as soldiers under orders, not as ordinary bandits. "The lives of the Confederate prisoners were hanging by a thread," observed John Headley, who must have considered himself luckier, having come out of the New York arson attacks unpunished. He was not exaggerating: if the St. Albans men were extradited to the Northern states, they faced certain imprisonment and probable execution.

Enter Sarah Slater.

From Seddon's point of view, the young woman was perfect for the job: fluent in French, she could easily pass as someone from Quebec.

And her appearance was another asset: "Union officers would surely be inclined to see a shapely ankle rather than an enemy agent." The secret documents she carried described the St. Albans men as authorized Confederate fighters, emblazoned with the Great Seal of the Confederate States "to establish . . . that they acted under orders."

On January 31, 1865, Sarah Slater, Confederate courier, set off towards Canada. As much as she was no doubt filled with excitement over her new adventure, Slater knew the risks were enormous. The route Confederate couriers travelled between Canada and Richmond was a danger-filled trek on horseback or in horse-drawn carriages, by ferry and rail across more than seven hundred miles through heavily defended Union territory. If she was discovered as a spy, it meant prison at the very least—if not the noose. What Slater did not know is that five days before she left Richmond, another courier for the Confederates in Canada was sitting in a Union jail, sentenced "to be hung by the neck until he is dead." It is possible that Slater got her first mission precisely because a committed Southern soldier named Lieutenant Samuel Boyer Davis had failed in his.

———

President Jefferson Davis (who was no relation) extolled the lieutenant as "a gallant true officer." Jacob Thompson insisted "no braver or truer soldier can be found." But the Union prisoners who knew Samuel Davis at a brutal Confederate prison in Georgia would not have agreed.

After being injured during the Battle of Gettysburg, Davis was assigned to help run the massive Andersonville camp. "Very much has been said of the cruelty to prisoners at Andersonville," Davis said, "but it is sensational bosh." The conditions, he insisted, "were sufficiently good." In reality, in just over a year, more than 13,000 men perished— an appalling one-quarter of the 45,000 Union captives held there. Among the many prisons on both sides of the war that became death camps, Andersonville was indisputably the worst. Crammed into barracks filled to four times their capacity, the starving men were described as walking skeletons. After the war, Davis's boss and camp commander,

Heinrich Hartmann Wirz, was found guilty of murder and hanged—one of the few Confederates executed for war crimes. Try as Davis might to deny the crimes at Andersonville, they would soon catch up with him.

Davis's spying career had been set in motion at a Christmas celebration in Richmond in 1864. He had been enjoying the liquor that flowed freely at the Spotswood Hotel when he bumped into an operative working for Secretary of State Judah Benjamin. His friend told him he was being dispatched to Canada with some important messages but he didn't care to go. Davis leaped at the chance. "I was anxious for some change, and seized by sudden impulse, I said I'll go if you do not want to," Davis recalled, "and that remark nearly cost me my life."

Davis got the assignment as a courier to carry documents to Canada proving that John Yates Beall, facing execution for his actions as a Lake Erie pirate and attempted train hijacker, was a legitimate soldier acting under Richmond's orders. Davis arrived in Toronto on January 4 and registered at the Queen's Hotel, foolishly using his own name, as "Lieutenant S.B. Davis, Confederate States Army, Richmond, Virginia." He then asked immediately to be taken to Jacob Thompson's room.

The head of Canada's Confederate Secret Services was somewhat flustered by the lack of subterfuge exercised by the inexperienced spy. He needed help to hide Davis and turned to the wealthy and willing George Taylor Denison III. "I assented," said a delighted Denison, "and after it was dark, he slipped out [of the hotel] and when it was certain that they were not followed, they came out to my house." The Toronto aristocrat had no compunctions about helping his Confederate friends hide a man he called "a gallant officer" who had helped run one of the most notorious prison death camps. On the contrary, Denison wrote in his memoirs about how his new house guest was connected to "the celebrated prison at Andersonville."

Davis stayed under Denison's protection, only going outdoors for exercise after dark. In less than a week, Thompson was ready to send the courier back to Richmond with more messages. According to several accounts, that included a request for copies of the same documents that Sarah Slater had been ordered to smuggle into Canada to help the St. Albans raiders. Davis would later admit only that he was carrying "closely written" secrets and "my head full of more important matters committed to memory."

Regardless of their content, the messages had to be kept as secure as possible. George Denison, perhaps reliving his years as a child listening to the war stories of his elders, came up with a scheme worthy of the highest intrigue. He knew the challenges if Davis got caught. "The Federal officers had learned nearly every trick of searching prisoners," he wrote. "Boots and collars were cut open, and folds of cloth in the clothing everywhere examined. Buttons were taken to pieces and carefully scanned under magnifying glasses."

How to fool the Union investigators?

"An idea struck me which I explained to Colonel Thompson," Denison recounted. "It was to write the despatches on thin white silk in pencil, and sew them in the back of the coat or vest, and in the sleeve near the elbow. The silk could not be felt, nor would it rustle." Five pieces of very thin silk were prepared and Denison recruited his wife, who worked from 1 a.m. to 4 a.m. to sew them into Davis's coat and vest under Thompson's supervision. Denison then got a friend to obtain Davis a passport from the US consul and drove him by sleigh in the middle of the night to the train station. Denison was relieved when he saw his companion get on board safely.

On his second day on the train, however, Davis had the misfortune to run into Union soldiers who had been freed from the Andersonville prison. They recognized the man they blamed for their torment and Davis was immediately arrested. In jail, he was searched, but nothing incriminating was found. Davis managed later to remove the messages in silk hidden in his clothing and destroy them.

Davis complained about the "filth and dirt besprinkled with vermin" in his cell, a rather hypocritical complaint considering his role in the hellhole that was Andersonville prison.

A swift military trial ended unsurprisingly with a guilty verdict. His execution was set for February 17.

———

The debacle with Lieutenant Davis's mission showed the Confederates how risky the courier routes were. With Sarah Slater on the road to Montreal, they were not going to take any chances. They had no way of knowing if their new young recruit would succeed in her mission. As a backup, they put their faith, if not in God, then at least in God's messenger.

Stephen Cameron was a fiery, almost fanatical chaplain for the Confederacy. He had written two patriotic songs, delivered the eulogy for Captain John Morgan, the leader of the Kentucky raiders, and sent Robert E. Lee a sword praying he would use it in "a sacred and glorious cause." In early 1865, Cameron was in Montreal, eager to help the St. Albans cause in any way he could. "They were my brother soldiers," Cameron later recounted. "I did what I could to save the lives of the boys." Thompson arranged for his passage to Richmond "and supplied the funds."

When he arrived in the Southern capital on February 1, he immediately went to see Judah Benjamin. The Confederate secretary of state told him that another messenger—Sarah Slater—had just left with her copy of the dispatches, but he was to be "entrusted with duplicates as a second messenger" in order to "assure the safe delivery of the papers." Cameron departed for Canada on February 4, just a few days behind Slater. He never disclosed his route, although according to Edward Sowles, the lawyer representing the St. Albans banks, he passed through the Vermont town dressed as a Roman Catholic priest, "accompanied by two women dressed in the robes of nuns."

Sarah Slater, meanwhile, had a smooth journey. Relying on a network of safe houses and sympathizers, she advanced along the well-travelled route that Confederates used to move across enemy lines: from Richmond, across the Rappahannock River, until arriving at a signal corps camp and waiting for safe passage into Washington. Her seasoned guide was "one of the most effective spies along the Potomac" named Gus Howell. He accompanied her to New York until she was on a Montreal-bound train.

In the dead of a frigid winter night on February 15, Slater went to the fashionable St. Lawrence Hall, the preferred Confederate hangout not far from the train station. It was 3 a.m. The registry shows her tidy, small signature as "Mrs. N. Slater, New York"—one of the few times she would use her real name. There was no risk. She could easily pass herself off as a French-speaking tourist from a neighbouring state. No doubt exhausted, she settled into Room 138.

It had taken her just over two weeks to make it to the Confederate North.

29.

'TOO GREAT A RISK'

The day before Sarah Slater checked into the St. Lawrence Hall, Jacob Thompson had arrived at the same Montreal hotel for what must have been serious business: he took over no fewer than four rooms. Three of them—numbers 107, 144 and 150—were not far from Slater's. There is no record of any meeting between the courier and the head of the Confederates' secret services in Canada, but it seems inconceivable that the two of them—both in town as the St. Albans trial was unfolding—would not have talked or at the very least crossed paths.

Thompson had been asked by his Richmond superiors to leave the Canadian operations in the hands of his successor, Edwin Gray Lee. But to his credit, Thompson hung on, determined to help the men he had sent on missions who were now facing death in American prisons. His other courier, Samuel Davis, was scheduled to be hanged on Johnson's Island—the same prison Thompson had tried so hard to liberate. At Fort Lafayette, John Yates Beall, who had tried to capture a Union gunship, and Robert Cobb Kennedy, who had helped set the fires in New York, also faced imminent execution.

"It was now Colonel Thompson's determination to stand by them to the bitter end," remarked John Headley. A veteran of Washington's backroom politics but a military amateur, Thompson had never been that effective directing Confederate soldiers and spies from Canada. As a cabinet minister in the years before the war, though, he had known Lincoln. Now was the time to exercise whatever diplomatic muscle he could bring to bear.

On February 2 he penned a long letter beseeching Lincoln to intervene on Davis's behalf.

"This young man's life is in your hands," Thompson pleaded. "You have a right to retain him as a prisoner of war, but I declare on my honour, he is not a spy." Lincoln was persuaded and commuted Davis's death sentence to imprisonment until the end of the war.

Beall, the man whose life Davis had been trying to save with the documents he was carrying from Richmond, was not as fortunate. On February 8, the military court found him guilty on all charges, condemning him to death. On February 24, he died on the gallows, his status as a Confederate hero enshrined when his memoirs were issued soon after by prominent Montreal publisher John Lovell, who did a booming business printing Confederate propaganda. On its front page, the *Gazette* reprinted a *Richmond Examiner* commentary promising that Beall "will be revered as a martyr" and calling for the hanging "of any Yankee officers . . . who might be found." Then in its own words, the *Gazette* later praised "the impetuous daring warrior" for the "sincerity of belief in the rightfulness of the cause for which he died."

Three days after Beall's execution, Robert Cobb Kennedy's trial in front of a military tribunal for his role in the arson attack on New York wrapped up. To no one's surprise, it also ended with a guilty verdict and a death sentence. Kennedy appealed, hoping that he would escape Beall's fate.

———

The same hope was shared by Bennett Young and the rest of his St. Albans gang.

When their trial resumed in early February, their strategy included delays and outright fabrications. "I knew nothing of the St. Albans raid or any other raid," George Sanders openly lied to the court on February 11—presumably with a straight face—even though his son in his testimony that same day admitted to being a conduit for some of the money. And Sanders himself from the start of the escapade had been all over the newspapers claiming credit for the raid as the start of a series of cross-border attacks.

Fortunately for Young and his men, around the same time Sanders was spinning his tales, Sarah Slater had made it safely to Montreal with her precious cargo of Confederate documents for their defence. What happened next, as is often the case with Slater, is shrouded in more myth and mystery than provable fact. "After only a few hours' sleep, Sarah, heavily veiled, entered the Montreal courtroom, clutching a large envelope in her hand," H. Donald Winkler wrote in his book *Stealing Secrets*.

The image of a veiled agent walking into court with the official papers from Richmond to rescue her Confederate comrades is exciting but probably exaggerated. Slater almost certainly did deliver the military papers that she had smuggled across the border to the lawyers. But in a twist, it was the second, backup courier, not Slater, who presented the documents in public court. Stephen Cameron had left Richmond later than Slater, but they arrived in Montreal around the same time. According to the court transcript, on February 15, it was Cameron who presented the judge with the official papers from Richmond, including muster rolls showing the regiments to which the men had been assigned. The secretary of state, Judah Benjamin himself, Cameron told the judge, "had sent the orders under which the young men had acted, previous to their making the raid."

It was all a bit of legal legerdemain. The raiders had been acting under the direction not of Richmond but of Clement Clay and George Sanders in Canada. By Cameron's own account, Benjamin produced the officially stamped papers only in February, almost four months after the bank robberies. In the conspiracy trials after Lincoln's assassination, Cameron was asked under oath if, as alleged, he had talked with his colleagues about the documents being "cooked up."

"The papers I carried were genuine," he answered, skirting around the question. The papers he brought from Richmond may have been genuinely official, but they were also "cooked up" after the fact. The Confederates would have to wait a few weeks to see if the judge agreed that the documents measured up to scrutiny.

Cameron's testimony in open court may have been a bold legal gambit, but it was foolish spycraft. He could hardly continue to be an effective secret courier having just admitted as much in public. Perhaps that is why the more cautious Sarah Slater stayed in the background in order to continue her work in the shadows. Confederate John Headley extolled Slater's "heroic interest," praising her as a "devotee of the South" for risking her life to bring the "necessary certified papers, well concealed," all the way from Richmond, even if they were not used in court. Having proven her worth, Slater intended to keep spying.

In his memoirs written forty years later, Headley also contributed to another myth about Slater and the St. Albans raiders. "[A] widow only 24 years old, employed by the Confederate Government for secret service in the Northern States, had come to Montreal and called on the prisoners at the jail," he recounted. "The prisoners never met this lady before or after her visits to the jail at Montreal. One of the survivors secured her photograph at the jail, but . . . her name is forgotten." Headley forgot more than her name. Slater was neither a widow nor twenty-four years old. He published a blurry photo of a petite young woman in his book. Like Slater, she is dark-haired, but she looks older and more proper than pretty; it also seems unlikely that as a secret courier she would let a picture of herself circulate in a Montreal jail.

Nevertheless, the saga of Sarah Slater had entered the lore of the South. "The woman's name was very conspicuous in Montreal during the trial of the St. Albans raiders," Union investigators were later told, "[a]s one of those who went to Richmond to help the raiders in their trial." Her mission to Montreal accomplished, Slater returned by train to New York, where she would meet a dashing young man who over the next two months would figure prominently in her life—and in the Confederate plots against President Lincoln.

———

John Harrison Surratt was a friend of John Wilkes Booth who would become closely entangled in Booth's conspiracies. Nowhere near as famous as the popular actor, he was almost as handsome, with wavy

dark hair, thick eyebrows and a well-trimmed goatee. "Tall, erect, slender and boyish," one acquaintance recalled. "His nose was sharp, thin
and aquiline; his face bore an unusually keen and shrewd expression."

He was born in Washington, DC, to a hard-drinking father and a
strict mother, Mary. At age fifteen, he was dispatched to a Roman
Catholic seminary. It was "severe, and the discipline rigid," and Surratt
was "a very orderly student," recalled a fellow classmate, Louis J.
Weichmann. "Surratt was a pronounced friend of the Southern cause
from the start," Weichmann explained, so it was hardly a surprise
when Surratt the seminarian plunged into action when what he called
the "stirring events" of the Civil War started just a day shy of his sev-
enteenth birthday.

Surratt began by spying in his teens: "I . . . was mostly engaged in
sending information regarding the movements of the United States
army stationed in Washington and elsewhere." He also became one of
the most successful couriers, smuggling secret military messages through
enemy lines and delighting in fooling what he saw as the incompetent
Union forces. "I devised various ways to carry the dispatches—sometimes in the heel of my boots, sometimes between the planks of the
buggy," he said. "I confess that never in my life did I come across
a more stupid set of detectives than those generally employed by the
U.S. government."

"It was a fascinating life to me," Surratt declared. "It seemed as if I
could not do too much or run too great a risk." Surratt's service to the
Confederacy was a family affair. The Surratts ran a tavern and stage-
coach stop with overnight lodging in a crossroads community in
Maryland that came to be known as Surrattsville, about a dozen miles
south of Washington. Conveniently located on the crossroads that led
from the capital south to Richmond or north to Canada, the Surratt
tavern became a "resort for blockade runners, spies . . . a regular secession headquarters," as Weichmann—who befriended the Surratt family
and visited their home—aptly described it.

When his father died in 1862, Surratt briefly took over his father's
job as a Federal postmaster—an ironic posting for a Confederate

courier—but was fired when his Southern sympathies became known. Late in 1864, his mother moved to a three-storey townhouse on H Street in Washington, and turned it into a boarding house. It too would become a frequent resting and meeting place for conspirators, including Sarah Slater and John Wilkes Booth.

When the Confederates needed someone to meet Slater in New York in February 1865 on her way back from Montreal with "urgent dispatches," John Surratt was the ideal man for the job. The dashing young Surratt, who had been working for the Confederacy since the start of the war, met up with one of the South's newest and most beautiful spies; it was the beginning of a close relationship. The two connected in New York and travelled together to Washington, arriving at Mary Surratt's boarding house on February 22.

Slater piqued the interest of Louis Weichmann, who by now was a regular boarder there. Weichmann seemed to straddle both sides of the war: he worked as a clerk in the Department of War in Washington, but his presence at the Surratt house kept him in constant touch with many of the Lincoln conspirators. He would become a key prosecution witness in the assassination trials.

"The woman was rather diminutive in height, but very active and sprightly in all her movements. She wore . . . a kind of short veil, covering the face only as far as the chin," Weichmann later recalled in his memoirs. "I did not succeed in seeing her face at all, and I believe that it was intended that I should not." Weichmann helped the mysterious woman out of the carriage and brought her trunk—"a very small affair"—into the house. He was also asked to give up his room for her, and he obliged.

Intrigued, Weichmann pushed Mary Surratt for more details later, when they sat in the dining room. She let on that Slater was from North Carolina, spoke French, "and that she was a blockade-runner, or bearer of despatches." By the next morning the lady in the veil was gone, though she did leave the fascinated Weichmann with a ghostly reminder of her presence, "a delicate pair of ladies' shoes" he found in his closet.

With the latest dispatches from Montreal in hand, Slater rode off towards the Potomac and, with the help of her escorts, was ferried across the river and eventually back to Richmond. She did not stay long in the Confederate capital, no more than a few days. The Richmond leaders had more secret—and apparently urgent—messages for her to carry back to the rebels in Montreal for her second mission to Canada. Civil War expert James O. Hall noted that "authorities in Washington later suspected that she was carrying instructions to trigger Booth's plot to assassinate Lincoln."

Perhaps, but their contents remain a mystery to this day. There is good reason to believe that, whatever other orders Slater may have been carrying, some of her messages dealt with the internal power struggle within the Confederate Secret Service in Canada—given the timing of her stay in Montreal in early March. Her visit to Canada coincided with the arrival at the St. Lawrence Hall on March 11 of General Edwin Lee, the man Richmond had sent to take over from Jacob Thompson. Lee was on much better terms with Richmond than his predecessor. He boasted, quite accurately, that he knew "most of the members of the Confederate States government and . . . had frequent, official intercourse with them."

On March 17, 1865, the day Slater signed in at the hotel, Lee recorded in his diary that Thompson "read me his dispatches from Richmond . . . extremely interesting news." Almost certainly, these were some of the dispatches Slater had carried. Then, on March 22, Lee noted that he had "fixed up and sent off my letter" to his secretary of state, Judah Benjamin. In an apparent reference to Sarah Slater, he added that he needed "to get the messenger off. I pray she may go safely."

This time, Slater would have to make it back from Montreal to the United States without any help from her new-found protector John Surratt. He was somewhat preoccupied at the time. Alongside his good friend John Wilkes Booth, Surratt had a president to kidnap.

30.

'KIDNAP PRESIDENT LINCOLN!'

In the pouring rain, they gathered by the tens of thousands at the Capitol building in Washington, eager to celebrate with the president who had led them through four years of unimaginable conflict and hardship.

The inclement weather on Inauguration Day, March 4, 1865, did little to dampen people's high spirits. As Lincoln settled into his second term in office, victory for his bleeding Union seemed, if not assured, then at least on the horizon. His armies were rampaging through South Carolina, the first state to secede, and were laying siege to Petersburg, Virginia, just twenty miles from the Confederate capital of Richmond. Fittingly, in the crowd that day in Washington were many Black soldiers from the Colored Troops that Lincoln's administration had set up a year ago. Once hesitant to confront the abolition of slavery, Lincoln now made it central to the battle. "One-eighth of the whole population were colored slaves," he told his supporters. "These slaves constituted a peculiar and powerful interest. All knew that this interest was somehow the cause of the war."

Despite the hatreds that had torn apart his country, Lincoln chose to be magnanimous towards his enemies, ending his speech with ringing words that have since gone down in history. "With malice toward none, with charity for all, with firmness in the right as God gives us to see the right," the President declared, "let us strive on to finish the work we are in, to bind up the nation's wounds."

But many in the country—and at least one man in the crowd—were not ready to bind wounds, much less forsake malice just yet. John Wilkes Booth stood not far from the President that day. "What an excellent chance I had to kill the President, if I had wished, on Inauguration Day!" he later boasted to a friend. At that moment in March, at least, killing was not Booth's immediate plan; kidnapping the President was.

————

Booth had begun seriously thinking about kidnapping the President as far back as the previous September, when he had recruited his two good friends, Samuel Arnold and Michael O'Laughlen, in Baltimore. His visit to Montreal the following month was crucial to solidifying the plot. It gave him money, encouragement from hard-liners like George Sanders, and helpful letters of introduction from Patrick Martin to the Confederate underground in Maryland.

Just three weeks after he had returned from Canada, the urgency of a kidnap attempt was obviously at the top of his mind. "My love . . . is for the South alone," he wrote. "Nor do I deem it a dishonor in attempting to make for her a prisoner of this man to whom she owes so much misery." Booth travelled to Maryland, using the letters from Martin to meet with Dr. Samuel Mudd, a well-connected Confederate sympathizer in the region.

On December 23, 1864, two days before Christmas, Mudd and Booth were walking in Washington when the doctor caught sight of a man he knew well—John Surratt, accompanied by Louis Weichmann. Surratt was just the kind of person Booth was looking for: a Confederate agent who knew the back roads and river crossings of Maryland and Virginia and had close ties to the underground Confederate network.

"I was introduced to John Wilkes Booth, who, I was given to understand, wished to know something about the main avenues leading from Washington to the Potomac," Surratt recounted later.

The four men went to Booth's room at the National Hotel. Booth huddled over a table with Surratt. The ever-curious Weichmann watched out of earshot as Booth drew lines on a piece of paper and talked animatedly. Booth told Surratt he would divulge his plans only if he promised secrecy. "I will do nothing of the kind," Surratt protested, adamant that such a vow was unnecessary. "You know well I am a Southern man. If you cannot trust me, we will separate."

Booth relented. "I will confide my plans to you; but before doing so I will make known to you the motives that actuate me," he said. Then he cautiously explained the dire situation with respect to Southern prisoners—the same dilemma that had motivated Confederates in Canada to launch multiple attempts to free them. "In the Northern prisons are many thousands of our men whom the United States Government refuses to exchange," Booth explained. "Aside from the great suffering they are compelled to undergo, we are sadly in want of them as soldiers . . . I have a proposition to submit to you, which I think if we can carry out will bring about the desired exchange."

There was what Surratt later described as "a long and ominous silence" until Surratt finally broke it by asking: "Well, Sir, what is your proposition?"

Booth sat quiet for a while, then stood up to look under the bed, in the closet, behind the doorway and along the hotel corridor before saying: "We will have to be careful; walls have ears." He then drew his chair close to Surratt and in a whisper said he intended to capture Lincoln and carry him off to Richmond.

"Kidnap President Lincoln!" Surratt exclaimed.

Years later, Surratt insisted he was initially shocked by Booth's plan. "I stood aghast at the proposition, and looked upon it as a foolhardy undertaking," he said. "To think of successfully seizing Mr. Lincoln in the capital of the United States surrounded by thousands of his soldiers, and carrying him off to Richmond, looked to me like a foolish idea."

Surratt claimed he told Booth as much, but he was gradually won over as the charismatic Booth divulged the minute details of the proposed capture, down to "the parts to be performed by the actors in the performance."

"I was amazed—thunderstruck—and in fact, I might also say, frightened at the unparalleled audacity of this scheme," Surratt recalled. "After two days' reflection, I told him I was willing."

In his telling, Surratt tried to pass himself off as a reluctant recruit, but in truth he was central to the operation. Surratt began putting together the team, starting with his friend David Herold. Weichmann described him accurately as an "excellent horseman, a good pistol shot" who knew "all the secret recesses and hiding places" in Maryland. His job at a pharmacy also offered access to chloroform to disable a kidnap victim.

By mid-January, Surratt—with money provided by Booth—purchased a boat to sneak the captured president across the Potomac and had signed up George Atzerodt, one of the most experienced river navigators. On January 21, Surratt travelled to Baltimore to rope in Lewis Powell, a strapping six-foot-two-inch former soldier who would be the team's muscle man. At Mary Surratt's H Street boarding house, Louis Weichmann remarked on his friend's new-found sense of urgency. "Surratt, in fact, at this time, was continually on the go and away from his home much of the time," he wrote. "He always appeared to have plenty of money and had the air and actions of a man thoroughly preoccupied with important business affairs." Indeed, Surratt was growing close enough to Booth that in February he joined the actor for a warm and friendly visit at the New York house of Booth's brother Edwin. It was also during that New York trip that Surratt, on February 22, met up for the first time with Sarah Slater, who was returning from one of her courier missions to Montreal. Surratt escorted Slater back to Washington, where she stayed overnight at his mother's rooming house, and then he arranged for his fellow plotter George Atzerodt to sneak her across the Potomac to Richmond. Surratt stayed in Washington to help Booth finalize the attack on the President.

On the evening of March 15, 1865, Surratt, Booth and the five other conspirators met at an upscale restaurant on Pennsylvania Avenue run by Charles Gautier. Gautier had come to America with his wife and daughters from France via Quebec, establishing a fine eatery with white marble counters, elaborate wallpaper and a gaslight chandelier. The conspirators consumed copious amounts of oysters, champagne and whisky while they talked—and argued—until the early hours of the morning. The original plan had been to try to nab Lincoln on one of his frequent trips to the Soldiers' Home, the President's summer residence located a few miles from the White House. Unexpectedly, that night Booth announced to his team that he wanted instead to grab Lincoln while he was attending a play at Ford's Theatre. The rest of the gang objected, quite rightly fearing that grabbing the President and getting him away in a crowded theatre would be much more difficult and dangerous.

Tensions mounted when Booth seemed to suggest that if all else failed, killing the President was always an option. The actor stood up and banged his fist on the table. "Well, gentlemen, if the worst comes to the worst, I shall know what to do." That prompted harsh words and threats, according to Surratt, with one member exclaiming: "If I understand you to intimate anything more than the capture of Mr. Lincoln I for one will bid you goodbye."

Everyone agreed and the men stood up to leave, putting on their hats. Probably sensing that he had pushed things too far, Booth apologized, saying that he "had drank too much champagne." "After some difficulty everything was amicably arranged," Surratt said, "and we separated at 5 o'clock in the morning."

In the early hours of March 16, an exhausted Surratt made his way back to his mother's boarding house, where later that day he likely saw Sarah Slater once again. She was passing through Washington on her way to Montreal. She stayed only one night, but Surratt would have more time to spend with her when she returned within a week—and by then he no doubt hoped he would have quite the tale to share with her.

———

On Saturday, March 17, Surratt and the other conspirators got sudden word from Booth that his plans had changed yet again. Booth had learned that the President would be travelling that day on a quiet road to attend a play for Union veterans at the Campbell Military Hospital. Surratt later recounted with pride how quickly he and the gang reacted to the news from their leader Booth: "The report only reached us about three quarters of an hour before the time appointed, but so perfect was our communication that we were instantly in our saddles on the way to the hospital."

Surratt—who as the best rider was assigned to leap into the President's carriage and take control of the horses—was certain with speed and surprise they could pull it off. What's more, they knew the countryside, and thanks to the contacts Booth had picked up in Montreal, they had a network of sympathizers along the route. But they waited for their prey in vain—Lincoln never showed. The plotters had no choice but to scurry away. Lincoln had made a last-minute change in his schedule, cancelling his trip to see the play and instead staying in Washington to address Union troops from the balcony of the National Hotel—the same hotel where Booth had been staying.

Their plot foiled, the conspirators took a break to watch their leader perform on a stage where success was more certain. Surratt—along with Weichmann, Atzerodt and Herold—went to Ford's Theatre to take in a play starring John Wilkes Booth, who had arranged for tickets for his friends. Booth portrayed the villain so well that the *New York Times* marvelled at how he "fills the centre of the picture, dealing out destruction to all who cross his path . . . reveling in the accumulation of horrors." Weichmann, perhaps revising history if not his memory, would insist that he was struck that night by Booth's "malevolent expression . . . the fierce glare and ugly roll of his eyes."

Off stage, Booth was busy rewriting the script for his plans to deal with the president he had despised for so long. Despite the failure of the kidnap plot against Lincoln that he had carefully orchestrated for half a year, Booth was not despondent. He was determined. "For six months we had worked to capture," Booth wrote, "but our cause being almost lost, something decisive and great must be done." Over the next twenty-nine days, he would finalize his plan to do just that.

John Surratt's account of that fateful restaurant meeting came in a public lecture five years after Lincoln's assassination. He maintained that while he was all in for what he had called the "foolhardy undertaking" of kidnapping the President, he had nothing to do with any plot to kill him. "Such a thing as the assassination of Mr. Lincoln I never heard spoken of by any of the party," he claimed. "Never!"

Surratt was being disingenuous at best. He was fooling himself if he thought any attempt to snatch the President from a speeding carriage and then sneak him all the way to Richmond was not likely to cause Lincoln serious injury if not lead to his death. His claim that he had "never heard spoken" any talk of assassination was belied by his own account that Booth had indeed raised that distinct possibility over drinks at the restaurant. Moreover, the team that Surratt had helped put together for Booth—almost to a man—was the same team that would strike on assassination day less than a month later. After the failed kidnap attempt, Surratt had told the gang to hide some of their weapons at the Surratt tavern, which is precisely where a fugitive Booth would retrieve them after killing the President.

Perhaps most importantly, Surratt bore at least an indirect responsibility for Lincoln's eventual murder by Booth: had he or any of the other conspirators gone to the authorities to alert them about the kidnapping plot, Booth would have been arrested and the assassination would never have taken place. But Surratt, of course, was not about to betray his close friend. And to his dying day, Surratt was proud of the role he played in trying to capture Abraham Lincoln. "Rash, perhaps foolish, but honorable," he later said. "I was led on by a sincere desire to assist the South in gaining her independence. I had no hesitation in taking part in anything . . . that might tend toward the accomplishment of that object."

So it is not surprising that, within days of the kidnap attempt, Surratt and Booth—along with Sarah Slater—were back together again, engaging in new intrigues. Around March 22, Slater was in New York carrying messages for Richmond from Montreal. John Wilkes Booth had also arrived in New York that morning, and one of his most respected biographers, Michael Kaufmann, surmises that this time he may have been the one who accompanied Slater back to Washington.

When she arrived in the capital on March 25, Slater—uncharacteristically—did not stay at the Surratt boarding house on H Street. "She stopped at the National Hotel," according to George Azterodt. That was where Booth almost always stayed when in Washington, the implication being that Slater shared the same hotel with the actor, if not his room. Like several of the other men in that circle, Azterodt seemed a bit taken by Slater. In a later confession, he described her as "good looking and well dressed. Black hair and eyes, round face."

"Mrs. Slater went with Booth a good deal," he reported.

Azterodt was the only witness to directly tie Slater to Booth. His confessions were rambling and confused; he called Slater by two other names (which could have been her aliases).

Still, his stories cannot be dismissed. He had no reason to lie about her and Booth—it did not help his own case or provide an alibi for him. Given Slater's ties to John Surratt, a connection to Booth was quite plausible. Surratt had just come back from working closely with his good friend to kidnap Lincoln. It seems inconceivable that he would not have talked about these exploits with his fellow courier, a woman he was getting to know better with each mission they shared.

It had been just three hectic months since Slater had signed up to be a courier, but she had travelled a lot more than the seven-hundred-mile journey each way on her missions. The wife of a Connecticut dancing instructor had become a Confederate agent who rubbed shoulders with some of the Confederate leaders in Montreal and Richmond and now was spending time with top conspirators such as Booth and Surratt.

Weichmann could sense that his long-time friend John Surratt was on edge. He wrote to a priest at the Catholic college they had both attended, telling him that Surratt was about to embark on a "perilous trip." The war was careening towards its final days. Booth was busy preparing for his final performance—and Surratt and Slater still had one last mission to Canada ahead of them.

31.

'HE WAS DONE PLAYING'

As the only New York arsonist to be publicly identified—never mind arrested—Robert Cobb Kennedy became somewhat of an outlaw celebrity as he awaited his execution in late March 1865. The prisoner displayed "a strange mixture of bravado, recklessness, timidity, hopefulness, malignity and goodness of heart," the *New York Times* reported. He would curse and rail against the "Yanks" but then listen attentively to a visiting pastor, before penning angry letters and asking for more cigarettes and whisky.

His trial before a military court lasted twenty-three days and was covered extensively, if at times sensationally. "Evidently a keen-witted, desperate man, he combines the cunning and the enthusiasm of a fanatic," the *Times* wrote. The military judges were determined to make an example of someone they saw as a callous terrorist. "The attempt to set fire to the city of New York is one of the greatest atrocities of the age," they ruled with judicial hyperbole as they handed down a death sentence. "There is nothing in the annals of barbarism which evinces greater vindictiveness."

The day before Kennedy's execution, the *New York Times* reporter who had followed the case so closely visited his cell. The doomed Confederate, rather remarkably, opened up and made a full confession to the *Times* about his role in the New York fires. "We only wanted to let the people of the North understand that there are two sides to war," he explained, "and that they can't be rolling in wealth and comfort, while we in the South are bearing all the hardships and privations." His guilt off his chest, Kennedy spent his last night on earth writing letters, smoking furiously and downing whisky "for his faintness." The next morning, Saturday, March 25, he dressed himself in Confederate grey, ate "a hearty breakfast" and walked slowly to the gallows. As the Union colonel read the charges, Kennedy kept interrupting. "It's a damned lie," he exclaimed. "This is a judicial cowardly murder."

The 29-year-old Kentuckian who had spent the final year of his life fighting from Canada would be the last Confederate executed during the Civil War.

———

Kennedy's hanging sent a message to the Southern soldiers operating out of Canada that the consequences of getting caught were deadly serious. Several of the St. Albans raiders were still on the run in Canada and desperate to get back to the Confederacy safely.

In early 1865, former Montreal chief of police Lamothe received a note from Confederate banker John Porterfield asking him to assist several St. Albans escapees. And so Lamothe hatched a plan. His thoughts and actions are revealed in a remarkable sixty-eight-page handwritten letter to his son. On the surface it was an angry condemnation of what he called "all the dirt and dishonesty" hurled at him, but what it amounted to was a confession.

Lamothe recounted how he told the fugitives to secure snowshoes, sleds, warm clothes and plenty of food, then directed them to cross the frozen St. Lawrence River and head to Lévis, across from Quebec City. Bad weather forced the men back. "You cannot abandon us," they pleaded. So, in the spring, Lamothe tried again. With funds from the Confederates, he bought a schooner named the *Canadian Eagle*, stocking it with food, guns and ammunition. Across rough waters, he guided the four escapees, impressed by how the Confederate fugitives "tried hard to be happy and full of courage."

It was, to say the least, shockingly illegal activity for a former chief of police of Canada's largest city. Yet he boasted about how, during his operation to smuggle the Confederates out of Canada, there were times he had to hide from police. Once, when he came across some of his own former officers on the hunt for the raiders, he lied and convinced them "it would be absurd for me to get involved with this affair."

Lamothe's actions during the trial in late 1864 while he was still police chief were dubious ethically and legally, but arguably he carried them out while under instructions from or in concert with the presiding judge and the defendants' lawyers. Now, as a civilian, he had consciously chosen to help accused criminals. "I had a lot of sympathy for the people of the South," he explained. "I admired their bravery and chivalry. All the preferences of my heart was for them."

By April, the Confederates under Lamothe's care had made it to Nova Scotia, and from there they would eventually reach safety in the slave South. Lamothe's role as a Confederate smuggler remained hidden in his family's personal papers for decades; he was never charged with anything to do with the escape of the fugitives.

―――――

Bennett Young and the four other raiders still in jail and on trial in Montreal must have been jealous of their comrades' successful escape. After many fits and starts, their case resumed in Montreal on March 21 before Justice James Smith. By now, the raiders were minor celebrities; crowds packed the courtroom as well as the corridor and the stairs outside, and, the newspapers reported, there were "very many ladies." John C. Abbott, still dean of the law faculty at McGill University, once again took up the defence of the Confederates. Talking to a reporter, George Sanders was confident: "There was plenty of money, [he] remarked, his eyes skewedly twinkling, . . . to pay for all law expenses." Bernard Devlin, who had successfully advocated for the removal of the controversial Montreal police chief, returned to do battle on behalf of the Canadian and American governments to get the men extradited as common criminals.

The next six days in court saw many testy exchanges between the two legal combatants. Devlin scorned the attempts to "elevate a daring act of robbery to the dignity of a manly deed of warfare." Abbott did exactly that, insisting that Young and his men were "performing a lawful warlike exploit." Echoing Confederate propaganda, he went so far as to claim that the raid was "more peacefully warlike" compared with the far worse crimes of war committed by Lincoln's forces. "I can find the record . . . of a thousand times worse acts than the St. Albans raid, committed in a thousand instances in the South, by Federal troops."

"That is beside the question!" an outraged Devlin responded.

Devlin also tried to undermine what he dismissed as the "unofficial and inauthentic" orders from Richmond sanctioning the raid and delivered with so much difficultly by the couriers. They had been written "long after the raid was committed," Devlin rightly pointed out, tainting them "with so much suspicion." But it was Abbott who had the last word. In his closing argument, he drew a "distinction between ordinary crimes and those of a political character . . . arising out of a civil war." He shrewdly noted that Lincoln's cabinet ministers and his generals themselves had denounced the St. Albans attackers not as common thieves but as "rebel men" and "rebel marauders." Abbott called on the judge to issue a verdict "dictated by justice, tempered by mercy."

Bennett Young and his band got the mercy they wanted, though perhaps at the expense of justice. It took two days for Smith to read his verdict, though he somehow never found time to mention that one civilian in St. Albans had been shot dead by Young's gang. He noted there was no doubt the men had stolen the money and pillaged the town but questioned "whether the prisoners are really robbers." On the contrary, he concluded that the testimony "established beyond controversy by the evidence" that they were indeed legitimate "soldiers in the Confederate army" and therefore had not violated any Canadian laws. In a striking example of dubious moral equivalence, he compared the fate of Young and his men to that of a fugitive slave in Canada fighting extradition for killing someone in defence of freedom. Both the slave and the Confederate rebels, he argued, were worthy of Canada's protection. He dismissed the case against all the accused. Cheers erupted in the courtroom, "which the authorities were unable to quell," and the celebrations continued down the stairs and outside into the street.

Devlin was enraged. "It was humiliating to the last degree to be obliged to listen to such statements," he declared. "Was it possible that the causes of law and order have no friends, in this city, that we are ruled by a mob?" The *Globe* echoed that fury, reprinting a commentary from the British papers that "such a decision meant that Canada was a lawless neighbour to be shunned." The Americans, predictably, were even more incensed. "Judge Smith discharged the prisoners and declared the raid justifiable and even commendable," the US consul in Montreal, John Potter, told Washington. The ruling, he warned, "was cheered most vociferously both in the courtroom and in the street."

The American newspapers said publicly what Lincoln and his officials must have been thinking. "Another Canadian Justice has decided that the St Albans burglars were guiltless," the *New York Times* sneered, noting sarcastically that Smith was as bad as "the notorious Coursol." "The St Albans raiders have been tried before a knave [and] were now . . . before a fool," the paper complained. "This is nonsense that is not even amusing."

To add monetary insult to legal injury, Canada agreed to use government money to reimburse the St. Albans banks for the $88,000 in stolen loot never retrieved. In a desperate attempt to save face, the Canadian government immediately laid new charges against Young and his men under a revised Neutrality Act and they were shipped to Toronto for yet another trial in the first week of April. But the results were the same. When the charges were dropped against all the men except Bennett Young, "the decision was received with loud applause," the *Globe* reported. George Taylor Denison, in what an appreciative Young described as "an act of friendship," put up $10,000 for his bail.

Young made his way out of the court "amid great enthusiasm." All charges against him were eventually dropped once the war was over. His raid into a Vermont town had made him famous—and he would build on his Canadian escapade to become a Confederate hero for decades to come.

———

Sarah Slater no doubt felt some relief when she heard the news that the St. Albans raiders—the men she had been dispatched to save on her first known mission to Canada—had escaped any punishment. But she had little time to revel in that rare victory for the South. She was too busy shuttling back and forth between Montreal and Richmond.

As March drew to a close, she was joined once again by John Surratt as her escort on her courier expeditions. "John Surratt began to be a bird of passage, riding to and from Montreal to Richmond," Louis Weichmann recalled. He remembered one day that March looking out the dining room window at the Surratt boarding house in Washington and seeing Surratt, his mother and Slater heading off in a carriage led by two white horses on yet another mission.

It was at the family tavern in Surrattsville that the travellers learned some distressing news: Gus Howell, Slater's frequent escort, had been arrested there the night before by Federal troops. If the authorities had waited a little longer, they likely would have been able to nab Slater and seize the secret dispatches she was carrying. In the end, after overnighting in Port Tobacco, Surratt decided he himself would accompany the intriguing woman the rest of the way to Richmond. He sent a friend back to Washington with the horses, which were owned by John Wilkes Booth. "As business will detain me for a few days in the country, I thought I would send your team back," he wrote to the livery owner on March 26. "If Mr. Booth should want my horses, let him have them but no one else."

Then Surratt added a more personal note: "I should have liked to keep the horses for several days but it is too expensive—especially as I have 'woman on the brain' and may be away for a week or so."

John Surratt was apparently falling for the lady in the veil.

———

As Slater and Surratt neared Fredericksburg, Virginia, a singularly dark incident was alleged to have taken place. The story comes from Dr. Lewis McMillan, a Canadian surgeon who had befriended Surratt in Montreal and later recounted what the Confederate man had told him. "After a great deal of trouble, they managed to cross the Potomac," McMillan later told a court when John Surratt stood trial for his role in the Lincoln assassination in 1867. "As they were drawn along, they saw some men coming towards them—five or six if I recollect right. They ascertained that these men were Union prisoners, or Union soldiers escaped from southern prisons."

"Let's shoot the damned Yankee soldiers," Sarah Slater called out.

"She had hardly said the word when they all drew their revolvers and shot them, and went right along, paying no more attention to them," McMillan testified.

———

By March 29, Surratt and Slater had arrived in the Confederate capital. They found Richmond teetering on collapse. That same day, President Jefferson Davis gave his wife Varina a pistol and taught her how to load and fire it before sending her and their four children on an escape route that would eventually bring them to Canada.

No sooner had Surratt checked into the popular Spotswood Hotel than he was told secretary of state Judah Benjamin wanted to see him— an indication of how important he and Slater were to the Confederate spy network. "He asked me if I would carry some dispatches to Canada for him," Surratt recounted. "I replied 'yes.' That evening he gave me the dispatches and $200 in gold with which to pay my way to Canada."

There is conflicting evidence about whether Slater attended that meeting, but it is quite possible considering she was the one who had messages from Montreal with her. The couple—whether they were a romantic pair or not, they certainly were a spy team—were seen together. A Confederate official later reported that Surratt was accompanied by a female "professional blockade runner." Slater and Surratt did not stay long in the besieged city; they left Richmond together on Saturday, April 1, for what would be their final mission to Montreal.

On Sunday, Davis, along with his government and military commanders, fled Richmond. Mobs of desperate Southerners, abandoned and angry, roamed the streets, setting the city ablaze.

On Monday, Federal troops moved in—including Black soldiers from the 36th US Colored Infantry, who helped put out the flames that were consuming the Confederate city. By Tuesday, Abraham Lincoln, almost four years to the day after the Civil War started, was walking through the smouldering ruins of the former secessionist capital. Blacks who had still been enslaved twenty-four hours before—they made up one-third of the city's population—huddled around him. "The colored population," wrote a Black journalist covering the event, "was wild with excitement."

"You are free—free as air," the President told them. "You can cast off the name of slave and trample upon it. It will come to you no more."

Back in Montreal, Edwin Lee poured out his grief into his diary: "First news of Fall of Richmond! God help us."

The Confederacy was in its dying days.

But its leaders—and their trusted spies and couriers—had not given up. Perhaps the Canadian connection still held out some faint possibilities.

———

Slater and Surratt arrived in Washington on April 3 at 4 p.m., just as Richmond fell. Surratt had hidden the money and secret messages Benjamin had given them in—of all places—a book about the life of abolitionist John Brown. On 7th Street in Washington, Surratt bumped into one of the kidnap conspirators—he never identified which one—who asked what had become of their leader, John Wilkes Booth. "I told him . . . that I was then on my way to Canada, and that I had not seen or heard anything of Booth since our separation," Surratt said.

Surratt decided to stay at a hotel after he learned that a Federal detective had been to his mother's boarding house. Still, he dropped by later to meet his friend Louis Weichmann. Weichmann was struck by how flush Surratt was with money, thanks to the twenty gold pieces Benjamin had given him. The two men went out for an oyster supper at a saloon near Pennsylvania Avenue. Then they walked back to Surratt's hotel and Weichmann bade his friend goodbye. "He said he was going to Montreal the next morning and would correspond with me," Weichmann recalled. "That was the final farewell. Little did I realize that we would never speak to one another again in this life."

Early the next morning, on Tuesday, April 4, Surratt and Slater took the train for New York. "Upon arriving in New York, I called at Booth's house," Surratt recounted, "and was told by the servant that he had left that morning suddenly, on the ground of going to Boston to fulfill an engagement at the theater." Booth was performing in Boston on April 5, but not at a theatre. He was possibly there to see his brother Edwin, who was wrapping up a successful engagement at the Boston Theater. One witness later told a newspaper that he saw Booth at Roland Edwards's Pistol Gallery on Green Street, "where Booth practiced pistol firing in various difficult ways such as between his legs, over his shoulder and under his arms."

That evening, Slater joined Surratt on the overnight train to Montreal. They arrived on April 6 at 10:30 a.m., a spring day that must have felt glorious compared with the blustery winter they had faced on earlier missions to Montreal. "I put up at the St. Lawrence Hotel," Surratt said, "registering myself as 'John Harrison' such being my first two names." It appears two rooms were assigned to him that morning—numbers 13 and 50—though one of the rooms, curiously, was vacated that same day. Slater's name—unlike for all her other trips—does not appear in the registry, indicating she either stayed for the first time in another hotel (which was unlikely) or shared one of the rooms Surratt had booked.

Surratt went straight to see Edwin Lee, who had formally taken over the Confederate operation in Canada from Jacob Thompson, to deliver the dispatches from Richmond to him. Lee's diary entry for that day used the code name "Charley Armstrong" that he had adopted for Surratt: "Letter by Charley from Mr. Benjamin, my last rec'd all safe." In part, the messages from Richmond must have concerned the huge funds the faltering Confederacy still had in Canadian banks. Thompson still had control over the money and Richmond wanted him to hand the fortune over to Lee. "I am unwilling to consent to this arrangement because it will hamper my movements," Thompson said, in essence admitting that with the South collapsing, he wanted to ensure his escape.

Did those secret dispatches contain anything else? Surratt later insisted the contents of the Confederate messages he and Slater had spirited across seven hundred miles were innocuous. "They were only accounts of some money transactions—nothing more or less," he claimed, "despite of the fact that the government had tried to prove that they had relation to the conspiracy to kill Mr. Lincoln." Maybe, but Surratt's activities over the next few days in Montreal certainly suggested he knew something was afoot with Booth, even if he did not have any specific details.

On his second day in the city, he dropped by the tailor shop of John J. Reeves on Notre-Dame Street, just a few steps from his hotel. Reeves—who would soon prove adept at providing his client with more than clothes—fitted Surratt with a new Garibaldi pleated jacket with four buttons down the front and a belt. Stylish, no doubt, but also distinctly un-American; Surratt apparently wanted to blend in as a "Canadian" over the next few fateful days.

He then took in the sights, especially the imposing Notre-Dame Basilica near his hotel in all its spring glory—a far cry from the ashes of Richmond. "Montreal is really a beautiful city and what pleases me more there are a great many pretty girls here," he wrote to a friend on April 10. "I am enjoying myself to my heart's content. Nothing in the wide world to do but visit with the ladies and go to church."

That same day, Surratt set out to take the train from Montreal to New York but turned back once he got to the railway station. Two days later, on April 12, he left the hotel again and this time boarded the 3 p.m. train to New York. Why the back and forth, and why the decision to head back to the States? The best clue comes from Lewis McMillan, the Canadian doctor who would accompany Surratt on his long boat trip to Europe later that year and who testified at his trial. Surratt told him that in the days before the assassination he "received a letter from John Wilkes Booth, dated 'New York,' ordering him immediately to Washington, as it had been necessary to change their plans, and to act promptly," McMillan said. "He told me that he started immediately on the receipt of the letter."

Surratt must have had a pretty good idea what change of plans Booth had in mind. By Surratt's own admission, a month earlier at the Washington restaurant Booth had made clear he was considering killing Lincoln if the kidnap plans fell through. More than anyone else on the planet, Surratt must have had a suspicion, if not a certainty, of what his good friend was planning. Adding to the intrigue, while Surratt was in Montreal in early April, he "had frequent interviews . . . with other noted rebels and villains," according to the spies working for US consul John Potter—including the meddling George Sanders, who, it is worth recalling, spent a lot of time with Booth during his visit to Montreal in the fall.

On the same day that Surratt left Montreal for Washington, back at the Surratt house an increasingly worried Louis Weichmann asked Booth why he was not acting anymore. "He answered he was done playing," Weichmann reported.

Well, not exactly. In three days, John Wilkes Booth would make one final appearance on the theatre stage.

32

'THAT AWFUL TRAGEDY'

Good Friday blessed Washington with blue skies and a little breeze. The lilacs were in full bloom on that April 14, 1865. The country was preparing for a much-needed resurrection after four years of a shattering, draining, gut-wrenching civil war. Five days earlier, the hero of the Confederacy, General Robert E. Lee, had surrendered to the Union army. There would be hardline holdouts in the Deep South and in Canada, and sporadic fighting for many months to come, but essentially the war was over.

Anderson Abbott, who had been serving as a doctor in the Union army for the previous two years, shared in the joyous celebrations that had been going on in the city all week. "The days . . . were devoted to festivities exceeding in brilliancy and grandeur anything I had before witnessed," he recalled. All week long, Washington had been ablaze with bonfires, lanterns and lamps. "Washington was brilliantly illuminated and decorated . . . to give appropriate expression to the intense feeling of joy which thrilled the heart of the nation," he wrote. "People who thronged Pennsylvania Avenue that memorable morning had no thought that a plot was brewing which would turn all that joy and splendor into sorrow's darkest night."

―――――

Dark plots were brewing, in Washington and in Canada. Edwin Lee, the man still running the Confederate operations north of the border, was one of those who refused to concede defeat. "Poor old Richmond and her gallant, glorious defenders have been overwhelmed," he wrote from Quebec on April 11. "No one here pretends to believe now that there is a shadow of doubt of hope for our cause—except myself." Lee was planning yet another attempt at a raid on a Northern prison—this time with John Surratt in charge. "I scoff at the idea of submission and everybody thinks I am a fool," Lee declared in a letter home. "I cannot and will not believe that because Lee has surrendered 22,000 men, that therefore we have no more armies and can wage no more war."

John Wilkes Booth shared Lee's fury and his determination to make one last effort to wage war. On the same day Lee was putting his thoughts on paper in Quebec, Booth was in Washington watching as President Lincoln addressed a large crowd, including many ex-slaves, from the balcony on the north side of the White House.

"We meet this evening, not in sorrow, but in gladness of heart," Lincoln began. He went on to address the thorny issue of what to do with former rebel states such as Louisiana that wanted to rejoin the Union—along with its tens of thousands of liberated enslaved Blacks. Lincoln made a proposal that enraged Booth: "It is also unsatisfactory to some that the elective franchise is not given to the colored man," the President declared.

Booth understood that Lincoln's cautiously phrased words amounted to endorsing the right to vote for Blacks, threatening the very core of the white supremacy that was paramount to him and so many Confederates. After all, Booth had proudly proclaimed that "this country was formed for the white not for the black man," and that slavery was "one of the greatest blessings that God ever bestowed upon a favored nation." Bad enough Lincoln had freed the slaves; now he was considering giving some of them the power of the ballot. As Lincoln spoke, Booth turned to his fellow conspirator Lewis Powell. "That means n----- citizenship. Now, by God, I will put him through," he vowed. "That will be the last speech he will ever make."

———

Three days later, Booth started his Good Friday with a late breakfast at 10 a.m. at the National Hotel—he had been out carousing and drinking the night before. He then walked four blocks to Ford's Theatre to pick up his mail. It was a sign of just how comfortable and at home Booth felt at a theatre where he had performed frequently and knew the owners and staff well. When he learned President Lincoln would be attending the performance that evening, Booth knew he had the perfect time and place to pull off his assassination plot. He was able to case out the presidential box without arousing suspicion.

Shortly after noon, he visited a nearby stable to rent a horse for his getaway. Then he dropped by the boarding house on H Street to see Mary Surratt, who was on her way to the family tavern in Surrattsville. Booth wanted to make sure that the guns John Surratt had stored there after the failed kidnapping would be ready during his escape. Booth was not just targeting a president he despised; as a last-ditch effort to save the Confederacy, he was planning a sort of coup by execution that Friday night, hoping to destabilize the entire government. He had instructed the muscular Lewis Powell to break into the home of Secretary of State William Seward, who was convalescing from a carriage accident, and slay him, while George Atzerodt was to kill Vice President Andrew Johnson.

The same lights throughout the city that had so thrilled Anderson Abbott only served to embitter the assassin. "Everything was bright and splendid. More so in my eyes if it had been a display in a nobler cause," he wrote in a final letter to his mother on April 14. "But so goes the world. Might makes right."

———

Abraham Lincoln was used to people wanting to kill him.

Back in 1861, he had to sneak into Washington on his first trip as president-elect because of a rumoured plot to kill him in Baltimore. "Frequent letters were received warning Mr. Lincoln of assassination, but he never gave a second thought to the mysterious warnings," noted Elizabeth Keckley, Mary Lincoln's dressmaker and friend.

Now, with the Civil War all but over, the ire of his enemies only seemed to mount. In early April, a Union general, concerned about reports of attempts to murder Lincoln, urged the President to take precautions and beef up his personal security. But the President declined. His habit over the years was to take little or no protection with him when he ventured out of the White House, and he was not about to change now. "I cannot bring myself to believe that any human being lives who would do me any harm," he told the worried general.

Lincoln was looking forward to catching a popular comedy at the theatre that evening. First, though, he had to get through the usual array of meetings, briefings, pleas and decisions. Lincoln's business that day— the last one of his life—started and ended with matters pertaining to Jacob Thompson, the Confederate commissioner from Canada. During his cabinet meeting at 11 a.m., Lincoln was not overly concerned when informed that Thompson had been spotted in Maine, attempting to flee to England. "If Jake Thompson is permitted to go through Maine unbeknown to anyone, what's the harm?" the President said.

Around 3 p.m., Jacob Thompson's name came up again. A dispatch from Portland, Maine, revealed that Thompson was expected to arrive there that night and board a Canadian steamer for Liverpool. Lincoln's secretary of war, Edwin Stanton, was itching to have Thompson arrested, but again Lincoln demurred. "I rather think not," he said. "When you have an elephant by the hind leg, and he is trying to run away, it's best to let him run."

The last person the President ever saw on official business was George Ashmun, a congressman from Massachusetts who had been Lincoln's unofficial emissary to Canada early in the war, tasked with trying to patch up the often strained relations with America's northern neighbour. But Lincoln did not have time to talk—it was 8:30 p.m. and he was already running late for his evening at the theatre with his wife. Lincoln scribbled a note to allow Ashmun to come see him the next morning. It went down in history as the last words the President ever wrote.

Mary Lincoln was excited to spend the night out with her husband; she had rarely found him so relaxed and at ease as he was on that Good Friday. "He was almost boyish," she wrote several months later. "I never saw him so supremely cheerful—his manner was even playful."

The streets of Washington were already dark when the couple set off for what they hoped would be an evening of cheer and laughter at Ford's Theatre.

———

Just after 9:30 p.m.—the play underway—Booth was in the narrow alley at the rear of the building. He asked a stagehand who knew him well, Edman Spangler, to watch his horse, at the ready for his escape. A calm Booth then walked slowly to a saloon next door, ordered a whisky and water, and waited until around 10 p.m. The actor then strolled through the front entrance of the theatre and chatted briefly with the doorkeeper before making his way up the stairs to the dress circle on the second floor.

There were no police or military personnel stationed there to guard the leader of the country that had just come through the bloodiest and most violent war in its history. Standing in the vestibule that led to the guest boxes, Booth took the piece of wood he had placed there earlier in the day and wedged it near the door, thereby blocking anyone else from entering from the outside. Peeking through a hole in the inner door—there is some dispute about whether Booth had drilled it earlier that day or whether it was already there—the assassin could see Lincoln in a rocking chair, directly beyond the door. He needed to know exactly where his target was because he knew he would have only a few seconds to shoot.

Booth was familiar with every line in the play that was unfolding, *My American Cousin*. He waited for a specific scene when he knew there would be only a single actor on the stage and the roar of laughter from the audience would cover the noise of his next move.

It was 10:15 p.m.

John Wilkes Booth stealthily entered the presidential box. He raised his single-shot derringer and pulled the trigger not two feet from President Abraham Lincoln's head.

"The audience heard the shot but supposing it fired in the regular course of the play did not heed it," the *New York Times* reported the next day, "till Mrs. Lincoln's screams drew their attention."

———

Anderson Abbott, like many Washingtonians, had spent the evening celebrating.

After supper, he had gone to watch a torchlight victory parade. "As far as the eye could reach from the elevated position which we occupied," he recalled, "it appeared like a fiery serpent winding its sinuous course through the streets and avenues of the city."

By 9 p.m., Abbott headed towards a friend's house, where he had settled in for a long night of music and merriment. A young woman had started to play the piano when she was interrupted by the "fierce ringing" of the doorbell. The host returned from the door with slow, hesitating steps and an expression of shock on his face that Abbott would never forget.

"I have sad news to tell you," he announced. "President Lincoln was shot at Ford Theatre tonight and Secretary Seward's throat has been cut and both are dying."

"Horrible!" exclaimed the women.

"The Lord have mercy on us!" Abbott and the others cried out.

———

The bullet had entered Lincoln's head about three inches behind the left ear and travelled about seven and a half inches through his brain before coming to a stop behind his right eye. Almost immediately, the President slumped down, unconscious.

Mary Lincoln burst out screaming and wailing.

Booth swung his legs over the balustrade and leaped onto the stage. Never one to miss a cue, the actor turned to the shocked audience to utter his most famous—and final—line on stage: *"Sic semper tyrannis."*

"Thus be to tyrants."

Like his Shakespearean hero Brutus, Booth in his mind had slain a despot who had dared to free the slaves and crush his beloved South. "I struck boldly," he wrote in his diary. "God simply made me the instrument of his punishment."

He dashed across the stage and out the rear door onto his waiting horse, disappearing into the night, as the city, the country and indeed the entire world were plunged into panic and fear.

———

As Booth was making his escape, a badly shaken Abbott and his friends headed outside into the streets of the capital at 11:30 p.m. Abbott remarked how the city's wide avenues, dimly lit by gaslights, were always dark at night, the "shadows of alleys and porches affording convenient lurking places for garroters, assassins and thieves." As a Black man hearing news of Southern assassins lurking in the nation's capital, he was frightened. "For the first time during my stay in Washington I was troubled with a feeling of uncertainty regarding my safety," he remembered. "To what extent does this infamous plot extend?"

As it turned out, Booth's murderous plots had failed to extend beyond the President. Lewis Powell had succeeded in barging into the house of William Seward, pretending to be bringing medicine from a doctor. Forcing his way into Seward's room, the would-be assassin stabbed the secretary of state five times in the face and neck. Seeing Seward's blood spurting everywhere, Powell thought he had accomplished his mission and fled away on horseback. But by sheer luck, Seward had survived.

As for Andrew Johnson, he was saved by cowardice. George Atzerodt lost his nerve and never followed Booth's orders to assassinate the vice president.

Still, panic spread through the city. "Senators, Congressmen, clerks in the departments, citizens, soldiers all rushed by in a frenzy of excitement," Abbott noted. "The soldiers seemed to be arresting anyone who looked or acted at all suspicious." Two men were dragged into the street in their bedclothes. An angry crowd was ready to lynch "an unfortunate man" found in Lafayette Park near the White House. There were reports of Union soldiers killing two men who dared to cheer the assassin's work.

"We thought it prudent to keep at a safe distance from the mob," Abbott wrote. "But my experience of tragedy had not ended."

———

Three doctors who happened to be at Ford's Theatre rushed to attend to the President. The prognosis was grim: "His wound is mortal. It is impossible for him to recover," said army surgeon Charles Leale, the first on the scene. They moved his body to a house across the street and laid his long, limp body diagonally on a bed. Mary Lincoln sat on a chair near her husband's head, kissing him several times and begging him to speak, even a single word to her.

A few close friends and leading politicians gathered for what amounted to a death watch.

The President's breathing grew faint; his pulse dropped to forty-four.

———

In the early hours of the morning, Elizabeth Keckley, the former slave who had become Mary Lincoln's dressmaker and confidante, was summoned to come to her aid. Anderson Abbott, who had befriended Keckley, later wrote that he had accompanied her, making it through the throngs of people and then the military cordon with some difficulty.

As her husband lay dying, Mary Lincoln "was lying in an adjoining room prostrate with anguish." Keckley did her best to comfort the sobbing, grieving woman.

"[T]he anguish of the widow in the privacy of her apartments, surrounded by her children and with Mrs. Keckley as her sole companion, was pitiable in the extreme," Abbott recounted.

He lingered for a short while and then, thoroughly exhausted, he made his way home.

Doctors told the Lincoln family an average man with the kind of brain damage the President had sustained would pass away in about two hours; the President hung on for nine.

Some medical experts say that with today's technology, an emergency airlift to a trauma centre and modern surgery, Lincoln could have survived. But in the nineteenth century there were no X-rays, no brain surgery, just guesswork. A silver shaft was used to probe the bullet hole and keep the wound open. It steadied his breathing and pulse, but the treatment was just easing his way into death.

At 7:22 a.m. on April 15, 1865, Abraham Lincoln passed away.

Abbott, the son of Blacks who had fled the slave South, who had grown up to become Canada's first native-born Black doctor, was beside himself with grief as Washington—and indeed the entire country and much of the world—slipped into mourning.

Heartbroken, Abbott wandered through the streets. "The city rapidly assumed a funeral aspect," he remarked. "The draping of the public buildings, business houses and residences was quite general . . . even if, as in one case, it was nothing more appropriate than a Black skirt hung over the door. There was an ill-disguised expression of anxiety on the faces of everyone as to the extent of the conspiracy."

On Tuesday morning, April 18, the White House gates were opened as President Lincoln's body lay in state in an open coffin. On that first day alone, the crowd stretched for blocks and numbered 20,000 to 30,000. Abbott was there. "As I looked upon the pale, cold face of the President as he lay in state in the Guest room, a great sorrow weighed heavily upon my heart," he wrote, "for I thought of the loss to the Negro race in the recent life of freedom, of the great guiding hand that now lay paralysed in death."

Elizabeth Keckley echoed his thoughts. "No common mortal had died. The Moses of my people had fallen in the hour of his triumph," she wrote. "The whole world bowed their heads in grief when Abraham Lincoln died."

Jefferson Davis, ex-president of the Confederate States, and his wife, Varina, photographed during their stay in Montreal in 1867 (Courtesy McCord Museum)

Dead Confederate soldiers after the Battle of Antietam. More men died in the Civil War than in all the wars combined in which Americans fought. (Courtesy Library of Congress)

Jacob Thompson headed the
Confederates' actions in Canada
from 1864 to 1865. (Courtesy
Mississippi Department of
Archives and History)

The order signed by
Jefferson Davis authorizing
$1 million for "secret
service"—most of which
went to Canada (Courtesy
US National Archives)

Clement Clay, the second-in-command directing Confederate agents in Canada (Courtesy US Library of Congress)

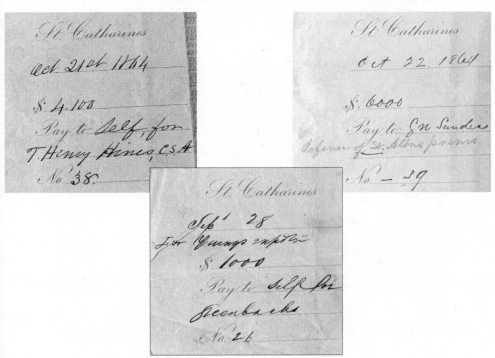

Receipts from Clay's bank book showing payments for the St. Albans raid, including $4,100 to Thomas Hines, $1,000 to Bennett Young and $6,000 to George Sanders (Clay Papers, Duke University)

In 1864, Bennett Young (seated far right) and his St. Albans raiders await trial in Montreal. (Courtesy Vermont Historical Society)

Fifty years later, Young addresses the crowd at the unveiling of the Confederate Memorial at Arlington National Cemetery in 1914, with US president Woodrow Wilson in attendance. (Courtesy US Library of Congress)

George Sanders (Courtesy
McCord Museum)

Edwin Lee (Courtesy
McCord Museum)

Dr. Luke Blackburn
(Courtesy National
Museum of Medicine)

Three of Morgan's Raiders went to Canada to carry out attacks on Northern targets.
From left to right: John Headley, who tried to burn down New York; Thomas Hines
and John Castleman, who plotted to attack prisons during the Northwest Conspiracy
(From Headley's book *Confederate Operations in Canada and New York*)

John Wilkes Booth and his friend
and accomplice John Harrison
Surratt (Courtesy US Library of
Congress)

SURRAT. BOOTH. HAROLD.

War Department, Washington, April 20, 1865.

☞ **$100,000 REWARD!**

THE MURDERER

Of our late beloved President, Abraham Lincoln,

IS STILL AT LARGE.

$50,000 REWARD

Will be paid by this Department for his apprehension, in addition to any reward offered by Municipal Authorities or State Executives.

$25,000 REWARD

Will be paid for the apprehension of JOHN H. SURRAT, one of Booth's Accomplices.

$25,000 REWARD

Will be paid for the apprehension of David C. Harold, another of Booth's accomplices.

LIBERAL REWARDS will be paid for any information that shall conduce to the arrest of either of the above-named criminals, or their accomplices.

All persons harboring or secreting the said persons, or either of them, or aiding or assisting their concealment or escape, will be treated as accomplices in the murder of the President and the attempted assassination of the Secretary of State, and shall be subject to trial before a Military Commission and the punishment of DEATH.

Let the stain of innocent blood be removed from the land by the arrest and punishment of the murderers.

All good citizens are exhorted to aid public justice on this occasion. Every man should consider his own conscience charged with this solemn duty, and rest neither night nor day until it be accomplished.

EDWIN M. STANTON, Secretary of War.

DESCRIPTIONS.—BOOTH is Five Feet 7 or 8 inches high, slender build, high forehead, black hair, black eyes, and wore a heavy black moustache.

JOHN H. SURRAT is about 5 feet, 9 inches. Hair rather thin and dark; eyes rather light; no beard. Would weigh 145 or 150 pounds. Complexion rather pale and clear, with color in his cheeks. Wore light clothes of fine quality. Shoulders square; cheek bones rather prominent; chin narrow; ears projecting at the top; forehead rather low and square, but broad. Parts his hair on the right side; neck rather long. His lips are firmly set. A slim man.

DAVID C. HAROLD is five feet six inches high, hair dark, eyes dark, eyebrows rather heavy, full face, nose short, hand short and fleshy, feet small, instep high, round bodied, naturally quick and active, slightly closes his eyes when looking at a person.

NOTICE.—In addition to the above, State and other authorities have offered rewards amounting to almost one hundred thousand dollars, making an aggregate of about TWO HUNDRED THOUSAND DOLLARS.

The reward poster for Booth, Surratt and David Herold (left) and the Presidential Box at Ford's Theatre where Booth shot Lincoln (Courtesy US Library of Congress)

A popular drawing of Booth's dying moments after he was tracked down and shot by the cavalry detachment led by Canadian Edward Doherty

The St. Lawrence Hall in
Montreal, the favoured hangout
for Confederate spies and agents
(Courtesy McCord Museum)

The registry book from the hotel showing John Wilkes Booth (second name from the bottom) checking into Room 150 on October 18, 1864. (Free Library of Philadelphia, Rare Book Department) Sarah Slater (second name from the bottom) took Room 138 at 3 a.m. on February 15, 1865. (Courtesy Library and Archives Canada)

33.

'A NATION WEEPS'

In 1865, news, even as earth-shattering as the slaying of a president, could only travel as fast as the telegraph wire and the printing press. The *New York Times* spread the shocking bulletin across its front page on Saturday morning, April 15: PRESIDENT LINCOLN SHOT BY AN ASSASSIN. But at that point the headlines also reported Lincoln was "still alive" though with "no hopes of recovery."

"Perhaps no news was ever flashed over the electric wire to this city which more startled and horrified our citizens," the *Globe* reported in Toronto. People huddled on street corners and outside newspaper offices, reading the news as it came in hourly over the telegraph. The paper managed only to slip in one short article on page two of its Saturday edition. Booth's name was still not mentioned, but as the *Globe* accurately put it, "that a fanatical Southerner was the author of this deed will be the conclusion of almost everybody."

Without the sound of radio or the power of TV images, the press had the almost impossible task of trying to capture the immediacy of such a calamity. As the *Buffalo Express* wrote: "The awful, terrible announcement which we have to make this morning to our readers— would that our type could refuse to set it forth. We cannot speak of it. We are too sick with the shock of horror and grief and apprehension . . . God pity us all!"

———

But from some, there were cheers instead of tears.

Confederate sympathizers gathered at the Queen's Hotel in Toronto, just hours after Abraham Lincoln was pronounced dead. "Southern refugees assembled in our chief hotel as soon as the deed was known early on Saturday morning, and entered into a noisy debauch in honour of the event," the *Globe* reported. At the bar in the hotel, two of the St. Albans raiders were heard heaping praise on the killer. The *Hamilton Evening Times* reported that "some Southerners drank [to] the health of the assassin in bumpers of champagne in a public barroom." In Halifax, there was a "demonstration of fiendish exultation over the event" aboard a Confederate vessel that was in the port.

At Montreal's St. Lawrence Hall, a clergyman at a breakfast celebration declared that "Lincoln had only gone to hell a little before his time." It is not known if Edwin Lee, a regular guest at the hotel and the man still in charge of Confederate activities in Canada, attended the party, but he reacted to the presidential assassination with a sort of grudging admiration. "News of Lincoln's death came this morning, exciting universal horror and amazement," he had written in his diary on April 15, striking out the word *shock*, presumably favouring amazement over revulsion.

David Thurston, one of the US consuls in Canada, could not contain his disgust at the actions of his fellow Americans in Canada. "There were some so . . . depraved, as to exult over this great crime. I am more grieved to say that these persons—I cannot call them men—were but a short time since citizens of the United States," he wrote to Washington. "Treason has transformed them to brutes."

Lady Elizabeth Owen Monck, the wife of Canada's governor general, paid a visit to the nuns at Montreal's Ursuline convent a week after the killing. "We talked about Lincoln's death," she wrote. "[T]he nuns thought he was 'daggered' as a judgement for going to the theatre on Good Friday." If that sounded somewhat extreme, the *Gazette des Campagnes*, a widely read farmers' publication in Quebec, made a similar point, arguing the assassination was God's punishment because the Union had held victory celebrations on a holy day.

In his death as in his life, Lincoln had captivated and cleaved his country—and Canada. Where people on both sides of the border stood on Booth's history-changing act said more about them than it did about either the President or his killer.

———

Within a day, the newspapers had identified John Wilkes Booth as the culprit. Jefferson Davis, the defeated Confederate president, got the news about the assassination by telegram while on the run in Charlotte, North Carolina. He recalled that his troops "cheered, as was natural at news of the fall of one they considered their most powerful foe." A witness recorded that Davis privately paraphrased a line from Lincoln's favourite play, *Macbeth*: "If it were to be done, it were better it were well done." In his memoirs written many years later, Davis denied he read the news "with exultation." Still, he could not bring himself to express any grief or regret over the slaying; he saw only the dangers it posed for his cause. "For an enemy so relentless in the war for our subjugation, we could not be expected to mourn," he wrote, "yet, in view of its political consequences, it could not be regarded otherwise than as a great misfortune to the South."

The *Richmond Whig* echoed that view, warning the assassination—because of the fallout it would bring—was the "heaviest blow which has fallen on the people of the south." Other Southern newspapers sounded a more vengeful tone. "Abe has gone to answer before the bar of God for the innocent blood which he has permitted to be shed, and his efforts to enslave a free people," cried the *Chattanooga Daily Rebel*.

In Canada, the pro-Southern press picked up the same themes, essentially arguing that Lincoln had it coming. "It must be remembered that as atrocious as was Booth's deed, his 'sic semper tyrannis' was literally justified by the facts," argued the *London Examiner*. "The man he killed had murdered the Constitution of the United States." The *Toronto Leader* opined that "it should not be forgotten that [for] all such deeds there is some cause," blaming Lincoln for the harsh treatment of "the oppressed people of the South."

The Montreal *Gazette*, astonishingly, found a way to focus most of its sympathy not on the slain president but on "the great loss which the South sustains in his death." The paper reminded its readers that it had questioned "the justifiableness of the war itself" and feared that if vengeance took over, "the calamity which his assassination causes to the Southern States is great." French Quebeckers got the same message from *Le Canadien*: in a special edition it published on April 15, its first worries were for "the terrible reprisals against the south that could come." It went on to chastise those "creating a pedestal for the deceased President . . . [when] just a few days ago he was but a mediocre man."

Henry Hogan, the owner of the St. Lawrence Hall where Booth stayed, couldn't bring himself to speak evil of the actor he admired. "His friends were unable to associate the man as they knew him . . . with his terrible doom," he said. "As the phantom fades away, we recollect only what was human in this rash, hot-headed youth of twenty-six."

———

On the Monday following the assassination, the city council in Toronto met in a solemn mood to express condolences to the American people. "A nation weeps," said one alderman in support of a resolution to shut down for two hours as a tribute to the slain president.

There was only one council member who opposed the idea: George Taylor Denison III, the inveterate Confederate backer and friend to the conspirators in Canada. Denison insisted, when it came to Lincoln's slaying, "we should pass the matter by without noticing it."

"We had plenty of things to attend to under our own Government without attending to those of another," he said.

Despite Denison's objection, the motion passed with all the other twenty-five aldermen voting in favour.

———

George Brown, the abolitionist publisher of the Toronto *Globe* and perhaps Lincoln's most loyal supporter in Canada, was of course appalled by his hero's murder and the pages of his newspaper reflected that. "The bells are tolling mournfully," the paper reported from Washington in its first edition after the news broke. "Strong men weep in the streets. The grief is widespread and deep."

"He was sagacious, patient, prudent, courageous, honest and candid," Brown wrote in an editorial. "He is dead, but his principles live after him."

Brown was perhaps more in tune with the mood of ordinary Canadian people than the pro-Southern elites in Canada who ran many of the other newspapers. The depth and intensity of mourning across the country for a foreign leader was something that had never been seen before. At a solemn gathering at a Toronto hotel presided over by the American consul, it was resolved that all American residents in the city should wear "a black badge of mourning" on their left arm for thirty days. So many other people took up the custom that there was a shortage of black cloth. The entire front of the American Express Company office on Yonge Street in Toronto was draped in black, as were many other buildings in other cities. In the small town of Galt, Ontario, bells tolled for two hours as the American flag fluttered over the local post office. From Victoria to Charlottetown, businesses were shuttered in remembrance.

Naturally, the grief ran strongest among Canada's Black communities, which had sent many men to join Lincoln's army. "Almost every colored man has worn a badge of mourning," Brown's *Globe* reported. They packed into the Queen Street Baptist Church, where a portrait of the slain president stood on the pulpit, draped in black. In St. Catharines, where Confederate commissioner Clement Clay made his base and plotted numerous operations, the Black church on Geneva Street was covered in mourning cloth as the choir sang "John Brown's soul is marching on." The newspaper noted that "none were more loyal and brave" than the Black Canadians who served as soldiers, scouts and spies for the Union army, "bringing about, for their oppressed people, for all time to come, Freedom, Liberty and Emancipation."

From one end of the country to the other, in large cities and small towns, people flocked to churches and town halls to express their sorrow and sympathy. Two thousand attended a service in London, Ontario. In Sherbrooke, Quebec, they gathered for "the largest meeting for many years on every public occasion" to condemn the "fiendish and dastardly murder of Abraham Lincoln." In Montreal, four thousand people attended a memorial at the Wesleyan Methodist Church.

As Brown's *Globe* put it, "almost all of us feel as if we have suffered a personal loss. Mr. Lincoln is spoken of in the same terms as are used towards a familiar friend. All mourn his untimely fate."

One Canadian would do more than mourn the murder of a president. He would go after Lincoln's killer.

34.

'NEVER TAKEN ALIVE'

The leaflet issued by the War Department on April 20—six days after Lincoln's assassination—looked like one of those "Wanted: Dead or Alive" posters pasted on saloon doors in the Wild West:

$100,000 REWARD!

THE MURDERER

Of our Late beloved President Abraham Lincoln

IS STILL AT LARGE

Plastered on buildings and lampposts of cities and towns across the United States, the notice reproduced three photographs: John Wilkes Booth in the middle flanked by two accused accomplices, David Herold and John Surratt. A reward of $50,000 was offered for Booth's capture and $25,000 each for his two accused accomplices. The total was a staggering amount—worth more than $1.8 million in today's figures.

The next day, the funeral train carrying Lincoln's body from Washington to its burial place in his hometown of Springfield, Illinois, began its pilgrimage through 180 cities and towns across seven states. On Friday morning, April 21, it rolled into Baltimore, where Alexander

Augusta led a procession of seventy-five thousand Black troops through the streets of the city. By Monday, April 24, it was leaving Philadelphia—even at 4 a.m. thousands lined the tracks—on its way to New York, where eventually as many as half a million people would gather to pay their respects to their slain leader.

On that Monday, Edward Doherty was sitting on a bench in Lafayette Park across from the White House with another officer of the 16th New York Cavalry "talking to a couple of ladies," as he put it. Amidst the gloom and grief that shrouded the city, it was a rare moment of rest for the Union army lieutenant. "It was my day off and I was rejoicing my soul in the bright rays of spring sun," he later recalled. Doherty was as shocked and saddened by Lincoln's assassination as most people, perhaps more so. After all, even though as a Canadian it was not his battle to fight, he had enlisted in Lincoln's army within days of the war's start. He had shaken the President's hand in 1861 when Lincoln had visited his regiment in Washington. He had been taken prisoner, saw his comrades die in battle, and won praise and promotion for his courage and leadership.

Now he was stationed in Washington, tasked with defending the capital from the Confederate armies. Doherty's respite in the park that day was interrupted when a messenger approached with urgent orders. The specifics of his new mission were not spelled out; all Doherty knew was that his commander at the 16th New York Cavalry had been told to find "a reliable and discreet commissioned officer" and twenty-five men with three days' rations.

Doherty rushed back to his barracks and sounded the call to his men for "boots and saddles." He had little time to pick and choose his team. Only one of them, an eager if at times edgy sergeant named Thomas H. "Boston" Corbett, was from his own company; the others were men he scarcely knew. Doherty made his way to the War Department at 211 Pennsylvania Avenue, where he reported to Lafayette Curry Baker, a burly man with a thick beard and dark, deep-set eyes.

"Colonel Baker handed me photographs," Doherty recalled.

They were pictures of John Wilkes Booth and his accomplice, David Herold.

Doherty suddenly grasped the gravity of his assignment: he had been charged with hunting down the accused conspirators behind the assassination of Abraham Lincoln.

————

Doherty was used to the discipline of the army; he had no idea he was about to be plunged into the pettiness and rivalries of Washington's political games. At the time, there was little in the way of sophisticated operations by law enforcement to call upon in the aftermath of Lincoln's slaying. The United States Secret Service would not be officially created until three months after the assassination, and even then, its main task for many years was fighting counterfeiting, not protecting presidents. A national crime-fighting organization like the FBI would not be set up until the next century.

Instead, the scramble to find Lincoln's killers fell to a loose collection of police and private detectives from across the country who were sent to Washington with little coordination or leadership. In addition, nearly a thousand Union soldiers were deployed, making it the biggest manhunt in US history to date. Edwin Stanton, the secretary of war, was nominally in charge of the operation, but as the search floundered, Stanton asked for help from Lafayette Baker, the head of what was called the National Detective Bureau. Baker had made a controversial name for himself running spy operations for the Union. He had a reputation for being brutal with suspects during the war; there had been allegations of torture and lynchings. What's more, he was conniving, known to steal clues and credit from other detectives. Eager for a piece of any glory (and reward) that came from capturing the Lincoln assassins, Baker appointed two of his own operatives to work with Doherty—his cousin, Luther Baker, and a man named Everton Conger.

"He . . . said they would accompany me," Doherty recalled, the implication being that, in his mind at least, as the army man he was in charge of the detectives. In Luther Baker's recollection, he was the one named as the leader. It did not take long for the rivalries and jealousies to set in.

Much of the manhunt for the killers to date had been in Maryland, but Lafayette Baker had told Doherty there was word that Booth and Herold were "somewhere between the Potomac and Rappahannock Rivers" in Virginia. Doherty and his men boarded a steamer to Virginia, then travelled through the night on horseback south towards the town of King George.

At first, there were scant clues and many false leads. Frustrated with the lack of any early results, the posse split up. Conger took a detail of five men "to scour the country" but returned empty-handed. "The detectives returned about 3 p.m. without any clue," Doherty recounted. "It was thought by the detectives that we would not find any traces of the assassins." As Doherty later told the *New York Times*, "It was tiresome work, the men . . . began to have very little faith in the detectives."

———

Under cover of darkness, and with the help of a network of Confederate sympathizers and soldiers, the most wanted man in America had thus far eluded capture.

Within two hours of killing the President, around midnight, Booth and Herold had made it to the Surratt tavern in Maryland, where they procured the weapons stored there after the kidnap attempt. Booth, though, was in pain; he had broken his left leg just above the ankle. (Most popular accounts attribute the injury to his dramatic leap onto the stage at Ford's Theatre, but more modern scholarship has suggested the injury came when his horse fell on him during his nighttime ride in the countryside.) Before first light on the morning of the fifteenth, Booth turned up at the comfortable home of Samuel Mudd in Charles County, Maryland. Booth felt he could trust Mudd; the doctor's name was on that important list of Southern sympathizers that Booth had obtained from his Confederate associate in Montreal, Patrick Martin. The doctor helped set Booth's broken leg as best he could and offered his home as a place of rest. The next day, he gave the fugitive directions for safe routes along the underground network that could take him from Maryland into Virginia across the Rappahannock River.

Booth spent the next six days in hiding, fearful of capture but equally furious that he was being seen as a villain. "After being hunted like a dog through swamps, woods . . . till I was forced to return wet cold and starving with every mans [sic] hand against me I am here in despair," he wrote in his diary on April 21. "And why; For doing what Brutus was honored for, what made Tell a Hero. And yet I for striking down a greater tyrant than they ever knew am looked upon as a common cutthroat."

Complained the fugitive: "I am abandoned, with the curse of Cain upon me."

———

Doherty and his men arrived at Port Conway on the shores of the Rappahannock late in the afternoon of April 25 at a spot where a local fisherman would use his boat to ferry people across the river. Doherty went over to some women by the water to show them pictures of the men they were hunting. "The women picked out the photograph of Booth and Harrold [sic] and told me they had been there [the] night before."

Doherty and Luther Baker then went to talk to William Rollins, the fisherman who ran the unofficial ferry. He too recognized Herold and Booth. For the first time, Doherty felt the hunt was beginning to turn his way: "After exhibiting the photographs, we concluded that we were on their track."

———

Just hours before, Booth and Herold had shown up at the landing, growing impatient as Rollins insisted on not helping them across the river until he had taken care of his fishing nets. Just then, three

ragged-looking soldiers rode up on horseback. Much to Booth's surprise and good fortune, they were not Union men but Confederate
brigands. Booth, who by this point had been on the run for ten days,
let down his guard for the first time.

"I suppose you have been told who I am?" Booth said, drawing his
revolver. "Yes, I am John Wilkes Booth, the slayer of Abraham Lincoln."
That bold admission impressed at least one of the men, First Lieutenant
Mortimer B. Ruggles: "His face was haggard, pinched with suffering,
his dark eyes sunken, but strangely bright. The coolness of the man
won our admiration."

Ruggles and his friends agreed to join Booth and help him escape
once on the other side of the river—but to which destination?

———

Doherty and the search party picked up a vital clue when Rollins's wife
told them she knew that one of the three Confederate soldiers who had
helped Booth was named Willie Jett. "The woman told me that Jett
was courting a young woman . . . whose father was keeping a hotel at
Bowling Green," Doherty recalled, "and she had no doubt that they
had all gone there."

The small town was just sixteen miles away. By 6 p.m., Doherty's
entire command of more than two dozen men and their horses had
made it across the river, racing towards Bowling Green.

They were closing in on their prey.

———

Once the Confederate men had spirited Booth to the other side of the
Rappahannock, for the first time since fleeing Washington the fugitive
assassin felt a moment of relief. "I'm safe in glorious Virginia, thank
God!" he exclaimed.

On their way to Bowling Green, the Confederate soldiers decided it
would be best to hide Booth at the home of a local man named Richard
Garrett. "I think they'll give him shelter there and treat him kindly,"
Jett said. Garrett ran a five-hundred-acre tobacco farm nearby called

Locust Hill. His sympathies for the Southern cause ran deep; his two eldest sons had served in the Confederate army and, unlike many, they had come home alive. So Jett was hardly taking any chances when he rode up on Monday, April 24, around 3 p.m. and asked Garrett if he would harbour a man they called "James Boyd," supposedly a wounded Confederate soldier on his way home.

"You who know anything of Virginia as it used to be will know that there could be but one response to such a request," Garrett's youngest son, also named Richard, recalled. "My father cordially invited his guests to alight."

Booth and Herold told convoluted stories to the Garrett family about their supposed wartime experience that didn't sit right. The Garretts' worries only grew when they saw a large party of Union soldiers dashing by their farm, clearly on the hunt for somebody. Richard remembered the sound and the fury of the Union posse. "[W]e saw a cloud of dust and a detachment of cavalry rode past in the direction of Bowling Green."

It was Doherty and his men, galloping towards the hotel in search of the Confederates who had helped Booth. About seven miles into their journey they had raced past the front gate of Locust Hill. As Doherty later wrote, "At dark we passed the Garrett farm, not then dreaming that the assassins were concealed there."

———

By midnight, the 16th New York Cavalry had made it to Bowling Green. Doherty and Conger headed to the Star Hotel, looking for Willie Jett. Doherty ordered his men to surround the building with their guns in hand. They knocked on the doors for about fifteen minutes without any reply. Eventually a sleepy and surprised Julia Gouldman, the mother of Jett's sweetheart, answered. Doherty was in no mood for politeness or niceties. He demanded to know who was in her house, "telling her that if my men were fired on, I should burn the building and take the inmates prisoners to Washington."

The searchers dashed up a flight of stairs and in a small room they found a half-dressed Jett and another man. Doherty, Baker and Conger

would later each give differing accounts of who played the lead in inter-
rogating Jett, but all agreed on the outcome.

Nerves were frayed. Doherty told one of his men, Corporal Herman
Newgarten, "to shoot the prisoner if I saw him make any move to get
away." Jett sprang up from his bed but initially denied knowing anything about Booth. Doherty was having none of it. "I had my revolver
in my hand ready cocked," he recounted.

"I know your movements for the last two days. If you lie to me, I'll
take you and hang you. If you tell the truth, I'll protect you," Doherty
told the Confederate. Jett knew the game was up. "I left him at Garrett's
house, three miles from Port Royal," Jett confessed. "You passed him
on your way here."

Doherty put Jett under guard and then went back to rouse his
troops. They had been riding for almost two days with little food and
less sleep. "They were very tired and had fallen asleep. With great difficulty I woke them up," Doherty noted. "But when they learned that
we were on Booth's track new life seemed to be infused into them."
The cavalry captain led his exhausted troops back up the road to the
farm, hoping at last to corner Lincoln's assassin. They were determined
to take the most infamous man in America alive. He would have vital
information about the planning and plotting of the assassination.

But Mortimer Ruggles, one of the Confederates who had helped
Booth find shelter at Garrett's farm, knew that Booth would go down
fighting. "He was wounded, desperate, and at bay," he remembered,
"and he said that he would never be taken alive."

———

Booth had now been on the run for just twelve days. It had not taken
long for Doherty and the search party to track him down.

Tuesday, April 25, began in all of Virginia's Southern splendour.
"That day was bright and warm," Richard Garrett recalled. "It was
an unusually early spring that year, and the grass in the yard was like
velvet, while the great orchard in front of the house was white with
apple blossoms." But the warmth of the Garrett hospitality for their

now unwanted guests had cooled. Garrett told "Boyd" that he and his companion could not spend a second night sleeping in the house; he offered the large barn where he cured his tobacco, about 150 feet from the main house. With little choice, the fugitives agreed. As they went to sleep that night, the Garretts took an extra precaution. Fearing the suspicious strangers might steal their horses, they put a padlock on the barn door.

Although they didn't yet know who they were harbouring, with that padlock the Garretts had just sealed the fate of President Lincoln's assassin.

———

It was still pitch-black when Doherty's forces arrived at the farm around 2 a.m. on Wednesday, April 26. They halted at the orchard fence as Doherty ordered his men to surround the property, sending six men to the rear of a barn and other buildings.

"They are in that house and we must take them," Private David Baker remembered his captain ordering his men. "Shoot any person you see running away."

Then Doherty, along with the detectives Baker and Conger, walked up to the porch and pounded on the door. In their later accounts, all three leaders more or less agreed on what happened in the next few vital hours; they just had different versions of the roles they played, each putting himself at the centre of all the action.

A confused Richard Garrett came out in his nightclothes. Doherty, in his telling, was the one to put a gun to his head. "A man standing on the step thrust a pistol into his face," his son Richard later recalled. "The yard was filled with men who with drawn swords or pistols crowded around the door."

"Where are these men that were here yesterday afternoon?" Doherty demanded.

"They went to the woods," came the nervous reply.

Baker and Conger insisted they were the ones who questioned the old man, but all witnesses agree he told his interrogators that his two visitors had fled to the woods. "Lies will do no good now, we know they are here," one of the detectives yelled. "Bring a rope, hang the damned old rebel and we will find the man afterwards."

The life of the Garrett patriarch was saved when another of his sons, John, came up to the soldiers and implored his frightened father to tell the truth. Doherty seized the younger Garrett by the collar, pulled him down the steps and put his cocked pistol to his ear.

"Where are those men?" he shouted.

"In the barn," John Garrett confessed. "We don't know who they are and told them they could pass the night there."

"Show me the barn!" Doherty barked.

Dragging John Garrett with them, Doherty and the detectives made their way to the barn. Doherty ordered his men to encircle the large wooden structure. Doherty noticed a large crack on one side and stationed Sergeant Boston Corbett to stand watch at that corner of the barn.

Doherty's instinct was to wait until daylight for his next move. "But the men told me they heard voices and the moving about of men in the hay. I then decided to get at them as soon as possible." The hunting party got the Garretts to retrieve the key to unlock the padlock on the barn door.

From inside the barn came the distinctive voice of one of America's most famous actors. "Who are you? What do you want? Whom do you want?"

"It doesn't make any difference" was Doherty's terse reply. "Come out."

That, at least, was Doherty's account, with him playing the lead role in the confrontation with Booth and Herold in the barn even though Baker and Conger, in their versions, would make themselves the centre of the verbal exchanges and action.

"I am a cripple and alone," Booth said, ever the actor.

"I know who is with you," Doherty stood firm, "and you had better surrender."

"I may be taken by my friends, but not by my foes," taunted the assassin.

"If you don't come out, I'll burn the building," Doherty warned.

It was not an empty threat. The men began to pile up some hay against one of the walls of the barn, but as the corporal began his task, Booth cried out:

"If you come back here, I will put a bullet through you."

Doherty again hesitated, pondering if it would be wiser to wait until daylight, charging the barn from all sides when they could better see— and overpower—their targets. Detectives Baker and Conger disagreed; according to Doherty, they wanted to move in quickly.

But then Booth changed the game.

"O Captain! there is a man in here who wants to surrender awful bad," Booth cried out. Herold apparently was not as willing to play the martyr in Booth's final performance.

Once again, Doherty in his account was at odds with the detectives. Baker was unsure about trusting Herold's offer of surrender, but Doherty felt he had a decent chance to get Herold out alive. "If we can't get both of you, we'll take one," one of the soldiers named John Winter remembered Doherty saying.

"Open the door!" Doherty ordered one of his men. "I will take that man out myself!" Then he cried out to Herold: "Hand out your arms and you can come out."

"I have none," Herold said.

"I own all the arms, and intend to use them on you gentlemen," Booth added.

Not willing to trust the man who had killed a president, Doherty wanted to make sure Herold was not a threat. "Let me see your hands," Doherty ordered Herold, and the man complied, thrusting his empty hands through the barn door. Doherty lunged, grabbed his wrists and pulled Herold into the yard. He frisked the fugitive and once he was assured Herold was unarmed, he secured the first of what he hoped would be two prisoners.

"You had better follow his example and come out," he yelled back to Booth. "Now it's your turn. Are you going to come out?"

"Tell me who you are and what you want of me," Booth replied. "Perhaps you are my friends."

"It makes no difference who we are," replied Doherty. "We want you and we will take you dead or alive. The barn is surrounded and it is impossible for you to escape."

"No, I have not made up my mind; but draw your men up fifty paces off and give me a chance for my life," said Booth, itching perhaps for a shootout.

"I did not come here to fight," replied Doherty, and then, with a bit of his own theatrical embellishment, he doubled the size of his forces. "I have fifty men and I can take you."

Not to be upstaged, Booth retorted: "Well, my brave boys, prepare me a stretcher, and place another stain on our glorious banner."

It was a standoff.

"Boston" Corbett—the only man in the 16th New York Cavalry whom Doherty knew personally—offered to enter the barn alone and confront Booth, even if it meant giving up his life to draw Booth out. Corbett had a well-deserved reputation for being somewhat of a religious fanatic. Before enlisting, he had adopted the name "Boston" from the city where he stopped drinking and found God. He had castrated himself with a pair of scissors when he was tempted by prostituted women. As a Union soldier, he carried a Bible with him, quoting from it frequently. So it was hardly out of character for this eccentric soldier to volunteer to martyr himself to capture Booth.

Doherty and the detectives wisely turned down his offer. Corbett was sent back to his post behind the barn. Instead, they would try to coax Booth out by setting the barn afire.

"The hay in the barn . . . was blazing up brightly," Doherty recalled. But then history turned in a few pivotal seconds.

From inside the barn, Doherty heard a gunshot. His first instinct: Booth had shot himself.

———

The single gunshot only added to the confusion as the flames crackled in the burning barn.

Doherty and the detectives raced into the burning building to grab Booth. Years later, Doherty recalled the scene vividly: "He was dazed for a moment and his eyes bore that piteous expression characteristic of a hunted deer. He bent forward as if to make a spring and, raising his right hand, ran his finger through his heavy hair as if collecting his thoughts." Then he slumped down and collapsed onto the floor of the barn.

It was not Booth who had fired what would turn out to be the fatal shot, but the mercurial Corbett. "He [Booth] was taking aim with the carbine, but at whom I could not say," Corbett later claimed. "I took steady aim on my arm and shot him through a large crack in the barn." Doherty later confirmed his soldier's story: "Corbett . . . seeing by the igniting hay that Booth was leveling his carbine at either Herold or myself, fired, to disable him in the arm; but Booth making a sudden move, the aim erred, and the bullet struck Booth in the back of the head, about an inch below the spot where his shot had entered the head of Mr. Lincoln."

The soldiers gathered around the dying assassin. Corporal Newgarten put his hand under Booth's sagging head. Doherty took a knife from Booth, and then Newgarten with three others carried out Booth's limp body from the flames of the barn to the front porch of the Garrett home. Even Booth's final minutes were contested in different accounts offered by Doherty and the detectives. Baker would later insist it was he who talked with the dying Booth.

"While he was lying there, I spoke to him," Doherty wrote. "He tried to raise his hands. He seemed powerless to do so and I took hold of his hands and raised them up . . . But he shook his head."

"Useless! Useless!" Booth muttered.

"The man looked defiant and wild, and would scarcely have been recognized as the dashing young actor of a few weeks ago," Doherty recalled.

They tried to offer Booth water and brandy, but he could not swallow anything, drifting in and out of consciousness. Doherty sent for a doctor, but there was nothing to be done. "At seven o'clock Booth breathed his last," Doherty recorded.

On the Garrett porch, Doherty and the team proceeded to go through the dead man's pockets. "He had on his person a diary, a large bowie knife, two pistols, a compass, and a draft [note from] Canada for £60," Doherty recorded. The bank note in Booth's pocket was the money he had withdrawn from the Ontario Bank branch in Montreal during his trip six months earlier. It was signed by the bank manager, the former and future mayor of Montreal, Henry Starnes.

———

"Did you consider it necessary to shoot Booth?" Doherty was asked many years later by a newspaper reporter.

"I think we could have taken him alive," he answered, "though the chances are he would have provoked a fire[fight]."

The death of Booth made Doherty famous, but sixty years after the event, Doherty's son Charles revealed that his father had mixed feelings about how things turned out: "This incident in the capture of the fugitives was always a source of great regret and disappointment to my father as it had been his intention to take the prisoners back to Washington alive."

Alive to face justice and answer questions about who else was behind the conspiracy. Who were Booth's accomplices? What support, if any, did he get from the Confederacy for his plots? Whatever secrets Booth may have been keeping died with him that morning. "[They] have sealed the only lips that could unravel this dark and mighty mystery," wrote Nathaniel Beverley Tucker, one of the Confederate leaders in Canada who himself would later be accused of being one of the conspirators. "Alas! We can never know all that died with this daring, yet misguided young man."

Doherty didn't see Booth as "daring." He had hunted down a president's killer across two states. Now he had a corpse to get back to Washington. He did so with surprising tenderness and care. "I took a saddle blanket off my horse, and, borrowing a darning needle from Miss

Garrett, sewed his body in it. The men found an old wagon," he wrote. "The body was placed upon it, and two hours after Booth's death I was on the way back to Belle Plain, where I had left the steamboat."

For Edward Doherty, that was the end of the hunt for Lincoln's murderer. But not the end of his battle.

Execution by hanging of four of the Lincoln conspirators, July 7, 1865
(Courtesy US National Archives)

PART FOUR

'TRAITORS IN CANADA'

(April 1865–May 1868)

I wish you to do nothing merely for revenge,
but that what you may do, shall be solely done
with reference to the security of the future.

—ABRAHAM LINCOLN, November 19, 1864

35.

'MAKE MYSELF SCARCE'

It did not take long for the Canadian connection to Lincoln's assassination to become front-page news—and John Surratt was at the centre of it.

THE PRESIDENT DEAD. BOOTH AND SURRATT THE ASSASSINS. THEY ARE SUPPOSED TO BE ESCAPING TO CANADA ran the triple headline in the *Globe* on Monday, April 17.

Surratt had been quickly and correctly identified by the American authorities as a close associate of Booth's. But in the early confusion, he was wrongly pegged as the attempted killer of Secretary of State Seward. "A man named John Surratt is supposed to be the criminal," the *Globe* reported. "It is said there is likelihood that the assassins will endeavour to escape to Canada."

Booth, of course, had fled not north but south to Virginia. Surratt had no need to escape to Canada in the wake of the assassination. He was already there—and police knew it.

At around 2 a.m. on Saturday, April 15, as Lincoln lay dying in a bed across the street from Ford's Theatre, detectives were ringing the doorbell of Mary Surratt's boarding house just five blocks away. The authorities were aware that the H Street home had been frequented by Southern sympathizers and that Mary's son had close ties to Booth. Questioned about her son's whereabouts, she told them he was in Canada; after all, she had received a letter posted from Montreal just a few days earlier.

When police returned to the boarding house on April 17, they found a nervous Lewis Powell, the man who had stabbed Seward, claiming implausibly to be a ditchdigger. They arrested him, and after a search of the home they took Mary Surratt as well. The next day, Samuel Mudd, the doctor who had treated an injured Booth, was questioned and brought into custody shortly thereafter. On April 20, George Atzerodt was arrested on a farm outside Washington.

The conspirators were being rounded up. Mary's son John was the key person who had introduced most of them to Booth in the first place. Unlike all of them—Booth included—Surratt was the only one who was a self-avowed agent of the Confederate government, a courier who was on Richmond's payroll and had met with top officials in Jefferson Davis's government. Those arrested were amateurs, drawn into the conspiracy by adventure or accident. Only Surratt, along with his companion Sarah Slater, was a professional in the high-stakes world of Civil War intrigue.

Which is why—despite all the attention and sudden infamy—he remained elusive.

———

John Surratt had arrived in Montreal with Slater more than a week before his associate John Wilkes Booth had killed the president. At the St. Lawrence Hall, Surratt huddled with the Confederate official Brigadier General Edwin Lee, for whom the war was still far from over. "The news of the evacuation of Richmond did not seem to disturb the General much in his plan," Surratt recounted, "as he doubtless thought then that the Confederacy wanted men more than ever." To supply those men, Lee sent Surratt to scout out a possible attack on a Union prison holding Confederate soldiers near the small town of Elmira in upstate New York.

That was where Surratt found himself on Saturday morning, April 15, when he woke up at a local hotel "little dreaming of the storm then brewing around my head." At the breakfast table, a fellow guest turned to ask him if he had heard the news about Lincoln's assassination, handing him the newspaper article. "[A]s no names were mentioned, it never occurred to me for an instant that it could have been Booth or any of the party," Surratt explained in his public lecture years later, "for the simple reason that I never had heard anything regarding assassination spoken of during my intercourse with them." It was one of Surratt's many lies. After all, in that same speech, he had made much of the fact that he and the others were aghast when Booth had floated the idea of assassination during the Washington restaurant meeting in March to plot Lincoln's kidnapping.

Surratt's next actions were hardly those of an innocent bystander. He rushed to the telegraph office and wrote out a message addressed to "John Wilkes Booth." Suddenly he realized he should be more discreet. "I hesitated a moment, and then tore the paper up," he recalled. This time he handed the telegraph operator a message addressed only to "J.W.B." The message was only nine words long:

If you are in New York, then telegraph me.

As he heard people talking about how Booth had been identified as the assassin, Surratt tried to grab back the note, but it was too late. "The whole truth flashed on me in an instant, and I said to myself, 'My God! What have I done?'"

Indeed. What had Surratt done? Was he simply worried that an impulsive telegram to a friend would tie him accidentally to a now-notorious killer? Or was he perhaps more concerned that the truth would come out about his close partnership with Richmond and Booth in plots against Lincoln?

He decided to run.

Surratt wanted at first to make it by train to Baltimore, but his plan changed on Monday morning, April 17, when he spotted the newspaper articles that by then had named him as the suspect in the attempted assassination of Seward. "I could scarcely believe my senses. I gazed upon my name, the letters of which seemed sometimes to grow as large as mountains," he recounted. "So much for my former connection with him I thought." As if the ties to his good friend Booth whom he had just tried to telegraph was a "former" connection.

It was urgent for Surratt to come up with a better escape plan—and the choice for any smart Confederate on the run was obvious. "After fully realizing the state of the case, I concluded to change my course and go direct to Canada."

_____

The fugitive took a strangely circuitous route through New York State and then Vermont, passing through St. Albans of all places. He wore the distinctive "Canuck-style" jacket he had made sure to buy in Montreal to escape any undue attention.

By April 18, he had checked in again at the St. Lawrence Hall in Montreal, taking Room 121. The other name that appeared in the registry underneath his was "Miss H.C. Slater." Presumably by pre-arrangement, Sarah Slater was back together with Surratt. Hardly a "former" conspirator but rather still a very active Confederate spy, Surratt immediately met with Richmond's man in Canada, Edwin Lee. He handed over the sketches and information he had gathered for a planned prison break at Elmira. Apparently satisfied, Lee paid his spy for the work. The page from Lee's diary for April 18 is mysteriously torn out, but his entry for April 19 reads "This day or the 20th, gave messenger $40 expenses and $100 services, (Charley)," using Surratt's code name.

Lee and his agent had a problem, though. Precisely because the hotel had proven to be such a welcoming spot for Confederates, it was hardly ideal for Surratt to hide there. "I was afraid the United States government would suspect me of complicity in the plot of assassination," Surratt told Lee. "He advised me to make myself scarce."

Later that day, Lee had some female guests over for tea, but Surratt stayed secluded in another room in the hotel suite. When the ladies asked why his mysterious guest was not joining them, Lee tried to put them off by suggesting he was not thirsty. "I expect you have got Booth in there," one of the ladies remarked.

"Perhaps so," Lee answered laughingly.

"That was rather close guessing," Surratt later quipped.

But it was far from fun and games. By April 20, the War Department in Washington had issued a Wanted poster offering $25,000 for the apprehension of Surratt as "one of Booth's accomplices." Federal detectives—following up on the information supplied by Surratt's mother—had arrived in Montreal on the prowl for the accused conspirator. With them was Louis Weichmann, Surratt's one-time classmate, a boarder at his mother's house—and now the chief witness against him. "I was convinced that I was doing the right thing in going to Canada in pursuit of Surratt," Weichmann later wrote, perhaps feeling somewhat guilty about his apparent betrayal. "I went with the kindest of intentions towards him."

"One day I walked out and saw Weichmann on the lookout for me," Surratt later boasted. But his old friend never saw him. For six days Weichmann and the detectives hunted for their prey through the streets of Montreal, Surratt keeping one step ahead of them through chance and cunning. According to a later news report, as the detectives had arrived at the St. Lawrence Hall to check the register, Surratt was slipping out the back door. On April 20, the detectives told Washington they had learned that Surratt had checked out with two companions but they felt confident they'd be caught. Surratt, though, had planted a false trail by telling the clerk he was heading to Quebec City. In reality, under the darkness of night, he slipped away to find brief refuge in the stately Montreal residence of someone Surratt considered "a most devoted friend"—John Porterfield, the Nashville banker and Confederate broker who had been so helpful in aiding the St. Albans robbers to escape with their loot.

But since Porterfield was a known Southern sympathizer, Surratt could not afford to stay there long. To throw the detectives off his trail, two carriages pulled up in front of the house; Surratt got into one while another man dressed like him got into the other. The ruse worked. A police report stated that officers "followed them from Porterfield's in the direction which they had taken, but all trace of them was lost about

15 miles from the city." Weichmann travelled all the way to Quebec City to look for Surratt while another team searched in Trois-Rivières.

But Surratt had secretly found yet another hiding place in Montreal, in a location the police would never think of looking: the home of the apparently very agreeable tailor John Reeves who had made the Garibaldi jacket for him. Surratt stayed at Reeves's place for two days, but he was growing nervous. "The detectives were now hunting me very closely," noted Surratt, "and would doubtless [have] succeeded in capturing me."

It was time to get out of the city that had long been a nest of Confederate spies but now was "swarming" with Union investigators, as Surratt put it. Just seven days had passed since the assassination. Surratt had become what he called "a wanderer in a foreign land." But not a lonely wanderer. He would remain well sheltered and hidden for the next five months in the remote Quebec countryside—an accused assassin kept safe by a network of men few would have suspected.

36.

'CAN SUCH A THING BE?'

Washington was still a city very much on edge. It had been just two weeks since Lincoln's assassination. John Wilkes Booth's body was being autopsied on a navy ship anchored in the Potomac. Most of his alleged fellow conspirators were behind bars, but John Surratt was still on the loose. Confederate general Robert E. Lee had surrendered, but there were still thousands of armed Southern troops operating in at least four Southern states. The rebel president, Jefferson Davis, had not been captured.

It was time to settle political scores.

On May 2, the new president, Andrew Johnson, issued a special proclamation that the *New York Times* turned into a stack of blaring headlines on its front page:

THE ASSASSINS.

MR. LINCOLN'S MURDER PLANNED
BY LEADING TRAITORS.

MOST OF THESE TRAITORS ARE
HARBORED IN CANADA.

JEFFERSON DAVIS IS THE HEAD
OF THE ASSASSINS.

AIDED BY JACOB THOMPSON, CLEMENT C. CLAY,
BEVERLY TUCKER AND GEORGE N. SANDERS.

"It appears from evidence in the Bureau of Military Justice that the atrocious murder of the Late President Abraham Lincoln . . . [was] . . . incited, concerted and procured by and between Jefferson Davis . . . and Jacob Thompson, Clement C. Clay, Beverly Tucker, George N. Sanders, W.C. Cleary and other rebels and traitors against the government of the U.S. *harbored in Canada*," the government pronounced. The last three words were italicized for emphasis in the *Times*.

Washington offered $100,000 for the arrest of Davis and $25,000 for most of the other men. Five of the six men whose names were plastered in headlines and posters—all but Davis—were in Canada, hardly the kind of publicity the country needed. STARTLING PROCLAMATION, the *Globe* headline read, CANADIAN REFUGEES ACCUSED. Canada had already been vilified in previous months as a base of operations for Confederate agents during the St. Albans bank raid, the Lake Erie piracy and the New York fires. But now the North Star was taking centre stage for sheltering the supposed assassins of a beloved president.

———

That front-page declaration carried all the weight of a solemn pronouncement from the White House, presumably based on solid military evidence. Yet the selection of the accused conspirators was an odd mixture. "I was obliged to issue it," Johnson later candidly admitted to Clement Clay's wife in a private correspondence, "to satisfy public clamour."

Singling out Davis made sense if you wanted to blame the Confederacy, but why not also his secretary of state, Judah Benjamin, who ran the Confederate Secret Service in Canada? Thompson and Clay were the senior commissioners in Canada, and Sanders was a renowned meddler, but W.C. Cleary was a lowly secretary (though he carried out some gun-running). Beverley Tucker was a financial operator on the fringes of the action, obscure enough that the Washington proclamation misspelled his first name.

Still, the allegations sent shock waves across Canada. "That the plot originated with the chief political rebels in Richmond, was planned in detail in Canada, and was to be carried out in Washington, there is also no doubt," the *Globe* reported on its front page, citing an "unequivocal statement" from the secretary of war, Edwin Stanton.

The *Globe* reprinted a strikingly accurate article by George Townsend, a correspondent for the *New York World*, who knew Booth well and would go on to write the first definitive biography of the assassin. "I assert that the Canadian agents knew Booth and patted his back, calling him, like Macbeth, the 'prince of cut-throats,'" Townsend wrote. He described how Booth had "abandoned the project of kidnapping" after it failed and moved on to murder; how Booth had visited Montreal, stayed at the St. Lawrence Hotel and handled his finances at the Ontario Bank. To its credit, amidst all the hysteria surrounding the conspiracy plot, the *Globe* showed some restraint when it came to Booth's alleged Canadian accomplices. "Dishonourable as their conduct has been while enjoying an asylum in this country," it cautioned, "it is still difficult to suppose them all guilty of the fiendish crime charged upon them by the American Government."

"Can such a thing be?" the *Globe* asked, warning with prescience: "That evidence may be found to consist of hearsay tales and ambitious outgivings of melodramatic villains."

———

The Confederates in Canada knew they had to defend themselves quickly and loudly. Edwin Lee was the first to speak out in a letter to the sympathetic Montreal *Gazette*, which, as was to be expected, endorsed his claim "as a Southern gentleman" that he knew nothing of the conspiracy. Lee denounced the "low slander" that his bosses in Richmond and their Canadian agents were "promoters of this murder." Yet his description of Booth's cold-blooded, murderous crime was subtly positive: "As the act of an individual, whose motives are, as yet, undeclared and unknown, it was a daring one . . . and each one may criticise it as his feelings dictate."

On May 4, just two days after Washington's proclamation, Beverley Tucker—who had also described Booth as "daring"—wrote a somewhat pompous letter "To the People of Canada" from his base in

Montreal. "I did not know that any such person as J. Wilkes Booth existed," he claimed. "I have never heard of him before." (That would have made Tucker one of the few people who knew nothing about one of the most famous actors in America. Moreover, witnesses put Tucker at the St. Lawrence Hall playing cards with Booth during his visit to Montreal in October 1864.)

Sanders, in another open letter he published with Tucker, called the allegations "a living, burning lie." But it was Sanders who was playing with the truth, ignoring the fact that eyewitnesses put him with Booth on multiple occasions. "We say we have no acquaintance whatever with Mr. Booth or any of those alleged to have been engaged with him," he insisted.

Throughout the month of May 1865, Sanders and Tucker stepped up their defence by going on the attack. In an angry statement that was later published as a pamphlet, Tucker planted the seed of misdirection for a conspiracy theory that has continued to be taken up by Confederate apologists to this day: it was Andrew Johnson, Lincoln's vice president, who was "the only solitary individual . . . who could possibly realize any interest or benefit from the perpetration of this deed." The *Globe* saw the "peculiar genius of George N. Sanders" behind that scurrilous accusation.

Then it was Jacob Thompson's turn. Before fleeing to Europe, he would take the time to pen a lengthy letter to the *New York Tribune* published on May 22. "I have never known, or conversed, or held communication, either directly or indirectly, with Booth, the assassin of the President, or any one of his associates," he insisted. He repeated the new Confederate conspiracy theory about "the complicity of President Johnson in the foul work upon President Lincoln." He complained that "the most unreasonable and unjust" thing to have happened in the Civil War was not slavery, nor the hundreds of thousands killed, but the indictment against him and his partners in Canada.

The *New York Times* in a blistering series of commentaries and articles noted that "Thompson's diatribe is simply a repetition of the trash by which the rebels . . . seek to justify their connection" to everything from cross-border raids to the yellow fever plot. "The man who would once lend himself to such business could scruple at nothing, however diabolical," the *Times* declared. "Yet this Jacob Thompson faces the world with protestation about his respectability and honor."

It was all too much for the *Times* and doubtless many of its readers on both sides of the border still reeling from the slaying of Lincoln. "From the painful ravings of these Confederate agents in Canada, . . . the people will inevitably conclude that these refugees protest too much to be honest."

———

Jefferson Davis had been on the run for a month, since the fall of the Confederate capital in early April. WHERE IS JEFFERSON DAVIS? the *Globe*, along with everyone else, asked. "Ever since the evacuation of Richmond this has been an every-day question."

As luck would have it, on the same day, May 10, that the *Globe* put that question in its headline, Davis was spotted by a patrol of Northern troops in Georgia and, after a brief chase, taken into custody. On that day as well, Clement Clay wrote to the Union army to offer his surrender, "conscious of my innocence . . . and confident of my entire vindication." The defeated president of the slave states and his Canadian commissioner met up in Macon, Georgia, as they were taken away together to a prison at Fort Monroe, where they were put in adjacent cells under the watchful guard of twenty-two soldiers. In her memoirs, Clay's wife, Virginia Clay-Clopton, captured the scene of "the weeping of children and wailing of women" as the families said goodbye to their jailed men.

By coincidence, on the same day as those arrests, the conspiracy trial of Mary Surratt, David Herold and the other accused accomplices of Booth opened in Washington. The government would try to prove that Davis and other leaders were involved in the assassination.

But just as the much-anticipated proceedings were getting under way in Washington, a shocking court case in Toronto would reveal the secrets of another dark plot—and the challenges in seeking justice against the Confederates.

37

'THE HIDEOUS DEVIL'

Just over a week before Lincoln's assassination, an unassuming man had walked in to see the US consul in Toronto. He was short in stature, dishevelled, wearing the shabby clothes of the poor, unemployed shoe-maker he was. But the explosive stories Godfrey Hyams came to tell on that Wednesday, April 5, about Confederate conspiracies in Canada would make him a star witness in the dramatic trials that soon unfolded in two countries.

Hyams was obviously still upset that he had never received the promised riches for carrying out Luke Blackburn's dirty work the year before, smuggling into the United States several trunks of clothing the doctor hoped would spread yellow fever and kill thousands. Hyams was so destitute he could not pay his rent; his newborn son had died a month earlier. Maybe, he hoped, the US government could pay him for his information as "an intimate associate of rebels" in Canada.

"He told me he had been connected with the rebels for several years and all their schemes and plots were known to him," David Thurston, the consul, told Washington. Hyams came through: he revealed details about the plotting behind the St. Albans raid; about how Jacob Thompson had worked with George Taylor Denison to outfit the *Georgian* as a warship; and, of course, about Blackburn's poisoned clothing plot.

The reaction was swift. Two days later, on April 7, the *Georgian* was seized by the government and Denison was in deep trouble, fighting to get his property back. On April 10, Hyams was on the stand, testifying in the final trial against the St. Albans bank robbers, describing plots hatched in the Queen's Hotel by Bennett Young "to take what money he could and burn down the town."

Then, on April 14, John Wilkes Booth walked into Ford's Theatre and the stakes were raised considerably. Suddenly, anything the shoemaker from Toronto could reveal about high-level Confederate conspiracies and plots of murder became of paramount importance.

———

On May 10, a Toronto detective named Francis McGarry swore out an arrest warrant charging that Blackburn and "other persons unknown" conspired to commit murder by importing large quantities of clothing "infected with the virus of yellow fever and other deadly, poisonous and noxious substances." The details and dates of the shipments clearly came from Hyams's insider information. Five days later, McGarry was in Montreal, where he had no trouble finding the good doctor in his suite at the St. Lawrence Hall. Arrest warrant in hand, the detective insisted Blackburn accompany him to Toronto immediately.

"Being seriously ill at the time, however, he could not take the trip without danger to his life," the officer recorded. It was a curiously sudden onset of health problems, considering that the doctor had the strength in the previous months to travel at least twice to Bermuda for his yellow fever work, play cards with John Wilkes Booth in Montreal and even consider taking part in an attack on Boston as part of the Northwest Conspiracy.

By the end of the week, Blackburn told the police he "was sufficiently restored to bear the fatigue of the journey" to Ontario. He bid his friends a tearful goodbye, insisting: "I am completely innocent." Upon arrival in Toronto, the physician claimed that "close confinement would be exceedingly prejudicial to his health," so he arranged to stay not in jail but at the Queen's Hotel under police guard until his court hearing began.

The sensational story of a yellow fever plot would have made headlines under any circumstances. But it took on a new importance now, after Lincoln's assassination. Washington wanted any kind of proof that Confederate leaders were behind the murder of the President. If they were willing to sanction the murder of thousands through chemical warfare, the reasoning went, why wouldn't they back the killing of Lincoln? The Blackburn case quickly became a media battle as much as a judicial one, with rival newspapers displaying their passions and prejudices for their favoured side in the Civil War.

———

Blackburn's escapades had already exploded onto the front pages of the North American press a few weeks prior to his arrest, thanks to the sensational trial of one of his accomplices in Bermuda. After sending Hyams to the United States from Halifax with several trunks of clothing during the summer of 1864, Blackburn had returned to St. George's Island in Bermuda in September, hiring a local man named Edward Swan to keep watch over another shipment of ten trunks he had stuffed with soiled material from dying or dead patients. Swan did so dutifully for the next six months, and everything seemed to be going according to plan. But then, in April, the US consul there—acting in part on the tips Hyams had provided to American officials in Toronto—notified Bermudian authorities of Blackburn's plot "to introduce yellow fever into New York and Philadelphia."

An arrest warrant was issued for Blackburn, but he had long since returned to Canada. Swan, however, was picked up and charged, and when the trial got underway in a St. George's police court in late April, the evidence of Confederate complicity in the poisonous plot was disturbing. "Blackburn represented himself as a Confederate agent, whose mission was the destruction of the Northern masses," Swan explained. Blackburn told him if he didn't return to Bermuda, Swan could collect his payment from the Confederate officials who ran a permanent blockade-running operation on the island.

Three of the original ten trunks were discovered at Swan's home, with address labels on them from hotels in Quebec City and Niagara Falls. A health officer testified they contained shirts, blankets, pillowcases and bandages "covered with black stains" similar to those made by Black Vomit. Nurse Dinah Amery testified that when an infected woman under her care was sweating profusely, Blackburn insisted on smothering her with more blankets and clothing. Overnight, the nurse removed the extra coverings from the suffering patient, but the next morning the doctor returned, scolded her and quickly bundled up the material into one of his trunks.

Swan was found guilty and jailed for four months; the mastermind behind the plot, on the other hand was safely back in Canada, enjoying the comforts of the St. Lawrence Hall. The revelations from the Bermuda trial caused an uproar when the stories were picked up by the papers back in the United States and Canada. "Blackburn is in Canada, where he will, no doubt, upon these facts becoming known be considered as great a hero as Bennett Young or George N. Sanders," the *Philadelphia Inquirer* snidely remarked. On May 7 and 8, the *Globe* in Toronto and the *New York Times*—the most prominent anti-Confederate papers in their respective countries—ran the same news story about the revelations, describing Blackburn as "a leading ultra-rebel." The *Times* went on to denounce him as "a prominent and particularly vindictive traitor."

Blackburn was surely relieved that he had escaped prosecution in Bermuda, but his reprieve lasted only a few weeks until his arrest in Montreal. That only intensified the propaganda war. In Nova Scotia, the *Halifax Unionist* rushed to defend Blackburn, insisting that "his antecedents are too magnanimous and gentlemanly to warrant this suspicion." The pro-rebel *Gazette*, which had covered his medical trips to Bermuda as "an event in the interest of humanity," reminded readers of the "high reputation in which he has always stood." The *Leader* ran a sympathetic account of his detention, describing him as "a gentleman well-known in that city for his many excellent qualities and for the high professional standing he occupies."

It was all a bit much for the *New York Times*, which could not resist a dig at what it saw as hypocrisy on the part of the pro-Confederate Canadian papers. "Dr. Blackburn, the gentle specimen of Southern chivalry, who is charged with trying to import yellow fever . . . in order to destroy as many of the Northern people as possible has been suddenly transformed into a martyr by some of the Canadian papers."

———

The crowds of curious onlookers and Southern sympathizers packed into the court when the doctor's sensational trial got under way in Toronto on May 20. The Americans were skeptical about the outcome, given Canada's spotty record when it came to prosecuting Confederate plotters and the repeated St. Albans legal fiascos. "Will they give us a new act in the farce of Canadian justice," the *Philadelphia Inquirer* asked, "or will they really do something to show their detestation of the demoniac malice of this benevolent physician."

On the bench for Blackburn's hearing was a police magistrate named George Boomer, a lower court official more accustomed to settling disputes over brawls and drunkenness. Now he was faced with a complex case of an alleged conspiracy to murder with no crime scene evidence—the trunks and the clothing having been destroyed. It was much like attempting to prosecute someone for murder without a dead body. The testimony of Hyams, as the self-confessed accomplice, was therefore crucial—and it was devastating. In a colourful and damaging first-person, eyewitness account, he described how, under the doctor's direction, he smuggled the trunks that had been brought to Halifax from Bermuda into various American cities.

The pro-Southern press turned on Hyams with venom, attacking his credibility. The *Gazette* pointedly referred to him as "the Jew witness." The *Leader* dismissed Hyams's account as the "hearsay information" of a "hired ruffian," denouncing the case against Blackburn as a "nefarious piece of devilry . . . contemptible as it is wicked." Blackburn's Confederate supporters denounced Hyams as a "notorious felon" and a "villain," dismissed him as a "beggar" and a "poor creature," and then finally settled on what they no doubt considered the ultimate insult: he was a "cock-eyed Jew."

In court, Blackburn's defence lawyer then tried to turn the tables by trying to make Hyams the chief culprit, arguing that even if his evidence was "true in every respect, it did not prove a conspiracy but the employment by Blackburn of Hyams to carry out the business already planned by Hyams." The *Toronto Leader* jumped on this specious line of reasoning, insisting that the shoemaker was "equally deserving of blame" and that both he and Blackburn should be punished or neither. The *Globe* angrily replied that it was clear who was the mastermind of the operation: "Dr. Blackburn is a man of education and standing, while Hyams is a poor and illiterate person."

Back and forth the two newspapers went, as if they were in court and not the lawyers.

The *Leader* tried arguing that "there is nothing to show that the yellow fever did break out at any of the places mentioned." To which the *Globe* replied in a pointed rebuke: "Blackburn is as guilty as if hundreds had perished by the dread disease, for he did everything that could be done to accomplish it . . . The *Leader's* reasoning would have excused Booth's guilt if the shot had not resulted in Lincoln's death."

Finally, out of desperation, the *Leader* noted that even if Blackburn committed the crimes alleged, did not the Americans in the past infect Indigenous peoples with smallpox blankets to wipe them out? "Will one infamy excuse another?" the *Globe* asked. "Because an outrage was committed . . . is a similar outrage now excusable? That is the high moral code of the *Toronto Leader*."

It was a debate in which neither side would budge. But then a bombshell was dropped in the courtroom—and it came not from a Union snitch but from a close Confederate associate of Blackburn's.

———

William C. Cleary, as the secretary to Jacob Thompson from the start of Confederate operations in Canada, was an ever-present observer and at times an active participant in many of their schemes. He remained to the very end a loyal and unrepentant rebel. So when he submitted a sworn affidavit to the court that was entered into evidence on May 23, he could not be accused of any of the animus Hyams carried as a spurned accomplice turned government agent.

Cleary started off by admitting he knew both Blackburn and Hyams and "met them on several occasions in Canada." In January, he met Blackburn in Montreal when the doctor explained he had hired Hyams to distribute clothing "infected with the yellow fever" into the United States. But Blackburn had his doubts about Hyams—"a great rascal" he called him—carrying out the mission. Cleary recounted how Blackburn, planning to replace Hyams with a more reliable accomplice, "had more goods prepared"—a reference no doubt to the ten trunks still sitting at the time with Edward Swan in Bermuda.

It was stunning testimony, confirming the gist of Hyams's accusations and the revelations from the Bermuda courts. Worse still, Cleary's testimony implicated the Confederate leaders in Canada. "Dr. Blackburn told me he expected to get money from Mr. Thompson to carry out this enterprise," Cleary continued. The three men were all staying at the St. Lawrence Hall and Blackburn proposed to accompany Cleary and Thompson on a planned trip to Halifax in early April "on his way to make his second attempt." According to Cleary, Thompson balked at financing the mission, insisting that he was "a man of family and had a reputation to sustain." It hardly seemed credible that Thompson—who had sanctioned and bankrolled an arson attack on New York City that, if successful, could have killed hundreds, not to mention numerous prison attacks and ship hijackings—had suddenly grown a conscience. Moreover, Hyams had testified that Thompson had already paid him some money for the first yellow fever plot. But even if true, Cleary's story about Thompson's sudden reluctance hardly made a difference. The truth was out: senior Confederate leaders in Canada—and perhaps their superiors in Richmond—knew about both Blackburn's first operation of biochemical warfare in the summer of 1864 and his second attempt in 1865.

Despite these damaging revelations, the *Toronto Leader* held firm, unwavering in its commitment to Blackburn as "a paragon of benevolence." But coming from inside the Confederate camp, Cleary's testimony had badly shaken other pro-Southern papers. The most striking reversal came from the influential Montreal *Gazette*,

Blackburn's hometown paper and up until that moment his consistent cheerleader. The newspaper admitted that for the longest time, when it came to the yellow fever allegations, "we took no more notice of them than of the many others of the absurd fictions" levelled against Confederates in Canada. But Cleary was "a man of character" who laid out "credible evidence."

The *Gazette* went on to a condemnation so virulent that it is worth quoting at length. The italics are from the original newspaper article:

> This evidence being accepted, *Dr Blackburn must be found guilty* . . . Such an act cannot be held to belong to civilized war. It is an outrage against humanity . . .
>
> No punishment can be too severe for such an offence . . . [I]t is an incident of human life to be profoundly deplored that a man could fall from so high a position as that which Dr Blackburn held into *so deep an abyss as the evidence seems to have placed him*. It was an evil hour for him in which *over-zeal for the cause of country . . . or temptation of the devil* led him to commit himself to so foul a crime. *He had better himself have died.*

It was such a no-holds-barred reversal that both the *Globe* and the *New York Times*, no doubt with more than a small dose of "we told you so" satisfaction, reprinted the *Gazette*'s commentary in full.

———

Thursday, May 25, was pretty much like any other day at the busy police magistrate's court in Toronto. An 80-year-old woman was sentenced to thirty days for drunkenness. A 50-year-old man was fined $1 for indecent exposure. The owner of a brothel—politely called "a low disorderly den"—was fined $5 for assaulting one of the women working there.

Then it was the turn of the well-dressed and well-heeled Luke Blackburn to hear the judge's decision in his case. His defence lawyer had conceded there was enough evidence that "disclosed a conspiracy to commit a crime abroad." But "abroad" was the key word: he argued that precisely because the attempted murders took place in the United States, the crime was beyond the court's jurisdiction "and was consequently not triable here." Another complication was that the criminal acts that did take place north of the border—the packing and shipping of the trunks—happened in Halifax, and at the time, Nova Scotia was not in the same country as Ontario.

The presiding judge, George Boomer, didn't buy the argument entirely. "I consider that there is sufficient evidence of a conspiracy in this country," he declared. But—and it was a big but—the lowly police magistrate was troubled by "the uncertainty of the English law." So he punted the case to a higher court "to give their opinion on the facts and credibility of the evidence."

It was as good as an acquittal. Blackburn was released on $8,000 bail. By the time the case would be heard in October, prosecutors had determined the evidence was "by no means sufficient to enable the Crown to prosecute Blackburn with any chance of success." Once again, as had happened with the St. Albans case, no one disputed the acts committed—be it bank robbery or shipping trunks of supposedly infected clothing—but the Canadian courts determined, under a dubious interpretation of law, there was nothing to be done.

Blackburn may have won his judicial battle, but he and his fellow Confederates had lost in the court of public opinion. "The result of the judicial investigation in Toronto," the *Globe* reported, "has caused the utmost horror" in New Bern, North Carolina, where people accepted the popular wisdom of the time that the yellow fever could be spread by Blackburn's soiled clothing shipments. "This hideous and long-studied plan to deliberately murder innocent men, women and children . . . is an act of cruelty without a parallel," cried one paper in the city that had been hard hit by the disease.

The *Globe* used the Blackburn scandal—"one of the most fiendish plots ever concocted by the wickedness of man"—to take a swipe at all the Confederates in Canada. "It shows what despicable characters the Southern refugees count in their ranks, and to what villainy these much-petted 'gentlemen' can resort . . . how shamefully they abused the asylum afforded them in this province."

Similarly, the *New York Times* saw in the actions of Blackburn— "the hideous devil of yellow fever notoriety"—a broader indictment of the entire hellish Confederacy and its leaders. "The virus of this rebellion seems to have rotted the entire moral nature of those who have had to do with it," it wrote. "The facts altogether point with strong emphasis to the moral and mental debasement to which the principal rebel conspirators, from Davis to Blackburn, must have sunk, as the hopelessness of their cause began to stare them in their face."

Exposing the rotten moral nature of the Confederacy was more important now than ever. At the same time as Blackburn was battling it out in a Toronto court, Jefferson Davis and the Canadian Confederate leaders were being named as conspirators in the Lincoln assassination trial that everyone was watching in Washington.

38.

'THE ASSASSIN IS OF THE SOUTH'

Guilty.

Most people, at least in the North, had made up their minds long before the trial of the Lincoln conspirators started: it was not just the accused accomplices of Booth but also the Confederate leaders in Richmond and Canada who had to be punished. "Jeff Davis and the other original conspirators have committed the most monstrous crime, and, in its consequences, the most terrible witnessed," the *New York Times* intoned in the days after the assassination. "If justice ever made a claim on earth, it claims these men for punishment."

Perhaps sensing it was pushing the bounds of balanced journalism, the *Times* had the wisdom to ask: "Is justice revenge?"

Revenge was on the minds of many and they pointed the accusing finger towards Canada. "The president's murder was organized in Canada and authorized in Richmond," declared the influential journal the *Atlantic*. "The assassination plot was formed in Canada, as some of the vilest miscreants of the Secession side have been allowed to live [there] . . . The Canadian error was in allowing the scum of Secession to abuse the 'right of hospitality.'" Privately too, American officials were convinced the guilt lay as much north of the border as it did in the Deep South. As John Potter, the US consul in Montreal, wrote to his superiors back in Washington about Booth, Jacob Thompson and the other Confederates: "There are many facts which tend to prove that these persons were not only cognizant of the conspiracy but the conspiracy was planned in this city."

But proving in a court of law what is true, much less what you fervently believe to be true, is not always easy.

———

"Trial of the Century" has become an overused expression in our times, but it was certainly apt when the court proceedings began on May 9, 1865, in Washington's Old Arsenal Penitentiary. In America and around the world, people devoured the pages and pages of transcripts and articles that filled the major newspapers almost every day for close to two months.

On trial for their lives were eight people who had the misfortune of collaborating one way or another with John Wilkes Booth: David Herold, caught in the Virginia barn with Booth; Lewis Powell, who had stabbed Secretary of State Seward; George Atzerodt, who had been assigned by Booth to kill the vice president; Mary Surratt, who ran the boarding house and tavern used by the conspirators; Michael O'Laughlen and Samuel Arnold, who joined in the kidnapping plot and stayed with Booth afterwards; Dr. Samuel Mudd, who had helped an injured Booth on the run; and Edman Spangler, a stagehand at Ford's Theatre who was accused of helping Booth make his getaway.

Hanging over the entire proceedings like ghosts were the unindicted co-conspirators, named in the charges but never present in the courtroom: Jefferson Davis, who was in prison; John Wilkes Booth, who was dead; John Surratt, who was on the run; and five Confederate agents from Canada: George Sanders, Jacob Thompson, Clement C. Clay, Beverley Tucker and William Cleary "and others, unknown." That meant there were in effect two trials going on at the same time. The prosecution would meticulously lay out the criminal actions of the eight individuals in the dock in the weeks and days before the assassination. But the government had the harder challenge of trying to convince the public it was all part of a broader and more sophisticated conspiracy orchestrated from Richmond and Canada.

This was a military tribunal, not a civilian court. The judges were nine serving officers who had all seen bloody combat during the war, so they were hardly unbiased. Only a simple majority was needed for a conviction and there could be no appeal to a higher court, only to the President.

"Is justice revenge?" the *Times* had asked. Maybe a better question would have been: Is revenge justice?

———

"I visited Canada."

Those were the words spoken on the first day of the trial by Richard Montgomery, a key prosecution witness. A Union soldier and spy who had infiltrated the Confederate operations, he carried messages to and from Canada for the South while also sharing the information with Washington. Montgomery was just the first of many people on the stand who talked about the Confederate men, money and machinations north of the border. For a country that has since prided itself as being the North Star for runaway slaves, a very different picture of Canada emerged during the trial of the Lincoln assassins. The judges and the public would hear all the details about Booth's banking in Montreal, the St. Albans raid, the yellow fever plots, the Lake Erie piracy and Sarah Slater's courier missions.

But what gripped the court—and avid newspaper readers—was the testimony about high-level Confederate leaders on both sides of the border allegedly orchestrating the murder of the President. Montgomery led off the prosecution's case in seemingly strong fashion by testifying that Thompson boasted he could have Lincoln "put out of his way" and he was just waiting for approval from Richmond "to rid the world" of the President. Montgomery confirmed that Booth had been in Montreal—he said, like others, that he saw him talking with George Sanders—but then he added the explosive allegation that Booth had met Jacob Thompson several times before and after that fall visit to Canada, once in the summer of 1864 and twice during the following winter.

Next came James B. Merritt, who told the court that, as a doctor in Canada close to the Confederates, he heard them discussing assassination plans in Toronto and alleged that George Sanders had a letter from none other than Davis supporting the killing. The most explosive testimony came from Sanford Conover, who explained that he was a former conscripted soldier in the Confederate army who made his way to Montreal, became a newspaper correspondent, and—under the alias of "James Wallace"—ingratiated himself with Jacob Thompson and his crowd. Conover said he was there in April 1865 when John Surratt delivered the messages he was carrying from Richmond to Thompson. Thompson, Conover alleged, laid his hand on the dispatches, which authorized the assassination, and declared: "This makes the thing all right."

The press in the Northern states and in Canada, naturally, ate it all up. THE REBEL LEADERS IN CANADA DIRECTLY IMPLICATED IN THE MURDER was just one of a series of headlines the *New York Times* ran on June 6: JACOB THOMPSON BOASTS OF HIS POWER TO KILL TYRANTS. A LETTER FROM JEFF. DAVIS APPROVING OF THE SLAUGHTER. As the *New York Tribune* put it succinctly: "It is either overwhelmingly conclusive of the complicity of the Confederate leaders in the assassination conspiracy or it is an unmitigated lie from beginning to end."

———

There may indeed have been complicity, but it quickly emerged that there were also plenty of lies.

The government case began to fall apart when it was revealed— thanks mainly to revelations that first emerged in Montreal newspapers and soon sent shock waves across America—that the central prosecution witness Sanford Conover was actually a polished imposter named Charles A. Dunham, who had used as many as a dozen aliases and had worked for both the Confederates and the Union. Dunham's testimony, it turned out, was full of holes. He had carefully weaved true events (such as Surratt's presence in Montreal in early April) with unverifiable or fabricated stories. Hotel records from Toronto showed Thompson was not in Montreal on the dates Dunham claimed to have met him. A letter was produced that Dunham had written to Thompson introducing himself for the first time, months after he claimed to have been conferring with Thompson.

Why did he lie? Dunham had been a fraudster most of his life, yet government prosecutors were all too keen to believe and use his stories because it suited their purposes. But Civil War author William Tidwell makes the convincing case that there was a darker conspiracy afoot: that Dunham, one way or another, was in cahoots with that expert Confederate manipulator George Sanders. They were known to each other and had crossed paths in Canada.

As Tidwell points out, Dunham returned to Canada immediately after his headline-grabbing testimony in May 1865 at the Lincoln conspiracy trials—to confer with none other than George Sanders and other Confederates. Soon after those meetings, a declaration signed by "James Wallace"—one of Dunham's aliases—appeared in the *Montreal Evening Telegraph*, repudiating his own testimony as "Conover." Southern sympathizers in Canada and the US gleefully reprinted the story and other rebuttals in widely read pamphlets and books, successfully sowing doubts about the main plank in the prosecution case that Lincoln's assassination had been plotted by senior Confederate leaders in Richmond and Canada.

Either from the start Sanders had manipulated Dunham and set him up to be the vital government witness, knowing he would end up sabotaging their case; or at the very least, he turned Dunham into a weapon against the prosecution after the fact. As Tidwell concluded, Sanders "was not going to let the trial take place without trying to influence it, and he was successful in shaping the way the country thought about the assassination—even to this day": it was all the crazed work of a lone assassin, not a Confederate-aided plot.

Dunham was eventually arrested for perjury and sentenced to ten years in prison. It turned out he had also recruited the witness James Merritt, who was not a doctor in Canada and had been paid to perjure himself. Richard Montgomery, for his part, at least had not lied about his identity: he was a Union spy, as he claimed. But his military record and credibility were sketchy and the dates for his alleged encounters with Confederates also did not add up.

The damage was done: the government's case against Davis and his Canadian leaders had unravelled.

———

The prosecution of the eight defendants who were actually sitting in the courtroom was on much firmer ground, thanks to more reliable witnesses and much more incriminating direct evidence. David Herold, after all, had fled alongside Booth on the night of the assassination, and Edward Doherty took the stand to testify about capturing him at Garrett's farm. Louis Weichmann gave a damning account of Mary Surratt's frequent dealings with Booth. Lewis Powell was identified by eyewitnesses who were attacked by him when he stabbed the secretary of state at his home. George Atzerodt gave a full and detailed confession.

All four were condemned to hang. It was a blistering hot afternoon on July 7, 1865, when they were brought to the gallows that had been constructed overnight, past the graves that had already been dug for them and the gun crates that would be used as their coffins. Mary Surratt would be the first woman executed by the United States government.

The other accomplices were luckier. Samuel Mudd, Michael O'Laughlen and Samuel Arnold were sentenced to life in prison. Edman Spangler, whom Booth had asked to care for his horse at Ford's Theatre, got six years.

The results of the trial pleased almost nobody. Confederate sympathizers turned those executed—especially Mary Surratt, presented as a devoted and innocent mother—into martyrs. "They were all murdered," cried Edwin Lee in a letter from Canada to his family in the South. "[N]o trial was ever more unjustly conducted." In contrast, many Northerners were frustrated that Jefferson Davis and his Canadian operatives seemingly got away scot-free.

———

How strong was the evidence of a wider conspiracy behind Booth's murder of Abraham Lincoln? The government had botched its case, but that didn't necessarily mean that the thrust of the allegations was wrong.

It was true that among the tens of thousands of written Confederate records recovered after the war, no one ever found a memo, letter or dispatch quoting Davis, Thompson, Sanders or others planning the assassination. But, as the saying goes, absence of evidence is not evidence of absence. Many valuable and doubtless incriminating documents, after all, had been systematically destroyed. Judah Benjamin, Jacob Thompson and Clement Clay all took care to dispose of much of their personal records. Furthermore, the rebel leaders were not foolish enough to commit dangerous instructions to writing.

After the trial, the Judiciary Committee of the House of Representatives looked through thousands of pages of Confederate documents and called many witnesses. It was their investigation that helped expose the perjury of Dunham and led to his arrest and conviction. So they were hardly gullible conspiracy theorists. Their final report, issued in July 1866—a year after the trials ended—discarded all the perjured testimony and yet it was still damning. Their report documented in painstaking detail the plots hatched, orchestrated or carried out from Canada. They concluded that "Davis, Benjamin, Clay and Thompson"— the four top leaders in Richmond and Canada—"planned, organized and incited the various schemes, expeditions and conspiracies," including the yellow fever attack, the Great Lakes piracy, the St. Albans raids and the Northwest Conspiracy. At the very least, the committee argued, these murderous crimes showed the Confederate leaders could not claim they were morally or politically "incapable of the great crime of assassination."

Proving culpability does not necessarily require finding a memo or a money trail linking Booth directly to Davis or his Canadian operatives. More than a century after the assassination, modern-day historians and writers such as James O. Hall, William Tidwell and Edward Steers amassed a mountain of convincing indirect and circumstantial evidence that puts Booth's action in a broader context of desperate measures in the final months of a desperate war. Booth was not a lone madman. He was operating within a framework in which the Confederacy cultivated a dirty war and dark intrigues.

In February 1864, the Union had launched a raid against Richmond with the goal of freeing Federal prisoners. On the dead body of a young cavalry officer, Confederates found handwritten orders from Washington that stated "once in the city it must be destroyed and Jeff Davis and cabinet killed." Whether genuine or not, that letter sparked what the *Richmond Examiner* called a "war under the Black Flag"—a wave of reprisal consisting of dirty tricks and deadly plots. That included Confederate operatives and agents on both sides of the border contemplating, planning and even attempting the assassination of Lincoln.

During the failed peace talks in Niagara in the summer of 1864, an exasperated Clement Clay told a woman from Virginia who had moved to Canada that if Lincoln "does not make peace with us he had better make peace with Heaven, for we will carry the war into the White House." The witness later told investigators that when she next saw Clay at her home in Toronto in November of that year, he boasted that "it would be easy enough to put old Abe out of the way."

There was more than just talk. Davis and his Canadian officials knew about Blackburn's schemes to kill innocent civilians—and Lincoln himself—with clothing infected by yellow fever. And Booth was also not the only one to attempt to kidnap Lincoln. A member of Richmond's secret service, Thomas Nelson Conrad, tried to carry out his own kidnap operation in the fall of 1864. In his memoirs, Conrad—who got at least $400 in gold from the Confederates' hefty secret service fund— says he was "frequently sent by President Davis" on spy missions "into Washington and sometimes into Canada." What's more, Davis knew very well that any effort to abduct Lincoln had a good chance of leading to the President's death.

Another agent named Thomas F. Harney was captured four days before the assassination, preparing to plant bombs underneath the White

House. At the very least, the Confederate leaders seemed willing to entertain the prospect of killing their arch-enemy.

Then there is the central and intriguing role played by John Surratt, Booth's close friend and associate. A special congressional investigation in 1866 concluded that the evidence "renders it certain that Surratt was employed in the secret service of the rebel authorities of Richmond." While on missions with Sarah Slater, Surratt met Judah Benjamin and carried dispatches for him—in the midst of the kidnap plot he was orchestrating with Booth. It seems inconceivable that an experienced agent like Surratt would not tell his boss, the secretary of state in charge of the secret service, about such important plans. As for Surratt's partner, Sarah Slater, convicted conspirator George Atzerodt was adamant in his confession about the assassination plot that "she knew all about the affair."

Finally, what of the actions of John Wilkes Booth himself?

Booth, like the Confederate leaders in Richmond, Montreal and Toronto, was obsessed with trying to free the badly needed Confederate soldiers being held prisoner in Northern jails near Canada. That was the motivation for his initial kidnapping plot. As far back as July 1864, when he was hatching that plan, Booth visited a small hotel in Boston at the same time as three men—all using aliases—arrived from Canada. Then, three months later, in October, Booth made his trip to Montreal. Even if Booth did not meet with Thompson in Montreal, as the perjurers suggested during the trial, it is indisputable that he met George Sanders, who, according to a family biography and his own boasting, "was in frequent consultation with the Confederate President, Jefferson Davis, and Benjamin." Is it credible that Sanders—always a meddler and self-aggrandizer—never discussed his meetings with the famous actor and Southern sympathizer with his contacts in Richmond?

Sanders may also have kept in touch with Booth after he left Montreal, according to one of the more reliable prosecution witnesses during the trial. Henry Finnegass was a Union officer from Boston who had commanded a Black regiment during the war. He recounted a conversation he overheard between Sanders and Thompson's secretary William Cleary in Montreal in February 1864:

"I suppose they are getting ready for the inauguration of Lincoln next month," Cleary reportedly said.

"Yes, if the boys only have luck, Lincoln won't bother them much longer," Sanders remarked.

"Is everything going well?" Cleary pushed.

"Yes, Booth is bossing the job," Sanders replied.

There was no way to verify Finnegass's story, but hotel records did put him and Cleary in Montreal in early February and Sanders was a frequent visitor there.

George Townsend, the respected New York newspaperman with impeccable sources, concluded that Booth's visit to Montreal and his meetings with Confederates there was central to his plots against Lincoln: "From this visit, whatever encouragement Booth received, he continued in systematic correspondence with one or more of those agents down to the commission of his crime," he wrote.

There is also the intriguing possibility that Booth may have made another, less publicized trip to Montreal. Townsend wrote that Booth visited Canada "once certainly and three times it is believed." In his reports to Washington right after the assassination, the US consul in Montreal, John Potter, noted: "Booth was here in the latter part of October and probably under an assumed name at a subsequent date."

What is certain is that Booth's well-documented trip to Canada in October 1864 gave him the connections he would use for his kidnap plot. He would then use some of the same people and the same escape route on the night of the assassination. As assassination expert Tidwell eloquently concluded: "To assume that Booth went to Montreal merely to ship his theatrical wardrobe through a blockade to the South is naive in the extreme, like believing in leprechauns." Though extreme, Booth's actions were but the logical conclusion to the Confederates' demonizing of Lincoln. Black rights leader Frederick Douglass perhaps most accurately connected Booth to the Confederacy by focusing on context, not conspiracy. "Booth the assassin is of the south . . . He fired his deadly shot in the interest of the south. His motto of defense after committing the atrocious crime, was copied from the south. From the first of the war, he took sides with the south. His first thought upon the commission of the crime, was escape to the south. There is nothing in his morals or manners, or in the crime itself to separate him from the south," Douglass said. "Booth the miserable assassin only did at the last what was meditated, threatened, and expected at the very outset of the rebellion. Great as was his crime, he is at this moment not one whit guiltier, than . . . other Leaders of the rebellion."

———

Could Booth—or anyone else for that matter—have managed to kill Lincoln at some other time without any help from the Confederacy in Richmond and Canada? Absolutely, given the intense level of Southern hatred against the President and, by today's standards, the low level of security around him. But it is equally true that John Wilkes Booth could not have carried out the most famous assassination in history when and how he did without the inspiration, tacit support and indirect backing from the highest levels of the Confederacy in Richmond and Canada.

There was one man who held the best clues to those intriguing connections. John Surratt was the only person who was close both to Booth and to the Confederate leaders. He talked, planned and schemed with them all. But as his mother and the other accomplices swung from the gallows and speculation swirled about the guilt of Jefferson Davis and his fellow leaders, Surratt was nowhere to be found.

39.

'HOPING NO ONE WOULD SEE US'

For years John Surratt had relied on a network of Confederate agents and soldiers to keep him safe. Now he turned to men wearing a different kind of uniform: the priestly garb of the Catholic Church. Outside of the busy city of Montreal and a handful of other towns, the province of Quebec was a sparsely populated countryside of small roads and even smaller villages—very French, very Catholic and very isolated. The perfect place for the most wanted man in the world—who, after all, had attended a Catholic seminary—to hide.

Surratt's benefactor and protector, Brigadier General Edwin Lee, knew how to run a clandestine operation with military precision. When surrounded deep in enemy territory—as Montreal was increasingly becoming—you look for allies wherever you can find them. The Confederate general benefitted from the fact that his aide-de-camp, Lieutenant Tom Dixon Davis (a cousin of Jefferson Davis), happened to speak French fluently. Lee managed to make good friends with Father Larcille Lapierre, an influential and well-connected Quebec priest who was canon to Ignace Bourget, the Roman Catholic bishop of Montreal.

Father Lapierre would prove instrumental in marshalling the network of the French Catholic Church in aid of John Surratt.

———

Surratt urgently needed help to sneak out of Montreal. He had already moved from the St. Lawrence Hall to John Porterfield's house to then hide out at his tailor's home. On April 22, Lapierre sent his brother to pick up Surratt there. They rode by carriage to a tavern in an east end neighbourhood of the city, where Surratt crossed the St. Lawrence River in a small canoe disguised as a huntsman. They were heading towards Saint-Liboire, a hamlet about fifty miles southeast of Montreal run by the parish priest, Father Charles Boucher. "We entered the village very quietly, hoping no one would see us," Surratt recalled. The priest was told his American guest—introduced under the alias "Charley Armstrong"—was recovering from the war. "He was in very poor health," Boucher remembered, describing a fever and chills that seemed to plague his visitor. "At such times he could hardly move. He was very pale and weak. Sometimes I was apprehensive that he might not live."

At thirty-three years old, Boucher was a young and apparently eager priest who had been ordained just eight years earlier. Saint-Liboire was his fourth posting in the small villages of rural Quebec. He gave the haggard-looking American his spare bedroom, where he would stay for the next three months. Saint-Liboire was the ideal hideout for the Confederate fugitive: close enough to Montreal that he could see the mountains on the south shore of the city, but isolated enough amidst the miles and miles of farmland.

Within "ten or twelve days," Boucher later admitted, he had discovered the true identity of his mysterious house guest. Which invited the question: Why would a good man of the cloth hide an accused assassin, at the time the most wanted man on the continent? It was a thorny problem that bedevilled Boucher later, at Surratt's trial. The Catholic priest displayed a Jesuitical talent for splitting hairs and evasion:

"Did you try to conceal it?" the prosecutor asked about hiding Surratt.
"I did not speak of it."
"Did you try to conceal it?"
"From whom?"

"From everybody . . ."

"I never spoke of it."

"I say, did you try to conceal it?"

"I do not remember."

"Don't you know whether you tried to conceal it or not?"

"If you don't speak of a thing, is it concealing it?"

"My question is whether you tried to conceal it?"

"He was in my house . . ."

"I ask you if you tried to conceal him in that house?"

"I do not understand your question."

"Did you let your parishioners know that you were keeping in your house a person published as one of the President's assassins?"

"Not to my knowledge."

Only later, under examination by Surratt's defence lawyer, did Father Boucher confess the truth:

"Why did you not, when you found the person at your house was Surratt, report him to the United States?"

"Because I believed him innocent."

The American authorities knew that Surratt was hiding in Quebec and they had pretty good suspicions the Church was helping him; they just didn't know where he was. A few hours from the city, Boucher was doing his best to keep his guest away from the prying eyes of the Americans, and of almost everyone else. Surratt's health was improving: he went on walks and enjoyed duck hunting with hand-picked guests who came up from Montreal to see him.

The sad irony, of course, was that while John Surratt was enjoying his relaxing if reclusive vacation in Quebec, his mother was on trial for her life back in Washington. It became one of the darkest accusations that would dog Surratt for the rest of the life: why he did nothing while his mother faced the gallows. Surratt later insisted—rather implausibly—that he knew little about the most famous trial of the day because his friends sent him newspapers with the articles blacked out, and then stopped sending him any news altogether.

One regular visitor who kept up Surratt's spirits was the devoted Father Lapierre. "Lapierre had taken a fancy to the dashing young Southerners and was very kind to them all," Bennett Young, the veteran Confederate fighter, recalled. Lapierre was concerned about Surratt's financial health as well. Edwin Lee noted in his diary over the summer that he had "Sent C. 100" dollars after meeting with the priest.

Whatever their personal sympathies or political beliefs, Lapierre and Boucher were being faithful to the Catholic Church's deep-seated conservatism, which during the Civil War tended to lean strongly towards the South. Father Boucher and his parishioners in Saint-Liboire would have been reading how Lincoln's America was "the most immoral country in the world," as *Le Canadien* put it, where "the most monstrous and disgusting doctrines are given free rein," as the *Courrier du Canada* warned. The *Gazette des Campagnes* decried the "dictatorial tyranny" of Lincoln while hailing the more traditional South for its "patriotism . . . and honor."

When details of the Quebec clergy's collaboration with the Lincoln conspirators later became public, the conservative Catholic press rushed to their defence. The *Courrier du Canada*, a prominent paper funded in part by the Church, refuted "accusations against the Catholic clergy that it thwarted justice and protected a criminal." The priests welcomed Surratt "solely out of charity in a spirit completely independent of politics, as they would have given asylum for an escaped slave," the *Courrier* insisted. By fleeing to Quebec before the assassination, Surratt had proved his innocence, the paper argued: his body was far from the scene of the crime and "so was his soul."

Surratt may not have had God on his side, but he clearly had the Catholic Church in his cheering section.

———

Concealing an infamous Confederate in the Quebec countryside could not last forever. One day, a servant girl at Father Boucher's house peered through a hole in the wall and spotted Surratt in the guest bedroom. The priest told his guest regretfully that he could hide him no longer.

Surratt next turned up in Murray Bay, a secluded resort town for the wealthy English-speaking elite in the Charlevoix region, on the north shore of the St. Lawrence. Almost certainly, Surratt's protector, Edwin Lee, had paid for and arranged the two-hundred-mile trek from Saint-Liboire to Murray Bay, where he met the Confederate he had been protecting. "Scenery gorgeous," Lee remarked. His diary entry notes a "dinner with Armstrong" on Friday, August 11.

Compared with the cramped room in Father Boucher's home, the fresh air and open water must have felt glorious to Surratt. Adding to his pleasure was the presence of a beautiful young woman from New York, identified in quotation marks by Lee as "Miss Young." Several Surratt researchers have speculated that she may have been the elusive Sarah Slater. "Young" is obviously an alias, like Charley Armstrong. Lee does not use quotes for the real names of prominent people he records in his diary, such as Father Lapierre or Jacob Thompson. Of course, "Miss Young" could be another random young woman from New York who travels hundreds of miles to be with a famous Confederate fugitive, however unlikely that may be.

If Miss Young was indeed Slater, she would have good reason to disguise her identity. Her name had come up numerous times during the conspiracy trials in May and June, but Federal authorities seemed unable to track her down. Then, in mid-June, her hometown papers in Connecticut started making uncomfortable connections. On June 5, the *Hartford Evening Press* ran a letter signed by an anonymous "Rebel Hater" that correctly revealed her maiden name as Gilbert and accurate details of her marriage. A week later, the *Hartford Daily Courant* picked up the story and asked: "Does any one here know of her?" Apparently, some answers came in quickly. "'Mrs. Slater' who has appeared in the assassination trial . . . is well known here," the paper wrote on June 16. "Her name was Sarah and she enjoyed (?) a doubtful reputation during the latter days of her residence here." (The snide question mark was in the original.)

Slater likely saw or heard about these disturbing news reports and realized she needed to stay underground somewhere. Some historians speculate that Slater may have been with Surratt in Canada for much of the summer. Was she disguised as one of the small men in the carriage used as a decoy when Surratt fled Montreal? Was she the woman Surratt mentions—but other witnesses do not—who brings him to Saint-Liboire? Impossible to know but, like all good spy stories, intriguing. In any event, we do know that Surratt and "Young" spent the weekend boating, fishing and swimming with Lee and his guests, including the Montreal publisher John Lovell.

But like all pleasant interludes, it had to come to an end.

By August 18, Surratt was back in Montreal. The Catholic Church connection came through again. This time, the man on the run was hidden in the home of the father of the priest Larcille Lapierre, who ran a thriving shoe business. On Old Cemetery Street, not far from the St. Lawrence Hall, from his second-floor window Surratt could see the garden of the Bishop's Palace.

There were some brief, guarded moments with the mysterious Miss Young who had returned to Montreal with Surratt—harder to arrange safely in a busy city compared with the isolated countryside. Next to his references about Young, Lee recorded in his diary on August 21 that Surratt was "very devoted"—he doesn't say to whom or to what, though the implication seems clear. Lee "made an opportunity for him in the Library," presumably not just to read books.

Then, "after his departure at 8 pm," Lee writes cryptically: "Had a very confidential conversation with 'the Young' after returning from the theatre," with the word *confidential* partially underlined for emphasis. If Young was Slater, their talk could not have been about her secret courier business as it had been in the past—there was no more Confederacy for Slater to service. Did Lee warn Young about Surratt or at least discourage her from hanging around—to protect either her, the delicate operation to keep Surratt away from the law, or both? We don't know, but on August 25, Lee wrote simply: "Armstrong arrived at 8 pm. Miss Young left at 12 M" (presumably midnight). It was their last four hours together.

Sarah Slater disappeared from John Surratt's life—and the pages of history, until intrepid historians would unearth the story of her final years.

———

Surratt had at least one regular visitor while he was cloistered near the Bishop's Palace. He must have forged a close bond with his summer host, Father Boucher, for the parish priest came down to Montreal several times a week to keep company with the lonely Confederate.

Still, four months after Lincoln's assassination, Surratt and Lee— and the ever-helpful priests Boucher and Lapierre—must have realized that Quebec, however vast its countryside and sympathetic its Church to the Southern cause, was diminishing as a safe hideout. "After visiting Quebec and other places, with the reward of $25,000 hanging over my head, I did not think it safe to remain there," Surratt later explained, "and so I concluded to seek an asylum in foreign lands." The Catholic Church in Quebec had been extremely helpful to Surratt, but why not go even higher, all the way to the Vatican? The Pope was recruiting devoted men to fight in the Papal Zouaves, a kind of foreign legion resisting the Church's secular enemies. With Father Lapierre's recommendation, Surratt got approval to join the Pope's army.

Next came the challenge of sneaking their famous fugitive out of the country and across an ocean and a continent, all the way to Italy. According to Lee's diary, on September 1 he "made inquiries about a boat." Three days later he conferred with Father Lapierre, and on the fourth day he sent Surratt another $100. Then, on September 14, Lee made some unspecified purchases, and met again with the priest and "Armstrong." A carefully planned operation was clearly under way.

The next evening, a carriage arrived outside the Lapierre family home on Old Cemetery Street. Three men got on. Father Boucher wore his appropriate priestly attire. Father Lapierre, however, broke with religious tradition and was dressed in ordinary clothes. Surratt also took precautions: he had put on glasses and dyed his hair a dark brown. The three men took the steamer *Montreal*, headed for a connection to a transatlantic vessel in Quebec City. Doubtless with huge relief, Lee noted in his diary that "Charley leaves Quebec today." The brigadier general had spent almost half a year hiding, financing and entertaining the Confederacy's most hunted man. His mission was now fulfilled.

His co-conspirator in the Surratt operation, Father Lapierre, had one more mission to complete. A few days earlier, in the streets of Montreal, he had met a country doctor he knew well. Lewis McMillan had started his practice in Lennoxville in Quebec's Eastern Townships and then moved to other small towns until—conveniently for Father Lapierre—he began serving as the ship doctor on the *Peruvian*, the ship that Surratt was going to take to Europe. The priest promised the doctor "he would give [McMillan] an introduction to a friend." Sure enough, while accompanying Surratt on board the steamer to Quebec City, Father Lapierre brought McMillan to his room, unlocked the door and introduced him to a handsome young man he called McCarty. They chatted as the boat made its way up the St. Lawrence. When it reached Quebec City, Father Boucher said what must have been a sad farewell to the man he had hidden most of the summer.

What the priest could not have known was that in entrusting the fugitive to the friendly doctor, he had led Surratt into what turned out to be a trap of Surratt's own making. Maybe it was McMillan's reassuring bedside manner. Maybe, as the waters of the Atlantic put more and more miles between him and the American authorities, he let down his guard. Certainly, the alcohol on board helped loosen his lips. For whatever reason, over the next ten days of the ocean voyage, Surratt opened up—slowly at first and then unreservedly—to the Canadian doctor. The very first day on board, "McCarty" pointed to another passenger on the vessel and told the doctor he suspected the man was an American detective; Surratt nervously pulled a small revolver from his pocket. In the following days, he went on to boast about running important dispatches for the Confederacy from Richmond to Montreal and described his adventures with "a lady from New York" who ran missions with him. Surratt told the doctor he had received at least two payments of $30,000 and $70,000 from Secretary of State Judah Benjamin—a much higher sum than documented records ever revealed. He confessed to planning Lincoln's abduction, "which was concocted entirely by John Wilkes Booth and myself." He described how he hid in Montreal and the Quebec countryside, thanks to Confederate sympathizers and collaborating priests. Then, on the final day of the voyage, a half-hour before they landed, the very intoxicated fugitive whispered in the doctor's ear: "My name is Surratt."

McMillan, his suspicions alerted and perhaps eager for a piece of the hefty reward offered for Surratt's capture, notified American consular officials in England about his surprising encounter with the wanted man. But the authorities were slow to act, and Surratt once again managed to slip away, headed towards the Vatican. Surratt, on the run thousands of miles from home, knew the stakes were high. "I know very well if I go back to the United States, I shall swing," he had admitted to McMillan.

For close to two years, it looked as though Surratt would get away with it, safely hidden while serving the Vatican. But a chance encounter in Italy with yet another Canadian would change John Surratt's life, and the story of the Lincoln assassination, forever.

40.

'VINDICATING MYSELF'

While John Surratt had spent most of the summer of 1865 hiding in Quebec, the Quebec man who had tracked down his friend John Wilkes Booth found himself in the midst of a very public and protracted battle.

Edward Doherty had told his story about the capture of Booth and Herold at the very public trial of the Lincoln conspirators. Once he stepped away from the witness chair on May 22, he must have hoped it was all over. Surely, after a few minutes in the judicial spotlight, he could return to the more comfortable and private shadows of military life. Instead, he was suddenly caught up in a much longer and twisted trial of sorts that would drag on for more than a year and reverberate for decades after—a conflict that endangered his very reputation as an army officer and an honest man.

Ever the efficient soldier, Doherty had filed a complete report of his actions to the army's chief of staff on April 29, just three days after the dramatic events at Garrett's farm. A dry and methodical chronology, it was not without its digs at the ineffectiveness of the detectives who had been assigned to join his 16th New York Cavalry for the hunt. Doherty took care, on the other hand, to highlight the determined efforts of his men. "Great credit is due to all concerned for the fortitude and eagerness they displayed in pursuing and arresting the murderers," he wrote. "For nearly 60 hours hardly an eye was closed or a horse dismounted until the errand was accomplished."

Doherty was not just being a conscientious commander. Like any good soldier, he was preparing for the next battle—a nasty one he must have known was brewing over the more than $100,000 that had been offered for the capture of Booth and his accomplices.

———

Doherty's suspicions had been aroused the day he arrived in Washington in late April, soon after Booth had been killed. He met Lafayette Baker, the man Secretary of War Edwin Stanton had named to oversee the manhunt, who told him Stanton wanted to see Doherty the next morning to express his gratitude. But the next day, Baker suddenly informed Doherty the meeting was off. "It is desirable that the matter for the present should be kept quiet, and its publicity might frustrate our plans," Baker said, according to Doherty. "Go to your Barracks, and keep your mouth shut and all will be right." Doherty followed the instructions, only to find that Baker soon called in reporters to boast about his own role in the story, writing Doherty out of the narrative.

Worried about what was afoot, Doherty wrote to the army's chief of staff, Colonel J.H. Taylor, on May 9. Doherty submitted the names of the twenty-six men who served under him with a simple message: "My command and myself claim the honor of having effected the capture of the assassins and we respectfully ask that the reward offered be properly distributed where it belongs." Doherty or someone close to him must have leaked the story to the local media, for there was a favourable article in an Albany, New York, newspaper in early June. "There appears to be some unfair work going on with respect to Lieut. Doherty and his men," it reported. "The two detectives, Baker and Conger, who accompanied them . . . appear to have official influence on their side."

To counter that political influence of his rivals Luther Baker and Everton Conger, Doherty stepped up his campaign inside the military, sending the army's top brass affidavits from no fewer than thirteen of his men. One after the other, they confirmed the leadership role Doherty had played in the hunt, at times adding colourful descriptions about his strict orders and warnings. Private Louis Savage noted that it was Doherty who approached the witnesses at the ferry in Port Conway who gave the hunters their first clue about where Booth had gone. "I am positive Captain Doherty was the first to speak to the . . . man that gave the information," Savage said. "I did not notice any Detectives at all." Private William Byrne backed that up, reporting that detective Luther Baker was not present when Doherty spoke to the ferryman. Having learned at that point that Booth and Herold had crossed the Rappahannock just the day before, Doherty ordered another soldier, Adolph Singer, to go find detective Everton Conger, who was staying in a nearby house. "I went and found Conger asleep in the house," Singer noted. "He got up but was in no hurry getting up." Corporal Charles Zimmer, who acted as an orderly to Conger, confirmed in his affidavit that the detective was asleep while Doherty was breaking the case.

Private William McQuade said that Luther Baker had wrongly dismissed the leads Doherty was following to the ferry crossing as "a wild goose chase."

Doherty's men also described his leading role during the confrontation at Garrett's farm. Sergeant Oliver Lonkey backed up Doherty's story of grabbing Garrett's son John by the collar and dragging him to the barn once the family gave up the location of the fugitives. Private Winter placed Doherty at the centre of the action at the barn. "A good deal of conversation took place between Captain Doherty and Booth— The Captain was in front and exposed to the men inside the Barn," Winter recounted. "The detectives were more in the rear."

The accumulated weight of the testimony was impressive. Of course, it was to be expected that enlisted men would back up their commanding officer. But the sworn accounts seem too consistent, too detailed to have been coaxed or manufactured. That didn't mean that Doherty was not above embellishing his story. In his various accounts given over the years to the army, the inquiries and the press, he put himself at the centre of almost every major twist in the hunt, diminishing or even erasing the actions of detectives Baker and Conger. Baker and Conger did likewise in their accounts, downplaying the role of Doherty and his men. Doherty also at one point claimed he had cradled a dying Booth in his arms, an act not mentioned by other eyewitnesses. Still, the main pillars of his story—down to the exact words spoken—remained remarkably constant and, where possible, were largely backed up by his own men, witnesses and the documentary evidence.

He soon learned those accounts would not be enough in the cut-throat battlefield of Washington politics.

———

From within the army, there were some signs of recognition and reward for Doherty's role in capturing Booth. He was promoted to captain a week after Booth's death. But the battle for the reward seemed stalled.

Six months after Doherty had first submitted the request on behalf of himself and his men, he was told by military officials that "your claim . . . was assured." That's when things started getting really messy.

Lafayette Baker and his underlings Conger and Luther Baker did not want Doherty and his men to get the glory or the cash. In late December 1865, they lobbied Secretary of War Edwin Stanton with an account filled with exaggerations, omissions and outright lies. In their version of events, Lafayette Baker masterminded the entire hunt from his office in Washington: "The chief remained at headquarters . . . constantly, anxiously, and exhaustively collating and exploring every outside rumor, theory, and source of information that sleepless labor, vigilance, and experienced sagacity could compass." It was Luther Baker and Conger who turned up the clues from the ferry at Port Conway (even though, according to several witnesses, Conger was asleep at the time). It was Baker who took Herold from the burning barn (when by soldiers' accounts it was Doherty). The detectives went so far as to malign Doherty—and spell his name incorrectly—by fabricating the story that, at Garrett's farm, "Lieutenant Dougherty was most of the time, in the early part of the affair, at the barn, and took a position under an open shed." Never one to be modest, Colonel Lafayette Baker concluded—despite the fact he stayed in Washington, uncovered no clues and was nowhere near the chase—that he was in effect the one who "apprehended both Booth and Harrold [sic] . . . and is entitled to the reward primarily." Baker downgraded "Lieutenant Dougherty [sic] and the cavalry" to nothing but "the subordinate, though necessary, instruments."

Furious, Doherty dashed off a lengthy letter to none other than the new president himself, Andrew Johnson. "I understand that efforts are being made by General Baker, and others to deprive me of the just reward that I am entitled to," he wrote. He gave a lengthy account of the instrumental role he and his men had played at every step of the hunt for Booth and his capture. He asked the President "to withhold the distribution of the reward from that quarter, until full and impartial developments and evidence will fairly decide as to who are entitled to the reward." A few months later, in early spring 1866, Doherty followed up with another letter to Stanton. "An effort is made that I was only an escort to two detectives and that they commanded," Doherty wrote, bristling at the belittlement of his command.

The battle lines had been drawn. Now all Doherty could do was wait.

————

Doherty and the detectives were not the only people competing for a share of the reward. Other members of Doherty's 16th New York Cavalry applied even though they'd had nothing to do with the chase. A West Virginia cavalry captain offered to bribe a congressman to get a piece of the prize money. To sort through the deluge of claims, the secretary of war appointed Judge Advocate General Joseph Holt—who had presided over the conspiracy trials—and General E.D. Townsend, the army's chief administrative officer. In April 1866 they handed down their report, and for a short while at least it appeared that Doherty and his men had won. His central role in the capture of Lincoln's assassin and his accomplice could not have been spelled out any clearer:

> The military element of the expedition for the arrest of these criminals Booth and Herold is therefore believed to have been that which was essential to its success, and without which its results could not have been attained. As the commander of the detachment employed upon this important duty, Lieutenant Doherty was solely responsible

for its discipline and efficiency. He is found to have been active and energetic, and it is believed to be established by the weight of testimony that it was he who personally made the actual seizure of Herold.

The report went on to establish that it was Doherty—along with Luther Baker—"who obtained the first reliable information which rendered the capture of the criminals almost certain." "Lieutenant Doherty is shown to have acted and been recognized as the commander of the expedition" and as such was worthy of the largest share of the reward—$7,500 (worth about $137,000 today). The two detectives, Conger and Baker, who "were of no doubt great value," would each get $4,000, while Colonel Lafayette Baker would have to settle for $3,750.

Baker and his detectives must have been enraged. But unlike a lowly military man like Doherty, they had political connections. Lafayette Baker had long been a fixture of Washington intrigue and had connections in Congress. Everton Conger, for his part, was assured by a congressman named Rutherford Hayes that he would get a hefty chunk of the reward money. Hayes was a family friend from Conger's hometown—and a future president. The fix was in. Just weeks after the Holt–Townsend report was issued, a Committee of Claims in the House of Representatives began to debate the "fairness and propriety" of the reward payments. The ensuing debate on the floor of the Congress late in July 1866 was anything but fair or proper.

Giles Waldo Hotchkiss, a congressman from New York, opened the proceedings with a full-frontal attack. "I believe Lieutenant Doherty was a downright coward in the expedition," said the politician, who had never seen battle in his life. Repeating the lie that Lafayette Baker had spread a few months earlier, Hotchkiss insisted that while Baker's man, Everton Conger—"as brave and gallant a soldier as any who fought in our army"—was leading the assault on the Garrett barn, "Doherty stayed under a shed, and no power could drive him out of it," while his frightened men were "lying around under the apple trees and elsewhere." Equally ludicrous claims were made by another congress-man, Rowland Ebenezer Trowbridge, who insisted it was Conger who was "in command of the expedition" since Doherty had in essence deserted: "on the night of the capture . . . he had abandoned his post and left the premises."

Of course, this made-up version of events stood in direct contrast to the eyewitness accounts among the soldiers and the Garrett family. Representative Columbus Delano of Ohio expressed outrage that the House was trying to reward Lafayette Baker, who stayed in Washington while Doherty and his men were risking their lives in the field. "He did nothing; he sat here." John Fletcher Driggs, a congressman from Michigan, hinted at corruption because of Baker's "remarkable power in the Government." He warned: "There must be some mysterious influence at work."

Their objections were to no avail. Unlike the Holt–Townsend report, which saw the manhunt as a largely military operation (there were two dozen cavalrymen and only two detectives, after all), the congressional committee concluded that "the capture of Booth and Herold was planned and directed by Colonel . . . Lafayette C. Baker." Accordingly, it voted to give the man who sat behind a desk in Washington during the entire manhunt the biggest share of the reward money—$17,500. It allotted the same amount to Conger. Doherty would get just $2,500—a third of what Holt had proposed.

Fortunately, there was some justice restored when the report was debated in front of the full House and then put to a vote on July 28, 1866. Lafayette Baker—whose machinations and lies had also earned him plenty of political enemies—saw his bounty massively slashed down to a paltry $3,750. Conger—who appeared to have the most friends in Congress—had his prize money reduced only slightly. Luther Baker had to settle for just $3,000. Doherty had his reward pushed back up to $5,250—not as much as Holt had originally recommended, but at least it was double what the congressional committee had sug-gested. His men got a little over $1,600 each.

———

It was a messy end to an ugly affair. Doherty had been an officer sitting on a Washington park bench when written orders thrust him into the political spotlight of the Lincoln assassination. Now he was slightly richer in his pocketbook but much poorer in stature. Worse than any squabble over money, the military man whose valour and leadership had been heralded by his men and his superiors had been denigrated as a coward in Congress, the most public forum in the country.

Doherty voiced his outrage in a letter to the *New York Times* that was published on August 8, expressing frustration that because Congress had adjourned for the summer, "I no longer had an opportunity of vindicating myself before that body." So he used the press to speak out. "I cannot remain quiet under such a charge, affecting my character as a soldier and my conduct as an officer," he declared.

"Chance has connected my name with a great historical event," wrote the Canadian who took up the Union cause, "and I simply desire that the army with whom I served, and the people for whom I fought, should know that in the performance of my duty, I was not a laggard and a coward."

It was not Doherty's last word on the capture and killing of John Wilkes Booth.

41.

'A PITIFUL CASE'

For all his bravado and bluster about serving the Southern cause, John Surratt, much like his friend John Wilkes Booth, never during the four years of the Civil War opted to enlist and put on the Confederate grey of the secessionist army.

By 1866, a year after the fighting was over, Surratt was finally sporting a grey military uniform—only it was the unusual outfit of the Pope's private army, the Papal Zouaves. A now famous picture of Surratt shows him sitting somewhat pretentiously, one leg folded over the other, wearing a fez with a long pompom, a red-trimmed jacket and baggy pantaloons. He was a Zouave Third Class in Company C of the 3rd Regiment, stationed outside Rome.

Surratt's journey to Italy from England, where he had landed after fleeing Quebec, was marked by the same luck that seemed to follow the fugitive everywhere. In Liverpool in September, he was hidden by yet another Catholic priest, then made his way to London by October. There, Surratt somehow managed to get a passport as a Canadian under the name of "John Watson." He headed first to France for some sightseeing and by the end of 1865 had enlisted with the Vatican's special army. Serving with the Zouaves was an ideal solution for anyone seeking anonymity; hundreds of single men from around the world wiped away their pasts and became armed servants of God.

Except even God couldn't protect John Surratt from bad luck.

In early April 1866, Surratt was with a group of his Zouave companions, enjoying the fine weather and lots of Italian wine. He was spotted by a fellow soldier named Henri Beaumont de Sainte Marie, a Zouave private born in Quebec, who approached Surratt, asking him if he was American.

"You remind me of an American named Surratt; are you he?" Sainte Marie asked.

"Oh, no" came the quick answer.

"All the better for you," said Sainte Marie, but he knew Surratt was lying. The two men had met before, in Maryland in 1863. Surratt had been with Louis Weichmann, visiting the Catholic college they had both attended. The friendly travelling Canadian stayed in Weichmann's home for a while and kept in touch with Surratt briefly by mail. Now, Sainte Marie was certain he had crossed paths again with a famous fugitive.

Eager for fame and the substantial reward money, Sainte Marie tipped off the American authorities. After much delay and confusion, Vatican authorities arrested the Zouave they knew as John Watson on November 7, 1866. The next day, while on a walk in the prison courtyard, Surratt jumped off a parapet and managed to break his twenty-three-foot fall by landing in a pile of garbage, then made it to a ship bound for Egypt. That's where American authorities finally caught up with him on November 27. He crossed the ocean one more time—this time as a prisoner, not a passenger—on February 16, 1867. It had been almost two years since John Surratt had first arrived in Montreal in the week Lincoln was assassinated.

Finally, he would stand trial as an accused conspirator for the assassination of the President. But Surratt was far more than just a single man accused of a heinous crime. A close friend of John Wilkes Booth and a trusted agent for the Richmond Confederate leaders, he alone could unlock some of the secrets behind Lincoln's assassination. The *New York Times* expressed the sentiments of many when it hoped that his trial "will shed the light of day upon the most difficult as well as the most interesting criminal mystery of our time."

John Surratt knew that when his trial began, in June 1867, the circumstances were dramatically different—and much more favourable to him—from when his mother faced similar charges two years earlier. When Mary Surratt and the other conspirators were before a military tribunal in the early summer of 1865, Lincoln's murder was just days old. The Civil War was still simmering and many—especially in the North—were thirsting for revenge. By 1867, passions had cooled; many wanted to put the bloody past behind them.

Even more importantly, Surratt faced a civilian court, so his fate lay in the hands not of Union generals but of twelve of his peers from the Washington area. Most of them hailed from the South, and some no doubt still had sympathies for the Confederate cause. "Lucky indeed is it for this, the . . . companion and alleged confidential confederate of J. Wilkes Booth that his capture occurred after the declaration of peace and the withdrawal of martial law," the *New York Times* observed.

That accurate assessment of Surratt's luck was part of an extensive prison profile featured in the *Times*, hardly a pro-Southern paper, which reflected the favourable mood—indeed, almost the celebrity status—that enveloped the most famous inmate in the country. "Not expecting to meet such a distinguished character in such a place," the *Times* correspondent was greeted with "a very friendly smile and a courteous shake of the hand." Dressed in a dark suit in the latest fashion, a new felt hat, and neatly cut and trimmed hair, "this somewhat remarkable man" seemed relaxed and confident. "Many poor prisoners whose crimes are scarcely worth mention in comparison with the great crime associated with Surratt's name, would rejoice could their lifetime be spent as comfortable as are the prison hours of this universally accused assassin," the paper noted. His luxuries included open-air walks in the courtyard, a wide assortment of books and fine cooking supplied by friends.

The American public must have still been in awe at Surratt's ability to hide from the law in Canada, for the reporter pushed for details of his escapades north of the border:

I ventured to ask him a leading question in regard to his escape and concealment in Canada. Putting on one of his most offensive smiles, he replied, "I have nothing to say about that." His manner of reply, more than his words, conveyed to my mind the impression that he considered it "a good thing," something to boast of, a great secret that would tend to make him famous hereafter, a mystery for the world to ponder on and with which to associate his name.

The *New York Times* story ended on what turned out to be a prophetic note: "An over-lenient jury may fail to find his actual complicity with the awful crime of murder . . . but the world will ever hold him guilty in connection with the death of his mother."

————

To try to impress any "over-lenient jury," the government charged Surratt under multiple indictments, hoping to have it both ways. On the one hand, it promised to prove that Surratt "did kill and murder" the President by being at the scene as an active participant that night at Ford's Theatre. On the other hand, if jurors did not buy that, the prosecution also attempted to nail Surratt for being guilty by association, part of a wide-ranging Confederate conspiracy.

For two months, more than three hundred witnesses were paraded into the courtroom. Many who took the stand either were from Canada or talked about Surratt's Canadian adventures. "The Surratt trial is watched here with keen interest," one Montreal paper reported, since there were many people "in certain circles of this place . . . who know more on the topic of the day than they choose to tell . . . and who have been behind the curtains." Those curtains were drawn back only slightly by witnesses on the stand. Father Boucher testified about hiding Surratt in Saint-Liboire; the tailor John Reeves recounted the help he offered; Louis Weichmann and the Federal detectives told of their unsuccessful hunt for the fugitive. The prosecution even brought back the Montreal bank teller who had testified at the first conspiracy trial to describe the Confederate Secret Service's finances in Canada.

The testimony of Lewis McMillan, to whom Surratt had spilled out his heart during that long transatlantic voyage, was among the most incriminating evidence, for if the Canadian doctor was to be believed, Surratt had confessed to many crimes in his own words. McMillan told the court how Surratt bragged about "shooting the damn Yankees" with Sarah Slater; how he carried money and dispatches for Secretary of State Benjamin; how Surratt and Booth together had planned to kidnap the President; and how in the days before the assassination Surratt heard from Booth that "it was necessary to change their plan."

Trials have a tendency to bring out the best and the worst in people, and things can turn nasty and personal. Father Lapierre had obviously trusted McMillan enough in 1865 to introduce him to Surratt aboard the *Peruvian* and ask him to take care of him. But now, at the trial, the defence used the priest to undermine the credibility of the doctor. Father Lapierre told the jurors McMillan was not a trustworthy fellow because they had had a falling-out over money for the Church and—presumably even more sinful—the doctor allegedly practised abortions. The prosecution in turn sought to discredit Father Lapierre by embarrassing him with the revelation that he had spent a week in Old Orchard—a favourite Maine vacation spot for Quebeckers even back then—using an alias and dressed not as a priest but in civilian clothes while being "quite attentive to the young ladies there."

On a more serious note, the government lawyers spent an enormous—and ultimately fruitless—amount of time trying to make the dubious case that John Surratt had indeed been with Booth on that bloody night of April 14 in Washington. They produced no fewer than fifteen eyewitnesses of various calibre and credibility who insisted they had seen Surratt in the city: a barber claimed he had cut his hair that day; an old school friend was certain he had spotted him on the street; a woman recognized him on a streetcar. The defence parried with four witnesses—including merchants from the store where he bought clothes and someone who saw him at the train station—to support Surratt's claim that he was hundreds of miles away from the assassination site, on a mission for Edwin Lee to scout out the Elmira prison in upstate New York.

Defence lawyer Richard Merrick—knowing that many of the jurors had roots in the South—also played on their political sympathies, as Surratt biographer Michael Schein carefully documented. In Merrick's courtroom oratory, the Civil War over slavery became the "late war for freedom and constitutional independence." Slavery itself became a system "which is passing away, and which hereafter will be remembered in romance and in story." Surratt was just one of "a number of young men . . . sympathizing earnestly with the South" who planned to kidnap the President purely as a "measure of war." Surratt's defence was not unlike the tactic deployed by the St. Albans raiders who had argued they were not robbers but Confederate soldiers doing their duty. Surratt's role in the attempted kidnapping of the President was not a crime but a "measure of war," the jurors were told. Surratt was basically admitting to taking part in one conspiracy, as a dutiful son of the South following "his honest convictions" to kidnap Lincoln—but who conveniently happened to be out of town when the rest of his gang planned to kill the President and two of the top officials in his government. Oh, and by the way, he could not have been committing a crime with Booth because he was busy working with Confederate official Edwin Lee to break another law by planning a prison attack.

In strict legal terms, it was a flawed argument. Under conspiracy law, you are guilty of all the crimes committed by your fellow plotters whether you are there or not. At no time did Surratt tell Booth to stop; at no time did he warn authorities about Booth's actions and plans. One of the men Surratt had recruited for the kidnapping of Lincoln, George Atzerodt, never followed through on his mission to kill the vice president, but he still was hanged for being part of Booth's conspiracy. Why was Surratt any different?

Because jurors are human beings, subject to their emotions and biases. After deliberating for four days, the jurors declared they were hopelessly deadlocked and the trial ended with a hung jury. Subsequent newspaper reports revealed the jurors had voted eight to four to acquit, with almost all those on Surratt's side coming from the South.

"[W]hat a pitiful case he had," Surratt gloated about the prosecutor's defeat.

———

In desperation, the government attempted again to try Surratt, filing a second and then a third indictment. They were rejected by the courts on various technical or legal grounds, and by the end of 1868, John Surratt was a free man. *Harper's Weekly*, speaking for many in a country still reeling from Lincoln's death, had expressed the hope that Surratt's capture and trial would unlock "the secret history of Lincoln's murder." But it was not to be. In no small part thanks to the help he received in Canada, Surratt was the one who got away. His friend and fellow conspirator John Wilkes Booth had been shot dead. His mother had been hanged. The other men he recruited for the kidnapping plot had also been executed.

Surratt's acquittal was only the first illustration of what would become a disturbing legacy of the Civil War over the years: the North may have won on the military battlefields, but on the legal, political and ideological fronts, the South and its vision of America was far from defeated.

42.

'THE BLESSING
OF CANADA'

For two years, Jefferson Davis had been held at the Fort Monroe prison in Virginia, his physical strength failing, his spirits lagging. Initially held in irons on his ankles in a small cell with no visitors or books allowed except a Bible, Davis was eventually moved to more comfortable quarters where his wife Varina could see him. There was understandably little sympathy for his plight in the Northern press. "Jeff Davis should be hung," bellowed one Connecticut paper, hastening to add that this should be done, of course, as soon as he was "convicted under law." In Canada, the *Globe*—though always a fierce supporter of Lincoln—took a more measured approach. "He has been charged with the foulest of felonies—complicity in the assassination of a great and good man—but we fancy that the evidence against him is too weak to justify his arraignment." That would prove to be an all too accurate observation.

Davis's prison mate and former commissioner in Canada, Clement Clay, fared little better, his health rapidly deteriorating in his cell. He wrote sad and pleading letters to his wife, his family and Union officials. "I defy any proof that I ever did anything mean or cowardly, or unwarranted by the rules and practices of War," he declared, conveniently forgetting that he had written about the potential mass killing of all adult enslaved males to protect what he saw as his endangered white race. Clay was released in the spring of 1866, further humiliated by being obliged to take an oath of allegiance to the Federal government he had so detested.

On May 13, 1867, Jeff Davis himself finally tasted freedom. The spectators who packed the Richmond courtroom erupted into cheers and applause when their hero was granted bail, still facing treason charges. An estimated five thousand well-wishers greeted him at the Spotswood Hotel, where, during happier times for the Confederacy, John Surratt and Sarah Slater had stayed while on secret missions for Davis and his government. In Quebec too there was enthusiasm for the deposed leader of the slave states. The *Journal de Québec* hailed his release as a "great act of justice and humanity."

Davis was free, but he was a broken man. The deposed president of the Confederacy at one point had over a hundred enslaved workers toiling on his plantation; now he had lost all his power and wealth. "Our plantations had been laid waste and seized," Varina Davis wrote in her memoirs. "Poor in pecuniary purse but moderate in our wants, we turned our faces to the world and cast about for a way to maintain our little children," she wrote. "As soon as practicable, we proceeded to Canada."

It says a lot about Canada's role in the Civil War that, for comfort and protection, the first place the former president of the Confederacy headed was not south to Memphis, Montgomery or Mississippi, but north to Montreal. Canada may well have been a North Star of freedom for runaway slaves before the Civil War, but during and after the war it had been a hideout and haven for Confederate agents, and now it became a refuge for their leader.

———

Jefferson Davis left the noisy crowds of Richmond behind him and boarded a train northwards to New York, where he rested for a few days before journeying across the border by the end of May.

Davis had already sent his three eldest children to Montreal, in the care of Varina's mother and sister, soon after the war ended. Jefferson Jr., at eight years old, carried a sword with him, vowing "to lick the Yankees." Their daughter Margaret attended school at the Catholic

Convent of the Sacred Heart—she had made "satisfactory improvement in French and other studies," a teacher assured her family—even though the Davises were Protestants. "The Catholics, God bless them, have been everything to me . . . The Catholic clergy have been so good to me I love the sight of one," Varina told her husband in a letter.

The Archbishop of Halifax, Thomas Connolly, who had long been supportive of the Confederates, offered to educate the Davis children. He visited Margaret at her school, giving her a prayer book and a small gold cross. An unnamed priest in Montreal—perhaps one of the Church fathers who had helped hide John Surratt—had sent Davis a bottle of fine liqueur, a green Chartreuse, from his private collection while he was in prison. Southern aristocrats that they were, the Davis clan was drawn to the traditional ways of French Catholic Quebec, as a *Chicago Tribune* correspondent found out when he spent time with the children and Varina's mother. "She likes the idea of caste that prevails in the Province," he reported, "and thinks that in this the people are like those of the South, who dislike the freedom of manner and equality that is in the North."

Money was tight and the family was forced to move from a home on Mansfield Street to a smaller place in the east end, on Viger Square. Varina's sister Margaret chose a strange way to keep her morale up. She carried around a bloodstained rag taken from a Union regiment during the war. "This thing," the *Tribune* remarked, "she looks upon with great pride."

Once Davis and his wife arrived to join the children, the family needed to find a larger place to live. The *New York Times* reported that apartments had been reserved—where else?—at the St. Lawrence Hall. But in the end, help and better housing came from local sympathizers. The wealthy Montreal publisher John Lovell, who had printed many pro-Confederate pamphlets and books, put the family up at his mansion on the corner of St. Catherine and Union, where the Bay department store now stands. "We could not but sympathize with the Southerners," explained Lovell's wife, "in the loss of their luxurious homes and of the many near and dear to them."

Eventually, the family settled in a three-storey, grey stone house with arched windows nestled in a quiet neighbourhood in the west end of the city known as Mountain Terrace, paid for by anonymous Confederate donors. The *Gazette* reported that Varina Davis had come to Montreal "accompanied by two servants of color," but it was not clear if they were former slaves from the old family plantation.

At first, Davis kept his stay in Canada low-key. "Mr. Davis is . . . keeping within doors, or going out incognito," the *Gazette* reported. "He shuns the crowd."

But not for long.

———

Friends and supporters urged "our gallant and noble chief" to come visit Toronto. Davis boarded a steamer heading westwards, stopping halfway at Kingston to disembark for a stroll. There, according to an account by one sympathizer, he was soon surrounded by a crowd, "all pressing around the President with cheers and congratulations, each begging to shake hands with him."

Meanwhile, in Toronto, "quite a flurry of excitement prevailed at the Queen's Hotel, where many of the Southerners congregate," the *Times* reported, among them the always eager Luke Blackburn, who had been notified by telegram ahead of time about Davis's pending arrival. Also tipped off early was George Taylor Denison III, the affluent benefactor of Confederates in Toronto who hosted many of them at his Southern-style villa. "I went around and started a number of friends to pass the word through the city for as many as possible to come down to the wharf and give him a reception," Denison wrote in his memoirs. "By the time the vessel arrived a crowd of several thousand filled the landing place. I got on a pile of coal with a number of friends to give the signal and start the crowd to cheer." Davis's Toronto fans waved their hats and handkerchiefs with "hearty rounds of cheers repeated again and again," according to press accounts. "So great was the rush to see him . . . police had to force a passage for him through the crowd."

Denison, however enthused, was shocked by the appearance of the newly released Confederate prisoner as he made his way down the gangway. "I was so astonished at the emaciation and weakness of Mr. Davis who looked like a dying man, that I said to a friend near me, 'They have killed him.'"

Perhaps his spirits if not his health were buoyed by what the press called a "handsome lunch" at the Toronto home of yet another top Southern official, Charles Helm, whom Davis had sent to Havana as his consul. There, "all the Confederates in the city, besides large numbers of Canadians, paid their respects to him." The adulation only intensified when Davis, accompanied by Denison, headed down Lake Ontario to Niagara (now Niagara-on-the Lake).

As Davis walked off the boat, Denison recalled the Confederate leader pointing to a large American flag fluttering in the wind at Fort Niagara, just across the river.

"Look there," Davis remarked, "there is the gridiron we have been fried on."

But on the Canadian side at least, Davis was a hero; his journey through southern Ontario looked more like a victory tour than a sad tribute for a defeated secessionist. "Niagara offered a ready shelter to many exiled or refugee Southerners," wrote William Kirby, a fervent supporter of the slave states and the influential editor of the *Niagara Mail* for twenty years. "They were welcomed and kindly treated by the townspeople." Kirby's next-door neighbour was John C. Breckinridge, who had served as the fourteenth vice president of the United States and became a Confederate general. Another general who had a comfortable home in Niagara was Jubal Early, who during the war once held a small Union town in Pennsylvania for ransom; when his demands for gold were refused, he burned it to the ground. John Porterfield, the Nashville banker who had helped Bennett Young and his men retrieve their stolen St. Albans bounty, also lived there. Davis's host while in Niagara was James Mason, a former senator and Davis's ambassador to England, who was about as hardline a Southern slave owner as they came. He had denounced Blacks as the "curse of the country" and helped write the infamous Fugitive Slave Act of 1850, which had driven so many runaways to Canada. Now he was the one in exile, living in what he called "quite a large and attractive Confederate circle."

So it was only natural that Davis's visit "created quite a sensation . . . in this little Niagara where a pleasant Confederate society is springing up," as even the *New York Times* was forced to admit. Davis was serenaded by the people of Niagara and their town band. "I thank you sincerely for the honor you have this evening shown to me," Davis told the large crowd that had gathered outside of Mason's house. "May peace and prosperity be forever the blessing of Canada, for she has been the asylum for many of my friends, as she is now an asylum to myself."

The adulation continued the next day, when "all the principal citizens called on him en masse, being introduced by the mayor," the *Times* reported. "He has been made to feel that, although in the land of strangers, he is in the midst of friends."

———

After his successful visit to Niagara, Davis returned to Toronto to attend what newspapers that were following his every move described as a fashionable wedding attended by the Southern celebrities who had flocked to the city. Davis gave away the bride, and as he left the church, a large crowd outside cheered noisily.

The cheers continued when Davis returned to Montreal. On July 18, he had agreed to join "the elite of the city" for a play at the Theatre Royal in support of a charity called the Southern Relief Association. Davis and his family arrived quietly, after the play had started. But he was soon recognized "and within moments the entire crowd from pit to box was on its feet cheering lustily." Someone in the audience shouted, "We shall live to see the South a nation yet." Amidst calls for "Dixie," the band played the Southern anthem and the theatre-goers gave the Confederate icon three cheers, which Davis acknowledged with repeated bows. "Not for half an hour did the shouting die down to allow the play to go on," according to news reports.

There was at least one note of dissent amidst all the accolades that night at the theatre. As Davis was getting into his carriage to depart, an unidentified man handed him a note. Only when he got home did Davis open it up to see the single word etched on the paper—*Andersonville*, the name of the infamous Confederate prison where thousands of Union prisoners had perished. "This . . . went like a dagger to heart," the *Herald* reported, perhaps with more wishful thinking than accuracy, claiming that the Davis women screamed and the former president nearly fainted.

Davis was undeniably haunted by the ghosts of the war. "His hair and beard are fast turning white," one Montrealer described him. "His face was haggard and care-worn, while his entire looks and demeanor showed an old and broken-down man." His wife Varina tried to encourage him to start writing his memoirs, but it only made his mood worse. She had carefully arranged for the treasure trove of his private letters and documents to be shipped to Canada, where she deposited them in the vaults at a branch of the Bank of Montreal. "All the anguish of the last great struggle came over us," Varina recalled. Her husband paced around the room distractedly and finally urged her to put away the files. "Let us put them by for awhile," he said. "I cannot speak of my dead so soon."

Jefferson Davis found some much-needed solace and solitude when, in September 1867, his family moved out of the bustle of Montreal and spent the next few months in tranquil Lennoxville, a largely English enclave in Quebec's Eastern Townships. "This is a very quiet place and so far agreeable to me," Davis told a friend. The Davis clan stayed at a small hotel, spending a lot of time at the home of a wealthy local family. Alexander Galt, the first finance minister of the newly formed Dominion of Canada, dropped by to visit the family and bring gifts for the children. Davis's older son attended Bishop's College, where he was surrounded by many other young Confederate children, who were known to break out into "war songs of the South."

When Varina's mother, who had taken care of the children during much of the war and Davis's imprisonment, died in November 1867, she was buried anonymously in a Montreal cemetery, far from her Southern home. "It is in the most beautiful part of the cemetery on the mountain," Davis wrote, "but it is unmarked and unprotected." Doctors urged an enfeebled Davis to avoid the Canadian winter, so in the late fall he and his wife left for an extended trip to the United States. In Mississippi, they came upon their old plantation in ruins. "We found our property all destroyed, our friends impoverished," Varina wrote, though they managed to reunite with the people she called "our Negroes." Davis returned to Lennoxville for a short stay in the spring, but by the summer he and his family returned to the South for good.

In December, President Andrew Johnson issued a general amnesty, granting a "full pardon and amnesty to all persons engaged in the late rebellion." Davis's treason trial had been continually delayed. Still stinging from the setback in the Surratt trial, the government feared a jury could rule in his favour. In early 1869 all proceedings against Davis were dropped. Almost four years after the war had ended, the once proud and powerful president of the Confederacy had escaped any legal repercussions.

The United States had become a more welcoming, or at least less menacing, place for the former leader of a secessionist rebellion.

———

Jefferson Davis had arrived in Canada in May 1867 a broken leader, an accused treasonous plotter out on bail, hated in much of his country. He returned as a hero to many, having stared down Lincoln's successors and won. The *Courrier du Canada* heaped praise on him as a man "who, despite everything, commands respect because of his deep soul and pure character," a leader "who fought, suffered courageously and would die if needed for his convictions."

Indeed, that kind of fulsome support from Canada proved vital to Davis's physical and political rehabilitation. Before he left Montreal for good, Davis, like so many of his Confederate colleagues, stopped by William Notman's photography studio to get his portrait taken. Next to his wife Varina, sitting elegantly at a desk, Davis stands erect and dignified, with a neatly trimmed beard and thoughtful gaze. Robert E. Lee, the foremost Confederate general, singled out "the warm reception" Canadians gave his leader. In a letter to George Taylor Denison, Lee recounted that Davis told him that, upon arriving in Canada, "he was received with the greatest enthusiasm and for the first time since his capture two years before, he drew a full breath, and felt that he was once more breathing free air." Lee concluded: "He said he instantly felt better, and told me earnestly that he believed it saved his life."

Nothing illustrates Canada's ambivalent role in the American Civil War better than Davis's stay in the country from 1867 to 1868. Canadians welcomed runaway slaves with open arms and held rallies to fight the extradition of Blacks back to the murderous slave South. Canada sent Black doctors and many soldiers to fight for the Union cause. Yet Canadians also cheered and serenaded the unrepentant head of the Confederate slavocracy, the leader who had sent agents, spies and saboteurs to Canada to keep alive a slave system. Davis himself acknowledged the special role Canada had played for him, recalling fondly: "Of my wanderings it is proper to say that in Canada the hospitality of the people was everywhere most cordial."

Escaped slaves in a "contraband" camp in Virginia, 1862
(Courtesy US Library of Congress)

PART FIVE

'ITS SHADOW STILL LINGERS'

(1868–1921)

History is not history unless it is the truth.
—ABRAHAM LINCOLN, 1856

43.

'WE ARE A POWER'

The betrayal of Abraham Lincoln's legacy and his singular triumph of the Civil War—the freeing of America's enslaved people—had begun even before the slain president's body was in the ground.

Millions of people lined the streets to pay tribute to Lincoln as his casket was driven through many Northern cities. Yet in New York— where Blacks had been lynched and killed in the ugly draft riots of 1863—the city council voted to ban Blacks from taking part in the funeral procession. The racist affront was reversed under pressure from Washington, but it showed how the battle for equality was only just beginning in earnest. In protest, Black leaders in New York organized their own event to honour Lincoln's life and death, with the famed civil rights leader Frederick Douglass as their featured speaker. "If in the coming reconstruction, we shall incorporate any of the seeds of injustice, any of the remains of slavery," he warned, "we shall repeat the mistake of our fathers, with the certainty that our children after us will reap a similar harvest of blood to that we have just experienced."

It did not take long for the seeds of injustice to be planted. The Reconstruction era, as the two decades after the Civil War were called, had begun with so much promise. The Thirteenth Amendment abolishing slavery was ratified by enough states to become law by the end of 1865. The Fourteenth Amendment, which guaranteed equal citizenship, and the Fifteenth Amendment, which protected voting rights, followed in the next five years. But Lincoln's vice president, Andrew Johnson, lacked his predecessor's popularity and his principles. He held—and expressed—deeply racist views, once saying of Frederick Douglass: "I know that damned Douglass; he's just like any n-----, and he would sooner cut a white man's throat than not."

Johnson allowed former slave states to return to the Union without enforcing any guarantees for Black voting rights. To add insult to injury, many of the men the South sent to Congress were recent Confederate generals and hardline secessionists. Johnson tried to use his veto to block the first Civil Rights Act and the Freedmen's Bureau Bill, which aimed to deliver health care, food and other basic needs to freed Blacks in the South, arguing that it infringed on states' rights. Emboldened and unrestrained by a compliant administration in Washington, the former slave-owning states unleashed a wave of violence and intimidation against Black Americans that would last decades, triggering what one historian called a "slow-motion genocide." A leading Confederate general, Nathan Bedford Forrest, set up the Ku Klux Klan—the shock troops in the Southern terror war on freed Blacks—just eight months after Lincoln's assassination; by 1870 it was rampaging throughout almost every Southern state. Federal troops were withdrawn from the South by 1877, giving the former slave owners a free hand to restore their power.

In words that ring true to this day, Frederick Douglass warned: "Slavery is indeed gone, but its shadow still lingers over the country and poisons more or less the moral atmosphere of all sections of the republic."

———

As Black doctors who left the Union army soon after the fighting was over, both Alexander Augusta and Anderson Abbott felt the sting of the postwar betrayal in civilian life.

Less than a month before the war ended, Augusta was promoted to lieutenant colonel, making him the highest-ranking Black officer in the Civil War period. But that stature in the military did not easily translate into meaningful change in postwar America. Augusta began his post-army career by running the Lincoln Hospital in Savannah, Georgia, part of the Reconstruction work of the Freedmen's Bureau that President

Johnson had tried to sabotage. Then he returned to Washington, teaching anatomy in the new medical department at Howard University. Though its student body was almost entirely Black, all the instructors were white—until Augusta became the first African American appointed to the faculty of any medical college in the US.

Still, it wasn't enough to earn him acceptance from his white peers. In 1869, Augusta applied to the local branch of the American Medical Association but was turned away. Charles Sumner, the outspoken senator who had taken up racial discrimination in public transit during the war when Augusta had been booted off a Washington streetcar, once again made discrimination against the doctor a national issue. On the Senate floor in 1870, he tried to get the charter of the Washington AMA society repealed because "they have undertaken to exclude persons otherwise competent simply on account of color."

The AMA did not budge. Augusta kept fighting but, like his fellow Blacks in postwar America, was confronted with the proverbial dilemma of one step forward, two steps back. Howard University awarded him the honorary degree of medicinal doctor—at the time a rare recognition for a Black man from an American university. But in 1877 the school insisted on replacing him as chair of the anatomy department with a white doctor. Augusta left Howard University in protest. Augusta's repeatedly unsuccessful attempts to join the whites-only medical associations led him finally, in 1884, to help found the Medico-Chirurgical Society, the earliest Black medical organization in the United States. Six years later, Dr. Alexander T. Augusta died just before Christmas 1890 at the age of sixty-five.

Dr. Alexander T. Augusta was buried at Arlington National Cemetery—the first Black military officer allowed to be honoured in the US military's official resting place for veterans. The famous cemetery was built on land that was first used during the Civil War as a "Freedman's Village" to settle freed slaves. It was a fitting tribute for the path-breaking doctor who had to flee his native America to get a degree in Canada, only to return to break down colour barriers in Lincoln's army.

But the shadows still lingered. Augusta's gravesite was kept in a segregated section of the cemetery, well away from those of the white soldiers.

———

Back in Canada, Augusta's colleague Anderson Abbott also found himself on the front lines of the battle for equality and recognition. Like Augusta, Abbott had worked for the Freedmen's Bureau after he was honourably discharged from the army. Caleb Horner, the chief medical officer of the Freedmen's Bureau, took "great pleasure in bearing testimony to the good and faithful service" Abbott displayed.

In the fall of 1867, Abbott received a precious gift from Abraham Lincoln's wife Mary. "Several articles that he valued very much and which were much used by him, were given away as mementos to his friends," Abbott wrote. "I received the plaid shawl which Mr. Lincoln was frequently seen wearing." The *New York Weekly News* reported that the shawl Lincoln wore over his knees in the cool Washington weather "was given to Dr. Abbott of Canada, who had been one of his warmest friends. During the war this gentleman, as a surgeon in the United States Army, was in Washington in charge of a hospital and thus became acquainted with the head of the nation." The description of Abbott as one of the President's "warmest friends" was an exaggeration, but the gift nonetheless was testimony to how Mary Lincoln felt about the Black Canadian doctor. Abbott kept the shawl in his family for decades "as a most precious heirloom."

In Washington, Abbott had been a witness to history, but it was time to head home. In 1867 he returned to Canada to pursue the medical studies he had suspended when he enlisted, working towards his bachelor's degree in medicine from the University of Toronto. In 1869 he received his licence from the College of Physicians and Surgeons of Ontario and became the acting resident physician for the Toronto General Hospital. In 1871, Abbott moved to Chatham with his new wife, Mary Ann Casey, the daughter of a prosperous Black barber, and established a private practice in the small southern Ontario town.

Much as his father had done, Abbott immersed himself in community affairs and Black civil rights. He broke barriers on the medical front when he was appointed as coroner for Kent County in 1874, the first Black man to hold that public medical office in the province. (It was, ironically, the same position Augusta had tried unsuccessfully to secure a few years earlier.) Abbott also became president of the Chatham Medical Association. He headed the Chatham Literary and Debating Society and was the associate editor of a widely read church newsletter. In the newsletter and in other public forums, he took up an issue that had been one of his father's passions, denouncing what he called the "unlawful, unjust and unreasonable" discrimination in education and segregated schools. To counter that, he served as president of the Wilberforce Educational Institute, which aimed to prepare Black high school students for college.

In Chatham, Abbott also began what turned into a decades-long obsession with writing lengthy and outspoken letters and commentaries to newspapers. For the smug Canadians who felt their country was immune from the rampant white supremacy in America, Abbott had harsh words. "[R]ace prejudice is growing to such an extent that there is scarcely a place in Canada where colored men are not discriminated against," he warned.

Yet Abbott was also defiant and proud. "I see thirty millions [sic] of my race on this continent," Abbott told a rally in Chatham for George Brown's Reform Party in 1874. "We are a power on the Continent which it would be folly to ignore. Like young giants, we are just beginning to feel our strength. . . . Within less than half a decade we have seen our men of our race step from the conditions of serfs," said the man who had enlisted in Lincoln's army to fight slavery. "There is no telling to what possibilities we may not attain."

———

In 1894, Abbott returned briefly to the United States to take up the prestigious post of surgeon-in-chief and later medical superintendent of Chicago's Provident Hospital, the country's first Black-owned and -operated hospital and training facility for Black nurses. The *Chicago Conservator*, a crusading Black paper in the city, hailed Abbott as being "well-known and universally recognized as one of the ablest colored surgeons in this country . . . [who] . . . has already identified himself with the people by earnest promotion of all movements designed to help his race."

After three years, Abbott—now sixty years old—moved back to Canada, settling in Toronto, where he eventually retired from private practice but not from public life. He became somewhat of a Renaissance man, writing poetry, playing and teaching music, and pursuing a prolific variety of intellectual endeavours. He wrote lengthy papers on everything from Iago, the man who takes down Shakespeare's Black tragic figure Othello, to the poets Browning and Tennyson. His thirst for scientific knowledge seemed unquenchable; he churned out studies on everything from the digestive system of plants to the chemistry of the kitchen and the history of insects in folklore.

As always, though, Abbott's primary passion remained civil rights and the race issue. In 1905 he was incensed when the *Chicago Evening Post* ran a commentary suggesting that Blacks should be excluded from voting in the South because "the negro race is so far below the white man's lane of civilization and . . . the whites of the South represent the highest type of Caucasian civilisation." With barely restrained fury, Abbott asked if the "bulldozing, fire-eating, negro-lynching white men [were] products of this civilisation." Echoing Frederick Douglass's warning about the shadow of slavery, Abbott concluded: "It is now proposed to establish a master class in the South upon a system of peonage or serfdom."

Still, Abbott ultimately saw salvation not in confrontation but in accommodation.

For Abbott, the road forward was assimilation, albeit as equals. "It is just as natural for two races, equally conditioned and living together on the same soil to blend as it is for the waters of two rivers tributary to each to mingle," he wrote, somewhat optimistically. "By the process of absorption and expatriation the color line will eventually fade out in Canada."

———

Decades after the end of the Civil War that left such an indelible mark on his life and his entire generation, Abbott wanted to keep the fires of that cause burning. In 1891 he was thrilled to be accepted as a Toronto member of the Grand Army of the Republic, an association of veterans, and then as an aide-de-camp on the staff of the Commanding Officers Department of the GAR in New York, one of the highest military honours given to a Black veteran at the time. "War is indeed a ghastly spectacle," he acknowledged in a speech he gave at a GAR gathering in 1907, but Lincoln's battle was "a righteous war and one justifiable in its purpose."

"Canadians should be especially proud of the part they took in that epoch-making period of the world's history," Abbott proclaimed. "When 30,000 of them left their homes and went forward to fight . . . thousands of our comrades poured out their blood upon the battle field as a libation upon the altar of freedom."

That, no doubt, is how Abbott wanted to be remembered—as one of what he called the "modern crusaders fighting for a just cause." In late 1913, the 76-year-old crusader suffered a bad case of appendicitis and never recovered from the complications. He passed away on December 29, leaving behind his wife and five children. The obituary in the *Globe* was five paragraphs long. It stated simply that he was a doctor "who practised for a great many years" but never mentioned his race. Perhaps in death, Abbott had achieved that fading out of the colour line for which he had wished so strongly.

Many more decades would pass before Anderson Ruffin Abbott got the historical recognition he deserved.

44

'BREAK THE SILENCE'

In the first few weeks and months after the war, there were gratifying spurts of attention for Edward P. Doherty, the man who had helped lead the manhunt for John Wilkes Booth. In May he had testified briefly at the Lincoln assassination trial. In July, at a ceremony in New York, he received "a magnificent pair of revolvers, richly mounted in gold and silver and pearl," from his fellow officers of the 16th Cavalry as "the avenger of the late lamented President."

The following year, Doherty transferred to the 5th US Cavalry as a second lieutenant, followed quickly by a promotion to first lieutenant. But clearly, he yearned for something bigger. In early February 1866 he wrote to President Andrew Johnson to apply for the posting as US consul in St. Petersburg, Russia—noting he spoke French fluently and was "fully cognisant of commercial matters," and, by the way, "I captured two of the assassins of our late President." He stepped up his campaign in April. He appears to have somehow pulled off a face-to-face meeting with the President, for a follow-up letter to Johnson dated April 11 references "your wishes expressed to me this morning when I had the honor of having a personal interview with you." Still, Doherty—who despite his fame in the Booth capture was after all just an army lieutenant, and a Canadian to boot—may have been aiming too high. There is no record of any reply from the White House or the State Department.

Instead, in 1868, Doherty got some of the excitement he craved, but not the kind of diplomacy he had in mind. As part of the 5th Cavalry, Doherty was sent to Kansas and Colorado to help the Federal army fight the Sioux and Cheyenne. If for four years Doherty had the honour of being in a Union army fighting slavery, now he and his men found themselves with the more dubious task of waging the American government's war against the Indigenous peoples. During one particularly bloody battle in July 1869, at least fifty Cheyenne fighters were surrounded and slaughtered. Doherty achieved minor fame by teaming up with probably the most famous cowboy in America, "Buffalo Bill" Cody, who became a scout for the regiment. "They bivouacked, scouted and fought together," according to one biographical sketch. Cody later wrote that, during those years, he was with Doherty "continuously, both at various forts and in the field . . . chasing or fighting Indians."

————

Doherty's new-found glory in the US Army was short-lived. The grumbling started in the fall of 1868, according to author James Carson, who carefully chronicled the history of Doherty's cavalry regiment. Doherty's commander at Camp Emory requested that he be transferred to another company for unspecified reasons, insisting "it would be best interest of the regiment." The army brass declined to act, but controversy then followed Doherty when he was posted to a procurement and supply station in Wyoming. There were charges of "inferior rations and improper punishments meted out to enlisted men for being several hours late from leave." Again, an army investigation found no fault and accepted Doherty's defence that he was harsh but fair.

Things took an even more bizarre turn in September 1870 when the military got reports that Doherty "has a wife and child whom he has utterly neglected to provide for and refused to recognize." A woman calling herself "Mrs. Nellie Doherty" claimed she had married him four years earlier, in 1865 or 1866, though there is no known record of any marriage for Doherty in those years, while he was in Washington. More allegations piled up. Doherty was accused of going to the house of "a common, public prostitute" in uniform and there were reports of unpaid debts to a military post trader and a laundress.

All these complaints could perhaps have been attributed to the petty rivalries and jealousies that plague any army; whether true or not, they clearly indicated Doherty no longer commanded the same respect from his men that he garnered during the Booth manhunt. What finally did him in was a return of the drinking problem that had led to his dismissal once before, early in the war. Formal charges were brought against Doherty in November 1870 for "conduct unbecoming an officer and a gentleman." It was alleged that he appeared publicly in uniform in Cheyenne, Wyoming, "in a state of intoxication thereby bringing scandal and discredit on the service." A special military board convened in Washington and investigated Doherty's case for a month. He escaped a court martial, but the army brass ruled that he was "unfit for the service by reason of lack of good moral character" and he was mustered out of the service on December 27.

Doherty complained that he never got an adequate chance of "explaining or disproving these malicious false charges." His friend "Buffalo Bill" Cody never believed the allegations. Years later he wrote: "Doherty was an uncomplaining man, brave and energetic and I am sure that he accomplished fully his duty as an officer of the United States Army."

Maybe. But either way, Doherty's military career was over.

————

Not all the news was glum for Doherty.

Within a year, he married a woman named Catherine Gautier, a union that lasted until his death. In a twist of fate, Catherine's father ran the famous Gautier restaurant in Washington where Booth, Surratt and their co-conspirators spent long hours in March 1865 plotting the kidnapping of the President. It is hard to imagine that the couple did not marvel at their shared connection to Lincoln's assassin.

Out of uniform and seemingly disgraced, Doherty was not out of luck or guile: for the next fifteen years he managed to secure a series of government jobs and positions all over the country. Three years after their marriage, Doherty's wife gave birth to a boy they named Charles and the family settled in New Orleans, where Doherty earned a decent living as a contractor for the state and city. In the mid-1880s he got a government appointment as what was described as "an Indian post trader in Dakota." By 1886 he had landed a well-paying if unexciting sinecure as General Inspector of Paving in New York's public works department.

Still, there was always an itch for past glory. In November 1885 he submitted a proposal to the copyright office of the Library of Congress for a "Dramatic Composition"—a play that he described as a "Panorama of the Assassination of Abraham Lincoln" about the flight and capture of the presidential killers. Then, in 1886, according to military author Carson, Doherty tried one last time to exonerate himself before the army. His request to clear his name went to the Senate Committee on Military Affairs and the secretary of war, but nothing came of it.

Doherty probably would have been content to live the rest of his life in relative obscurity. But then, an old nemesis forced his hand. Of the three men who each claimed they had played a leading role in capturing Booth—Doherty and the two detectives Luther Baker and Everton Conger—Baker had received the smallest share of the reward money, and arguably the least attention. Perhaps that was why, after simmering for more than twenty years, his frustration boiled over. In 1886, Baker gave a series of public lectures about the manhunt in the Chicago area, where he was living. In Baker's version of events, he—who had been appointed to the job by his cousin, the self-serving head of detectives Lafayette Baker—was the star of the show. Doherty was reduced to being simply an escort, "to go with us wherever we should order and protect us."

In February 1889, Baker—by then an unassuming clerk in the office of Michigan's auditor general—related his version of the manhunt to the *Chicago Tribune*, which splashed it on its front page as "the story with details never published." Indeed, many of the details had never been published for the simple reason that they were not true. Baker insisted he had been put in charge of the entire operation, a claim not backed up by the other participants. He maintained that at the Garrett farm he was the one brandishing the revolver that made the Garretts reveal that Booth was in their barn—when by the accounts of the soldiers at the scene it was Doherty. In the *Tribune* account, it is Baker who does all the talking with Booth in the barn. Baker made no mention at all of Doherty in the *Tribune* article, and towards his fellow detective Conger he exhibited nothing but scorn.

Much as they had squabbled over the reward money twenty years earlier, the fight to be remembered as history's hero was now back on. When Doherty's local paper, the *Brooklyn Citizen*, reprinted the *Tribune* story, it provoked him to step out of the shadows. "Your article has, after a quarter of a century of silence, caused me to break the silence I have strictly observed regarding the event . . . in justice to my men and myself," he wrote in a letter to the editor. That prompted the newspaper to run a lengthy interview with Doherty under the straightforward headline:

HE CAPTURED BOOTH

CAPTAIN DOHERTY TELLS HOW HE CAUGHT LINCOLN'S ASSASSIN

"He has remained silent," the newspaper reported, "allowing the honor to go to others."

"My only son who is now growing up holds that it is due to him that I talk and I finally decided to do so," Doherty explained. "It made me mad to see news articles making a hero out of Det. Baker when he did not deserve it." As evidence, the newspaper quite rightly cited the reward settlement that gave Doherty more than Baker and quoted excerpts from the congressional report that credited Doherty as "the proper commanding officer of the expedition." The *Chicago Globe*, a rival to the *Tribune*, the paper that had first run Baker's account, reprinted the Brooklyn newspaper story. Doherty got more publicity—unsolicited this time—when in 1890 the popular and prestigious *Century* magazine published in full the detailed military report he had

filed soon after Booth's capture and death. That same year, the definitive ten-volume biography of Lincoln written by his private secretary
John G. Nicolay and the future secretary of state John Hay was
published, and it credited the hunt to "a party under Lieutenant E.P.
Doherty." A two-volume Lincoln biography in 1893 by the respected
historian John Torrey Morse came to the same verdict, declaring that
Doherty's "squad of cavalry traced Booth to a barn in Virginia." In
1895 the *New York Times* added its prestige to the scales of history
with a lengthy story about the city's paving inspector who "commanded the company of cavalry which tracked Booth to his hiding
place." Much more than he had in the battle for the reward money,
Doherty, it seemed, had emerged victorious.

Doherty also strengthened his ties with his fellow army veterans.
He became a commander of a local branch of the Grand Army of the
Republic and served twice as Grand Marshal for New York's Memorial
Day celebrations. In 1895, Doherty invited "Buffalo Bill" Cody to
attend one of the parades, but the famous cowboy sent his regrets in a
warm reply, hoping to see Doherty the next time he was in the city.

They never got to meet again. Doherty died of heart disease at his
New York home on April 3, 1897. The headline for the obituary that
ran the next day in the *New York Times* was simple and to the point:
HE COMMANDED THE MEN WHO HUNTED DOWN THE ASSASSIN OF
ABRAHAM LINCOLN.

Edward P. Doherty was buried in the military's hallowed grounds at
Arlington National Cemetery in Washington, DC. His tombstone
reads: "Commanded detachment of 16th N.Y. Cavalry which captured
President Lincoln's assassin April 26, 1865."

The boy from small-town Quebec had won his battle with history.

45

'TEARS ARE IN MY EYES'

Emma Edmonds, like Edward Doherty, had been somewhat adrift after her adventures and turmoil in the army. She took a break from her postwar work in hospitals to study at Oberlin College in Ohio, a progressive school that supported Black civil rights and the women's suffrage movement. Despite sharing the college's philosophy, Edmonds by her own admission found it "too much monotonous, after so much excitement."

In the spring of 1866, she returned to the farming community in Magaguadavic, New Brunswick, where she had grown up. It gave her a chance to re-establish a bond with her sister and brother; their parents had died during Edmonds's long absence. She also reconnected with a friend named Linus Seelye, a handsome, hard-working carpenter who had spent time working in the United States. That led to a new chapter in her life. In April 1867, the 26-year-old woman who had always been convinced that marriage was "not a safe investment" wedded Seelye in a small ceremony in Cleveland. The couple were inseparable for decades, though the free-spirited Edmonds still chafed at the marital conventions imposed on women. "You know how the census takers sum up all our employments with the too easily written words 'married woman,'" she said scornfully in a later newspaper interview. "That is what I became; and of course, that tells the entire story." Then she added, almost as an afterthought, "We have been now for a goodly number of years very happy together."

It was a happiness tinged with sorrow. Edmonds's first two children, both boys, died at birth. In 1873 a daughter named Alice survived and the couple also adopted two infant orphan brothers. The Seelyes moved to Louisiana, where Edmonds—displaying the same devotion that had driven her to the Union army—helped to run an orphanage for Black children whose fathers had served and died as Colored Troops in the war. But tragedy struck her family again in 1880 when a measles outbreak took young Alice's life on Christmas morning. The health of a once robust young soldier known as "Frank Thompson" was also failing. Edmonds was "taken with congestive chills," fighting off recurring attacks of malaria and at times in bed for weeks with a fever. Short of money and perhaps also hungry for a new fight, she decided—twenty years after she had left Lincoln's army—now was as good a time as any to clear her name as a deserter and push for the military pension that was due her.

———

To convince the government bureaucracy she was deserving of a pension, Edmonds had to do two things she no doubt dreaded: to the authorities, she had to disclose her real identity behind the persona of Franklin Thompson; perhaps more frighteningly, she had to reveal herself as a woman to her wartime buddies.

In March 1882, Edmonds submitted her formal Application of Discharged Soldier, attesting that she and the private who had served in the 2nd Michigan Infantry were one and the same and that she "left the command for fear her sex would become known." Filing paperwork was easy. Now came the hard part: Edmonds had to find witnesses to support her rather unusual claim.

That same month, Edmonds walked into a small store in Michigan. Damon Stewart, the owner and a former Union soldier, was behind his desk that morning and sensed something odd about the "grave, mature woman" coming straight towards him. "She looked directly at me as I approached her and I looked directly at her," he recalled.

"Are you Damon Stewart?" the stranger asked, lifting her veil. She asked if he could give her the address of Franklin Thompson.

"I forgot that twenty years had passed since the war ended," Stewart recounted as he blurted out a question to the woman with the familiar face:

"Are you Frank Thompson's mother?"

"No, I am not his mother."

"His sister perhaps?"

Just then, someone else entered the store. The woman took a pencil from his hand and wrote on a card: "Be quiet! I am Frank Thompson."

Stewart, who had been wounded at Williamsburg in 1862 and carried off the battlefield by the nurse he knew as Thompson, was stunned. "I sat down, wilted . . . but if I was non-plussed the woman before me was not," he remembered. "She was as tranquil and self-possessed as ever my little friend Frank had been."

Once he had recovered, Stewart invited Edmonds back home to meet his wife and family. Eager to help one of his favourite comrades-in-arms, Stewart offered to reach out to other men in their former regiment. One by one—after they too overcame their initial shock at the truth behind Frank Thompson—they filed affidavits and letters supporting Edmonds's claim and her military record. Milton Benjamin confirmed that she "performed cheerfully and fully and at all times any duty which was assigned to her." Sumner Howard, who had become the Speaker in the Michigan House of Representatives, wrote that her "soldierly qualities, kindness and devotion to the sick deserve to be recognized in a liberal substantial manner." John Dietz wrote that she was "brave to last degree."

No fewer than ten former members of her regiment confirmed that Edmonds had indeed been the soldier they knew as Frank Thompson. The support was encouraging, but so far everything had remained discreetly hidden in lawyers' offices and government files. Edmonds's battle was about to become very public.

———

Damon Stewart had suggested to Edmonds that, to help her cause, they should get in touch with a friend of his who worked at the *Detroit Post and Tribune*. "While doing service in the Union army . . . I had a companion, chum, campfellow," Stewart wrote to the reporter. "I thought it was a man! I hope to die if it was not a woman! She's up at our house now. Come out!"

The lengthy article that ran on May 23, 1883, under the title THE STORY OF A REMARKABLE LIFE changed Edmonds's life forever. The first of what would become several newspaper accounts, it meant the anonymous author behind the bestseller *Nurse and Spy* could hide no more. In her newspaper interview, Edmonds talked about her childhood on the New Brunswick farm, the life-inspiring exposure to the fictional account of the cross-dressing pirate Fanny, the success of her own book and what up until then had been her quiet life afterwards.

Edmonds's campaign now moved to the political stage. On January 7, 1884, the local newspaper in Fort Scott, Kansas, where she and her family had settled, took up her cause, devoting a full page to "the story of a heroic woman." Edmonds may not have been too pleased with the part of the headline that assured readers her path-breaking days were behind her: SHE IS NOW A HAPPY WIFE AND MOTHER. But the article recounted military exploits in her own words—and then added supporting testimony from several fellow soldiers. The editor began to lobby Congress on her behalf. It helped that Bryon Cutcheon, a former major in her regiment who remembered her bravery at the Battle of Fredericksburg, now sat on the Congressional Committee on Military Affairs. He spearheaded the drive to get her request for redress approved.

Edmonds was astute enough to realize that her claim as a woman fighting in the Union army was politically explosive. "My case is so very peculiar," she wrote to Cutcheon on March 5, "that the Honorable Gentlemen in Congress may look upon the granting of a pension to me as a sort of premium offered for women to step outside their legitimate spheres—consequently a dangerous precedent." It was an insightful recognition that breaking gender barriers publicly was a lot more challenging than hiding in a man's uniform.

Luckily, though, there was little opposition when two bills were introduced in Washington in late March 1884 to remove the stain of the deserter label from Edmonds's record and to secure her a $12-a-month pension. "Truth is of times stranger than fiction, and now comes the sequel," said a report that was filed to Congress. It went on to say that "though by the rules of war a deserter," Edmonds had shown the "same zeal in the service of her country" after leaving the army by taking care of the sick and wounded soldiers—both as a nurse and by donating "many hundreds of dollars" in profits from her book to the needy men.

On March 28, the House of Representatives passed legislation known as "H.R. 5335" to formally place on the pension roll "the name of Sarah E.E. Seelye, alias Franklin Thompson." On July 5, the President signed it into law.

———

Edmonds had reunited with her closest fellow soldiers and friends to wage a public battle right up to the halls of Congress and the White House. But what must have frightened her even more was the prospect of meeting large numbers of Civil War veterans outside her tight circle of wartime companions. She had turned down an earlier invitation to a reunion of her 2nd Michigan Regiment in late 1883, feigning illness. She told a friend to send her best wishes to the men—"every one of whom I love as if they were my own brothers."

When an invitation to a second reunion in her American hometown of Flint came in October 1884, Edmonds—perhaps emboldened by her victory in Congress—nervously accepted. She showed up at the Casino Hotel to greet her former regimental comrades. All of them, like her, were a little greyer, a little heavier. But their former mail carrier stood out as "the somewhat fleshy middle-aged matron, Mrs. Linus Seelye," as one newspaper indelicately put it.

Everything at first seemed to go much better than Edmonds had expected. She was happily reunited with her former commander, General Orlando Poe, and other long-lost friends. There were songs by a local glee club and music from a band. Then, "at the urgent solicitation" of one of her former colonels, Edmonds walked to the stage to say what few words she could manage to get out without breaking down. "My dear comrades, my heart is so full I cannot say what I would to you," she declared. "Tears are in my eyes, but I shall never, never forget your love and kindness to Frank Thompson. All that I can say is, that I am deeply grateful, and may God bless you."

But at some point in the evening, things suddenly turned dark for Edmonds. A woman at the gathering—probably a jealous wife of one of the soldiers—seems to have said something spiteful, perhaps an unkind reference to Edmonds's troubled relations with two men in the unit, Jerome Robbins and James Reid. A distraught Edmonds later penned an angry, sorrowful letter to one of her friends who had attended the reunion. "Who was that lady who volunteered the information?" she wrote without elaboration. "I was properly punished for going to the reunion." She complained that the "slurs upon my character" had made her "sick at heart" to the point that she even considered returning to Canada: "I shall return to my native land, a wiser if not a happier woman."

Whatever the insult was, Edmonds recovered and never did go back home. She stayed in the US and kept in touch with her military friends, who kept writing her warm and appreciative letters. In the summer of 1886 a second bill in Congress that lifted her status as a deserter was passed into law. By the spring of 1889—seven years after she had begun her legal battle and twenty-six years after she had left the Civil War battlefield—Emma Edmonds was granted an honourable discharge with a small amount of back pay.

———

Over the years, Edmonds became somewhat of a local legend in her new home of Fort Scott, Kansas. Her biographer Sylvia Dannett reported that Edmonds fascinated the young girls in the neighbourhood when she stood outside in men's boots chopping wood. A less tolerant neighbour was upset that the now famous war veteran "couldn't get used to dresses." Edmonds was also known to put on pants and take a horse out from the local livery stable to ride an old military road called the Seven Mile Loop, perhaps reliving her adventurous rides as a mail carrier.

She connected to her military past in a more meaningful way as well: in 1897 she was accepted into the Grand Army of the Republic, the organization for honorably discharged veterans. It must have thrilled the woman who all her life—albeit in unusual ways—had sought nothing but respect and equal treatment from her male peers.

Edmonds never got much of a chance to enjoy her new status as a full-fledged Civil War veteran. Nor did she ever get the time to finish a new, presumably more accurate autobiography, which she said would be "something like a sequel" to her first book, which she felt was "the hastily written work of a novice." After repeated illnesses, Edmonds died in her sleep in La Porte, Texas, in 1897 and was buried in a family plot. A short obituary in the local paper said that as a local hero she "had won the respect and esteem of all who knew her."

The farm girl from New Brunswick who became the Union army's most famous nurse had one more military manoeuvre to pull off. Her comrades in the Grand Army of the Republic felt she deserved a special final resting place. In 1901 she was buried again with full honours in the military's section of Washington Cemetery in Houston. On her headstone was a short, gender-neutral description of her life that would have pleased her:

"Emma E. Seelye, Army Nurse."

46.

'GREAT GOOD
OR GREAT EVIL'

Unlike his fellow Canadians Anderson Abbott, Edward Doherty and Emma Edmonds, George Taylor Denison III had chosen the losing side of the war. He would pay for it in his pocketbook and his prestige.

In one of his final and more audacious efforts to bolster the Confederate war effort, the wealthy Toronto landowner and city councillor had bankrolled Jacob Thompson's scheme to refit the steamer *Georgian* into a warship that could attack Union targets on the Great Lakes. The authorities had seized the vessel in Collingwood in early April 1865, as soon as the informant Godfrey Hyams had revealed the plot to the American authorities. After Lincoln's murder, Denison rather shamelessly figured it would be an opportune time to get back the boat for which he had paid $16,500. But his credibility took a hit when one of Thompson's underlings named Larry McDonald was arrested and put on trial in late April in Toronto for his role in the plot. A senior Canadian customs official testified that Denison was indeed the registered owner of the vessel. McDonald would later admit in an affidavit that Thompson's sale of the *Georgian* to Denison "was a mere blind" to cover up the truth that it was to be a refitted warship owned and paid for by the Confederacy. It didn't help that the authorities found Denison and McDonald "engaged in suspicious carpentry" on board the boat. When two police officers raided McDonald's house in

Toronto, they found bullet moulds, cartridges and—rather startlingly—twenty-six torpedoes in a cellar he had filled with water.

It all led to more sensational reports in the American papers, hardly the kind of publicity Denison, much less Canada, needed less than two weeks after Lincoln's assassination.

The *New York Times* summed up the damaging revelations in three succinct headlines:

MORE REBEL PLOTS IN CANADA

An Armed Expedition Ready to sail from Toronto

A TORONTO COUNCILMAN IMPLICATED

George Brown's *Globe* laid into the "ignoble" Confederates and "their tool Mr. Denison" with particular delight. "We now know . . . why he did not want to pay any mark of respect to the memory of Mr. Lincoln," the *Globe* wrote, referring to his city council dissent from its condolence message. "He was too careful of the feelings of his Southern accomplices."

In March 1866, the chief justice of the Court of Queen's Bench threw out Denison's lawsuit against the Canadian government. The following year he also lost his case against the US, which had appropriated the vessel as Confederate war property. But the loss he suffered was pocket change for the wealthy aristocrat. He had the wherewithal to rebuild his Heydon Villa into an even more impressive eighteen-room mansion with imported marble fireplaces, fine carpets and "assorted weapons collected from battlefields of the world." The mansion continued to offer a warm welcome to Denison's Confederate allies.

One of his most frequent post-war visitors was the former Confederate general Jubal Early, who had taken refuge in Canada. "We became very close friends and he was often at my house," Denison wrote. "We used to discuss military problems for hours together . . . He was very extreme in his views." Indeed. Early's troops were known to have abducted hundreds of escaped slaves—and even freed Blacks—to send them back to Southern bondage.

Denison also befriended the South's most famous military leader, Robert E. Lee. He travelled to New Orleans to spend two days with Lee and then corresponded with him regularly. "He is one of those men that made the ancients believe in demigods," Denison gushed.

When the former Confederate president Jefferson Davis returned briefly to Canada in June 1881, he dropped by Heydon Villa to have tea with the South's most outspoken ally in the country. Davis returned the favour, inviting Denison to his home, a former plantation in Mississippi. In March 1882, Denison spent a week with his hero "on the broad veranda, looking through the orange and magnolia trees upon the sea, discussing the events of the war and the inside history of it from the Southern side."

Nostalgia was fine, but the Confederacy's power was dead. Denison threw himself into new causes based on similar beliefs. In 1868, Denison was one of the co-founders of the Canada First movement, which promoted a strident brand of Canadian nationalism heavily tinged with racism. It campaigned for exclusively British immigration and Anglo-Saxon, Protestant values—churning out propaganda that was virulently anti-French and anti-Catholic. Later, Denison led the British Empire League to promote the colonial message around the world.

Denison also got a chance to impose his world view from a formidable seat when he was named a police court judge in 1877. The patronage appointment came with a yearly salary of $40,000, a princely sum in those days. But it was power, not the purse, that intrigued Denison.

"He constituted a one-man 'Vigilante Committee,'" as his family biography put it, handling no fewer than 90 percent of the indictable offences that came before the court over his four-decade career as a judge. Justice in Denison's court was swift: he was known to have 250 cases in three hours. The speed and showmanship made his sessions a popular attraction. One newspaper quipped that, for a tourist, a visit to Toronto without seeing Denison in action "would be like going to Rome and not seeing the Pope."

Denison's law was fast but not fair. "He is not above trifling away a prisoner's liberty and ruining his life in order that he can get through the day's work before eleven a.m.," one Toronto newspaper complained. Denison was steadfastly anti-union and pro-police. He admitted that he relied on "an intuitive feeling as to a man's guilt or innocence." But he was openly contemptuous of the Irish, Jewish, Italian and Chinese immigrants who appeared before him. He devoted an entire chapter in his book *Recollections of a Police Magistrate* to what he called "the Negro element." As he put it, "The negroes, many of whom were escaped or freed slaves, were a source of amusement in the court because of their many peculiarities."

Denison never lost his affection for the slave owners, nor did Confederates ever forget his devotion to their cause—even a half century after the war. In 1916, 20,000 Confederate veterans marched past a cheering throng of 190,000 spectators in Birmingham, Alabama. GREATEST PARADE IN THE HISTORY OF THE SOUTH MARCHES TO STRAINS OF BELOVED DIXIE bellowed the banner front-page headline in the *Birmingham News.* COL. GEORGE DENISON GIVEN MAGNIFICENT RECEPTION HERE, an accompanying headline read. The visitor from Canada got a standing ovation from the crowd at the Bijou Theatre. Bennett Young, the leader of the St. Albans raiders, hailed Denison as "a friend and helper."

Back in Toronto, the unrepentant Confederate sympathizer stayed on the bench dispensing his peculiar form of justice until 1921. After a brief illness, he died four years later, on June 6, 1925.

———

Like Denison, the two Montreal officials caught up in the St. Albans scandal—Guillaume Lamothe and Charles-Joseph Coursol—did quite well for themselves after the war. Forced out as Montreal's police chief, Lamothe's political connections got him a federal appointment as Montreal's postmaster, a job he held from 1874 until 1891. He died in 1911.

Coursol was reinstated as a judge in April 1866 on the grounds that his errors during the St. Albans trial "had been made in good faith."

He didn't remain on the bench long. He was elected mayor of Montreal by acclamation in 1871 and again in 1872. The change of jobs apparently did not alter his character: his administration was marred by corruption, though that did not seem to harm his political career. He was picked by the Conservatives to run in the 1878 federal election and won his seat again in 1882 and 1887. He died in office the following year.

Henry Starnes, the banker whose institution was so instrumental to the Confederates' operations, was also tainted by corruption. The bank draft signed by Starnes that was found on Booth's dead body did not seem to bother anyone: he went on to serve as Montreal's mayor from 1866 until 1868. In 1871 he left the Ontario Bank to set up the Metropolitan Bank, serving as its first president. In the same way Starnes's Ontario Bank had sparked controversy by assisting the St. Albans raiders in making off with their illegal funds, his new bank found itself embroiled in an even bigger scandal. Starnes's institution funnelled hidden contributions from a railway baron to the ruling federal Conservatives in exchange for a lucrative railway contract. When another financier threatened to disclose correspondence that could expose the corruption, Starnes paid him off to buy the incriminating documents—in effect, paying a bribe to hide a bribe. But once the sordid details came out, the resulting Pacific Scandal forced the collapse of the government and the resignation of Canada's first prime minister, John A. Macdonald.

Controversy continued to plague Starnes. His bank collapsed in 1876, prompting lawsuits alleging illegal banking schemes. As a Quebec cabinet minister, he was accused of profiting from land sales for the construction of a provincially owned railway. The stink of corruption never seemed to bother his fellow aristocrats, though, and Starnes went on to hold other government posts until his death in 1898.

———

George Brown, the crusading publisher of the *Globe,* took particular delight in making sure his paper chronicled all the tawdry details of the

Pacific Scandal that plagued his political opponents. For many years after the war, Brown remained active in politics, though his unfaltering anti-slavery views did not always extend to other causes. He was staunchly anti-French and anti-Catholic, denouncing Quebec and its "Popish schemes." As a businessman, he was also sternly anti-union. When printers went on strike in 1872 to fight for the nine-hour work day, Brown pushed for the labour leaders to be charged with criminal conspiracy. Eight years later, he was shot in the leg by a disgruntled worker and died of the subsequent infection at the age of 61.

Bernard Devlin, the eloquent lawyer who had tangled with Lamothe, Coursol and Starnes's bank while representing the US government in the St. Albans trials, continued to fight for progressive causes. As a city council member, he was instrumental in creating Mount Royal Park, which to this day crowns the mountain in the middle of Montreal. He moved into federal politics as a Liberal, sitting in the House of Commons from 1875 until 1878. In one of his best-known speeches in Parliament, he proposed a radical idea back then, "giving better representation to minorities through a transformation of the electoral system." When Devlin died of tuberculosis in 1880, hundreds lined the streets for his funeral. His body lay in state for three days at the St. Lawrence Hall, which was in the district he had long represented at city hall. From there, his coffin was carried to the cemetery on Mount Royal.

Devlin had been a singular voice speaking out against the financial, political and judicial elites in Montreal who had sided with the Confederates. "Great good or great evil will mark the result of this decision," he warned in his closing remarks to city council late in 1864, during the height of the St. Albans scandal. "Have we not . . . if not directly, indirectly aided, countenanced and sanctioned aggression upon the United States by the emissaries and agents sent here from the South for that purpose?"

His words could apply not just to that infamous raid but to Canada's entire conduct during the war.

47

'JUDGE ME KINDLY'

Alexander Augusta and Anderson Abbott had to keep struggling for their rights as Black men in a postwar society of white privilege. Edward Doherty and Emma Edmonds had to battle for their reputation and their legacy. But the American Confederates who had used Canada to wage their war against Lincoln had a much easier time.

With little difficulty, most of them went on to secure successful careers, wealth, power and in some cases a measure of fame. It was the tragic irony of the Civil War that once the guns were silenced, the losers in many ways scored louder victories than the winners.

———

In his postwar surroundings in Toronto, Luke Blackburn was either a disreputable drunk or a wealthy nobleman, depending on the political slant of the newspaper. The anti-Confederate *Philadelphia Inquirer* in August 1865 spotted him in the bar in the Queen's hotel: "Dr. Blackburn, of yellow fever notoriety, is there also, fat and pompous, but deploringly neglected, and wearing a worn and seedy appearance." A few months later, a more sympathetic Southern newspaper in Nashville painted a much brighter picture of the doctor, successfully practising medicine and residing in a "splendid mansion" with an extravagantly furnished suite of rooms. "The Doctor is looking wonderfully fine, and seems to be enjoying himself like an English nobleman."

Whichever account was more accurate, the noble doctor clearly yearned for the comforts of his native South. In the spring of 1866, and then again in May 1867, Blackburn unsuccessfully appealed to the American authorities for a pardon. When yellow fever began rampaging through Louisiana and Texas in September 1867, he saw another chance. Blackburn wrote to the President offering his help. "I have had much experience in the treatment of this disease," he said unabashedly, "and feel confident I could render essential service to my suffering and dying countrymen." Blackburn's experience with the disease, of course, included trying to kill thousands of his countrymen through biological warfare. It's hard to imagine why Blackburn, having been exposed in three separate trials in Bermuda, Washington and Toronto for his poisonous plots, thought the American government would welcome him back with open arms. Secretary of State William Seward—who had narrowly escaped a stabbing death the night Lincoln was killed—insisted that Blackburn was not worthy of a pardon, having committed a "detestable crime against mankind."

But laws or principles had never stopped Blackburn before, and he was not going to start obeying them now. That September, he crossed the loosely guarded American border with no apparent problem and made his way to New Orleans to handle a yellow fever outbreak there. He did the same when the disease struck Memphis in 1873 and Florida in 1877. In September 1878, yellow fever panic spread through the small town of Hickman in Blackburn's home state of Kentucky. Blackburn came to the rescue; for his efforts he was awarded a gold watch, a parade with street banners and a brass band, and the title of "Hero of Hickman."

Never one to be shy or humble, Blackburn capitalized on his new-found fame to run for governor of Kentucky. Some Northern papers, aghast at the surprising rehabilitation of the "hideous devil" behind the Black Vomit scare, ran exposés on the yellow fever plot. But Blackburn shrugged off the stories as "too preposterous for intelligent gentlemen to believe." Most Kentuckians apparently either didn't care about or were quite proud of the doctor's efforts to help the Confederacy; he easily swept the elections in August 1879. As the New York Times and other papers continued to question the new governor's dubious past, most of his supporters in the public and the South dismissed the attacks as lies, going so far as to question whether Blackburn had even been in Canada during the war.

Blackburn ruled as a popular governor of Kentucky for four years, until 1883. When he fell ill and died in 1887, to honour him the state erected a monument over his grave. Even in death, though, Dr. Luke Blackburn couldn't quite escape the ignominy of his plans for mass murder. The inscription on the tombstone insisted the "sordid aspirations held no sway" in tarnishing the reputation of a man who was "an example of heroism and fidelity."

Atop his tombstone was a carving depicting the biblical story of the Good Samaritan.

———

Jacob Thompson, who had financed part of Blackburn's yellow fever plots and most of the other Confederate operations from Canada, also had to deal with nagging questions about his conduct, only in his case, the sniping came from movement insiders.

Thompson had made a well-timed retreat out of Canada, fleeing on the day Booth had chosen to carry out the ultimate Confederate attack by assassinating Abraham Lincoln. Before he left Montreal, Thompson cleared out the account in Henry Starnes's Ontario Bank that had been used as a Confederate slush fund. According to testimony from the chief teller during the conspiracy trials, the account that had as much as $649,873.28 at its peak had been drained down to as little as $1,766.23. In the weeks before his departure, Thompson made personal withdrawals of $300,000, $100,000 and then $19,000. The last cheque he issued, fittingly, went to hotelier Henry Hogan for the extended stays at the St. Lawrence Hall.

And these sums were just what was on the books officially. Thomas Hines, one of Thompson's operatives, estimated that with the bank robberies and other thefts he and other Confederates pulled off, there may have been as much as $2 million under Thompson's control, with no detailed accounting or paper trails.

Leaving the messiness of spies and cross-border raids behind, Thompson embarked on a sumptuous two-year jaunt across Europe with his wife, stopping in elegant hotels in Rome, Naples, Venice, Vienna, Munich, Frankfurt, Cologne, Brussels and Paris. In that city, he was joined by former raider John Castleman, who recorded that "together we studied French saw the sights and went nightly to the opera." Across the English Channel, they visited the Scottish Highlands, Ireland and northwest England.

Thompson's lavish lifestyle prompted questions from his former partners in crime Beverley Tucker and George Sanders, who "complained bitterly of Mr. Thompson's conduct," alleging he had absconded to Europe with $300,000 in Confederate cash. Confronted about this "most repulsive subject," Thompson insisted any money he kept was for his services and the losses he suffered during the war. But the airing of dirty financial laundry was not in the interest of a defeated Confederacy still licking its wounds, so a compromise was reached, with Thompson paying back a modest sum and the affair being quietly swept away.

Mollifying his friends, Thompson also sought relief from his enemies. He tried to get a pardon from the American government, lining up the Mississippi legislature to endorse his bid. The Northern press would have none of it. "This man was the organizer and disburser of the money which paid for the Lake Erie piracy, the St. Albans raid, the hotel-burning at New York, the introduction of the yellow fever," the *Philadelphia Inquirer* reminded its readers, stressing that Northerners would "scarcely endure such a wretch as Thompson walking among them as though he were an honest and honorable man."

After his European jaunt, Thompson spent two more years in Canada until a general amnesty for Confederates allowed him to return to his native South in May 1869. He found his old plantation in Mississippi "in ashes and the whole town in ruins," according to one sycophantic biography, but all was not lost. "Mrs. Thompson had saved her silver by having it buried by some of her faithful slaves." There was more than silverware to keep Thompson comfortable: one historian estimates that with properties in four states and two planta-tions, Thompson's net worth exceeded $500,000.

Jefferson Davis frequently visited "his friend and advisor" in the comfort of Thompson's new estate in Tennessee, where Confederates gathered to relive and commiserate over what they saw as the glories of the Civil War and the ghastly prospect of Black freedoms. "They had not lost their proud spirits," according to one account. "They discussed the horrors of Reconstruction and they planned how to regain their power." Thompson succumbed to illness and died in March 1885 at the age of seventy-five, taking care to destroy his personal papers so that the secrets of his operations in Canada went with him to his grave.

———

Thompson's successor as the Confederate man in charge in Canada, Edwin Lee, died in 1869 of the lung disease that had plagued him most of his life. His cousin, General Robert E. Lee, praised him as "a benefit to his race."

George Sanders, who never held an official position in Canada but had wielded so much influence and caused so much mayhem, passed away in 1873. The notorious publicity seeker was buried in an unmarked grave in New York.

Thompson's fellow commissioner in Canada, Clement Clay, lived until 1882. He never lost his dread of Black emancipation, which he feared would "recast society and create unaccustomed, strange and hitherto repugnant relations between whites and blacks."

Judah Benjamin, the secretary of state who was in charge of the Canadian secret service, was the only member of the Confederate cabinet never to return to the South. He became a prosperous and successful lawyer in London, England. He died in Paris in 1884, though not before taking meticulous care to burn all his papers.

Jefferson Davis, the man who had first sent Thompson and Clay northwards, returned to Montreal in 1881 to arrange for the publica-tion of his memoirs in Canada. He addressed a crowd of supporters at the St. Lawrence Hall. Davis died in 1889, ever unrepentant about the slave system he had built and protected until his dying day. "Nothing fills me with deeper sadness than to see a Southern man apologizing for the defense we made of our inheritance," he proclaimed.

By the end of the century, the top Confederate leaders in Richmond and Canada were all gone. They were survived well into the twentieth century by the two couriers who had loyally shuttled their secret dispatches back and forth across the border: John Surratt and Sarah Slater.

———

With the cost of admission just 50 cents for adults and 25 cents for children, they packed into the old building in Rockville, Maryland, on December 6, 1870, to hear a special guest. Three years after he had walked away from a trial a free man, John Surratt was beginning a public lecture tour with a speech in, of all places, a courthouse.

The Rockville Cornet Band struck up a lively tune as Surratt walked up to take his place at the judge's bench as the crowd filled the courtroom seats. Surratt threw off his overcoat and looked distinguished in a grey suit, not at all like "a performer of desperate deeds," as the *Washington Evening Star* reported the next day in an account that took up most of its front page.

Surratt joked that he was more nervous in front of this crowd than he had been in front of a jury. "I hope you will all judge me kindly," he said. Surratt needn't have worried. For ninety minutes he charmed the crowd with humour and feigned nonchalance. "I am not here to surprise you by any oratorical effort—not at all—but only to tell a simple tale," he told the crowd, delighting them with stories of his daring days as a spy and courier with the Confederacy, his plots with Booth to kidnap Lincoln, his flight to Canada and his ultimate triumph in the court. He justified trying to capture the President but denied endorsing or even knowing about any plans to kill him. After his lecture the band played "Dixie" and a small concert was improvised. According to a newspaper account the next day, Surratt's fans did not leave "till a late hour, during which time Surratt was quite a lion among the ladies present."

Surratt received a decidedly cooler reception when he made a speech in New York three days later to what the *Times* dismissed as "a beggarly array of empty benches." The *Washington Evening Star* chastised him for "the flippancy with which he dwells upon his love adventures in Canada in the same breath with his reference to his mother's death upon the gallows." By the time he made it to Washington for a scheduled talk on December 30, there was enough of an uproar—the first venue was embarrassingly supposed to be a site known as the Lincoln Hall—that the event was cancelled. Surratt's hopes to return to the spotlight had dimmed.

Harking back to his days as a seminarian, Surratt secured a teaching job at a Catholic school in a small town in Maryland, where he earned a reputation for inflicting physical punishment on unruly students and being "rather a good shot" at target shooting with the local men in town. In 1872, Surratt got married and moved to Baltimore, where he found a job as a clerk for a steamship line. He stayed there for four decades, moving up to become the auditor of the company by the time he retired in 1915. The next year he fell ill and died on April 21, 1916.

Family lore has it that Surratt had been working on a book about his escapades. Not long before he died, he took his manuscript and notes—along with all the details about the plots against Lincoln—and burned them in a furnace.

———

Surratt's partner in spycraft, Sarah Slater, kept her secrets even more closely guarded. "The Government did its best to find out who the woman was but was unable to get any trace of her," wrote Louis Weichmann, the boarder in Washington who, like many, was entranced with her. "She has passed into the future as one of the mysteries of the Surratt house."

The government didn't even know her correct name, much less her location. It was only more than a century later that Civil War expert James O. Hall was able to piece together her biography and trace her whereabouts up until 1865. Researcher John F. Stanton picked up the trail and discovered that in August 1866 she filed for divorce in New York—a rare occurrence back then—from her husband, the dance instructor who must have seemed exceedingly plain and boring after the spies and conspirators with whom she had been consorting during the war. A year later she married a man who conferred upon her more status (and presumably wealth)—a power company official and alderman twenty years her senior.

Writer Susan Higginbotham picked up the next clue, locating Slater in the census records in 1902 living in Poughkeepsie, New Jersey, working as a nurse. Once her second husband died, in 1913 she found a third partner, William White Spencer. There were two aspects that were intriguing, not to say calculating, about that marriage: Spencer was her brother-in-law; he had been married to Slater's sister Laura, who had passed away just a year previous. He had also served as a captain in the Union Army, fighting at Gettysburg. When Spencer in turn died the following year, Sarah Slater, the Confederates' star courier, apparently was only too happy to enjoy collecting his Civil War pension.

Slater lived quietly for another four years. She died in June 1920, the short notice in the *Poughkeepsie Eagle News* saying only that she was taken to the cemetery in an "automobile hearse" to be laid next to her mother and sister. Her tombstone gave her birth year as 1855, shaving twelve years off her age.

Sarah Slater the spy practised deception even in her death.

48.

'THE LOST CAUSE'

Four Kentuckians—Thomas Hines, John Castleman, John Headley and Bennett Young—had all ridden with the much-feared Morgan's Raiders in the early years of the war. All four fled to Toronto to continue their cross-border attacks and violence. All four flourished after the war.

John Castleman, who had been captured and jailed in the United States during the Northwest Conspiracy, was freed during a prisoner swap at the end of the war and quickly returned to Canada. While at the University of Toronto's Trinity College studying French, he also got tutoring in law from his prominent relative John C. Breckinridge, the Confederacy's last secretary of war, who had taken up residence in Niagara and Toronto. Breckinridge became a sort of mentor to the former Confederate raiders. Rooming with Castleman in a small home on Hayden Street was Thomas Hines, who also took up French and law under Breckinridge's tutelage. (The handsome and dashing Hines paid for his good looks when, two days after Lincoln's assassination, while in Detroit, he was mistaken for John Wilkes Booth and had to make an escape at gunpoint on a ferry boat to get to Canada.) Bennett Young, the leader of the St. Albans attack, tutored Breckinridge's children and joined Breckinridge for a brief European trip. Young returned to the University of Toronto in 1868 to study law.

Breckinridge's guidance and teachings paid off for the former lawbreakers. After he was pardoned by the US government, Castleman set up a successful practice in Louisville, Kentucky. Hines passed his bar exam in Tennessee and eventually became chief justice of the Kentucky Court of Appeals. John Headley, for his part, served as Kentucky's secretary of state from 1891 to 1896. He published his memoirs, *Confederate Operations in Canada and New York*, in 1906. "It should not be a question of who was right or who was wrong," he concluded in his book, epitomizing the mantra of moral equivalence that has continued to be pushed to this day by Southern apologists.

No one promoted that lie with more vigour and success well into the twentieth century than Bennett Young.

———

Young spent time studying law and literature in Ireland and Scotland before returning to Kentucky in 1868 to become a prominent lawyer. Perhaps because of his religious upbringing and studies, or perhaps because he had always been a little more contemplative than his colleagues, Young displayed a surprising willingness, for a Confederate, to reach out to Blacks in the South. He helped set up what was called the Colored Orphan Home in Louisville in 1879 and stayed on as its president for twenty-five years. Most remarkably, in 1899 he represented a former slave who sued the Ku Klux Klan after they attacked his home—and won the case.

Still, for Young, the Civil War was "the most wondrous military tragedy of the ages." He became an early and leading proponent of what became known as the Lost Cause movement, which sought to rewrite history and bury the slave states' crimes. "The very fact that the South lost lends pathos and sentiment to the story of what her sons accomplished," Young declared.

In 1889, Bennett Young joined the United Confederate Veterans, eventually rising to become its commander-in-chief as he worked to restore the glory of the Southern war effort. The 17-year-old who had joined Morgan's Raiders and then brought his determination and wits to Canada now became an honorary "general" in a Confederate army that no longer existed. In 1900 and again in 1905 he brought thousands of former soldiers in Confederate grey to march in the streets of

Louisville. He led efforts to erect a 351-foot obelisk in honour of Jefferson Davis at the site of his birthplace—considered to this day to be the tallest unreinforced concrete structure in the world and the fifth-tallest monument in the United States. In 1913 he was the highlighted speaker for the South at the fiftieth anniversary of the Battle of Gettysburg, which brought together over fifty thousand Union and Confederate veterans in the largest Civil War reunion ever held.

———

The crowning achievement of the campaign by Young and his Southern comrades to rid the Confederacy of its shame and sins came in 1914, when an imposing Confederate Memorial was placed at the Arlington National Cemetery in Washington, the most important gravesite in America. A bronze female figure adorned with olive leaves stood atop a thirty-two-foot pedestal; carvings of brave Southern soldiers and their families encircled the monument underneath. Enslaved people were depicted as submissive and supportive. One scene showed what the United Daughters of the Confederacy described as a faithful Negro servant following his master. Another featured a weeping Black "mammy" cradling her master's child as he marches off to war. A Latin inscription makes explicit the message that "the lost cause" of the Confederacy "was pleasing to the gods." The terrible irony was that while the Confederate dead were being honoured, the graves of Black soldiers remained in the "Lower Cemetery" alongside former slaves. The Arlington National Cemetery remained segregated until 1948.

On hand at the ceremony to unveil the Confederate Memorial on June 4—the 106th anniversary of the birth of Jefferson Davis—were President Woodrow Wilson and Bennett Young, by then seventy-one years old. The one-time leader of the St. Albans raiders was the first speaker to address the crowd of four thousand, which included every member of Congress. "The dead for whom this monument stands sponsor died for what they believed to be right," Young declared. "True patriotism does not require that either the North or the South should give up its ideals. Are they not stronger and better for each maintaining its devotion to the history and achievements of those who fought?"

Young's words crystallized the new mythology of the South: Forget about four million people in bondage and the battle to end slavery. The Civil War was just about patriotic ideals, both sides being equally worthy in their devotion and justness.

———

Young brought that message to Canada when he returned in 1915 for a remarkable visit to the country that had sheltered him during the war.

It began with what the Montreal *Gazette* rightly called "an extraordinary function" on Wednesday afternoon, July 14, at the swank downtown Ritz-Carlton. "Four leading citizens of St. Albans Vermont entered the hotel and paid their respects to General Bennett H. Young," the newspaper reported. Among the delegates was the editor of the *St. Albans Messenger*, which had five decades earlier denounced Young as a marauder with blood on his hands, as well as Frank L. Greene, a Vermont congressman. They were "warmly welcomed" by Young, who regaled them with stories of his escape from justice in Canada. On hand as well for the happy reunion were local Montrealers whose relatives had helped the Confederates. They included Louis Payette, the son of the jailer who had treated Young and his men so well at "Payette's Hotel"; Jack Abbott, the son of the illustrious lawyer and eventual prime minister whose "splendid ability," in Young's words, had kept him safe from extradition and a probable hanging; and C.O. Lapierre, the nephew of Father Lapierre, who had been instrumental in hiding John Surratt.

"I never could have imagined so much friendliness as has been shown to me in this city," Young said, "and I am quite determined to come back again fifty years hence just to see if the rebel sentiment is as strong."

The St. Albans raider journeyed on to Toronto, to thank George Taylor Denison for his generous support to the Confederate cause.

Then he travelled to St. Catharines, where he had first plotted the attacks with Clement Clay. "Oh yes, bygones are bygones long since," Bennett Young said in a speech to his enthusiastic Canadian admirers. The local paper headlined his talk about the "Stirring Events" of a bloody four-year war that it dismissed as "the Late Unpleasantness."

Such was the power of the Lost Cause lie in Canada and the United States that the valiant war against slavery and the murderous plots against Abraham Lincoln had been reduced on both sides of the border to an unpleasant memory to be forgotten—or, better still, to be rewritten in order to justify the inequalities and injustices that never went away. Lincoln's assassination was dismissed as the crazed act of a lone assassin, not as the ultimate outcome of the Confederacy's determination to keep millions enslaved.

It is hard to overstate the complete turning of the tables that this represented: the defeated Confederates like Young become the winners to be cheered as heroes, their victims overlooked. The *Gazette*, which had long favoured the South during the war, aptly summed up the success of Young's trip to Canada this way: "The old sores of the Civil War are healed."

Like other Lost Cause myths, that was decidedly not true. Old sores that are ignored and go untreated are never healed. They ooze and fester and poison the body politic until they explode with an anger that demands attention.

One hundred and fifty years after the Civil War started, its troubled legacy is still with us.

In August 2017, workers remove a plaque honouring the Confederacy, which had been on a wall of the Bay store in Montreal for almost six decades. (John Mahoney, Montreal Gazette/Postmedia)

'THE MISFORTUNES OF HISTORY'

History, as the saying goes, is written by the victors. Except in the case of the Confederates and their supporters: they got to remake and rewrite history to their own liking.

Abraham Lincoln had won the war, but not the peace. His successors allowed the South to reinstitute servitude and segregation under other names. For decades, what racist laws could not do, the Ku Klux Klan accomplished with terror. Well into the twentieth century, the mythology of the glorious Lost Cause promoted by Bennett Young and others endured in popular discourse and culture. The 1915 silent classic *The Birth of a Nation*—considered the first Hollywood feature film—idealized the Klan as heroic figures rescuing whites from the newly freed Black hordes after the war. The 1939 blockbuster *Gone with the Wind*—to this day the highest-grossing film in history—turned history on its head, propagating the same kind of apologies for an anguished South while downplaying the real suffering of slavery.

In Canada, Civil War amnesia was more benign but equally inaccurate and deceiving. If you asked ordinary Canadians today what they know about their country's role during that period, most would repeat the dominant myth propagated in books and taught in schools: Canada was an honourable refuge for thousands of ex-slaves on the Underground Railroad. That is only a partial truth. In 1865, if you had asked Abraham Lincoln and Jefferson Davis—or their supporters in the press and the public—what they thought of Canada as the war raged on, you would have found surprising agreement from the bitter foes. The North cursed and the South cheered Canada for the same reason: it was seen by all sides as a base of operations and haven for Confederate operations and murderous plots.

This historical whitewashing occurred not just on big Hollywood screens but in small, everyday gestures. In 1957, the United Daughters of the Confederacy—the same group that helped erect the monument that glorified the Southern slave states at Arlington National Cemetery in Washington—erected a plaque in the middle of downtown Montreal honouring Jefferson Davis. The bronze plate affixed to the west wall of the Hudson's Bay department store on Union Street paid tribute to the place where Davis and his family stayed in 1867 at what was then John Lovell's home.

On a grey November morning in 1959, a dozen people huddled around a gravesite in the cemetery on the slopes of the mountain that dominates the city of Montreal. Jefferson Davis's mother-in-law had been buried there in 1867 in an unmarked grave. A lawyer from Lennoxville, where the Davis children had gone to school, reached out to descendants of the family and raised money for a proper headstone. "Draped over the tombstone was a specially-made Confederate flag," the *Gazette* reported on its front page, with a large photo. The newspaper, having still not entirely shaken its enthrallment with the Southern cause a century later, praised the ceremony in an editorial as "an act of gracious remembrance" for a family "sorely tried by the misfortunes of history."

———

The explosion of the Black civil rights movement in the 1960s forced a long-overdue re-examination of the Civil War. Even Lincoln's reputation came under a critical questioning. "Our truly great presidents were tortured deep in their hearts by the race question," Martin Luther King Jr. noted while praising the man who issued the Emancipation Proclamation. "Lincoln's torments are well known, his vacillations were facts." In the 1970s, the gripping TV series *Roots* galvanized a nation into confronting its history of slavery. In the twenty-first century, many Oscar-winning movies, celebrated documentaries and Pulitzer Prize–winning books have sharpened that uncomfortable focus as a new generation of Black storytellers gave voice to uncomfortable truths.

In 2008, 145 years after Anderson Abbott fought his way into the Union army as a Black surgeon, Barack Obama was elected president, making history in the White House where the levee attendees had been so scandalized when Abbott dared to show up to shake the hand of Abraham Lincoln. That same year, the American Medical Association issued a formal apology for what it admitted had been its "past history of racial inequality towards African-American physicians." Abbott's friend and colleague Alexander Augusta would have welcomed those words, even if the regrets came more than a century too late for him.

Then the statues and monuments started to come tumbling down, and with them the distorted myths they represented.

"It has been said, and it is probably true, that there are more monuments erected to commemorate Confederate valor and sacrifice than were ever built to any cause," said Bennett Young—who helped erect many of them. But sparked by a wave of police killings of young Black men and the Black Lives Matter movement, America in recent years has been forced to reconsider its Civil War legacy as never before. In 2017, a large statue of Jefferson Davis was dragged away through the streets of New Orleans over the protests of people carrying Confederate flags and firearms. In 2020, Mississippi lawmakers voted to remove the Confederate emblem from the state flag. A fifteen-foot bronze statue of John Castleman, one of Morgan's Raiders, sitting astride his horse, was taken down in Louisville, Kentucky. In 2021, the residents of Franklin, Tennessee, replaced a sculpture of a Confederate soldier in a city square with a life-sized soldier from the US Colored Troops.

The Southern Poverty Law Center estimates that close to four hundred Confederate symbols have been removed across the United States since 2015, but thousands remain. One of the largest monuments still stands in Savannah, the capital of Georgia. In the middle of a city park, it towers over forty-eight feet, a bronze soldier standing defiantly on top. It was built for the Confederates during the Civil War by the Montreal Marble Works.

Many conservative politicians opposed taking down any memorials to the "heroes" of America's past. Worse still—much like what had happened in the Civil War—more than a few powerful politicians and media outlets have been all too eager to stoke the same fears of "the other" by peddling exaggerations and outright lies. The rhetoric meant that America once again was tipping towards chaos: if not a new civil war then certainly a bitter and dangerous period of uncivil hatreds, violence and division.

———

History is catching up with Canada as well.

In 2021, the Canadian federal government designated August 1 as Emancipation Day, to commemorate the day in 1834 when slavery was officially abolished in the British colonies. Black leaders have since called on the government to issue a formal apology for the impact and legacy of enslavement in this country.

In small but significant ways, the country has been reckoning with its difficult past. In 2012, the Montreal city council named a small downtown square after Marie-Josèphe-Angélique, the slave who had been executed three centuries earlier for daring to fight for her freedom. In August 2017, prompted by objections from citizens and probing by the local CBC newsroom, the Bay was forced to unceremoniously remove the Jefferson Davis plaque that had adorned its flagship Montreal store since the 1950s. It was hard to decide what was more unsettling: that an avowed Confederate group had been allowed to honour its leader almost a hundred years after a bloody war to end slavery, or that a major corporate empire in Canada had kept that memorial on its wall for another sixty years.

Another pillar of the Canadian establishment also had a small but embarrassing remnant of the Civil War on its hands. The Bank of

Montreal, which had acquired Henry Starnes's Ontario Bank in 1906, disclosed that John Wilkes Booth's bank account stayed open with a balance of $455 for "an undetermined length of time following his death." A bank spokesperson said that over the years the cash had been described anecdotally as "blood money." No details were given about where the money ended up.

———

A hundred years after her death, Emma Edmonds witnessed something of a historical rebirth.

She was inducted into the Military Intelligence Hall of Fame in 1988. Two years later, she was elected to New Brunswick's Hall of Fame, and in 1992 she was selected for the Michigan Women's Hall of Fame. The state also erected a "Historic Site" marker in Flint, Michigan, detailing her life and triumphs. On the official website of the US Congress, several historical pages are devoted to her story.

Several young-adult books came out with a fictionalized version of her story. One cover featured a dashingly beautiful woman with a blue Union army cap and a grey dress running through a smoke-filled battlefield—perhaps captivating girls from a new generation the same way a child on a farm in New Brunswick in the 1850s had marvelled at the adventures of a woman who had dared to disguise herself as a swashbuckling pirate.

Like Edmonds, Anderson Abbott's legacy also gained new prominence in books, newspaper articles and museum exhibits. Abraham Lincoln's shawl that Mary Lincoln had given him stayed with the family for generations and then was donated to the State Historical Society of Wisconsin. In 2002, Abbott was honoured as one of the University of Toronto's "Great Minds." Atop a lamppost on the corner of Bloor and St. George Streets, a banner with his name and picture fluttered in the wind.

It was a fitting marker of the Civil War and Canada's connections to the conflict. All too often, history remembers the rich and the powerful, who traditionally have been white men.

In their time, wealthy aristocrats such as George Taylor Denison III and Henry Starnes sat on city councils and in parliaments, attended glittering banquets and balls, made fortunes and newspaper headlines. Today, they are largely forgotten except by a few historians. But in schools, museums, books and memorials, a generation of young people will grow up learning about a brave soldier named Edward P. Doherty, a dedicated nurse named Sarah Emma Edmonds and a path-breaking doctor named Anderson Ruffin Abbott.

History is not written; it is rewritten again and again. You cannot erase the stains of a country's past by removing a plaque on a wall or taking down statues. But those actions help. They are part of the necessary struggle to confront our past, not bury it. "History is not history unless it is the truth," a wise president slain by an assassin's bullet once said.

We need to remember the crimes and complicity of those in Canada who fought to preserve a world of slavery and inequality—and the heroism of those who sought to change it.

ACKNOWLEDGEMENTS

When I was a history student at McGill University in my hometown of Montreal far too many decades ago, I would stroll off-campus through the nearby downtown streets. Much to my surprise, one day I came across a plaque honouring the Confederacy that was embossed along one of the walls of the Bay department store. I remember thinking: Why would someone memorialize the slave states of the Civil War—and why is this plaque still here?

Flash forward almost fifty years. In the summer of 2017, during the protests against Confederate statues that is sweeping the United States, I am sitting at my desk at the CBC in Toronto. I call my daughter Myriam, who at the time was working at the local CBC newsroom in Montreal, and tell her about the infamous plaque. Journalists begin to investigate and, as recounted in the Epilogue you just read, the rest is history.

History—and the lies we tell ourselves—has always fascinated me. My first book, back in 1983, was *White Hoods*, about the little-known story of Canada's own Ku Klux Klan. So it is appropriate that four decades and seven books later, I return to the subject of our past and what it means for our future.

There is only one name on the cover of this book, but writing in reality is quite a collective effort.

A journalist's best friends when it comes to researching the past are the amazing librarians and archivists who work largely unheralded across Canada and the United States. First and foremost, my deepest thanks to Colleen Puterbaugh, who was the collections manager and archivist at the James O. Hall Research Center at the Surratt House

Museum in Maryland and did an amazing job. At the Duke Universities Libraries, special thanks to Trudi Abel, cultural historian and archivist at the David M. Rubenstein Rare Book & Manuscript Library, along with Jennifer Baker and Heather Martin, librarian for African and African American Studies. Much appreciation as well to Heather Thomas, for helping me navigate the Library of Congress in Washington, DC; Simon Walter, Projects Coordinator, Saint Albans Museum, for digging up some gems; and the people at the Historical Society of Michigan, the Connecticut Historical Society, the Clarke Historical Library at the Central Michigan University and Abraham Lincoln Presidential Library and Museum in Springfield, Illinois.

In Canada, the staff at the McCord Museum, the City of Montreal Archives, the Bibliothèque et Archives nationales du Québec, the Toronto Reference Library and the Library and Public Archives in Ottawa were extremely helpful.

William P. Binzel, vice president of the Surratt Society and vice president of the Civil War Round Table of the District of Columbia, kindly agreed to share his immense knowledge and passion on this topic to painstakingly review my manuscript. The value of his help and advice was immeasurable. Any remaining errors are mine alone.

The book publishing business in Canada is not an easy one in which to find success, and I have been blessed over the years by long-time supporters: John Pearce, my indefatigable agent at Westwood Creative, Anne Collins, executive editor at Random House Canada, who has always championed my work, and the amazing Pamela Murray, who is any author's dream editor, with her sharp eye and even sharper pen. Thanks to John Sweet for his careful copy editing and to Wendy Thomas for proofreading.

My family as always has been there to support me through all those absent days as I sat hunched over my computer: my children and grand-children who had to tolerate long absences and silences; my mother-in-law, Shirley, who let me stay in her house in California and write several chapters when I came down with Covid; my sister Ilona and her husband Sam, who put me up in Virginia while I did research there; and especially my wife and fellow writer, Lisa Fitterman, who knows what a madness and a joy it is to tell people's stories in the best way you can.

Julian Sher
Montreal, December 2022

SOURCES AND ENDNOTES

There have been more than 100,000 books written about the Civil War and Abraham Lincoln, not to mention innumerable magazine articles, academic papers and specialized websites. Far less has been written about the important Canadian connection to the conflict.

Historian Robin Winks wrote the definitive book in 1960, *The Civil War Years: Canada and the United States*, which remains to this day unparalleled in its scope and details. More recently, John Boyko's *Blood and Daring* does an excellent job of explaining the impact of the war on the creation of the Canadian Confederation, and Adam Mayer's *Dixie and the Dominion* is rich with portraits of the important characters. Barry Sheehy's *Montreal, City of Secrets* is full of photographs and documents; Claire Hoy's *Canadians in the Civil War* highlights some little-known people; while Greg Marquis's *In Armageddon's Shadow: The Civil War and Canada's Maritime Provinces* is a comprehensive look at that region.

Other works devoted to some of the characters or events in this book are described in more detail below. For simplicity, the references in these endnotes are kept as short as possible; full details of the sources are in the lengthy bibliography that follows.

PROLOGUE: 'ABE'S CONTRACT WAS UP'

"a pleasure trip" Testimony from John Deveny's testimony, *Assassination of President Lincoln*, 38.

"I was introduced to J. Wilkes Booth" *New York Times* (hereafter *NYT*), May 7, 1865, reprinted from the *Hamilton Times*. All other quotes from Dion from the same source.

1. 'A MAGNIFICENT SPECTACLE'

Emma Edmonds, alias Franklin Thompson, told her own story in her some-what unreliable memoir *Nurse and Spy in the Union Army*. Sylvia Dannett's *She Rode with the Generals*, published in 1960, is the most detailed biogra-phy, including interviews with family members living at the time, but lacks the new findings from recent research. For a more modern approach, see Laura Leedy Gansler's *The Mysterious Private Thompson*. Elizabeth D. Leonard, an expert on women in the war, published an annotated version of *Memoirs of a Soldier, Nurse and Spy* with an excellent introduction and helpful endnotes.

Several of Edmonds's letters are found in the "Sarah Emma Seelye Edmonds Papers, 1885, 1897" in the Clarke Historical Library at Central Michigan University (hereafter called "Edmonds Papers"). Testimony from her fellow soldiers and her own accounts of her army years are in the "Edmonds Pension File" in the US National Archives.

There are no books devoted to Edward P. Doherty, but much of his army service record (hereafter referred to as "Doherty Military Files") is found in *Letters Received by Commission Branch of the Adjutant General Office, 1863–1870*, held at the US National Archives. The Edward P. Doherty Papers in the Abraham Lincoln Presidential Library and Museum (referred to below as "Doherty Papers") include letters, affidavits and newspaper clippings. James Carson's extensively researched book, *Chasing Mosby, Killing Booth*, details Doherty's service with the 16th New York Volunteer Cavalry.

"The sight of that field is perfectly appalling" And other descriptions by
   Edmonds come from *Nurse and Spy*, 32–46.
"We waded in great confusion" *NYT*, August 6, 1861.
"brave to the last degree" and other comments are in the Edmonds Pension
   File, Letters from John Deitz, William Shakespeare.
"never absent from duty" Edmonds Pension File, House of Representatives
   48th Congress, 1st Session, Report No. 849.
"the beardless boy was a universal favourite" Dannett, 262.

2. 'THE WILDEST COLT'

"set him off into a temper" Early biographical details from Dannett, 18–22.
"hatred of male tyranny" and Edmonds's quotes from *Detroit Post and
   Tribune*, May 26, 1883.
"When I was 13 years old" *Nurse and Spy*, 218.
"When her father made arrangements" *Detroit Free Press*, May 30, 1915.
"She had the appearance" *NYT*, May 30, 1886.

3. 'THE BETTER ANGELS'

If you have to read just one book on Lincoln, make it Eric Foner's Pulitzer Prize–winning study *The Fiery Trial: Abraham Lincoln and American Slavery*. Two of the best biographies on Booth are Michael Kaufman's *American Brutus* and Terry Alford's *Fortune's Fool*. Some of Booth's own writings are contained in *Right or Wrong, God Judge Me: The Writings of John Wilkes Booth*, published after his death.

"His weak, wishy-washy, namby-pamby efforts" *Salem Advocate*, 1861. Cited by the National Park Services, Abraham Lincoln Resources.

"fourth-rate Illinois lawyer" *Ottawa Citizen*, May 22, 1860, cited by Wells, "Icy Blasts to Balmy Airs."

"a significant slaveholding family" Foner, 12. See Foner 48–49 for Lincoln's legal work on behalf of a slaveholder.

"I am not, nor ever have been" September 18, 1858, *Collected Works of Abraham Lincoln*, vol. 3, 146.

four million people in bondage The U.S. Supreme Court had just ruled that the ringing words of the American Constitution—that "all men are created equal"—explicitly did *not* apply to Black men regardless of whether they were enslaved or free. In its now infamous Dred Scott decision of 1857—in which a slave made the case that he should be liberated since his masters had taken him over the border into a free state—the Court declared that Blacks were "not included, and were not intended to be included, under the word 'citizens' in the Constitution."

"Instead of looking upon slavery as a sin" Booth unpublished speech, December 1860, *NYT*, April 12, 1992. The document only came to light in 1991, unearthed at a theatrical club in New York, the former home of John Wilkes's older brother Edwin.

"We recognize the negro" Jefferson Davis speech, March 1861, cited in Davis, *Look Away*, 137.

"but one feeling, all-absorbing" Letter to President John Buchanan, June 7, 1861, quoted in *Hamilton Weekly Spectator*, May 10, 1865.

"The Hall was crowded to excess" Montreal *Gazette* (hereafter *Gazette*), January 18, 1861.

"There is no country in the world" Ward, *Autobiography*, 158.

"War . . . seemed inevitable" / **"But the great question"** *Nurse and Spy*, 17, 18.

4. 'I FELT CALLED TO GO'

"As I was proceeding" and other Doherty quotes from Doherty Letters, *Gazette*, May 4, 20, 24, 30, 1861.

on September 23, 1838, in Wickham There is some confusion about Doherty's birthdate. His tombstone puts his birth year as 1840, as do many books and articles and some of his army records. His death certificate gives no birthdate. But the most official record—the baptismal records at the Catholic church in Wickham—indicate a boy named Edward was born to Joseph and Margaret Doherty on September 23, 1838. See "Québec Catholic Parish Registers, 1621–1979."

Doherty moved to Montreal to go to school, See Steven G. Miller's excellent research in "More on Capt. Doherty."

found himself working in New York City Doherty was not alone working as a Canadian in America. An estimated 250,000 people living in the US at the time were from British North America, and many, like Doherty and Edmonds, enlisted while on American soil.

"the enthusiastic and vehement cheers" Doherty Letters, *Gazette*, May 4, 1861.

"Every window, door, stoop, balcony" *NYT*, April 22, 1861.

"with their bright bayonets" and other quotes from *Nurse and Spy*, 18–28.

"I could best serve" Affidavit by Emma Seelye, January 1, 1884, Edmonds Pension File. Edmonds's plan to disguise herself as a man in order to get into Lincoln's army was not entirely unusual, though she perhaps had more experience than most women in hiding her gender. Historians estimate that as many as a thousand women joined the ranks of the Union and Confederate armies. Some did it to be with their husbands or lovers; others for a regular salary that was otherwise unavailable to most women; and some, like Edmonds, did it out of conviction. (See Leonard, *Memoirs of a Soldier, Nurse and Spy*, xiv.)

women were slowly becoming more common Florence Nightingale had become renowned for her work in the Crimean War, which had ended just five years earlier. Clara Barton did the same as a pioneering health care giver in the Civil War and went on to found the American Red Cross.

"had always been a remarkably strong, healthy girl" Affidavit by Emma Seelye, February 1884, Edmonds Pension File.

An estimated 750,000 soldiers would die For more than a century after the war ended, the accepted number of Civil War dead was 618,222—still the heaviest toll of any war in American history. But more recent historical research has increased the number by more than 20 percent—to 750,000 (*NYT*, April 2, 2012).

"The first blood has been shed" Doherty Letters, *Gazette*, May 26, 1861.
"Marching orders received today" *Nurse and Spy*, 29.

5. 'DESTRUCTION AND DEATH'

"We found many engaged" and Edmonds's other battle descriptions in *Nurse and Spy*, 36–38, 41–51, 56–57. Doherty later chronicled "The Battle of Bull Run: Interesting Statement by Edward P. Doherty," *NYT*, August 6, 1861.

and then killed the colonel Miller, "More on Capt. Doherty."

"The strife and carnage was fearful" Levin, *This Awful Drama*, 28.

"We have broken the back bone" Furguson, "Battle of Bull Run."

an estimated 30,000 to 50,000 English and French Canadians Most historians today accept this broad estimate, though Winks cautions against exaggerating the numbers (Winks, *The Civil War Years*, 179–85). Quebec historians Jean Lamarre and D.C. Bélanger estimate as many as 10,000 to 15,000 French Canadians enlisted.

at least twenty-nine earned Medals of Honour The Grays and Blues of Montreal, thegraysandbluesofmontreal.com.

an estimated 5,000 to 7,000 died Ibid. See also Lamarre, *Les Canadiens français*, 128, 53.

"Such unfortunate young men" *La Minerve*, October 21, 1864, June 16, 1864, cited by Rountree, "A 'Military Despotism,'" 5.

"A report of the Confederate victory" Boyko, 9.

6. 'THE STAR OF HOPE'

"the gallant defence" Creighton, *John A. Macdonald*, 369. What is all the more problematic is that the man heralded as the Father of Confederation in Canada was praising the South not at the start of the war but late in 1864, long after Lincoln had issued his historic Emancipation Proclamation making slavery a clear and central issue in the conflict.

"Our Canadian neighbors are imitating" *NYT*, August 17 1863.

reflected their anti-Lincoln bias Winks analyzed eighty-four newspapers and found that forty-three were "consistently anti-Northern," thirty-three were anti-South, and only eight were "neutral or varied." In French Quebec, according to Winks, four out of the five most important publications were anti-North (Winks, *The Civil War Years*, 210, 219–23).

a laudatory biography of Jefferson Davis and other quotes from *Le Canadien*, February 27, 1861, March 12, 1861, and *Courrier du Canada*, April 15, 1861, cited by Savard, 113, 115, 120.

"the most intelligent armies we have known" *La Minerve*, July 30, 1861, cited by Jacob, "La Perception de la Guerre de Sécession."

the bravery of Southern troops *La Minerve*, June 14, 1864, cited by Rountree, 6.

"Such a gigantic wrong" *Montreal Witness*, December 22, 1860.

"unlawful war" *Gazette*, August 24, 1861. The *New York Times* accurately described the *Gazette* as "the most prominent in its support of the South" (*NYT*, June 16, 1865).

"massacre their masters" *Gazette*, May 13, 1861, October 19, 1861.

"a French-Canadian gentleman" *Quebec Morning Chronicle*, December 16, 1863.

"mad, blood-stained despot" *Niagara Review* quoted in the *Toronto Leader* (hereafter the *Leader*), August 5, 1863.

"innocent women and helpless children" *Leader*, April 25, April 18, 1865.

"By far the greater number of the leading journals" *New York World*, November 21, 1861.

"the South's only adversary" Report to Confederate Secretary of State, Judah Benjamin, cited by Whyte, "Confederate Operations in Canada," 160. The report ignored two pro-Lincoln papers in Montreal, the French-language *Le Pays* and the *Montreal Witness*.

"The question is often put" and other quotes in *Life and Speeches of Hon. George Brown*, 260, 289, 290.

"the largest and most enthusiastic meeting" *Globe*, February 26, 1851.

"her Body then Reduced To Ashes" *Final sentence by the judge and by his four counsellors*, June 4, 1734, Archives nationales du Québec. For more on her story, see Cooper, *The Hanging of Angélique*.

"FOR SALE: A Young healthy Negro wench" Extian-Babiuk, "'To Be Sold,'" 13.

"To millions, now in our boasted land of liberty" *North Star*, December 3, 1847, all caps in the original.

"Almost every ship or boat" *Toronto Colonist*, June 17, 1852, cited by Hill, 32.

"determined to die rather than be captured" Walls, "Freedom Marker."

Osborne Perry Anderson As the only Black survivor of the raid, Anderson went on to write a gripping account, *A Voice from Harper's Ferry*, in 1861.

a company of US Marines arrived One of their commanders was a young officer named Robert E. Lee, still part of the Federal army. Alongside him, serving "with great bravery and firmness," was his cousin, a lieutenant in the volunteer militia named Edwin G. Lee (Levin, 30). Both of them went on to fight at Bull Run and play important roles in the Confederacy.

"I saw John Brown hung" Booth unpublished speech, December 1860, *NYT*,
April 12, 1992.

"brave old man" Clarke, 81.

" brave man" and other quotes in *Globe*, November 4, December 9, 16, 1859.

"John Brown is still remembered" *Nurse and Spy*, 289.

7. 'FIELD OF CARNAGE'

"I did not enjoy taking care of the sick" *Nurse and Spy*, 101.

"that Private Franklin Thompson be appointed" / "as a soldier 'Frank
Thompson' was effeminate looking" Dannett, 93, 211.

"the thunder of cannon" and other battle descriptions in *Nurse and Spy*, 71,
72, 121–28, 186–91, 217.

"My colt took fright" Affidavit by Emma Seelye, January 1, 1884, Edmonds
Pension File.

"her faithfulness, bravery and efficiency" Affidavit from William Morse,
Edmonds Pension File.

"with a fearlessness" Dannett, 213.

"complete disguise" and other spy stories in *Nurse and Spy*, 107, 147,
163-165.

"while in the 'Secret Service'" *Nurse and Spy*, 5.

"no information attributed" Fishel, 599.

"a daring spy" *Globe and Mail*, December 1, 2020. See also Robertson, 205.

"I make no statement of any secret services" Affidavit by Emma Seelye,
Edmonds Pension File.

8. 'THE PROMISE OF FREEDOM'

Two compelling books on Black Canadians in the American Civil War—and
Drs. Abbott and Augusta—are Richard M. Reid's *African Canadians in Union
Blue* and Bryan Prince's *My Brother's Keeper*. Catherine Slaney's *Family
Secrets: Crossing the Colour Line* is a moving and very personal portrait of
Abbott, while Dalyce Newby's *Anderson Ruffin Abbott, First Afro-Canadian
Doctor* tracks his medical career and political views. Several boxes of Abbott's
personal files, writings and articles (hereafter called the "Abbott Collection")
are in the Baldwin Collection of Canadiana in the Toronto Public Library.

"plumed hats, scarlet lined riding cloaks" *Nurse and Spy*, 237.

"I made no report" Letter, September 6, 1897, Edmonds Papers.

"*I would have rather been shot dead*" Letter, September 24, 1896, Edmonds
Pension File. Cited by Gansler, 217.

"I am very busy" Dannett, 200, 208.

"While I write the roar of cannon" *Nurse and Spy*, 302.

"stunning defeat to the invader" Freeman, 418.

"If there is a worse place than hell" Goolrick, 92–93.

"If slavery is not wrong" and other Lincoln quotes cited here can be found in his letters in *Collected Works*, vol. 7, 281, vol. 2, 320, and vol. 5, 388–89.

"You and we are different races" Foner, *Fiery Trial*, 224. "I strongly favor colonization," Lincoln stated in late 1862 at a White House meeting.

"President Lincoln was a white man" Douglass, "Speech at Unveiling."

Lincoln did not free all the slaves Foner, 240–43.

"the proclamation will be little more" *Gazette*, January 7, 1863.

"wise and right" *Globe*, January 3, 1863, cited by Reid, 38.

"the heaviest blow" General Ulysses S. Grant to Lincoln, August 1863 (Foner, 251).

9. 'THE TIME HAD NOW COME'

"Having seen that it is so intended" Augusta Letter to Lincoln, January 1, 1863, US National Library of Medicine.

"large and respectable attendance" *Globe*, February 4, 1863.

"I learn by our city papers" Letter to Edwin Stanton, February 4, 1863, Abbott Collection.

while working as a barber Butts, 106.

Augusta applied to the Faculty Henig, 23.

soon became Canada's first Black medical student Historians agree Augusta came to Canada in 1850. Some accounts have him starting medical school that same year. The more reliable writer Richard Reid sets the date in 1853 (Reid, 153).

"one of his most brilliant students" Simpson, 412–13. Cited by Henig, 24.

"the greatest curse" Henig, 24.

"the disgusting and despotic language" *Black Abolitionist Papers*, 383–84.

his mother had lost her first three children Slaney, 24.

"incurred the hatred" "Personal History" in Abbott Collection.

owning several dozen real estate holdings Hill, 206. See also Winks, *Blacks in Canada*, 328–29.

"They did not come in response" "Personal History" in Abbott Collection.

the first Black person elected to office See the entry for Wilson Abbott by Robin Winks in the *Dictionary of Canadian Biography* .

a petition with eighty-five signatures Abbott Collection. See also Hill, 109.

"not singing Negro songs" Slaney, "Process and Implications," 46, 76.

"removing the stain" Zackodnik, 200.

first president of the Queen Victoria Benevolent Society Henry, 125.
white parents eagerly sought Slaney, "Process and Implications," 39.
medical school at King's College Newby, 31–32; Reid, 156.
supported Abbott's work Reid, 155.
Canada's first native-born Black doctor There remains some confusion over
    when Abbott became a full-fledged doctor, in part because records are
    missing and the names and affiliations of colleges and medical boards
    changed. An ad he placed in a Chatham newspaper in 1874 claimed he
    was a "licentiate of the College of Physicians and Surgeons Upper Can-
    ada" as of 1861 (Abbott Collection). When he applied to join the Union
    army in 1863, he repeated that fact to Stanton but also wrote that it was
    his "intention to go up for my degree of Bachelor of Medicine in the
    spring"—which implied that he was licensed to practise but was not a
    full-fledged doctor. He did eventually return to university to get his full
    degree in 1867 from the University of Toronto and got a licence from the
    renamed College of Physicians and Surgeons of Ontario (Newby, 124).
"thrown in the scrap basket" Abbott Collection.

10. 'I DO NOT LOVE YOU LESS'

"nervous, whining woman" and other quotes from *Nurse and Spy*, 356,
    359.
"We jested about the ridiculous little boots" *Detroit Post and Tribune*,
    May 26, 1883.
"except no one thought" Poe Letter, January 4, 1884, cited by Gansler,
    212.
who shot herself *Louisville Daily Democrat*, April 16, 1863, cited by
    Dannett.
"From my standpoint, I never" Letter, April 15, 1883, cited by Fladeland,
    "New Light," 455.
"[H]er health became greatly impaired" Undated petition sent to Senate and
    House of Representatives, Edmonds Pension File.
the US Congress to Canada's History Society Canada's History Society in its
    biography of Edmonds says she was "unable to admit herself for treatment
    for fear of betraying her true sex." Even the *New York Times*, in one of its
    regular flashbacks to the Civil War called "Disunion," told of Edmonds's
    "harrowing adventure" as she remained "unwilling to reveal her gender in
    a military hospital" (April 21, 2014).
"One of the noble-hearted nurses" *Nurse and Spy*, 214.
Betty Fladeland, a legendary historian See bibliography for her two articles.
"a handsome man" Gansler, 63.

in the early fall of 1861 Gansler, 65.

"good noble-hearted fellow" All diary quotes from Jerome J. Robbins
    Papers, 1861–1913, Bentley Historical Library, University of Michigan.

They went to prayer meetings together Gansler, 66, 137.

"A mystery seems to be connected with him" Robbins Diary, October 30,
    1861, cited by Fladeland, "New Light," 358.

"Not for the world" Robbins Diary, November 11, 1861, cited by Flad-
    eland, "New Light," 359.

"Dear Jerome, I am in earnest" January 16, 1863, letter in Robbins Papers,
    cited by Gansler, 166. Not wanting to reveal her true feelings about
    Robbbins, Edmonds instead in her book wrote this stiff passage about
    reuniting with the newly freed prisoner: "[A]fter he had undergone the
    hardships of imprisonment and had been exchanged, I had the honor of
    meeting and congratulating him. I felt that it was a greater honor than
    to converse with many of our major generals" (*Nurse and Spy*, 214).

tall, blue-eyed Gansler, 164.

Poe . . . left the regiment Ibid., 173.

he and Edmonds had become lovers. Ibid., 176.

"This Sabbath afternoon" May 10, 1863, letter in Robbins Papers, cited by
    Gansler, 176.

some of the lines written in pencil had been erased Fladeland, "New Light,"
    358.

11. 'THE NEW DESTINY'

"I don't know why he should have been sanguine" Abbott Collection.

"Augusta had his misgivings" Ibid.

A COLORED ASPIRANT *NYT*, March 30, 1863.

"I have come near a thousand miles" Letter, March 30, 1863, cited by
    Henig, 25.

"exceptionally qualified" Reid, 160.

the Surgeon General spoke to Clymer While quite plausible, it is hard to verify
    how accurate this story is. Abbott recounted this story in an undated article
    he wrote called "Dr. Augusta Goes to Washington" (Abbott Collection).
    Abbott got the name of the review board chairman wrong, calling him
    Cronyn while the *New York Times* identified him as Clymer. It is not clear
    how Abbott found out about this incident—presumably from Augusta, but
    that only invites the question of how Augusta learned about the private
    conversation. Perhaps it was from a sympathetic member of the Lincoln
    administration who had pushed the medical board to act on Augusta's file.

highest-ranking Black officer at the time Henig, 25.

"the colored surgeon from Canada" *Douglass' Monthly*, June 1863.

"I have been a pupil of Dr. T. Augusta" Letter, April 30, 1863, Abbott Collection.

"I am a Canadian first and last" Notes for GAR address, Abbott Collection.

"The appearance of a colored man" *Evening Star*, April 17, 1863.

"splendid among the shabby field hands" Leech, 253.

DR. AUGUSTA MOBBED *Globe*, May 8, 1863, reprinting a *New York Tribune* story.

"Baltimore secessionists" *Douglass' Monthly*, June 1863.

"a boy about fifteen years of age" Augusta's account appears in a letter published in the Washington *National Republican*, May 15, 1863, reprinted in C. Peter Ripley, *The Black Abolitionist Papers*, vol. V, *The United States, 1859–1865*, 205–10.

"Lynch the scoundrel" Undated *Baltimore Gazette* article reprinted in *Douglass' Monthly*, June 1863.

"I hold that my position" *National Republican*, May 15, 1863.

"The attack was entirely unprovoked" *New York Herald*, May 20, 1863.

"It was a wonder that he escaped" Undated essay "Dr Augusta Goes to Washington," Abbott Collection.

"began to abuse us" and other quotes about the attack in Abbott Collection.

"It seemed to be an understood thing" *NYT*, July 14, 1863.

An estimated 2,500 Black Canadians signed up Reid, 4.

"It wasn't because" Abbott Collection.

offered money to help the families Prince, 86.

12. 'BEAUTIFUL RIGHT AND UGLY WRONG'

"under the influence of alcohol" Chaconas.

"I can cheerfully testify" and other words of praise from Doherty Military Files.

"that gallant officer" "Major Ruggles Narrative," *Century*, January 1890.

"on lonely scout and daring raid[s]" *National Intelligencer*, July 20, 1865.

undisclosed "family reasons" Chaconas.

"gallant and stubborn resistance" Doherty Military Files, Letter from Headquarters, April 1865.

"The war still continues" *Nurse and Spy*, 384.

visiting wounded soldiers Letter, May 19, 1863, cited by Gensler, 176–77.

forty thousand of them perished Elsie Freeman, "The Fight for Equal Rights," *Social Education*.

rain-soaked tents, wooden barracks Newmark.

the first Black man in American history Reid, 166. Reid puts the posting in September; Newmark and others place it in May 1863.

"**The water inside the camp**" cited by Downs, 31.

Anderson Abbott was at Augusta's side The exact date of Abbott's deployment is unclear. Prince says he was at the Contraband Hospital by July 26, 1863. Reid says he joined Augusta on September 2 (Reid, 174). Newby quotes an Abbott letter putting it in June (Newby, 65).

Together with other newly recruited Black doctors. Some historians say that Abbott and Augusta were among eight Black doctors at the start, which then grew to thirteen. Reid says there were "a dozen or so" (Reid, 147).

By October 1863 Reid, 16; Prince, 125–26. Butts has Augusta staying on at Camp Barker until the spring of 1864 (Butts, 107).

"**It became a struggle between beautiful right and ugly wrong**" Abbott Collection.

13. 'A NEW BIRTH OF FREEDOM'

"**Twice Booth in uttering disagreeable threats**" Katherine Helm, *The True Story of Mary, Wife of Lincoln* (New York: Harper and Brothers, 1928), 243. The story by Mary Clay is discounted by some historians since it was reported as a second-hand account (with some inaccuracies) more than sixty years later in a book by a niece of Lincoln, Katherine Helm.

the Gettysburg Address changed the course of the war Even in extolling "the birth of freedom," Lincoln was not in favour of the immediate and total end to slavery, telling a colleague the day before he left for Gettysburg that any rushed destruction of slavery would "be attended with great ruin," which was why he would be "glad to see" a more "gradual emancipation" (Foner, 269).

"**We claim to be behind no one**" Prince, 126–27.

"**this unexpected, unusual, and most unpleasant relationship**" Henig, 27.

Augusta remained as a senior surgeon Prince, 126; Reid, 162.

"**An incident like this**" *Congressional Globe*, 38th Congress, 1st Session, February 10, 1864, 553–54.

"**It was through Dr. Augusta**" Undated file, "Augusta Goes to Washington," Abbott Collection.

"**One evening we appeared at the White House**" Abbott Collection. It is not clear how the two doctors secured an invitation to the event. Possibly they were helped by Elizabeth Keckley, the Black seamstress and confidante to Mary Lincoln, who happened to be friends with Abbott and Augusta's wife Mary. Keckley established the Contraband Relief Association to provide help and care to recently freed slaves, and perhaps that is where she met Abbott and Augusta.

"whether we were really the first colored guests to visit the President" The doctors may have been among the first Black guests to attend a party at the White House, but as Foner has pointed out, "Lincoln opened the White House to black guests as no president had before"—meeting civil rights leaders like Frederick Douglass and others starting in 1862 (Foner, 257). See the following note as well for an account of four Blacks attending a levee in January 1864.

"During the evening Dr. Augusta" *Washington Star*, February 24, 1864. The *Star* article would seem to place the event on February 23, although many accounts in recent books and articles put the two doctors at a New Year's levee in January 1864 (Prince, 130–32). That timing is based on an article that appeared early in the new year in the *Washington Chronicle* and was widely reprinted (see *Pittsburgh Daily Post*, January 4, 1864). The article talked about "four colored men of genteel exterior" attending the event. But the story does not name Abbott and Augusta while the *Star* article from late February does explicitly reference them. Abbott also never mentions four Black men being at the levee, only he and Augusta. Whatever the date, it was an event that broke racial boundaries.

14. 'A SECRET MISSION'

"The year of 1864" Hines, *Southern Bivouac*, December 1886, 437.
"If your engagements will permit you" Jefferson Davis letter, April 7, 1864, *War of the Rebellion*, 278.
"a typical Southern gentleman" Headley, 463.
"a traitor" *New York Daily Tribune*, January 9, 1861.
"the ideas of cotton-growing chivalry" *NYT*, February 26, 1861.
"The slaves all gathered together by their master" and other biographical quotes from Oldman, 5, 55, 83, 127, 129.
"Richmond, Va., April 27th, 1864" Castleman, 221.
"A commission . . . was accordingly appointed" Davis, *A Short History*, 455.
$5 million . . . was set aside *Journal of the Confederate Congress*, vol. 6, 690–91.
　　William A. Tidwell, one of the leading experts on Confederate spy operations, estimated the slave states spent at least four times more than Lincoln's government did on that kind of warfare (see "Confederate Expenditures," 220–22). According to Tidwell, a second version of the $1 million appropriation letter was issued with the name "Thompson" handwritten on the document.
"hesitated to accept the appointment" Claiborne, *Mississipppi*, 460.
"painted gray . . . so that she could scarcely be seen" Hines, *Southern Bivouac*, December 1886, 444.

"the intimate friend" Clay-Copton, 68.

advocated restarting the African slave trade Encyclopedia of Alabama,
    "Clement C. Clay."

"No sentiment is more insulting" Pollard, 89.

the powerful position of Confederate secretary of war Whyte, 6.

he doubted his fitness for the mission Undated letter to Davis, Clay Papers.

"I am on my way to Canada" Nuermberger, 232.

"peevish, irritable and suspicious" Castleman, 133.

"the source of constant embarrassment" Hines, *Southern Bivouac*, January
    1887, 502.

"We waited until it was quite dark" Cleary quoted by Hines, *Southern
    Bivouac*, December 1886, 444.

"a hot Southern town" Marquis, 35.

"the treatment of defenceless" Marquis, 223.

flew Confederate flags Hoy, viii.

An unapologetic supporter of the Confederate States Flemming, 71.

"a good type of true Southern gentleman" Whyte, 57.

"to traverse the United States as an advocate of peace" Clay letter, June 14,
    1864, to Judah Benjamin, Clay Papers.

"one of the eminent men" Connolly letter, May 20, 1864, Clay Papers.

15. 'PROCEED TO CANADA'

The memoirs of Confederate soldiers in Canada, while obviously self-serving
and framed by Southern political blinders, are at times frank and they also
contain many official documents and letters. Among the most important are
Bennett H. Young's *Confederate Wizards of the Saddle*, John B. Castleman's
Active Service and John W. Headley's *Confederate Operations in Canada and
New York*. Thomas Hines authored four lengthy articles on the Northwest
Conspiracy in *The Southern Bivouac*. Much of Hines's adventures and related
documents are told—with some creative licence—in James Horan's *Confeder-
ate Agent: A Discovery in History*.

George Ellsworth wrote an account of his exploits, "Telegraph Strategy in
Warfare," that ran in several newspapers in 1882 and have since been reprinted
and edited in an excellent article by Stephen E. Towne in the *Register of the
Kentucky Historical Society*.

The David M. Rubenstein Rare Book & Manuscript Library at Duke University has Edwin Gray Lee's diary (hereafter called "Lee Diary") and some
personal letters (called "Lee Archives") as well as the "Clement C. Clay
Papers, 1811–1925" (referred to below as "Clay Papers").

"Colonel Morgan issued a stirring proclamation" and other quotes in Young, *Confederate Wizards,* 105, 111, 125.

"made up of the cream of Kentucky's gentility" *St. Catharine Constitutional,* July 17, 1915.

"outrageous insult" Kinchen, *Daredevils,* 23.

"gave war a new glamour" Young, *Confederate Wizards,* xii.

"All wanted to get with Morgan" and other quotes in Headley, 30, 61, 210, 217, 468.

"the ties of affection" and other quotes from Castleman, 15, 52, 56, 59.

"the daring deeds" and other quotes from Ellsworth, 19, 25, 32, 47. The *Cincinnati Daily Inquirer,* one of the many anti-Lincoln papers in the North, hailed Ellsworth's escapades as "a rich affair . . . in a new field of operations" (August 24, 1862). The news spread across the ocean as the *Times* of London on September 12, 1862, called it an "uncommonly pretty story," praising Ellsworth for his "remarkably good intelligence"—and his "impudence." (Both cited by Towne, 42.) See also Towne's article "The Adventures of Lightning Ellsworth," *NYT,* December 23, 2012, and Bakeless, 260.

"vivid delineations of the wonderful escapes" Hines, "Escape," 160.

"You are detailed for special service" Letter from James Seddon, March 16, 1864, reprinted in Headley, 218.

16. 'ENTERPRISES OF WAR'

"Within a few days" Headley, 215, 216.

"Toronto at the time" Horan, 79.

"his heart was with us" Clay letter, June 14, 1864, to Judah Benjamin, Clay Papers.

The Montreal police chief estimated Guillaume Lamothe statement to US Consul, January 6, 1872, in Papiers Lamothe, Library and Archives Canada (hereafter LAC).

"We can't stand here" Horan, 84.

to open a bank account Castleman, 134.

general manager for the Montreal branch Rudin, "Starnes." See also obituary, *Montreal Star,* March 4, 1896.

"Thompson has bought from us" All quotes from Campbell come from his testimony at the trial. *Assassination of President Lincoln,* 45–46.

"his authority . . . was almost autocratic" Hines, *Southern Bivouac,* January 1887, 500.

"effecting any fair and appropriate enterprises of war" Seddon orders to Hines, March 16, 1864, *Southern Bivouac,* December 1886, 443.

"the elastic verbal instructions" Castleman, 10, 134.

"It may be said" Headley, 214.

"Colonel Thompson cautioned us" Headley, 215.

17. 'A STRONG FRIEND'

George Taylor Denison III writes at length about his pro-Confederate passions in his memoir *Soldiering in Canada: Recollections and Experiences*. David Gagan's *The Denison Family* offers a detailed if largely uncritical biographical treatment.

"The red-brick mansion" Lundell, 46.

"I became very friendly with Colonel Thompson" and other quotes from Denison, 59, 21.

one of the wealthiest landowners in Upper Canada Gagan, 18. As Gagan notes, many of Toronto's modern street names reflect the Denison legacy, starting with Denison Avenue in what is now Kensington Market, along with Dovercourt, Esther, Borden and Ossington.

As a boy, Denison had devoured books and other biographical details from Gagan, 45–48.

Confederate secretary of state had dispatched Dewson Winks described Dewson as "the personal agent of Judah P. Benjamin" (Winks, *The Civil War Years*, 310).

18. 'THE WORK OF MURDER'

Nancy Baird's biography *Luke Pryor Blackburn* covers his life extensively but underplays his dubious actions. H. Leon Greene's *The Confederate Yellow Fever Conspiracy* has rich details about his crimes and escape from punishment.

"an infallible plan" Greene, 95.

three months before his nineteenth birthday and other early biography from Baird, 6, 13, 15–18.

he acquired eighteen slaves Greene, 15.

Blackburn easily made friends, Headley, 214, 281.

"of small stature, of dark complexion" *NYT*, May 30, 1865.

immigrated to the United States / claimed in a letter Greene, 53, 63.

"I have not a cent to help her" Letter, January 15, 1865, reprinted in *Montreal Herald*, May 26, 1865.

"He took me upstairs" All quotes from Hyams in this chapter, unless otherwise indicated, come from his testimony, May 29, 1865, *Assassination of President Lincoln*, 54–56.

some rather odd behaviour *Royal Gazette*, April 25, 1865.

"One of the hospital nurses said" Greene, 41.

"very nice valise with some very elegant shirts" *Washington Evening Star*, May 22, 1865.

"[I]t cannot be our policy" Steers, *Blood on the Moon*, 53.

"I asked the doctor for money" *NYT*, May 26, 1865.

"a sweeping pestilence" Benjamin, *Great Epidemic*, 3.

19. 'A CONSTANT MENACE'

There are no books devoted to the irrepressible George Sanders, but two unpublished theses cover his life and career well: George H. Whyte's "Confederate Operations in Canada" and Melinda Squires's "The Controversial Career of George Nicholas Sanders."

"All that is needed for our success" July report to Richmond by Thompson, quoted in Headley, 224.

"I never knew of another man like him" Horan, 87.

"a zealous and unscrupulous Southerner" *Daily Telegraph* (London), cited in *Gazette*, December 21, 1864.

"drunken, unprincipled adventurers" *New York Herald*, May 5, 1865.

"the notorious rebel" *Harper's Weekly*, August 26, 1865.

thoroughbred horses / underhanded tactics Whyte, 14, 28–30.

"became attracted by the power" Parker, 101.

"He sees everybody" Castleman, 136, 135.

"do[ing] away with the Crown Heads" Whyte, 83, 108.

he walked across the suspension bridge *The Gray Jackets*, 85–87. According to the *Montreal Herald*, "Sanders reported himself . . . in the garb and character of a Cornish miner seeking work in Canada," August 26, 1862, quoted in *NYT*, September 1, 1862.

Sanders recruited his family Whyte, 114.

"constantly unkempt" / "living affluently" Winks, *The Civil War Years*, 275–76.

"encouraged by your approval" Letter to Davis, March 7, 1865, published in *New York Herald*, July 8, 1865.

"It is said that he borrowed" Curtis, 80-81.

"Mr. Sanders is remarkably well-adapted" Parker, 103.

"Between him and myself" Sanders, letter to Jeff Davis, August 13, 1872, in *Jefferson Davis, Constitutionalist*, vol. VII, 346.

"There is such a thing as spoiling broth" Thomson to Clay, June 9, 1864, cited by Whyte, 64.

"a haven for fugitives" *St. Catharines Standard*, July 17, 1915.

"Commissioner Clay soon yielded" Castleman, 135.

"the Canadian junta" *Philadelphia Inquirer*, November 7, 1865.

"Conscious of the fast-waning vitality" Letter to Davis, March 7, published in *New York Herald*, July 8, 1865.

"Tens of thousands of white men" Hoy, 307.

"The Yankees are sick of war" Letter, August 24, 1864, Clay Papers.

Sanders at his manipulative best Whyte, 120, 122.

"Instead of the safe-conduct" *NYT*, July 22, 1864.

"the grinning, chattering, autocrat Lincoln" Hoy, 308–9.

"we lost nothing and gained much" Letter to Judah Benjamin, September 12, Clay Papers.

"[W]e need peace even more than the NORTH does" Letter, August 24, 1864, Clay Papers. Capitalization in the original.

"the harm they are doing" Boyko, 169.

"His long imprisonment" Squires, 123.

20. 'OUR PLAN WAS DARING'

"enemies of the United States" Alford,186.

"Leading rebels unusually busy" August 19, 1864, in Canadian Links folder, James O. Hall Research Center.

"In 1864 Confederate prisoners held by the United States" Castleman, 143.

Jacob Thompson was eager to step up the attacks Lincoln was facing a difficult re-election campaign in the fall of 1864. "It seems probable that Lincoln will be defeated," an elated Jacob Thompson wrote in a secret dispatch to Richmond in July 1864. "Nothing less, however, can accomplish this end . . . In short, nothing but violence can terminate the war."(Headley, 224)

"plunged the country into a cruel, bloody and unnecessary war" Vallandigham, 34.

plenty of support for his cause among the country's elites. In Quebec City, Charles J. Brydges, the head of the Grand Trunk Railway, gave Vallandigham a tour of the town. Brydges invited his American guest to the exclusive Stadacona Club. The crowd there, including such prominent politicians as John A. Macdonald, toasted Vallandigham as a "refugee . . . in distress." Vallandigham was asked by Thomas D'Arcy McGee, a member of Parliament from Montreal and a future Father of Confederation, to join him on the stage at a political rally in Quebec attended by two thousand people. Later, McGee went further and invited Vallandigham to be his honoured guest at the Legislative Assembly. (See Klement, 151,158,162; Boyko, 158; and *Globe*, July 21, 1863.)

two-room suite of a Windsor hotel Klement, 163.

Thompson offered generous amounts cash Just how much financial support
   Thompson shovelled to the Sons of Liberty was kept secret, but court
   testimony later revealed that Thompson had sent as much as $75,000
   "to be used for the purchase of arms and for releasing rebel prisoners."
   (NYT, April 4, 1865) Hines, for his part, diligently kept receipts, which
   included $3,000 for holsters and ammunition, $2,000 "for bribes for railroad
   employees who were to turn their trains over to the raiders for the prison
   camp assaults," and $3,000 for messengers who delivered reports back to
   Thompson in Canada. (Hines, *Southern Bivouac*, February, 1887, 567.

"waiting in breathless suspense day after day" Towne, 95.

"Our plan was daring enough," *St. Catharines Standard*, July 17, 1915.

gave them each $100 and a train ticket Boyko, 178.

"Arms were ready" Headley, 228, 229.

"promised so much and did so little," Towne, 95.

"fiasco at Chicago" Hines, *Southern Bivouac*, April 1887, 669.

with his fellow Kentuckian Confederates Baird, 26.

"being desirous only of benefiting" American Consular Reports—Civil War
   Period, 25.

"the philanthropic conduct" Note from British Admiralty, November 16,
   1864, cited by NYT, May 29, 1865.

PIRACY ON LAKE ERIE! Mayer, 73.

"With the failure of Beall's enterprise" Hines, *Southern Bivouac*, April 1887, 704.

21. 'REIGN OF TERROR'

There have been several books written about the St. Albans raid and there
exists a rich amount of primary source material. Edward A. Sowles's *History
of the St. Albans Raid* provides a first-hand perspective. All the court cases
are contained in the 1864 publication called *The St. Albans Raid* (hereafter
called "Court Transcript"). The full inquiry by the Montreal city council was
published the same year as *The St. Albans Raid: Investigation by the Police
Committee* (referred to as "Police Committee").

"It is but right that the people of New England and Vermont" *House of
   Representatives Report*, No. 104, 39th Congress, 10–11.

"He proposed . . . passing through the New England States" Clay letter to
   Judah Benjamin, November 1, 1864, cited in the transcripts of the conspiracy trial, *Assassination of Abraham Lincoln*, 26.

"I will never return" Young letter, September 20, 1864, *House of Representatives Report*, No. 104, 15.

Bank receipts preserved in Clay's family papers Clay Papers.

"They know how defenceless the town is," Prince, 131.

"tall, good-looking" *Burlington Times*, October 2, 1864, cited in *Globe*,
October 26, 1864.

"In the name of the Confederate States" Court Transcript, 54.

"We are Confederate soldiers" *Burlington Times*, October 20, 1864, cited in
Globe, October 26, 1864.

"pointed large navy revolvers at me" and other quotes in Sowles, 12, 14, 19.

"They have shot me through the body," *St. Albans Messenger*, February 15,
2014. Despite allegations that Young fired the fatal shot, another raider
named Erasmus Fuller was accused of the murder in Montreal courts.
But nothing came of the charges. See Torrance, 7.

"We're coming back" *NYT*, October 21, 1864.

"fearful that another train" *Gazette*, October 26, 1864.

"With our homes sacked" *New York Herald*, November 9, 1864.

"a simple bank robbery" and the following quotes from *Gazette*, October
21, 24, 25, 26, 1864.

Fourteen men were now behind bars The exact numbers of those arrested and
brought to trial is not clear. Affidavits from Justices of the Peace and arrest
warrants presented at trial list fourteen names (Court Transcript, 18–20, 42;
see also Lamothe, letter to son, 1885, Papiers Lamothe). But on October 24,
according to the *Globe*, only thirteen men appeared before Judge Coursol.

"Since then, all traces of them have been lost" *Gazette*, October 24, 1864.

"manifested the warmest friendship for the prisoners" Headley, 261. See
also *Globe*, October 26, 1864. The *Gazette* on October 27 reported that
in St. Johns "the sympathy of the majority of the townspeople still runs
strongly for the prisoners."

"providing wine and a variety of edible delicacies." Squires, 125.

"I went there for the purpose of burning the town" Cited by *Gazette*,
October 24, 1864, and *NYT*, October 24, 1864. See also Young's letter to
Gazette, October 27, 1864.

"merely the starting point of a system of warfare" Squires, 128.

"The notorious George Sanders is here," *Globe*, October 26, 1864.

"My mission here is one of peace" *Gazette*, December 21, 1864. See also his
October 26 letter to *Evening Telegraph*, reprinted in *Globe*, October 27, 1864.

a police magistrate Ste. Croix, "Coursol."

"He was what we should call a fast man" *NYT*, December 22, 1864.

"I always took an active part in politics" Lamothe, *Mes Mémoires*, 30.

"for their safe-keeping" Sowles, 28.

"Nothing transpired at that interview" Sanders statement in Police Committee, 34.

"Canada was so friendly" Sowles, 41.

22. 'I AM GOING TO HELL'

"stormy words" Asia Booth Clarke, cited by Alford, 183.

"We drank and freely conversed" Arnold memoirs, cited by Edward Steers, Jr., *Lincoln's Assassination*, 20.

"I am going to Hell" Alford, 185.

"He was a most genial gifted man" *Montreal Star*, March 8, 1902.

"in the most salubrious" Collard, 134, 139.

"elaborate and gilded" Ibid., 139.

a peephole in his office *Gazette*, February 4, 2012.

"A victory for the soldiers in gray" and other quotes from Hogan in *Montreal Star*, December 6, 1902.

"[Blackburn] was one of that clique of men" Hosea Carter testimony, May 29, 1865, *Assassination of President Lincoln*, 38.

"A Canadian winter was a novelty to Booth" Loux, 169.

Not far from Booth's hotel stood the Theatre Royal Several books and news articles about Booth's stay in Montreal insist that he thrilled Montreal audiences with a reading from Shakespeare's *Merchant of Venice* and Tennyson's "The Charge of the Light Brigade." Booth himself reportedly told his family that he was heading to Montreal "to fulfill an engagement" (Junius Booth Jr. Statement, *Investigation and Trial Papers*, April 1865). But the evidence that Booth actually performed onstage while in Montreal is unreliable and has been misinterpreted. The story originates from a confusing account in a book about Montreal's theatre history called *Histrionic Montreal* (145–46). It cites hotel manager Hogan, who said, "John Wilkes Booth played a short engagement under the Buckland management, preliminary to the regular opening." But the dates Hogan gave were impossible—he said the performance took place in 1865, "just a week or ten days before the assassination of Lincoln." The book also referred to a theatre program, but that listing was for a performance Booth gave in January 1864 in Missouri—not in Montreal.

"What are you going to do?" John Deveny testimony, May 12, 1865, *Assassination of President Lincoln*, 38.

"His spending was profuse" *Gazette*, April 17, 1865.

Booth had arranged to transport his trunks Unfortunately for Booth and Martin, their plans did not work out. Martin, along with Booth's trunks, was lost at sea—in a storm, not by the Union blockade.

"a rather excitable, meddlesome man" *Daily Graphic*, March 22, 1876. Steers concludes that Booth's dealings with Martin "must have been known at some point by the leadership in Richmond" (Steers, *Blood on the Moon*, 73).

a well-connected doctor named Samuel Mudd Steers, *Blood on the Moon*,
73 and 305. Kaufman disputes that Mudd's name was included in the
letters. See Kaufman, 430.

"How often did you see J. Wilkes Booth?" All quotes from Campbell's
testimony, May 20, 1865, *Assassination of President Lincoln*, 45–46.

Both men were in Quebec City Tidwell, *Come Retribution*, 329.

at least four days to meet up with Booth. John Deveny told investigators
after the assassination that he saw Booth with both Thompson and Clay:
"He was in their society constantly" (Deveny witness statement, *Investigation and Trial Papers*).

Sanders stayed in Room 169 St. Lawrence Hall Arrival Book, LAC (hereafter
referred to as Arrival Book, LAC).

"in intimate association with Sanders" Carter testimony, *Assassination of
President Lincoln*, 38.

"always confidential, always whispered," Deveny witness statement, *Investigation and Trial Papers*. See also Deveny testimony, *Assassination of
President Lincoln*, 38–39.

"urging a plan to assassinate Lincoln" Tidwell, *Come Retribution*, 332.

"In fact, Sir, we shall do such deeds" *Daily Telegraph* story quoted in
Gazette, December 21, 1864, and *Globe*, May 10, 1865. Sanders later
confirmed that he spoke to Sala at length, but he complained that "Sala
misrepresents me in the grossest and most infamous manner" (*Gazette*,
December 21, 1865). Sala stood by his story, insisting "that Sanders told
him distinctly of the plotting of atrocities which would make the world
shudder." See *NYT*, May 6, 1865.

"My opponent seemed" *NYT*, May 7, 1865.

"To Whom It May Concern" *NYT*, April 21, 1865.

23. 'TO BURN NEW YORK'

"There is one effectual way" *Richmond Examiner*, October 1, reprinted in
NYT, October 19, 1864.

"was deemed an opportune time" Headley, 264. All quotes from Headley
are from his memoirs, *Confederate Operations*, 264–81.

Blackburn . . . would set fire to Boston Ibid.

Thomas Hines would handle Chicago Mayer, 138. See also *Globe*, February
10, 1865.

"[H]e was regarded as wholly useless" *NYT*, March 26, 1865.

"there is a conspiracy afoot" *NYT*, November 3, 1864.

"Let trouble show itself" *NYT*, November 8, 1864.

"confidential agents and detectives" Butler, 73.

"lately urging the rebels stationed in Canada" and following quotes *NYT*, November 7, 16, 27, 1864.

"They were described as being rather gentlemanly" *New York Herald*, November 27, 1864.

"was simply a reckless joke" and other quotes from Cobb, *NYT*, March 26, 1865.

"[it] was a proud moment for their mother" *Montreal Herald*, June 7, 1893.

As the second scene of Act 2 was unfolding Alford, 194–97.

"However shrewd and skilful" *New York Herald*, November 26, 1864.

A furious Booth Alford, 198.

"A most daring raid" Thompson letter to Judah Benjamin, December 3, 1864, Headley, 288–96.

"I was restless" *New York Herald*, March 26, 1864.

they arrested several men *Globe*, December 5, 1864.

"unkempt, roughly clad, dirty" Beall, 57, 62.

24. 'KINDNESS TO THE PRISONERS'

"My jailer, Payette" and other quotes from Bennett Young, unpublished interview 1908, Vermont Historical Museum.

"The jailer set aside his parlors" Headley, 262.

"countenanced the robbers" *NYT*, June 16, 1865.

"the table of a prince" Sowles, 29.

regular shipments of chilled wine Horan, 180.

"This enterprise was conducted" *Gazette*, October 27, 1864.

"I am no less surprised" Letter, October 22, 1864, cited by Whyte, 148.

"defense of St. Albans prisoners" Bank receipts, Clay Papers.

"the 'Southern Junta' at 'the Hall'" *Montreal Star*, March 8, 1902.

"daring and devoted patriots" Court Transcript, 444.

"justice and equality to all classes and creeds" *Canadian Parliamentary Companion*, 119.

visiting the men when they were in jail Winks, *The Civil War Years,* 313.

"Whatever was done at St. Albans" Court Transcript, 79. See also *Leader*, November 14, 1864.

"Has Mr. Jefferson Davis power" *Globe*, October 25, 1864.

"Beautiful women" / "the raid on St. Albans is merely the starting point" Horan, 180.

"did not come into Young's possession honestly" Horan, 253.

Sanders talked again with Montreal police boss and following quotes about the actions of Sanders and Porterfield can be found in Police Committee, 34, 33 and 22.

"Where other men were carried away" *Montreal Star*, March 4, 1896.

he received two visitors at his home All quotes and details of these visits come from Lamothe's unpublished letter to his son, March 1, 1895, Papiers Lamothe, LAC. Lamothe claimed that Judge Coursol had told Bernard Devlin at the start of the trial that he should arrange to "seize" the stolen loot being held by the police chief, "otherwise you could lose the money." It is a difficult story to believe. Why would a judge give the money to the police chief only to then tell the prosecutor to seize it? Why did neither Lamothe nor Coursol ever bring up such an important defence of their actions during the various inquiries into the scandal? Why would Lamothe wait thirty years to recount this story and then only in a confidential letter to his son?

25. 'CONSPIRED WITH SOUTHERN AGENTS'

"The whole of the proceedings are wrong" Court Transcript, 117.

What few in the court knew Torrance, 11, 13. Torrance reported that on the eve of Coursol's ruling, Lamothe deposited the money "perceiving that it was likely to be favourable to the prisoners."

"She came often" Young, unpublished interview, 1908. About his seduction of the judge's daughter, Young said: "I was justified in my love making on the grounds that all is fair in love and war."

"I have and possess no jurisdiction" Court Transcript, 127.

"When men charged with robbery" *Globe*, December 14, 1864.

"rounds of applause and screams" Sowles, 32.

"I had understood that Mr. Devlin was very sharp" Police Committee, 31.

"It was in a sealed and labelled carpet bag" Ibid., 24.

"The money, all right and a little plus." Ibid., 31. The *Gazette*, displaying wilful blindness to the actions by its Confederate heroes, continued to insist that "they have taken away no money . . . whoever profits from this booty they do not" (December 15, 1864).

Coursol was wrong Torrance, 34. Torrance wrote that Coursol's ruling that he had no jurisdiction was "an abdication of his judicial functions." Torrance also expressed "grave doubts" about Coursol meeting privately with the defence lawyers.

"after the usual hour of business" All quotes from Ritchie come from his testimony, Police Committee, 38–44.

"I was not in a good mood" Unpublished letter, March 1, 1895, Papiers Lamothe, LAC.

he found refuge with the Saint-Jean-Baptiste Society At least three accounts verify the society's role. See Rush and Pewitt, *St. Albans Raiders*; Trépanier, "Guillaume Lamothe," 155; and David, *Mes Contemporains*, 164–65. David, a respected Quebec journalist and lawyer in the nineteenth century, writes that the Saint-Jean-Baptiste Society even thought of organizing a jail break to free the raiders. The society had powerful political connections: police chief Lamothe later became an active member and Judge Coursol served as the society's president.

Higbee was more than a mere bank robber Rush, 50–51. After his escape from Montreal, Higbee eventually settled in Fort Worth, Texas, where, ironically, he set up a bank.

"has not only written himself down" Kinchen, *Daredevils*, 75.

the stolen loot had been "liberally divided" *NYT*, December 22, 1865.

"Take her by the throat" *Chicago Tribune*, December 15, 1864.

"When all this was going on" *Montreal Witness*, October 22, 1864.

"illegally arrested" Police Committee, 6.

"I cannot really recollect" Ibid., 22.

John Porterfield was equally cagey Ibid., 20–26.

"No portion of this money" Ibid., 30.

"Seldom has a public official" *Globe*, December 20, 1864.

"Feeling that personal motives" Police Committee, 19.

Bernard Devlin made a speech Ibid., 66–71.

The final vote was fourteen to eleven Typical of the linguistic divide that continued to mark Montreal in the years since, the vote to condemn the police chief was split along language lines, with all the francophone members on city council siding with Lamothe.

"this wretched prig of a police magistrate" Letter by John A. MacDonald, March 10, 1865, in Tupper, 113.

"grave dereliction of duty" Torrance, 35.

"Whatever we had" Young, unpublished interview. Young's claim may have been a self-serving attempt to hide the possibility that the raiders pocketed a lot of the loot for themselves. But Montreal police chief Guillaume Lamothe also recounts that the raiders told him that "the money was handed over to Southern agents" (unpublished letter to son, March 1, 1895, Papiers Lamothe, LAC).

26. 'THE CURSE IN THIS COUNTRY'

"Now many of our best" Headley, 308.

"I have relaxed no effort" All quotes from Thompson in this chapter come from his letter to Judah Benjamin, December 3, 1864, reprinted in Headley, 288–96.

"rebel agents [were] being reinforced" Potter memo, December 10, 1864, in "Canadian Links" folder, James O. Hall Research Center.

"I do not see that I can achieve anything" *Assassination of President Lincoln*, 37.

"Ran aground . . .," Diary, January 3, 1865, Clay Papers.

"he destroyed a number of papers" Mayer, 202.

"From reports which reach us" Greene, 83.

"Certificate given" Levin, 121.

27. 'A WAR FOR HUMANITY'

"Should any of her readers object" *Nurse and Spy*, 6.

her regiment never fought there Leonard, 139.

"Not strictly so" *Detroit Post and Tribune*, May 26, 1883.

"The book was widely read" *Detroit Free Press*, October 6, 1935.

it sold 175,000 copies Edmonds letter, March 8, 1865, in Edmonds Pension File.

a much higher mortality rate National Archives, "Black Soldiers in the U.S. Military."

under the control of the Bureau of Refugees Newmark, "Contraband Hospital."

"The Hospital contained a capacity for 300 beds" Undated note, Abbott Collection.

"indulging in the use of intoxicating drinks" Reid, 169; Prince, 132.

a monthly salary of $169 as a major Henig, 28. See also Butts, 108.

By June 1864, Congress passed legislation Nazarian, "Civil War: The Struggle for Equal Pay." See also Foner, 253.

"There never was such a gathering" May 22, 1907, Grand Army of the Republic Speech, Abbott Collection.

"to be officered exclusively by colored men" According to Reid, the War Department did eventually appoint about ten Black officers, though many got their commissions after the war ended. Reid, 128–29.

28. 'SHE WORE HER VEIL'

The best source on the elusive Sarah Slater is the *Surratt Courier* (www.surratt-museum.org), a newsletter put out by the Surratt Society. It was not until 1982 that acclaimed assassination expert James O. Hall began to piece together the hidden story of Sarah Slater's life. Over the next forty years, other sleuths uncovered more of her secrets. See bibliography listings for James O. Hall, John Stanton, Joan Chaconas and Susan Higginbottom in the *Surratt*

Courier. Todd Holbrook's *Mrs. Slater in the Confederate Secret Service* is the only work entirely focused on her story. There is a chapter about her in H. Donald Winkler's book *Stealing Secrets.*

"She was a rather slim, delicate woman" David Barry testimony, Surratt Trial, vol. II, 754.

he sold three of his horses Holzer, "Cease Fire."

"She has lost her only brother" Hall, "Saga of Sarah Slater."

Slater was already a Confederate agent Holbrook makes the intriguing case that Slater was in Montreal at the end of 1864, based on an entry dated December 17 in the St. Lawrence Hall arrival book for "A. Reynaud"—the same alias she would use later—and another entry for an "N. Slater" on December 21 (Holbrook, 14–16; see also Stanton in the *Surratt Courier*). Indeed, the handwriting for the December 17 entry appears to closely match the signature Slater would use later. However, unlike the supporting evidence we have for her trips in early 1865, there are no references by Confederate operatives in Montreal to her presence there in December 1864; no sighting of her at that time by eyewitnesses at the Surratt boarding house in Washington or on the courier network; and no mention of documents brought from Richmond in any of the St. Albans court proceedings until the early months of 1865.

"He liked what he saw" Winkler, 33.

"The lives of the Confederate prisoners," Headley, 309.

"Union officers would surely be inclined" Hall, "Saga of Sarah Slater."

"a gallant true officer" and other quotes from Denison, *Soldiering in Canada,* 65, 60–62.

"no braver or truer soldier" Jacob Thompson letter to Lincoln, February 2, 1865, cited by Headley, 325.

"Very much has been said" and other quotes from Davis, *Escape of a Confederate Officer,* 33, 44, 45.

the same documents that Sarah Slater had been ordered to smuggle The accounts of what secret documents Davis was carrying are confusing. Denison *Soldiering in Canada,* (60) writes that Davis had *already* brought the papers necessary for the defence of the St. Albans raiders on his first trip to Toronto. But Mayer (184–85) writes that Davis was sent back to Richmond to retrieve those documents, as does Headley (324). To further complicate matters, Thompson, in a February 2, 1865, letter that he wrote to Lincoln after Davis's capture, insisted that Davis was on a mission to help not the St. Albans prisoners but another jailed Confederate. (See *Southern Bivouac,* April 1887, 703.)

"filth and dirt besprinkled with vermin" Davis, *Escape of a Confederate Officer,* 47.

how risky the courier routes were Aside from Slater, Davis and Cameron, there may have been other spies deployed to save the Confederates jailed in Canada. Whyte and Mayers suggest there may have been a fourth (Whyte, 16; Mayers, "Spies Across the Border," *Civil War Times Illustrated*).

"They were my brother soldiers" Cameron testimony, Surratt Trial, vol. II, 804–5. See also *NYT*, February 19, 1865.

"accompanied by two women" Sowles, 40.

"one of the most effective spies" Hall, "Saga of Sarah Slater."

her tidy, small signature Arrival Book, LAC.

29. 'TOO GREAT A RISK'

Under the headline JOHN SURRATT TELLS HIS STORY, the *Washington Evening Star* on December 7, 1870, published a transcript of his speech in Rockville (hereafter referred to as "Rockville Lecture"). Many quotes and actions attributed to him are in the full transcripts of *The Trial of John H. Surratt*, vols. I and II (hereafter called "Surratt Trial"). One of the best books on Surratt is Michael Schein's insightful *John Surratt: The Lincoln Assassin Who Got Away*.

he took over no fewer than four rooms Arrival Book, LAC.

"It was now Colonel Thompson's determination" and other quotes in Headley, 311, 376, 378.

"This young man's life is in your hands" Letter to Lincoln, February 2, 1865, cited by Headley, 325.

"will be revered as a martyr" *Gazette*, March 13, 1865.

"the impetuous daring warrior" Ibid., September 1, 1865.

"I knew nothing of the St. Albans raid" Court Transcript, 127.

"After only a few hours' sleep" Winkler, 34.

"The papers I carried were genuine" Cameron testimony, Surratt Trial, vol. II, 804.

"The woman's name" McMillan testimony, Surratt Trial, vol. I, 467.

"Tall, erect, slender and boyish" and other quotes in Weichmann, 14, 15, 21.

"I . . . was mostly engaged in sending information" Rockville Lecture.

"It was a fascinating life to me" Ibid.

"The woman was rather diminutive" Weichmann, 85–86.

"she was a blockade-runner" Weichmann testimony, May 13, 1865, *Assassination of President Lincoln*, 114.

"authorities in Washington" Hall, "Saga of Sarah Slater."

the arrival at the St. Lawrence Hall Arrival Book, LAC.

"had frequent, official intercourse with them" Letter to *Gazette*, April 25, 1865, in Lee Archives.

On March 17 There is some uncertainty around when Slater arrived at the St. Lawrence Hall and how long she stayed. On March 9, there is an entry at 11:30 p.m. for an "A. Reynaud"—her mother's maiden name—from New York. On March 17, there is a similar registration. If both those people are her, what she did in those intervening eight days is unclear. See Schein, 92–93.

"read me his dispatches from Richmond." Lee Diary, March 17 and 22, 1865.

30. 'KIDNAP PRESIDENT LINCOLN!'

"One-eighth of the whole population" Lincoln's Second Inaugural Address, March 4, 1865, *Collected Works*, vol. 8, 332.

"What an excellent chance" Trial testimony reported in *NYT*, May 17, 1865.

Booth had begun seriously thinking about kidnapping Another Canadian connection to the kidnap plot may have come as early as July 26, 1864. Booth stayed at the Parker House in Boston at the same time as three mysterious men who checked in from Toronto, Hamilton and Montreal. Tidwell suggests all three names they used were aliases and they probably discussed a kidnap plot. Tidwell, *Come Retribution*, 262.

"My love . . . is for the South alone" Clarke, 109.

"I was introduced to John Wilkes Booth" Rockville Lecture. All Surratt quotes in this chapter are from this 1870 speech.

"excellent horseman, a good pistol shot" and other quotes from Weichmann, 30, 78, 119.

His job at a pharmacy Steers, *Blood on the Moon*, 81–82.

"fills the centre of the picture" *NYT*, March 18, 1865, cited by Schein, 87.

"For six months we had worked" Tidwell, *Come Retribution*, 421.

he may have been the one who accompanied Slater Kaufmann, 192. Hall ("Saga of Sarah Slater"), on the other hand, suggests it was probably John Surratt who once again picked her up in New York.

"She stopped at the National Hotel" Azterodt Confession, *Baltimore American*, January 18, 1869.

"Mrs. Slater went with Booth a good deal" Ibid.

"perilous trip" Hatch, 59.

31. 'HE WAS DONE PLAYING'

"a strange mixture of bravado" *NYT*, March 26, 1865. All other quotes from Kennedy from the same article.

"The attempt to set fire" Headley, 327.

"You cannot abandon us" All quotes and details about Lamothe's activities taken from his unpublished letter to son, March 1, 1895, Papiers Lamothe, LAC.

"very many ladies" *NYT*, April 2, 1865.

"There was plenty of money" *Daily Telegraph* (London) report cited by *Gazette*, December 2, 1864.

"elevate a daring act of robbery" and other quotes from trial from Court Transcript, 274, 398, 438, 447–74.

It took two days for Smith to read his verdict Ibid., 447–74. See also Mayers, 204.

"which the authorities were unable to quell" *NYT*, April 2, 1865.

"such a decision meant" *Globe*, May 1, 1865.

"Judge Smith discharged the prisoners" Mayer, 203. See also *Gazette*, April 6, 1865.

"Another Canadian Justice has decided" *NYT*, March 30, 1865.

"the decision was received" *Globe*, April 11, 1865.

"an act of friendship" *St. Catharines Standard*, July 17, 1915.

"John Surratt began to be a bird of passage" Weichmann interview, *New York Tribune*, May 20, 1867, reprinted in *Surratt Courier* XVI, no. 8 (August 1991).

"As business will detain me" Surratt letter, March 26, 1865, cited by Hall, "Saga of Sarah Slater."

"Let's shoot the damned Yankee soldiers" McMillan testimony, Surratt Trial, vol. I, 467. How reliable is this account, which, remarkably, is the only description we have of any words spoken by the elusive Sarah Slater? Granted, it is double hearsay—a witness at a trial three years after the fact repeating what he says he was told by John Surratt. Still, among a collection of uneven witnesses, McMillan was one of the most credible; he had no obvious political axe to grind and many of his other statements were corroborated by other evidence. If he was making up tales about what Surratt told him, a yarn about a female accompanying him in a deadly shootout seems an odd and very detailed choice. For his part, Surratt could have been lying or exaggerating to his doctor friend; but what would be the motivation for him to invent such a tale?

"He asked me if I would carry some dispatches" All other quotes from Surratt in this chapter are from his Rockville Lecture.

"professional blockade runner" Townsend article, January 5, 1867, cited by Hall, "Saga of Sarah Slater."

"The colored population" Foner, 329.

"You are free—free as air" *Washington Post*, March 27, 2015.

"First news of Fall of Richmond!" Lee Diary, April 1, 1865.

"He said he was going to Montreal" Weichmann, 128.

"where Booth practiced pistol firing" *Boston Evening Transcript*, April 15, 1865, cited by *History of Massachusetts*.

two rooms were assigned to him that morning Arrival Book, LAC.

"Letter by Charley" Lee Diary, April 6, 1865.

"I am unwilling to consent" Levin, 152.

the tailor shop of John J. Reeves Surratt Trial, vol. II, 842.

"Montreal is really a beautiful city" Letter from the St. Lawrence Hall, April 10, 1865, cited by Schein, 122.

"received a letter from John Wilkes Booth" McMillan testimony, Surratt Trial, vol. I, 467, 471.

"had frequent interviews" Potter dispatch, in Canadian Links folder, James O. Hall Research Center.

"he was done playing" Weichmann, 131.

32. 'THAT AWFUL TRAGEDY'

"The days . . . were devoted to festivities" Abbott, "Some Recollections," in the Abbott Collection. This is the source for all quotes in this chapter from Abbott.

"Poor old Richmond" Lee Diary, April 11, 1865.

"I scoff at the idea of submission" Letter, April 11, 1865, Lee Archives.

"this country was formed for the white" Letter, November 1864, printed in *NYT*, April 21, 1865.

"That means n----- citizenship" *Army History*, Winter 2013, 10. Booth's words about "n----- citizenship" are disputed by some historians (see Lawrence, "Yes, Booth Did Speak Those Notorious Words") but are accepted by leading biographers (Alford, 257; Kaufman, 210).

"Everything was bright and splendid" Alford, 259.

"Frequent letters were received" Keckley, 120.

"I cannot bring myself" Gen. Edward H. Ripley, Proceedings of the Reunion Society of Vermont Officers.

"If Jake Thompson is permitted" *NYT*, May 7, 1865.

"I rather think not" Dana, 273–74.

"The audience heard the shot" *NYT*, April 16, 1865.

"As far as the eye could reach" Abbott, "Some Recollections."

"I struck boldly" Booth Diary, Surratt Trial, vol. I, 310–11.

Anderson Abbott . . . accompanied her It is impossible to confirm Abbott's

account. In her memoirs, Keckley describes Abbott as one of Lincoln's
"warmest friends." (Keckley, 346). But she puts the summons at 11 a.m. on
Saturday morning, not 2 a.m. in the middle of the night, as Abbott writes.
She says she went to the White House to comfort a distraught Mary
Lincoln, not to the home across the street from the theatre. Even if Abbott
did accompany Keckley, he never was at Lincoln's bedside as many historical accounts have since written. Over the years, many articles, books and
websites—including the *Dictionary of Canadian Biography*—identify
Abbott as one of the doctors standing vigil over him. But Abbott himself
never made such a claim. Reid suggests that people may have confused him
with Dr. Ezra W. Abbott, who was present during the vigil (Reid, 160).

Some medical experts say "Modern Medicine May Have Saved Lincoln,"
  Baltimore Sun, May 18, 2007.

"No common mortal had died" Keckley, 190.

33. 'A NATION WEEPS'

"Perhaps no news" *Globe*, April 17, 1865.

"The awful, terrible announcement" *Buffalo Express*, April 15, reprinted in
  Globe, April 17, 1865.

"Southern refugees assembled in our chief hotel" *Globe*, April 17, 1865.

two of the St. Albans raiders Winks, *The Civil War Years*, 364.

"some Southerners drank" *Hamilton Evening Times*, April 17, 1865, cited
  by Wells.

"Lincoln had only gone to hell" *Montreal Daily Witness*, April 18, 1865,
  cited by Wells.

"News of Lincoln's death" Lee Diary, April 15, 1865.

"There were some so . . . depraved" Alford, 236.

"We talked about Lincoln's death," Monck, 350.

the Union had held victory celebrations *Gazette des Campagnes*, April 18,
  1865, cited by Wells.

"cheered, as was natural" Davis, *Rise and Fall*, 580.

Davis privately paraphrased a line Holzer, "What the Newspapers Said."

"For an enemy so relentless" Davis, *Rise and Fall*, 580.

"Abe has gone to answer" Holzer, "What the Newspapers Said."

"It must be remembered" Alford, 236–37.

"it should not be forgotten" *Leader*, April 17, 1865. Historian Cherly Wells
  compiled a depressing litany of similar comments from across the country.
  In Ontario, the *St. Thomas Weekly Dispatch*—unsure if the assassination
  was for "better or for worse"—blamed Lincoln's "lust of power and

ambition." The *Northern Advance* in Barrie blasted Lincoln for waging "a fratricidal and unjustifiable war." In New Brunswick, the *Weekly Freeman* called out the "many illegal and tyrannical acts" committed by Lincoln's government, while the *Prince Edward Island Vindicator* castigated him for "more butchery than could even be charged Napoleon" (Wells, "Icy Blasts to Balmy Airs").

"the great loss which the South sustains" *Gazette*, April 17, 1865.

"the terrible reprisals against the south" *Le Canadien*, April 15, 1865, cited by Savard, 121.

"creating a pedestal" *Le Canadien*, April 21, 1865, cited by Rountree, 9.

"A nation weeps" *Globe*, April 19, 1865.

"we should pass the matter" Ibid.

"The bells are tolling mournfully" *Globe*, April 17 and 20, 1865.

"none were more loyal and brave" *Maple Leaves from Canada*, 39–40.

"the largest meeting for many years" Wells.

34. 'NEVER TAKEN ALIVE'

James Swanson's *Manhunt: The 12-Day Chase for Abraham Lincoln's Killer* is gripping and meticulous. Edward Doherty's detailed account of the "Capture of J. Wilkes Booth," which he filed on April 26, 1865, is in *A Compilation of the Official Records of the Union and Confederate Armies* (referred to below as "Doherty Report").

procession of seventy-five thousand Black troops Undated file, "Dr. Augusta Goes to Washington," Abbott Collection. See also Taylor, "Doctor of Courage."

"It was my day off" Undated magazine interview, in Hall Files, Doherty folder, James O. Hall Research Center.

"a reliable and discreet commissioned officer" Doherty Report. Unless otherwise indicated, all quotes in this chapter from Doherty come from this official report.

He was conniving Swanson, 282.

"It was tiresome work" *NYT*, January 18, 1895.

modern scholarship has suggested he broke his leg during his nighttime ride Kaufman, 273.

"After being hunted like a dog" Booth diary, reprinted in Surratt Trial, vol. I, 310–11.

"we were on their track" In Luther Baker's telling of the story, he did most of the questioning of these and other witnesses; in Doherty's subsequent accounts, he was the one who uncovered the evidence. See Swanson, 298–300.

"His face was haggard" Ruggles.

"The woman told me that Jett" *NYT*, January 18, 1895.

"I'm safe in glorious Virginia" Ruggles.

"You who know anything of Virginia" Garrett, "Chapter of Unwritten History." All quotes from Garrett come from the same source.

"to shoot the prisoner" Herman Newgarten affidavit in Doherty Papers.

"I know your movements" and following quotes from *NYT*, January 18, 1895. Conger later insisted it was he who questioned Jett.

"That day was bright and warm" Swanson, 292.

"They are in that house" Private David Baker affidavit in Doherty Papers.

"Where are these men" *Daily Picayune*, August 18, 1879.

"Who are you?" Swanson, 322.

That, at least, was Doherty's account For Baker and Conger's version, see Swanson, 323–24.

"O Captain! there is a man in here" Doherty testimony, May 22, 1865, *Assassination of President Lincoln*, 95.

"If we can't get both of you" John Winter affidavit in Doherty Papers.

"Open the door!" Swanson, 326.

"Hand out your arms" Doherty testimony, *Assassination of President Lincoln*, 95.

"You had better follow his example" Undated article, 1889, "He Captured Booth: Captain Doherty How He Caught Lincoln's Assassin," *Brooklyn Citizen*, in Doherty File, Hall folder, Surratt Society.

"The hay in the barn" *NYT*, January 18, 1895.

"He was dazed for a moment" *Brooklyn Citizen*, "He Captured Booth."

"He [Booth] was taking aim with the carbine" Swanson, 334–35.

"Corbett . . . seeing by the igniting hay" Letter from Doherty's son Charles, February 13, 1931, in Doherty Papers.

"The man looked defiant and wild" *Brooklyn Citizen*, "He Captured Booth."

"Did you consider it necessary to shoot Booth?" Ibid.

"This incident in the capture" Letter from Doherty's son Charles, Doherty Papers.

"[They] have sealed" Winkler, 194.

35. 'MAKE MYSELF SCARCE'

"A man named John Surratt" *Globe*, April 17, 1865.

"The news of the evacuation" Rockville Lecture for this and all other Surratt quotes in this chapter.

"Miss H.C. Slater" Schein surmises that one reason for Surratt's roundabout journey from Elmira across New York State to Vermont may have been to pick up Slater (Schein, 150). Curiously, Slater's signature is quite different from the other time she signed in as "Slater," and also different from the way she registered as "A. Reynaud," perhaps another subterfuge.

"This day or the 20th" Lee Diary, April 19, 1865.

"He advised me to make myself scarce" Surratt does not name Lee; he only says, "I immediately went to the hotel, got my things, and repaired to the room of a friend"—which can hardly be anyone but Lee.

"I was convinced that I was doing" Weichmann, 220.

On April 20, the detectives told Washington Note from police in Canadian Links folder, James O. Hall Research Center.

he was heading to Quebec City Hatch, 65.

"a most devoted friend" In his Rockville speech in 1870, Surratt never explicitly names Porterfield as the friend who provided his second hideout but police reports and other testimony identify the house as Porterfield's.

"followed them from Porterfield's" Hatch, 65.

Weichmann travelled all the way to Quebec City Schein 162.

36. 'CAN SUCH A THING BE?'

blaring headlines on its front page NYT, May 4, 1865.

STARTLING PROCLAMATION Globe, May 6, 1865.

"I was obliged to issue it," Clay-Copton, 319.

"That the plot originated" Globe, May 6, 1865.

"I assert that the Canadian agents" Townsend, 79.

"Can such a thing be?" Globe, May 4, 1865.

"as a Southern gentleman" Letter dated April 26, 1865, in Lee Archives.

"To the People of Canada" Gazette, May 4, 1865.

"a living, burning lie" Letter dated May 4, 1865. Printed in NYT, May 7, 1865.

"peculiar genius of George N. Sanders" Globe, May 4, 1865.

"I have never known" New York Tribune, May 22, 1865. Booth scholar Terry Alford unearthed an unpublished interview with Thompson in which he acknowledges knowing of the kidnap plot at the very least (Alford, 252, 411).

"From the painful ravings" NYT, May 25, 1865. See also NYT, May 23, 27, 1865.

WHERE IS JEFFERSON DAVIS? Globe, May 10, 1865.

"conscious of my innocence" NYT, May 10, 1865.

"the weeping of children" Clay-Copton, 256, 262.

37. 'THE HIDEOUS DEVIL'

"He told me he had been connected" Letter to Seward, April 7, 1865, in Canadian Links folder, James O. Hall Research Center. See also Mayers, 56.

the *Georgian* was seized Gagan, 49.

"to take what money he could" *Leader* and *Globe*, April 11, 1865.

a Toronto detective named Francis McGarry *Globe*, May 22, 1865, reprinted in *NYT*, May 24, 1865.

"Being seriously ill at the time" *Leader* quoted in *NYT*, May 22, 1865.

"I am completely innocent" *Leader*, May 23, 1865.

"to introduce yellow fever" *NYT*, May 7, 1865.

"Blackburn represented himself" *Bermuda Advocate*, April 26, 1865, reprinted in *Globe*, May 17, 1865.

Swan was found guilty, Greene, 139.

"Blackburn is in Canada" *Philadelphia Inquirer*, May 17, 1865.

"his antecedents are too magnanimous" *Halifax Unionist*, May 19, 1865, cited in *Globe*, May 29, 1865.

"high reputation in which he has always stood" *Gazette*, May 27, 1865.

"a gentleman well-known in that city" *Leader*, cited in *NYT*, May 22, 1865.

"Dr. Blackburn, the gentle specimen" Ibid.

the doctor's sensational trial got under way *Leader*, May 22, 1865, reprinted in *Philadelphia Inquirer*, May 26, 1865.

"Will they give us a new act" *Philadelphia Inquirer*, May 20, 1865.

"the Jew witness" *Gazette*, May 27, 1865.

"hearsay information" *Leader*, May 19, 1865. See also *Globe*, May 8, 1865.

"cock-eyed Jew" *Globe*, May 24, 1865, and *NYT*, May 26, 1865.

"true in every respect" and the following quotes from *Globe*, May 23 and 24, 1865.

"met them on several occasions in Canada" Cleary's affidavit was reprinted in the *Leader*, May 25, 1865.

"a paragon of benevolence" *Leader* and *Globe*, May 27, 1865.

"we took no more notice of them" *Gazette*, May 27, 1865.

"and was consequently not triable here" Greene, 147, 149.

"The result of the judicial investigation" *Globe*, June 6, 1865.

"This hideous and long-studied plan" *Bermuda Royal Gazette*, June 13, 1865, cited by Steers, *Blood on the Moon*, 51.

"one of the most fiendish plots" *Globe*, May 24, 1865, reprinted in *NYT*, May 26, 1865.

"the hideous devil" *NYT*, June 6, 1865, May 27 and May 29, 1865.

38. 'THE ASSASSIN IS OF THE SOUTH'

The most reliable transcripts of the conspiracy trial were published by Benn Pitman (*Assassination of President Lincoln*). The questions by prosecutors come from the version published by T.B. Peterson and Brothers. The three best books on the conspiracy and the role of the Confederate leaders are *Blood on the Moon* by Edward Steers, *Come Retribution* by William Tidwell, James O. Hall and David Gaddy; and Tidwell's *April '65*.

"Jeff Davis and the other original conspirators" *NYT*, April 21, 1865.

"The president's murder was organized in Canada" *Atlantic*, July 1865.

"There are many facts which tend to prove" Potter letter, April 27, 1865, cited by Bokyo, 242.

"I visited Canada" Richard Montgomery testimony, May 12, 1865, *Assassination of President Lincoln*, 24.

"put out of his way" Ibid.

Booth had met Jacob Thompson several times *NYT*, June 6, 1865.

discussing assassination plans in Toronto Merritt testimony, May 12, 1865, *Assassination of President Lincoln*, 25.

The most explosive testimony came from Sanford Conover Conover testimony, May 20, 1865, *Assassination of President Lincoln*, 28–34.

"It is either overwhelmingly conclusive" *Tribune*, June 6, 1865, cited by Evans, 358.

He had been a fraudster See Cummings, *Devil's Game*.

William Tidwell makes the convincing case Tidwell, *April '65*, 150–52 and also Tidwell's article "The Man Who Shifted the Blame."

Edward Doherty took the stand For his brief testimony, see *Assassination of President Lincoln*, 95.

the first woman executed by the United States Five of the nine military judges who sent her to the gallows asked for clemency, but President Johnson never signed the order for clemency.

"They were all murdered" Letter, July 9, 1865, in Lee Archives.

"planned, organized and incited" *House of Representatives Report*, No. 104, 21.

"war under the Black Flag" Tidwell, *Come Retribution*, 45. In Toronto, the *Leader* acknowledged that meant introducing "barbarities unknown in civilized warfare" (September 16, 1864).

"does not make peace with us" Deposition taken at the Bureau of Military Justice, February 6, 1866, in *War of the Rebellion*, Series II—Volume VIII, 878.

"frequently sent by President Davis" Steers, *Blood on the Moon*, 55–57.

Davis knew very well "He would undoubtedly resist being captured," Davis was quoted as telling a colleague. "I could not stand the imputation of having consented to let Mr. Lincoln be assassinated" (Schein, 44).

Another agent named Thomas F. Harney From Canada, Confederate Thomas Hines also had killing on his mind when he planned the Northwest Conspiracy. He had written to Secretary of War James Seddon that

"the State governments . . . will be seized and their executive heads
disposed of." Tidwell, *Come Retribution*, 237.

"renders it certain" *House of Representatives Report*, No. 104, 30.

"she knew all about the affair" Atzerodt confession, *Surratt Courier.*

"was in frequent consultation with the Confederate President" Parker, 104.

"I suppose they are getting ready" Finegass testimony, May 26, 1865,
Assassination of President Lincoln, 39.

hotel records did put him and Cleary in Montreal Tidwell, *April '65*, 146.

"From this visit, whatever encouragement Booth received" Townsend in
New York World, reprinted in *Leader*, May 5, 1865.

"once certainly and three times it is believed" Townsend, 78. Booth biographer
Terry Alford makes a strong case that Booth returned briefly to Montreal in
early April 1864, just days before the assassination (Alford, 252).

"To assume that Booth" Tidwell, *Come Retribution* 328.

"Booth the assassin is of the south" Frederick Douglass, "Eulogy for
Abraham Lincoln," June 1, 1865, Frederick Douglass Papers, Library
of Congress.

39. 'HOPING NO ONE WOULD SEE US'

canon to Ignace Bourget *Gazette*, July 15, 1915.

happened to speak French fluently Levin, 178.

"We entered the village very quietly" Rockville Lecture for this and all other
Surratt quotes in this chapter.

"He was in very poor health" Boucher testimony, Surratt Trial, vol. II, 896,
906, 914.

The American authorities knew The US consul in Montreal, John Potter,
informed Washington on May 22, 1865: "Surratt is, I think, secreted in
this city in some of the Roman Catholic institutions" (Hatch, 95).

"Lapierre had taken a fancy" *Gazette*, July 15, 1915.

"the most immoral country in the world" *Le Canadien*, October 2, 1861,
cited by Preston, 63.

"the most monstrous and disgusting doctrines" *Courrier du Canada*, August
23, 1865, cited by Savard, 124.

"dictatorial tyranny" *Gazette des Campagnes*, October 15, 1862, August 1,
1863; Preston, 63.

"accusations against the Catholic clergy" *Courrier du Canada*, August 14,
1867. As late as 1915, Catholic religious papers like *La Vérité* insisted that
"there is nothing to reproach the priests for," defending Surratt as a
"respected citizen" who had to endure a "terrible tragedy" of prosecution
(*La Vérité*, July 24, 1915).

"Scenery gorgeous" Lee Diary, August 11, 1865. Murray Bay's name was
  eventually changed to the French name La Malbaie, as it is known today.
she may have been the elusive Sarah Slater On the other hand, researcher
  John F. Stanton found divorce records for Slater and her husband Rowan
  that suggest they were in New York between May and October of 1865
  (Stanton, "A Mystery No Longer").
"Rebel Hater" *Hartford Evening Press*, June 5, 1865.
"Does any one here know of her?" *Hartford Daily Courant*, June 12 and 16,
  1865, cited by Hall, "Saga of Sarah Slater."
from his second-floor window Schein, 180; Levin, 168.
"Armstrong arrived at 8 pm" Lee Diary, August 25, 1865.
With Father Lapierre's recommendation Schein, 181.
The three men took the steamer Boucher testimony, Surratt Trial, vol. II,
  910–12.
"Charley leaves Quebec today" Lee Diary, September 16, 1865.
pulled a small revolver from his pocket and following quotes from McMillan
  testimony, Surratt Trial, vol. 1, 464, 468, 476.

40. 'VINDICATING MYSELF'

"Great credit is due to all concerned" Doherty Report for this and other
  quotes in this chapter, unless otherwise indicated.
"It is desirable that the matter" and other letters from Doherty Papers.
"There appears to be some unfair work" *Albany Daily Witness*, cited by
  Miller.
sworn affidavits from no fewer than thirteen All quotes from Doherty's men
  come from affidavits found in the Doherty Papers.
"The chief remained at headquarters" and following quotes from Lafayette
  Baker, *History of the United States Secret Service*, 532, 536, 539.
"The military element of the expedition" *Awards for the Capture of Booth
  and Others*, 39th Congress, 1st Sessions (Executive Document No. 90).
he would get a hefty chunk Wick, "Battle for the War Department Rewards."
"fairness and propriety" *Reward for the Capture of Booth*, House of
  Representatives, 39th Congress, Ist Session, Report No. 99, July 24, 1866.
"I believe Lieutenant Doherty" and following quotes in *Congressional
  Globe*, July 26, 1866, 4188–90.
"I no longer had an opportunity" *NYT*, August 6, 1866.

41. 'A PITIFUL CASE'

to get a passport as a Canadian Schein, 197.
"You remind me of an American" *NYT*, February 16, 1867. "[E]xcited by

wine, Surratt confessed . . . greatly to the astonishment of Ste. Marie and the delight of his associates, many of whom were Canadian refugees and raiders like himself." For a less fanciful account, see Schein, 206.

"will shed the light of day" *NYT*, November 26, 1866.

"Lucky indeed is it" *NYT*, April 6, 1865, April 8, 1867.

"The Surratt trial is watched here" Hatch, 150.

McMillan told the court McMillan testimony, Surratt Trial, vol. I, 467.

"it was necessary to change their plan" Schein, 185.

doctor allegedly practised abortions McMillan testimony, Surratt Trial, vol. II, 942.

"quite attentive to the young ladies there" Boucher testimony, Surratt Trial, vol. II, 913.

Merrick's courtroom oratory Schein, 287–91.

Why was Surratt any different? Ibid., 274.

"[W]hat a pitiful case he had" Rockville Lecture.

"the secret history of Lincoln's murder" *Harper's*, December 29, 1866.

42. 'THE BLESSING OF CANADA'

"Jeff Davis should be hung" *Hartford Daily Courtant*, June 12, 1865.

"He has been charged" *Globe*, May 22, 1865.

"I defy any proof" Letter to his wife, November 14, 1865, Clay Papers.

"great act of justice and humanity" Lacroix, "A Confederate in Canada."

"Our plantations had been laid waste" Varina Davis, vol. II, 796–97.

"to lick the Yankees" *Gazette*, September 6, 1986.

"satisfactory improvement in French" Whellams, "Jefferson Davis Comes to Canada."

"The Catholics, God bless them" Allen, 439.

Connolly . . . offered to educate *Gazette*, August 30, 1986.

a green Chartreuse Allen, 480.

"She likes the idea of caste" *Chicago Tribune* article reprinted in *NYT*, October 11, 1866.

apartments had been reserved . . . at the St. Lawrence Hall *NYT*, May 17, 1867.

"We could not but sympathize with the Southerners" *Gazette*, September 6, 1986.

"accompanied by two servants of color" *Gazette*, May 27, 1867. A young girl whose father ran a general store at the foot of Mountain Street later recalled that "Negro servants" from the Davis household frequently came by to buy supplies "for their master's household" (*Gazette*, August 18, 1962). Another article, though, suggested the servants may have been local people (*Gazette*, May 7, 1960). For more on his stay in Montreal, see *Gazette*, October 22, 1945, July 30, 1960, June 29, 1968, August 30, 1986, and November 25, 2017.

"Mr. Davis is . . . keeping within doors" *Gazette*, May 27, 1867.

"our gallant and noble chief" *NYT*, June 17, 1867.

"all pressing around the President" *Baltimore Gazette*, June 6, 1867, reprinted in *NYT*, June 13, 1867.

"quite a flurry of excitement" *NYT*, June 8, 1867.

"I went around" Denison, *Soldiering in Canada*, 68.

"hearty rounds of cheers" *Montreal Herald*, May 31, 1867.

"I was so astonished" Denison, *Soldiering in Canada*, 69.

"Niagara offered a ready shelter" Kirby, *Annals of Niagara*, 247–49.

"quite a large and attractive Confederate circle" Young, *Senator James Murray*, 198.

"created quite a sensation" *NYT*, June 6, June 12, June 13, 1867. See also *Niagara Mail*, June 6, 1867; *Montreal Herald*, June 14, 1867.

"I thank you sincerely" *NYT*, June 12, 1867. A month after Davis's speech to his friends, the Dominion of Canada was officially born as a new nation on July 1, 1867. The timing was not coincidental. As John Bokyo and other historians have noted, Canada united in no small part because its inhabitants watched in horror as the divisive Civil War tore apart its neighbour to the south. What added more impetus towards nationhood was the never-ending clamour for annexation coming from the United States.

   At least six so-called Fathers of Confederation, as well as other top founders of Canada, had demonstrated sympathies with or had connections to the Southern cause. Canada's first prime minister, John A. Macdonald, had praised "the gallant defence" of the slave states in 1864. *La Minerve*, Montreal's leading French-language paper and rabidly pro-South, was seen as a house organ for George-Étienne Cartier, Macdonald's chief ally from Quebec. Thomas D'Arcy McGee, though he had mourned Lincoln's death, had played enthusiastic host to Lincoln's nemesis and Southern apologist Clement Vallandigham. Joseph Howe from Nova Scotia had privately expressed support for the Confederates, according to historian Greg Marquis, even while his son fought in the Union army. Alexander Galt, the first minister of finance of the new Dominion, was friendly enough with Jefferson Davis to visit him in Quebec. John Abbott, who was elected to the House of Commons in 1867 and went on to serve as the country's third prime minister, had made a name for himself successfully defending the St. Albans raiders.

"all the principal citizens" *Baltimore Gazette*, June 6, 1867, reprinted in *NYT*, June 13, 1867.

a fashionable wedding *NYT*, June 5 and June 7, 1867; *Montreal Herald*,
   June 5, 1867.

Davis and his family arrived quietly and other quotes about the theatre are
   from *Gazette*, July 19, 1867, August 18, 1962, and June 29, 1968.

"like a dagger to heart" *New York Herald*, July 19, 1867, reprinted in
   Gazette, July 25, 1867.

"His hair and beard" *Gazette*, November 25, 2017.

"All the anguish of the last great struggle" Davis, *A Memoir by His Wife*,
   vol. II, 796.

"Let us put them by" Boyko, 292.

"This is a very quiet place" Cooper, 614.

bring gifts for the children Boyko, 289.

"war songs of the South" Boyle, 90. Occasionally, though, other boys would
   retort with chants of "We'll hang Jeff Davis to a sour apple tree" (*Gazette*,
   January 7, 1946).

"It is in the most beautiful part" *Gazette*, October 1, 1966.

"We found our property all destroyed" Davis, *A Memoir by His Wife*, vol. II,
   804.

"who, despite everything, commands respect" *Courrier du Canada*, October
   18, 1869.

"he was received with the greatest enthusiasm" Denison, *Soldiering in
   Canada*, 81.

"Of my wanderings" Richardson, "Jefferson Davis, Lennoxville."

43. 'WE ARE A POWER'

"If in the coming reconstruction" *NYT*, June 2, 1865.

"slow-motion genocide." Hannah-Jones, 261.

set up the Ku Klux Klan See my book *White Hoods: Canada's Ku Klux Klan*
   (Vancouver: New Star Books, 1983).

"Slavery is indeed gone" *NYT*, June 2, 1865.

the highest-ranking Black officer Henig, 29.

"they have undertaken to exclude persons" Summer, 148.

Augusta kept fighting Butts, 108. See also Baker, "The American Medical
   Association and Race."

honourably discharged from the army. Letter, May 14, 1866, Abbott
   Collection.

"great pleasure in bearing testimony" Newby, 114, 115.

"Several articles that he valued" Abbott Collection.

"was given to Dr. Abbott" *New York Weekly News*, October 19, 1867, in
   Abbott Collection.

working towards his bachelor's degree in medicine In 1869 he received his
   licence (see Newby, 90–91, and obituary in *Globe*, December 29, 1913).
"unlawful, unjust and unreasonable" *Messenger* newsletter, in Abbott
   Collection.
"Race prejudice is growing" Newby, 148.
"I see thirty millions" and following quotes from Abbott Collection.
"who practised for a great many years" *Globe*, December 30, 1913.

44. 'BREAK THE SILENCE'

"a magnificent pair of revolvers" *National Intelligencer*, July 20, 1865.
"fully cognisant of commercial matters" Letter to President Johnson,
   February 3, 1866, Doherty Papers.
"your wishes expressed to me" Ibid.
Doherty was sent to Kansas Miller, "More on Capt. Doherty."
the most famous cowboy in America, "Buffalo Bill" Cody Cody's father, who
   was born in the Toronto area, had settled in Kansas and became an ardent
   anti-slavery advocate in a territory deeply divided over the issue. He died
   from wounds sustained in a knife attack during one of his speeches. Bill
   Cody eagerly signed up with the Union army when he was only seventeen.
"They bivouacked, scouted and fought together" Miller, "More on Capt.
   Doherty."
"continuously, both at various forts" Letter from Cody to Doherty's wife,
   1908, in Doherty Papers.
James Carson, who carefully chronicled All quotes from Doherty's disciplin-
   ary problems are from Carson, 168–70.
"unfit for the service" Miller, "More on Capt. Doherty."
"Doherty was an uncomplaining man" Letter from Cody, 1908, in Doherty
   Papers.
"an Indian post trader in Dakota" Undated clipping in Doherty Papers. See
   also *Daily Picayune*, August 18, 1879.
"Panorama of the Assassination" Doherty Papers.
"to go with us" Baker, *Lecture on the Capture*, 10.
"the story with details never published" *Chicago Tribune*, February 17, 1889.
"Your article has, after a quarter of a century" *Brooklyn Citizen*, undated
   clipping around March 1889. The *Chicago Globe* reprinted the *Brooklyn
   Citizen* story on April 3, 1889. Doherty's claim was not entirely true. He
   was tracked down by a reporter in New Orleans more than a decade
   earlier and the story appeared in the *Daily Picayune*, August 18, 1879.
"a party under Lieutenant E.P. Doherty" Nicolay and Hay, vol. 10, 311.
"squad of cavalry traced Booth" Morse, 350.

"commanded the company of cavalry" *NYT*, January 18, 1895.

sent his regrets in a warm reply Letter from Cody, May 10, 1895, in Doherty Papers.

45. 'TEARS ARE IN MY EYES'

"too much monotonous" Affidavit, January 1, 1884, in Edmonds Pension File.

"You know how the census takers" *Detroit Post and Tribune*, May 26, 1883.

"taken with congestive chills," Dannett, 242.

"left the command for fear" Application of Discharged Soldier for Arrears of Pay, March 22, 1882, Edmonds Pension File.

"She looked directly at me" *Detroit Post and Tribune*, May 26, 1883.

"performed cheerfully" and other quotes from Milton Benjamin, Sumner Howard and John Deitz affidavits, in Edmonds Pension File.

"the story of a heroic woman" *Fort Scott Weekly Monitor*, January 7, 1884, in Edmonds Pension File.

"My case is so very peculiar" Letter to Cutcheon, March 5, 1884, in Edmonds Pension File.

"Truth is of times stranger than fiction" *Sarah E.E. Seelye, Alias Franklin Thompson*, House of Representatives, 48th Congress, 1st Session, Report No. 849, in Edmonds Pension File.

"every one of whom I love" and following quotes from Dannett, 255, 264, 279.

"Who was that lady" Letter, January 27, 1885, in Edmonds Pension File.

"something like a sequel" Letter to Cutcheon, March 5, 1884, in Edmonds Pension File.

"the hastily written work of a novice" Dannett, 254–56.

"had won the respect" Undated clipping in Edmonds Papers.

46. 'GREAT GOOD OR GREAT EVIL'

"engaged in suspicious carpentry" Gagan, 50. See also *Globe*, December 5, 1864.

twenty-six torpedoes in a cellar *NYT*, April 29, 1865, *Globe*, April 27, 1865.

"More rebel plots in Canada" *NYT*, April 23, 1865.

"their tool Mr. Denison" *Globe*, April 27, 1865.

"assorted weapons" Gagan, 65.

"We became very close friends" and other quotes from Denison, *Soldiering in Canada*, 59, 70, 76.

he dropped by Heydon Villa Denison diary, June 4, 1881, in Library and
  Archives Canada.
Denison led the British Empire League Gagan, 72–81.
"He constituted a one-man 'Vigilante Committee'" Ibid., 65.
90 percent of the indictable offences Homel, 171, 173.
"would be like going to Rome" Ibid., 172.
"He is not above trifling away" *Toronto Telegram*, February 15, 1896, cited
  by Kluckner, 202.
"an intuitive feeling" Denison, *Recollections*, 12, 39.
GREATEST PARADE IN THE HISTORY *Birmingham News*, May 18, 1916.
his administration was marred by corruption Even the official website of the
  city of Montreal, in its history section, admitted "his administration was
  unfortunately marked by actions for his personal benefit."
"giving better representation to minorities" Bonenfant, "Devlin."
"Great good or great evil" Police Committee, 66.

47. 'JUDGE ME KINDLY'

"Dr. Blackburn, of yellow fever notoriety" *Philadelphia Inquirer*, August 4,
  1865.
"The Doctor is looking wonderfully fine" *Nashville Daily Union and
  American*, December 31, 1865, cited by Greene, 205.
"detestable crime against mankind" *Harrisburg Telegraph*, September 26,
  1867, cited by Greene, 208.
"Hero of Hickman" Culver, 284.
"too preposterous for intelligent gentlemen to believe" Greene, 212, 213.
"sordid aspirations held no sway" *Find a Grave*.
testimony from the chief teller Campbell testimony, May 20, 1865, *Assassination of President Lincoln*, 45–46.
as much as $2 million Horan, 293–95.
"together we studied French" Castleman, 188.
"complained bitterly of Mr. Thompson's conduct" 1865 letter found by
  historian William C. Davis, "Conduct of 'Mr. Thompson.'"
"This man was the organizer" *Philadelphia Inquirer*, November 7 and 9, 1865.
"in ashes and the whole town in ruins" Oldman, 120, 125.
one historian estimates William C. Davis, "Conduct."
"They had not lost their proud spirits" Oldman, 125.
"a benefit to his race" Lee, *Recollections and Letters*, 431.
"among the ladies present" *Washington Evening Star*, December 7, 1870.
"a beggarly array of empty benches" *NYT*, December 10, 1870.

"rather a good shot" Isacsson, 342.

and burned them in a furnace Schein, 332.

"The Government did its best" Weichmann, 123.

Stanton picked up the trail See "A Mystery No Longer."

to enjoy collecting his Civil War pension See Higginbotham, *Surratt Courier*.

her birth year as 1855 *Find a Grave*.

48. 'THE LOST CAUSE'

got tutoring in law from . . . Breckinridge Mayer, 222.

tutored Breckinridge's children Ibid.

"who was right or who was wrong" Headley, 464. George "Lightning"
Ellsworth had a less illustrious career. His skills got him a job working with
Thomas Edison, but he shot and killed a saloon keeper for refusing to serve
him a drink. He was arrested, but he escaped from jail three times and
resurfaced as part of an armed robbery gang a few years later in Texas. He
published his memoirs in 1882 and died in 1899 of a heart attack, fittingly
while working at a telegraph station. See Towne, "Everything Is Fair in War."

a former slave who sued the Ku Klux Klan *Tampa Bay Times*, January 21,
2021. See Montgomery, *A Shot in the Moonlight*.

"the most wondrous military tragedy of the ages" Young, xi, xii.

"The dead for whom this monument stands" Young, "Address at Unveiling,"
298.

"an extraordinary function" *Gazette*, July 15, 1915.

"Oh yes, bygones are bygones long since" *St. Catharines Constitutional*, July
17, 1915. Young died four years later. His grave marker had a five-word
inscription: "I have kept the faith."

EPILOGUE: 'THE MISFORTUNES OF HISTORY'

"Draped over the tombstone" *Gazette*, November 25, 1959.

"an act of gracious remembrance" *Gazette*, November 24, 1959.

"Our truly great presidents" Martin Luther King, speech, September 12,
1962.

"past history of racial inequality" *NYT*, July 11, 2008.

"It has been said" Young, "Address at Unveiling," 297.

close to four hundred Confederate symbols *NYT*, February 23, 2021.

unceremoniously remove the Jefferson Davis plaque CBC News, August 15,
2017.

"an undetermined length of time" *Toronto Star*, October 13, 2014.

BIBLIOGRAPHY

Memoirs, Speeches, Diaries, Letters

Abbott, Anderson Ruffin. Abbott Collection, Baldwin Collection of Canadiana, Toronto Public Library.

———. "Some Recollections of Lincoln's Assassination." *Anglo-American Magazine*, May 1901. Typed transcript in the Abbott Collection.

American Consular Reports—Civil War Period. *Bermuda Historical Quarterly* 19 (Spring 1962).

Anderson, Osborne P. *A Voice from Harper's Ferry.* Boston: 1861.

Anonymous Confederate. "The Adventures of George Sanders." *The Gray Jackets: How They Lived, Fought, and Died for Dixie*, 85–87. Richmond: Jones Brothers and Co., 1867.

Atzerodt, George. Confession printed in *Baltimore American*, January 18, 1869. Reprinted in *Surratt Courier* XLVI, no. 3 (May/June 2021).

Augusta, Alexander. Letter to President Lincoln, January 1, 1863. US National Library of Medicine.

Bainbridge, A.R. Letter about Booth's escape, in "Major Ruggles Narrative." *Century*, January 1890.

Baker, Lafayette C. *History of the United States Secret Service.* Philadelphia: King & Baird Printers, 1867.

Baker, Luther Byron. *Lecture on the Capture of John Wilkes Booth.* Undated typescript, Michigan History Center.

Beall, John Yates. *Memoir of John Yates Beall: His Life, Correspondence, Diary.* Montreal: John Lovell, 1865.

Benjamin, W.S. *The Great Epidemic in New Berne and Vicinity, September and October, 1864. By One Who Passed Through It.* New Berne, NC: Geo. Mills Joy, 1865.

The Black Abolitionist Papers: Vol. II, Canada 1830–1865. Ed. C. Peter Ripley. Chapel Hill: University of North Carolina Press, 1986.

Booth, John Wilkes. Diary excerpts. *The Trial of John H. Surratt*, vol. 1, 310–11. Washington: Government Printing Office, 1867.

———. Unpublished speech, December 1860. Excerpted in *New York Times*, April 12, 1992.

————. Unpublished letter, November 1864. Reprinted in *New York Times*, April 21, 1865.

Butler, Benjamin F. *Butler's Book: Autobiography and Personal Reminiscences of Major-General Benjamin Butler*. Boston: A.M. Thayer & Co., 1892.

Castleman, John B. *Active Service*. Louisville: Courier-Journal Job Printing, 1917.

Clarke, Asia Booth. *John Wilkes Booth: A Sister's Memoir*. Jackson: University Press of Mississippi, 1996.

Clay, Clement. "C.C. Clay Papers, 1811–1925." Duke University Libraries.

————. "Speech on slavery issues, delivered at Huntsville, Alabama, September 5th, 1859." University of Michigan Library.

Clay-Copton, Virginia. *A Belle of the Fifties: A Memoir of Mrs. Clay of Alabama*. New York: Doubleday, Page & Company, 1904.

Claiborne, John Francis Hamtramck. *Mississippi, as a Province, Territory, and State: With Biographical Notices of Eminent Citizens*. Jackson: Power & Barksdale, 1880.

Cleary, William W. *The protest of W.W. Cleary against the proclamation of President Johnson, of May 2nd: with a complete exposure of the perjuries before the Bureau of Military Justice upon which that proclamation issued*. Toronto: Lovell & Gibson, 1865.

Dana, Charles A. *Recollections of the Civil War*. New York: D. Appleton and Company, 1898.

David, Laurent-Olivier. *Mes Contemporains*. Montréal: Eusèbe Senécal & Fils, 1894.

Davis, Jefferson. Speech on December 8, 1859. *Congressional Globe*, Senate, 36th Congress, 1st Session.

————. *Jefferson Davis, Constitutionalist, His Letters, Papers and Speeches*. 10 vols. New York: J.J. Little & Ives Company, 1923.

————. *The Rise and Fall of the Confederate Government*. Vols. I and II. New York: D. Appleton and Company, 1881.

————. *A Short History of the Confederate States of America*. New York: Belford Company, 1890.

Davis, Samuel B. *Escape of a Confederate Officer from Prison*. Norfolk, VA: Landmark Publishing, 1898.

Davis, Varina. *Jefferson Davis, Ex-President of the Confederate States of America: A Memoir by His Wife*. Vols. I and II. New York: Bedford, 1890.

Denison, George Taylor. *Diary 1863–1923*. Library and Archives Canada.

————. *Recollections of a Police Magistrate*. Toronto: Musson Book Company, 1920.

————. *Soldiering in Canada: Recollections and Experiences*. Toronto: George N. Morang, 1900.

Doherty, Edward P. Doherty Papers. Abraham Lincoln Presidential Library and Museum, Springfield, Illinois. Box: 19 Identifier: 02-08-001-Small Collection 410.

————. Letters published in the *Gazette* (Montreal), May 13, May 25, May 30, May 31, June 5, 1861.

————. "The Battle of Bull Run: Interesting Statement by Edward P. Doherty." *New York Times*, August 6, 1861.

———. "Booth's Death: An Interview with the Officer Who Commanded the Pursuing Detachment." *Daily Picayune* (New Orleans), August 18, 1879.

———. "Capture of J. Wilkes Booth and David E. Herold, at Garrett's Farm, near Port Royal Va., April 26, 1865." In *The War of the Rebellion: A Compilation of the Official Records of the Union and Confederate Armies.* Series 1, vol. 46, part 1, 1317–22. Washington: Government Printing Office, 1880–1901.

———. *Letters Received by Commission Branch of the Adjutant General Office, 1863–1870.* US National Archives. https://www.fold3.com/search?keywords= edward+p.+doherty&offset=20.

Douglass, Frederick. "Eulogy for Abraham Lincoln." Address at Cooper Union, New York City, June 1, 1865. In Frederick Douglass Papers, Library of Congress.

———. "Speech at Unveiling of the Freedmen's Monument in Lincoln Park," Washington, DC, April 14, 1876.

Douglass, Lewis. Petition from Lewis Douglass and Others to the Secretary of War. Records of the Adjutant General's Office, US National Archives.

Edmonds, Sarah. "Emma Seelye Papers, 1885, 1897." Clarke Historical Library, Central Michigan University.

———. *Nurse and Spy in the Union Army, comprising The Adventures and Experiences of a Woman in Hospitals, Camps and Battlefields.* Hartford: W.S. Williams & Co., 1865.

Edmonds Pension File. "Application of Sarah Emma Edmond Seelye, Discharged Soldier, for Arrears of Pay." March 24, 1882. US National Archives, catalog.archives. gov/id/306649.

Ellsworth, George A. "Telegraph Strategy in Warfare." *New Orleans Times-Democrat,* June 4 and June 11, 1882; *Little Rock Daily Arkansas Gazette,* June 25, 1882. Reprinted and edited by Stephen E. Towne. *Register of the Kentucky Historical Society* 108, no. 1/2 (Winter/Spring 2010).

Garrett, Richard B. "A Chapter of Unwritten History: Richard Baynham Garrett's Account of the Flight and Death of John Wilkes Booth." *Virginia Magazine of History and Biography* 71 (October 1963).

Headley, John W. *Confederate Operations in Canada and New York.* New York: Neale Publishing Company, 1906.

Hines, Thomas H. "The Escape." In *Famous Adventures and Prison Escapes of the Civil War,* edited by G.W. Gable, 158–83. New York: Century Company, 1913.

———. "The Northwest Conspiracy." *Southern Bivouac,* December 1886, January 1887, February 1887, April 1887.

Howe, Samuel Gridley. *Report to the Freedmen's Inquiry Commission.* 1864.

Keckley, Elizabeth. *Behind the Scenes, Or, Thirty Years a Slave, and Four Years in the White House.* New York: G.W. Carleton & Co., 1868.

Kellogg, Robert H. *Life and Death in Rebel Prisons.* Hartford: L. Stebbins, 1865.

Kirby, William. *Annals of Niagara.* Niagara Falls, ON: Lundy's Lane Historical Society, 1896.

Lamothe, Guillaume. Papiers Lamothe. Manuscript Group 19, A.12, Vol. III, Library and Archives Canada.

———. *Mes Mémoires*. November 1899. Typewritten manuscript in Montreal Archives.

Lee, Edwin Gray. "Canadian Diary 1865" and personal letters. In Edmund Jennings Lee II papers, 1746–1963. David M. Rubenstein Rare Book & Manuscript Library, Duke University Libraries, Durham, NC.

Lee, Robert E. *Recollections and Letters of Robert E. Lee*. New York: Doubleday, 1904.

Lincoln, Abraham. *Collected Works of Abraham Lincoln*. Abraham Lincoln Association, quod.lib.umich.edu/l/lincoln/. Accessed August 23, 2022.

Mackenzie, Alexander. *The Life and Speeches of Hon. George Brown*. Toronto: Globe Printing Company, 1882.

Maple Leaves from Canada for the Grave of Abraham Lincoln. St. Catharines, ON: E.S. Leavenworth, 1865.

Monck, Frances E.O. *My Canadian Leaves: An Account of a Visit to Canada in 1864–1865*. London: Richard Bentley and Son, 1891.

New York Times Book of the Civil War 1861–1865: 650 Eyewitness Accounts and Articles. Edited by Harold Holzer and Craig Symonds. New York: Black Dog & Leventhal, 2010.

Proceedings on the Reunion Society of Vermont Officers. Vol. 11, 1865–1909. Burlington, VT: Fire Press Printing, 1906.

Rankin, McKee. "The Story of J. Wilkes Booth's Wardrobe." Typescript, 1909. Chicago History Museum.

Robbins, Jerome J. Robbins Papers, 1861–1913. Bentley Historical Library, University of Michigan. quod.lib.umich.edu/b/bhlcivilwar/2011410.0011.001/

Robertson, John. *Michigan in the War*. Lansing: W.S. George & Co., 1882.

Robinson, Stuart. *The infamous perjuries of the "Bureau of Military Justice" Exposed: letter of Rev. Stuart Robinson to Hon. Mr. Emmons*. Rare Book Collection, Library of Congress.

Ruggles, Mortimer B. "Major Ruggles Narrative." *Century*, January 1890.

Sowles, Edward A. *History of the St. Albans Raid, Annual Address before the Vermont Historical Society*. St. Albans, VT: Messenger Printing Works, 1876.

Summer, Charles. *His Complete Works*. Boston: Lee and Shepard, 1990.

Surratt, John. "John Surratt Tells His Story." Rockville Lecture, December 6, 1870. Transcript in *Washington Evening Star*, December 7, 1870.

Têtu, Henri. *David Têtu et les Raiders de Saint-Albans*. Quebec: N.S. Hardy, 1891.

Thompson, Jacob. *Letters to and from Jacob Thompson*. Edited by P.L. Rainwater. *Journal of Southern History* 6, no. 1 (February 1940): 95–111.

———. Letter to Judah Benjamin, December 3, 1864. In *Official Records of the Union and Confederate Navies in the War of the Rebellion*. Series 1, vol. 3, *The Operations of the Cruisers from April 1, 1864, to December 30, 1865*, 714–19. Washington: Government Printing Office, 1896.

Townsend, George Alfred. *The Life, Crime and Capture of John Wilkes Booth*. New York: Dick & Fitzgerald, 1865.

Tupper, Sir Charles. *The Life and Letters of the Rt. Hon. Sir Charles Tupper*. Edited by Edward Manning Saunders. New York: Frederick A. Stokes Company, 1916.

Ward, Samuel Ringgold. *Autobiography of a Fugitive Negro: His Anti-slavery Labours in the United States, Canada, & England*. London: 1855.

Weichmann, Louis J. *A True History of the Assassination of Abraham Lincoln and of the Conspiracy of 1865*. New York: Alfred A. Knopf, 1975.

Young, Bennett H. "Address at the Unveiling of Confederate Monument at Arlington." *Confederate Veteran* XXII (1914), 297–300.

———. *Confederate Wizards of the Saddle: Being Reminiscences and Observations of One Who Rode with Morgan*. Boston: Chappie Publishing Company, 1914.

———. Unpublished interview with George P. Anderson, 1908. Vermont Historical Museum archives.

Vallandigham, Clement L. *Speeches, Arguments, Addresses, and Letters of Clement L. Vallandigham 1820–1871*. New York: J. Walter & Co., 1864.

Trial transcripts, Investigations, Reports

CANADIAN ARCHIVES:

The Canadian Parliamentary Companion and Annual Register, 1878. Edited by C.H. Mackintosh. Ottawa: Citizen Print and Publishing Company, 1878.

"Québec Catholic Parish Registers, 1621–1979." FamilySearch. Index 1816–1876 Baptêmes, mariages, sépultures 1816–1844. familysearch.org/pal:/MM9.3.1/ TH-1942-28000-5937-33?cc=1321742.

CANADIAN TRIALS:

Archives nationales du Québec, Centre de Montréal. Procedure Criminel contre Marie Joseph Angélique negresse—Incendiere, 1734. TL4 S1, 4136. Juridiction royale de Montréal, Final sentence by the judge and by his four counsellors, June 4, 1734.

Benjamin, L.N. *The St. Albans Raid or Investigation into the Charges against Lieut. Bennett H. Young and Command for Their Acts at St. Albans, VT., on the 19th October 1864*. Montreal: John Lovell, 1865.

The St. Albans Raid: Investigation by the Police Committee of the City Council of Montreal into the charges prepared by Councillor B. Devlin against Guillaume Lamothe, Esq., Chief of Police, and the proceedings of the Council in reference thereto. Montreal: Owler and Stevenson, 1864.

Torrance, F.W. *Report on the Case of C.J. Coursol*, in "Return to Addresses of the Legislative Assembly, February 6, August 14, 1865." Toronto Public Library.

AMERICAN TRIALS:

The Assassination of President Lincoln and the Trial of the Conspirators. Compiled and arranged by Benn Pitman. New York: Moore, Wilstach & Baldwin, 1865.

Investigation and Trial Papers Relating to the Assassination of President Lincoln. National Archives Microfilm Publication M599. Witness statements by Junius Booth Jr. and John Deveny.

Steers, Edward, Jr. *The Trial: The Assassination of President Lincoln and the Trial of the Conspirators*. Lexington: University Press of Kentucky, 2003. Contains the Pitman transcript and introductory articles by leading scholars.

The Trial of the Assassin and Conspirators for the Murder of President Abraham Lincoln. Philadelphia: T.B. Peterson & Brothers, 1865.

The Trial of John H. Surratt. Vol. I and II. Washington: Government Printing Office, 1867.

Archives

JAMES O. HALL RESEARCH CENTER:

(Surratt Museum, Maryland)

William A. Tidwell—Drawer 1: Atzerodt; 2: Booth diary; 3: Canadian links; 4: Confederate Secret Service; 5: Conover; 6: S.B. Davis; 8: Hines, Hyams; 9: Martin; 11: Sanders; 12: Slater, Surratt.

James O. Hall—Folder 128: Canada; 152: S.B. Davis; 154: Doherty; 353, 354: Patrick Martin; 499: St. Albans; 502: George Sanders; 500, 501: St. Lawrence Hall; 508, 509: Slater; 589: Surratt escape; 592: Thompson; 617: Weichmann.

LIBRARY AND ARCHIVES CANADA:

St. Lawrence Hall Arrival Book. Item ID number: 100055, 1864–1865.

LIBRARY OF CONGRESS:

Awards for the Capture of Booth and Others. 39th Congress, 1st Sessions (Ex. Doc. No. 90). Washington: Government Printing Office, 1866.

Congressional Globe. 38th Congress, 1st Session. 1864.

House of Representatives Report. No. 104, 39th Congress, 1st Session, 1865–66. Vol. 1. Washington: Government Printing Office, 1866.

House of Representatives. 48th Congress, 1st Session. Report No. 849, "Sarah E.E. Seelye, Alias Franklin Thompson."

Journal of the Congress of the Confederate States of America, 1861–1865. U.S. Serial Set, Numbers 4610–4616, Vol. 6.

Reward for the Capture of Booth. House of Representatives. 39th Congress, 1st Session. Report No. 99. July 24, 1866.

The War of the Rebellion: A Compilation of the Official Records of the Union and Confederate Armies. Series IV, Vol. III–Vol. XXXIX. Part 1—Reports; Series II—Volume VIII, Prisoners of War and State. Washington: Government Printing House, 1892, 1899.

MCCORD MUSEUM (MONTREAL):

Notman Photographic Archives.

Unpublished theses and papers

Extian-Babiuk, Tamara. "'To Be Sold: A Negro Wench': Slave Ads of the Montreal *Gazette* 1785–1805." Department of Art History, McGill University, Montreal, February 2006.

Jacob, François. "La Perception de la Guerre de Sécession dans la Presse Québécoise, 1861–1865." Master's thesis, Université Laval, Quebec, 2010.

Oldman, Dorothy Zollicoffer. "Life of Jacob Thompson." Department of History, Master of Arts, University of Mississippi, 1930.

Rountree, Lillian. "A 'Military Despotism' and a Danger: Montréalais Perception of the American Civil War." Gilder Lehrman Institute of American History, New York, 2018.

Slaney, Catherine, L. "The Process and Implications of Racialization: A Case Study." Department of Sociology and Equity Studies, Ontario Institute for Studies in Education, University of Toronto, 2004.

Squires, Melinda. "The Controversial Career of George Nicholas Sanders." Western Kentucky University, Bowling Green, 2000.

Whyte, George H. "Confederate Operations in Canada during the Civil War." Department of History, McGill University, Montreal, 1968.

Newspapers

CANADA:

Le Canadien
Courrier du Canada
Gazette (Montreal)
Gazette des Campagnes
Globe
Halifax Unionist
Hamilton Times
Minerve
Montreal Herald
Montreal Star

Montreal Witness
Niagara Mail
Niagara Review
Ottawa Citizen
Quebec Morning Chronicle
St. Catharines Constitutional
St. Catharines Standard
Toronto Colonist
Toronto Leader
Toronto Star

UNITED STATES:

Baltimore Gazette
Baltimore Sun
Birmingham News
Boston Evening Transcript
Brooklyn Citizen
Buffalo Express
Century
Chicago Tribune
Cincinnati Daily Enquirer
Daily Picayune
Detroit Free Press
Detroit Post and Tribune
Douglass Monthly
Fort Scott Weekly Monitor
Harpers Weekly
Harrisburg Telegraph
Hartford Daily Courant

Hartford Evening Press
Louisville Daily Democrat
Nashville Daily Union and American
National Intelligencer
National Republican
New York Daily Tribune
New York Herald
New York Times
New York Weekly News
New York World
North Star
Philadelphia Inquirer
Richmond Examiner
Salem Advocate
Tampa Bay Times
Washington Evening Star
Washington Post

Academic Journals, Magazines

Baker, Robert. "The American Medical Association and Race." *AMA Journal of Ethics*, June 2014.

Bélanger, D.-C. *Canada, French-Canadians and Franco-Americans in the Civil War Era (1861–1865)*. Last modified August 13, 2001. faculty.marianopolis.edu/c.belanger/quebechistory/frncdns/studies/dcb/preface.htm.

Boyle, Virgina Frazer. "Jefferson Davis in Canada." *Confederate Veteran* XXXVII (March 5, 1929): 89–93.

Butts, Heather M. "Alexander Thomas Augusta—Physician, Teacher and Human Rights Activist." *Journal of the National Medical Association* 97, no. 1 (January 2005): 106–9.

Carter, George E. "A Note on Jefferson Davis in Canada—His Stay in Lennoxville, Quebec." *Journal of Mississippi History* 33, no. 2 (1971): 133–39.

Chaconas, Joan L. "President's Message." *Surratt Courier* XIV, no. 1 (January 1989).

Culver, Gregory K. "The Impact of the 1878 Yellow Fever Epidemic on the Jackson Purchase and the Mississippi Valley." *Filson Club History Quarterly*, July 1997, 285–300.

Curtis, Merle E. "George N. Sanders—American Patriot." *South Atlantic Quarterly* XXVII (January 1928): 79–87.

Davis, William C. "The Conduct of 'Mr. Thompson.'" *Civil War Times Illustrated*, May 1970.

Fladeland, Betty. "Alias Franklin Thompson." *Michigan History* 42 (December 1958).

———. "New Light on Sarah Emma Edmonds, Alias Franklin Thompson." *Michigan History* 47 (December 1963).

Flemming, David B. "Archbishop Thomas L. Connolly, Godfather of Confederation." Canadian Catholic Historical Association, *Study Sessions* 37 (1970): 67–84.

Furguson, Ernest B. "The Battle of Bull Run: The End of Illusions." *Smithsonian Magazine*, August 2011.

Hall, James O. "The Lady in the Veil." *Maryland Independent*, June 25, July 2, 1975.

———. "The Saga of Sarah Slater." *Surratt Courier* VII, no. 1 (January 1982) and VII, no. 2 (February 1982).

Henig, Gerald S. "The Indomitable Dr. Augusta: The First Black Physician in the U.S. Army." US Army Center of Military History, *Army History* 87 (Spring 2013): 22–31.

Higginbottom, Susan. "The Last Years of Sarah Slater." *Surratt Courier* XL, no. 12 (December 2015).

Holzer, Harold. "Cease Fire: How Jefferson Davis Lost His Slaves." *America's Civil War*, July 2013.

———. "What the Newspapers Said When Lincoln Was Killed." *Smithsonian Magazine*, March 2015.

Homel, Gene Howard. "Denison's Law: Criminal Justice and the Police Court in Toronto, 1877–1921." *Ontario History* 73 (September 1981): 171–86.

Isacsson, Alfred. "Surratt and the Lincoln Assassination Plot." *Maryland Historical Magazine*, December 1957, 316–42.

Jones, Preston. "Civil War, Culture War: French Quebec and the American War between the States." *Catholic Historical Review* 87, no. 1 (January 2001): 55–70.

Klement, Frank L. "Vallandigham as an Exile in Canada, 1863–1864." *Ohio History* 74, no. 3 (Summer 1965): 151–68.

Kynoch, Gary. "Terrible Dilemmas: Black Enlistment in the Union Army during the American Civil War." *Slavery and Abolition* 18, no. 2 (August 1997): 104–27.

Lutz, Stuart. "Terror in St. Albans." *Civil War Times Illustrated*, June 2011.

Mayers, Adams. "Spies across the Border." *Civil War Times Illustrated*, June 2011.

McKnight, Alanna. "Borders, Battles and Bigotry: The Trials of Dr. Alexander and Mary Augusta." *Études canadiennes/Canadian Studies* 85 (2018): 49–65.

Miller, Steven G. "More on Capt. Doherty." *Surratt Courier* XV, no. 9 (September 1990).

Savard, Pierre. "La presse québécoise et la guerre de Sécession." In Réal Bertrand et al., *Mosaïque Québécoise*, 111–28. Québec: Société historique de Québec, 1961.

Stanton, John F. "A Mystery No Longer: The Lady in the Veil." *Surratt Courier* XXXVI, no. 8 (August 2011) and XXXVI, no. 10 (October 2011).

———. "Some Thoughts on Sarah Slater." *Surratt Courier* XXXII, no. 2 (February 2007).

Taylor, Alice. "Doctor of Courage." *University of Toronto Magazine*, February 2015.

Tidwell, William A. "Confederate Expenditures for Secret Service." *Civil War History* 37, no. 3 (September 1991): 219–31.

———. "The Man Who Shifted the Blame." *Civil War Times Illustrated*, June 2011.

Towne, Stephen E., and Jay G. Heiser. "'Everything Is Fair in War': The Civil War Memoir of George A. 'Lightning' Ellsworth, Telegraph Operator for John Hunt Morgan." *Register of the Kentucky Historical Society* 108, no. 1/2 (Winter/Spring 2010).

Trépanier, Léon. "Guillaume Lamothe (1824–1911)." *Cahiers des Dix* 29 (1964): 143–58.

Wells, Cheryl A. "Icy Blasts to Balmy Airs: British North America and Lincoln's Assassination." *Journal of the Abraham Lincoln Association* 36, no. 2 (Summer 2015): 26–47.

Whellams, David. "Jefferson Davis Comes to Canada." *Surratt Courier* XVIII, no. 4 (April 1993).

Wick, Robert G. "Battle for the War Department Rewards for the Capture of John Wilkes Booth." *Journal of the Abraham Lincoln Association* 32, no. 2 (September 2011): 1–15.

BOOKS

Allen, Felicity. *Jefferson Davis Unconquerable Heart*. Columbia: University of Missouri Press, 1999.

Baird, Nancy Disher. *Luke Pryor Blackburn: Physician, Governor, Reformer*. Lexington: University Press of Kentucky, 1979.

Bakeless, John. *Spies of the Confederacy*. Philadelphia: J.B. Lippincott, 1970.

Blanton, DeAnne, and Lauren M. Cook. *They Fought Like Demons: Women Soldiers in the Civil War*. New York: Random House, 2002.

Boyko, John. *Blood and Daring: How Canada Fought the American Civil War and Forged a Nation*. Toronto: Alfred A. Knopf, 2013.

Carson, James. *Chasing Mosby, Killing Booth: The 16th New York Volunteer Cavalry*. Jefferson, NC: McFarland, 2017.

Collard, Edgar Andrew. *Montreal Yesterdays*. Don Mills, ON: Longmans, 1962.

Cooper, Afua. *The Hanging of Angelique: The Untold Story of Canadian Slavery and the Burning of Old Montreal*. Toronto: HarperCollins, 2006.

Cooper, William J. *Jefferson Davis, American*. New York: Knopf, 2000.

Creighton, Donald. *John A. Macdonald: The Young Politician*. Toronto: Macmillan, 1952.

Cummings, Carmen. *Devil's Game: The Civil War Intrigues of Charles A. Dunham*. Champaign: University of Illinois Press, 2004.

Dannett, Sylvia G.L. *She Rode with the Generals: The True and Incredible Story of Sarah Emma Seelye, Alias Franklin Thompson*. New York: Thomas Nelson and Sons, 1960.

Davis, William C. *Look Away! A History of the Confederate States of America*. New York: Free Press, 2002.

Dewitt, David Miller. *The Assassination of Abraham Lincoln and Its Expiation*. New York: MacMillan Company, 1909.

Downs, Jim. *Sick from Freedom: African American Illness and Suffering during the Civil War and Reconstruction*. New York: Oxford University Press, 2012.

Evans, Eli. *Judah Benjamin: The Jewish Confederate*. New York: Free Press, 1988.

Fishel, Edwin C. *The Secret War for the Union: The Untold Story of Military Intelligence in the Civil War*. Boston: Houghton Mifflin, 1996.

Freeman, Douglas Southall. *Lee's Lieutenants: A Study in Command*. New York: Scribner, 1998.

Gagan, David. *The Denison Family of Toronto, 1792–1921*. Toronto: University of Toronto Press, 1973.

Gansler, Laura Leedy. *The Mysterious Private Thompson: The Double Life of Sarah Emma Edmonds, Civil War Soldier*. New York: Free Press, 2005.

Goolrick, William K. *Rebels Resurgent: Fredericksburg to Chancellorsville*. Alexandria, VA: Time-Life Books, 1985.

Greene, H. Leon. *The Confederate Yellow Fever Conspiracy: The Germ Warfare Plot of Luke Pryor Blackburn, 1864–1865*. Jefferson, NC: MacFarland & Co., 2019.

Hannah-Jones, Nikole. *The 1619 Project: A New Origin Story*. New York: One World, 2021.

Hatch, Frederick. *John Surratt: Rebel, Lincoln Conspirator, Fugitive*. Jefferson, NC: McFarland, 2016.

Hedrick, Joan D. *Harriet Beecher Stowe: A Life*. New York: Oxford University Press, 1995.

Henry, Natasha L. *Emancipation Day: Celebrating Freedom in Canada*. Toronto: Dundurn Press, 2010.

Hill, Daniel. *The Freedom-Seekers*. Agincourt, ON: Book Society of Canada, 1981.

Holbrook, Todd. *Mrs. Slater in the Confederate Secret Service*. Charleston, SC: Evening Post Books, 2002.

Horan, James. *Confederate Agent: A Discovery in History*. New York: Crown Publishers, 1954.

Hoy, Claire. *Canadians in the Civil War*. Toronto: McArthur & Company, 2004.

Jampoler, Andrew C.A. *The Last Lincoln Conspirator: John Surratt's Flight from the Gallows*. Annapolis, MD: Naval Institute Press, 2008.

Kinchen, Oscar A. *Confederate Operations in Canada and the North*. North Quincy, MA: Christopher Publishing House, 1970.

———. *Daredevils of the Confederate Army: The Story of the St. Albans Raiders*. Boston: Christopher Publishing House, 1959.

Kluckner, Michael. *Toronto the Way It Was*. Toronto: Whitecap Books, 1988.

Lamarre, Jean. *Les Canadiens français et la guerre de sécession*. Montreal: VLB, 2006.

Leech, Margaret. *Reveille in Washington: 1860–1865*. New York: Garden City Publishing, 1941.

Leonard, Elizabeth D. *All the Daring of a Soldier: Women of the Civil War Armies*. New York: W.W. Norton & Co., 1999.

———. Introduction and annotations to *Memoirs of a Soldier, Nurse and Spy*, by Sara Emma Edmonds. DeKalb: North Illinois University Press, 1999.

Levin, Andrea Lee. *"This Awful Drama": General Edwin Lee, C.S.A. and His Family*. New York: Vantage Press, 1987.

Loewen, James W., and Edward H. Sebesta. *The Confederate and Neo-Confederate Reader: The "Great Truth" about the "Lost Cause."* Jackson: University Press of Mississippi, 2010.

Loux, Arthur F. *Booth: Day by Day*. Jefferson, NC: McFarland, 2014.

Lundell, Liz. *The Estates of Old Toronto*. Erin, ON: Boston Mills Press, 1997.

Marquis, G. *In Armageddon's Shadow: The Civil War and Canada's Maritime Provinces*. Montreal: McGill-Queen's University Press, 2014.

Montgomery, Ben. *A Shot in the Moonlight: How a Freed Slave and a Confederate Soldier Fought for Justice in the Jim Crow South*. New York: Little Brown Spark, 2021.

Morse, John Torrey. *American Statesman: Abraham Lincoln*, vol. 2. Cambridge: Riverside Press, 1893.

Newby, Dalyce. *Anderson Ruffin Abbott, First Afro-Canadian Doctor.* Toronto: Fitzhenry & Whiteside, 1998.

Nicolay, John G., and John Hay. *Abraham Lincoln: A History,* vol. 10. New York: Century Co., 1909.

Nuermberger, Ruth Ketring. *The Clays of Alabama: A Planter-Lawyer-Politician Family.* Lexington: University of Kentucky Press, 1958.

Parker, Anna Virginia. *The Sanders Family of Grass Hills.* Madison: Coleman Printing Company, 1966.

Pollard, Edward. *The Lost Cause: A New Southern History of the War of the Confederates.* New York: E.B. Treat, 1867.

Prince, Bryan. *My Brother's Keeper: African Canadians and the American Civil War.* Toronto: Dundurn Press, 2015.

Prince, Cathryn J. *Burn the Town and Sack the Banks! Confederates Attack Vermont!* New York: Carroll and Graf, 2006.

Reid, Richard M. *African Canadians in Union Blue: Volunteering for the Cause in the Civil War.* Vancouver: UBC Press, 2014.

Rush, Daniel S., and E. Gale Pewitt. *The St. Albans Raiders.* Papers of the Blue and Gray Society, Number 19. Saline, MI: McNaughton and Gunn, 2008.

Schein, Michael. *John Surratt: The Lincoln Assassin Who Got Away.* Seattle: Bennett & Hastings Publishing, 2015.

Sheehy, Barry. *Montreal, City of Secrets.* Montreal: Baraka Books, 2017.

Simpson, Donald George. *Under the North Star: Black Communities in Upper Canada before Confederation (1867).* Trenton, NJ: Africa World Press, 2005.

Singer, Jane. *The Confederate Dirty War.* Jefferson, NC: McFarland, 2005.

Slaney, Catherine. *Family Secrets: Crossing the Colour Line.* Toronto: Dundurn, 2003.

Steers, Edward, Jr. *Blood on the Moon: The Assassination of Abraham Lincoln.* Lexington: University Press of Kentucky, 2005.

———. *Lincoln's Assassination.* Carbondale: Southern Illinois University Press, 2014.

Swanson, James. *Manhunt: The 12-Day Chase for Lincoln's Killer.* New York: HarperCollins, 2006.

Tidwell, William A. *April '65: Confederate Covert Action in the American Civil War.* Kent, OH: Kent State University Press, 1995.

Tidwell, William, with James O. Hall and David Winfred Gaddy. *Come Retribution: The Confederate Secret Service and the Assassination of Lincoln.* Jackson: University Press of Mississippi, 1988.

Trudeau, Noah Andre. *Like Men of War: Black Troops in the Civil War.* Boston: Little, Brown, 1998.

Winkler, H. Donald. *Stealing Secrets: How a Few Daring Women Deceived Generals, Impacted Battles, and Altered the Course of the Civil War.* Napierville, IL: Sourcebooks, 2010.

Winks, Robin W. *The Civil War Years: Canada and the United States* Baltimore: Johns Hopkins Press, 1960.

———. *The Blacks in Canada: A History*. Montreal: McGill-Queen's University Press, 1971.

Wodson, Harry M. *The Whirlpool: Scenes from Toronto Police Court*. Toronto: 1917.

Young, Robert W. *Senator James Murray, Defender of the Old South*. Knoxville: University of Tennessee Press, 1998.

Zackodnik, Teresa. *Press, Platform, Pulpit: Black Feminist Publics in the Era of Reform*. Knoxville: University of Tennessee Press, 2011.

Online Resources

Bélanger, D.-C. *Canada, French-Canadians and Franco-Americans in the Civil War Era (1861–1865)*. Last modified August 13, 2001. faculty.marianopolis.edu/c.belanger/quebechistory/frncdns/studies/dcb/preface.htm.

Bonenfant, J.-C. "Devlin, Bernard." In *Dictionary of Canadian Biography*, vol. 10. University of Toronto/Université Laval, 2003. biographi.ca/en/bio/devlin_bernard_10E.html. Accessed August 29, 2022.

Boyko, John. "A Canadian in the American Civil War: Sarah Emma Edmonds." JohnBoyko.com, May 10, 2014. johnboyko.com/2014/05/10/a-canadian-in-the-american-civil-war-sarah-emma-edmonds/.

Brooks, Rebecca Beatrice. "Boston during the Civil War." *History of Massachusetts* (blog), December 13, 2016. historyofmassachusetts.org/boston-in-the-civil-war/.

City of Montreal website. "Mayors of Montreal—Charles-Joseph Coursol (1871–1873)." ville.montreal.qc.ca/archives/democratie/democratie_en/expo/maires/coursol/index.shtm. Accessed August 29, 2022.

Clay, Clement Claiborne. Encyclopedia of Alabama. Last modified January 6, 2022. encyclopediaofalabama.org/article/h-2951.

Derreck, Tom. "Soldier Girl: The Emma Edmonds Story." *Canada's History*, March 14, 2017. canadashistory.ca/explore/women/soldier-girl-the-emma-edmonds-story.

Find a Grave. "Luke Pryor Blackburn." findagrave.com/memorial/10042/luke-pryor-blackburn. Accessed August 29, 2022.

Find a Grave. "Edward Doherty." findagrave.com/memorial/2278/edward-paul-doherty. Accessed August 29, 2022.

Find a Grave. "Emma Edmonds." findagrave.com/memorial/6843300/sarah-emma-seelye. Accessed August 29, 2022.

Find a Grave. "Sarah Slater." findagrave.com/memorial/114786320/sarah-antoinette-spencer. Accessed August 29, 2022.

Find a Grave. "Bennett Young." findagrave.com/memorial/7404128/bennett-henderson-young. Accessed August 29, 2022.

Grays and Blues of Montreal, The. "US Civil War Round Table Presentations." thegraysandbluesofmontreal.com. Accessed August 29, 2022.

Higginbotham, Susan. "The Veiled Lady's Will." susanhigginbotham.com/the-veiled-ladys-will/. Accessed August 29, 2022.

Kennedy, Robert C. "On This Day: August 1, 1863." *New York Times* and *Harper's Weekly*. archive.nytimes.com/www.nytimes.com/learning/general/onthisday/harp/0801.html. Accessed August 29, 2022.

Lacroix, Patrick. "A Confederate in Canada." Querythepast.com, August 2, 2018.

Lawrence, Ken. "Yes, Booth Did Speak Those Notorious Words at Lincoln's Last Speech." *History News Network*, May 10, 2020. historynewsnetwork.org/article/175394.

Leavitt, Sarah. "Confederate Plaque on Montreal Hudson's Bay Store Removed." CBC News website, August 15, 2017. cbc.ca/news/canada/montreal/jefferson-davis-confederate-plaque-montreal-1.4248206.

Masur, Kate. "Winning the Right to Ride: How D.C.'s Streetcars Became an Early Battleground for Post-emancipation Civil Rights." *Slate*, December 26, 2017. slate.com/human-interest/2017/12/black-activists-post-emancipation-battle-for-d-c-s-city-streetcars-one-of-the-first-civil-rights-victories-on-public-transportation.html.

National Archives. "Black Soldiers in the U.S. Military During the Civil War." https://www.archives.gov/education/lessons/blacks-civil-war. Accessed August 29, 2022.

National Park Service. "Emma Edmonds." nps.gov/people/sarah-emma-edmonds.htm. Accessed August 29, 2022.

Nazarian, Sara. "Civil War: The Struggle for Equal Pay." Veterans Legacy Program, University of Central Florida. vlp.cah.ucf.edu/aa/aaequalpay.html. Accessed August 29, 2022.

Newmark, Jill. "Contraband Hospital, 1862–1863: Health Care for the First Freedpeople." BlackPast.org, March 28, 2012. blackpast.org/african-american-history/contraband-hospital-1862-1863-heath-care-first-freedpeople.

Nicklemen. "Marine Villa's Lost Marine Hospital." *St. Louis History* (blog), December 5, 2014. stlouishistoryblog.com/2014/12/05/marine-villas-lost-marine-hospital/.

PBS. "The Civil War by the Numbers." *American Experience*. pbs.org/wgbh/americanexperience/features/death-numbers/. Accessed August 29, 2022.

Richardson, Robert. "Jefferson Davis, Lennoxville." Author's website, August 18, 2017. robertgrichardson.wordpress.com/2017/08/18/jefferson-davis/.

Rudin, R.E. "Starnes, Henry." In *Dictionary of Canadian Biography*, vol. 12. University of Toronto/Université Laval, 2003. biographi.ca/en/bio/starnes_henry_12E.html. Accessed August 29, 2022.

Ste. Croix, Lorne. "Coursol, Charles-Joseph." In *Dictionary of Canadian Biography*, vol. 11, University of Toronto/Université Laval, 2003. biographi.ca/en/bio.php?id_nbr=5446. Accessed August 29, 2022.

Southern Poverty Law Center. "SPLC Reports over 160 Confederate Symbols Removed in 2020." SPLCenter.org, February 23, 2021. splcenter.org/presscenter/splc-reports-over-160-confederate-symbols-removed-2020.

Taylor, Dave, ed. Lincolnconspirators.com. Accessed August 29, 2022.

United States House of Representatives. "The 'So Very Peculiar' Case of Sarah Seelye." history.house.gov/Blog/2020/March/3-20-SarahSeelye/. Accessed August 29, 2022.

US National Library of Medicine. "Binding Wounds, Pushing Boundaries: African Americans in Civil War Medicine." *History of Medicine*. nlm.nih.gov/exhibition/bindingwounds/index.html. Accessed August 29, 2022.

United States Senate. "Senators Witness the First Battle of Bull Run." Senate.gov. senate.gov/artandhistory/history/minute/Witness_Bull_Run.htm. Accessed August 29, 2022.

Walls, Dr. Bryan. "Freedom Marker: Integrity and Spirituality." PBS.org. pbs.org/black-culture/shows/list/underground-railroad/stories-freedom/abolition-slavery-canada/. Accessed August 29, 2022.

Weber, Jennifer L. "Abraham Lincoln Resources." National Park Services website. nps.gov/common/uploads/teachers/lessonplans/The-Legacy-of-Abraham-Lincoln-Readings.pdf. Accessed August 29, 2022.

Winks, Robin W. "Abbott, Wilson Ruffin." In *Dictionary of Canadian Biography*, vol. 10. University of Toronto/Université Laval, 2003. biographi.ca/en/bio/abbott_wilson_ruffin_10E.html. Accessed August 29, 2022.

INDEX

as viewed by others, 130, 133–34

assassination of Lincoln, 281–84, 304–05

Booth, John Wilkes, 160–61, 223, 240, 304

conspiracy trial, 297–300

death, 373

Dunham, Charles, 300

early political career, 131–33

Niagara peace plan, 135–38

St. Albans raid, 96, 147, 151–52, 177–80, 216, 232

St. Albans money, 154, 180–86, 189–92

son Reid's death, 138

Schein, Michael, 329, 419, 425, 431

Seddon, James, 110, 117, 146, 207, 209, 406, 428

Seelye, Linus, 356

Seward, William, 243, 246, 247, 275–77, 297, 370, 426

Seven Days Battles, 70

Shadd, Mary, 46, 84

Slater, Sarah

courier missions 209–10, 212–13, 221, 237–39, 298

Booth, John Wilkes, 228–29

death, 376

early life, 207–09

Surratt, John, 226, 228–29, 236–39, 276, 278, 304, 311–13, 420

later life, 375–76

Lee, Edwin, 311

marriages, 208, 376

photograph, 207

St. Albans trial, 213, 217–18, 235

St. Lawrence Hall, 214–15, 278, 418, 425

shooting Yankee soldiers, 236, 328, 421

Thompson, Jacob, 221

Weichmann, Louis, 220, 375

Slavery (*See also* Underground Railroad)

abolition in England, 42–43

Anti-Slavery Society, 22, 41, 64

Canada, 42

Davis, Jefferson, 20, 48, 58, 208

Emancipation Proclamation, 59

Fugitive Slave Act, 43–44

Lincoln, Abraham, 7, 17–18, 44–45, 48, 57–58, 203, 222, 242, 384

Thirteenth Amendment, 203

Smith, Justice James, 187, 232–34

Sowles, Edward, 149–50, 153–54, 177, 185, 213

Sons of Liberty, 142–43

Spangler, Edman, 245, 297, 301

Stanton, Edwin M., 61, 244, 259, 283, 317–20, 375, 399, 400

Starnes, Henry (*See also* Ontario Bank)

bank draft for Booth, 160, 270, 387

Confederate bank account, 115, 159–60, 371

early career, 114

St. Albans money, 182–83, 186

scandals after war, 367

Steers, Edward, 127, 302, 412

Stewart, Damon, 55, 67–8, 357–9

Stowe, Harriet Beecher, 44–45, 48, 197

Sumner, Charles, 93, 345, 358

Surratt, John

arrest, 325

assassination of Lincoln, 257, 275, 299, 305, 306

Benjamin, Judah, 213, 236–37, 304, 328

Booth, John Wilkes, 223–28, 239–40, 277–78, 328–29

JULIAN SHER is an award-winning journalist and the author of seven books, including *White Hoods: Canada's Ku Klux Klan* and *"Until You Are Dead": The Wrongful Conviction of Steven Truscott*. He co-authored two books on biker gangs, *The Road to Hell* and *Angels of Death*, and wrote two books on crimes against children, *One Child at a Time* and *Somebody's Daughter*. As an investigative reporter, he worked for the *Toronto Star* and the *Globe and Mail*. He was the Senior Producer of CBC's *the fifth estate*, Canada's premier investigative TV program, for five years. He has directed and written major documentaries, covering wars and intrigue across the globe. His documentary *Nuclear Jihad*, produced for the *New York Times* and CBC, won the broadcast equivalent of the Pulitzer Prize. His 2021 film, *Ghosts of Afghanistan*, won three top Canadian Screen Awards, including Best Documentary. He is also active in protecting media freedoms, as a Senior Fellow at Toronto Metropolitan University's Centre for Free Expression, and working with Journalists for Human Rights. More information at www.juliansher.com.